One-Day Trips
through History

*For my mother, Jessie Bradley Ockershausen,
who always made coming home the best part of
any trip.*

One-Day Trips
through History

200 Excursions Within 150 Miles of Washington, D.C.

Jane Ockershausen Smith

EPM Publications, Inc.
McLean, Virginia

Library of Congress Cataloging in Publication Data

Smith, Jane Ockershausen.
  One-day trips through history.

  Bibliography: p.
  Includes index.
  1. Washington region—Description and travel—Guidebooks.
  2. Historic sites—Washington region—Guidebooks. I. Title.
F192.3.S58   917.53'044   82-4995
ISBN 0-914440-54-3   AACR2

Notice: Telephone numbers and admission fees change so frequently that they have not been included in most listings. For those sites where appointments are necessary or special events are scheduled, addresses and phone numbers are cited. Days and hours of operation are given, but it is always best to call ahead and check. Consult telephone directories for numbers.

Book design by Michael J. O'Brien
Cover photograph by Fred J. Maroon

Contents

COLONIAL AGRICULTURE

COLONIAL PLANTATIONS

COLONIAL CHURCHES

COLONIAL TOWNS

THE DECLARATION OF INDEPENDENCE

REVOLUTIONARY WAR YEARS

WAR OF 1812

ERA BETWEEN THE WARS
PRESIDENTIAL HOMES

HOMES

TRANSPORTATION

INDUSTRIES

CIVIL WAR PERIOD
HOMES

CIVIL WAR FORTS

BATTLEFIELD SITES

The Capital Beltway

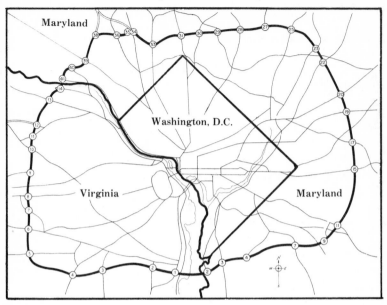

NOTE: The Beltway is I-495 clockwise from Virginia Exit 4 to Maryland Exit 27. The Beltway is I-95 clockwise from Maryland Exit 27 to Virginia Exit 4.

Virginia Exits

Exit 1
18. Mount Vernon
19. River Farm
22. Woodlawn Plantation
29. Gunston Hall
48. Christ Church
59. Ramsay House
60. Carlyle House
66. George Washington's Gristmill Historical State Park
67. Stabler-Leadbeater Apothecary Shop Museum
74. Gadsby's Tavern Museum
127. Lee-Fendall House
154. Boyhood Home of Robert E. Lee
163. Fort Ward Park
203. U.S. Army Engineer Museum

Exit 3
8. Moyaone
24. The National Colonial Farm
112. Smallwood's Retreat
116. Fort Washington

Exit 4
4. Jamestown Festival Park
5. Pamunkey Indian Reservation
6. Mattaponi Indian Reservation
7. Kecoughtan Indian Village
12. Jamestown Colonial Historical Park
17. Epping Forest
20. Mary Washington House
21. Kenmore
30. Carter's Grove
31. Shirley Plantation
33. Smith's Fort Plantation House
34. Scotchtown
36. Weston Manor
46. Bruton Parish Church
47. St. John's Church—Richmond
49. St. John's Church—Hampton
53. Peyton Randolph House
54. Brush-Everard House
55. James Geddy House, Shop and Foundry
56. Adam Thoroughgood House
57. Moses Myers House
58. Willoughby-Baylor House

Virginia Exits *(continued)*

Exit 4 *(continued)*
68. Hugh Mercer Apothecary Shop
71. Raleigh Tavern
72. Rising Sun Tavern
82. Governor's Palace
83. Capitol
89. George Wythe House
92. Nelson House
93. Berkeley
114. Yorktown Victory Center
115. Yorktown Battlefield
122. James Monroe Law Office-Museum
     and Memorial Library
124. Sherwood Forest
128. Chippokes Plantation
132. John Marshall House
133. Centre Hill Mansion
139. Chesapeake & Ohio Canal
     National Historical Park
158. Chatham
165. Fort Monroe
170. Richmond National Battlefield Park
172. Fredericksburg National Military Park
173. Chancellorsville Battlefield
175. Wilderness Battlefield
176. Spotsylvania Battlefield
178. Sayler's Creek Battlefield Historical State Park
179. Petersburg National Battlefield
181. Museum of the Confederacy
     & the White House of the Confederacy
183. The Valentine Museum
184. Siege Museum
185. Portsmouth Naval Shipyard Museum
195. Bassett Hall
198. General Douglas MacArthur Memorial
200. Shannon Air Museum
201. U.S. Marine Corps Aviation Museum

Exit 4 *(continued)*
204. U.S. Army Transportation Museum
205. U.S. Army Quartermaster Museum

Exit 8
32. Castle Hill
35. Red Hill Plantation
73. Historic Michie Tavern Museum
91. Monticello
155. Booker T. Washington National Monument
186. Culpeper Cavalry Museum

Exit 9
1. Thunderbird Museum
   and Archeological Park
123. Ash Lawn
129. Sully Plantation
157. Belle Grove
168. Manassas National Battlefield Park
177. New Market Battlefield Park
180. Appomattox Court House
     National Historical Park
182. Warren Rifles Confederate Museum
187. The Woodrow Wilson Birthplace
191. Frying Pan Farm
193. Camp Hoover
197. George C. Marshall Library and Museum

Exit 10
37. Abram's Delight
130. Oatlands
131. Morven Park
145. Colvin Run Mill
169. General Stonewall Jackson's Headquarters

Exit 14
26. Turkey Run Farm

Maryland Exits

Exit 4
199. Paul E. Garber Facility

Exit 7
2. St. Clement's Island Interpretive Center—
   Potomac Museum
13. St. Clement's Island
14. St. Mary's City
16. George Washington Birthplace
    National Monument
25. The Godiah Spray Plantation
39. Sotterly
50. St. Ignatius Church
84. Reconstructed State House of 1676
90. Stratford Hall
162. The Mary Surratt House

Exit 11
151. Duvall Tool Collection

Exit 19
3. Island Field Museum
44. John Dickinson Mansion
52. Hammond-Harwood House
64. Corbit Sharp House
65. Wilson-Warner House
75. London Town Publik House and Gardens
85. State House
94. Chase Lloyd House
95. William Paca House and Gardens
141. Chesapeake & Delaware Canal
     Waterwheel and Pumphouse Museum

Exit 22
10. Susquehannock Ceremonial Site
38. Montpelier
40. Mount Clare
51. Ephrata Cloister
80. Red Rose Inn
96. Carroll Mansion

Maryland Exits *(continued)*

Exit 22 *(continued)*
117. Star Spangled Banner Flag House
     & 1812 War Military Museum
118. Fort McHenry National Monument
     & Historic Shrine
119. U.S.F. *Constellation*
142. Baltimore & Ohio Railroad Museum
152. Shot Tower
207. U.S.S. *Torsk*

Exit 25
76. George Washington House 1760

Exit 27
9. Indian Steps Museum
11. Lenape Land
27. The Colonial Pennsylvania Plantation
28. Peter Wentz Farmstead
42. Pennsbury Manor
43. Landingford Plantation
45. Daniel Boone Homestead
62. Betsy Ross House
63. John Bartram's House and Gardens
69. Batsto Historic Area
70. Bethlehem Historic District
77. City Tavern
78. A Man Full of Trouble Tavern
79. Golden Plough Tavern
81. The Indian King Tavern
86. Independence Hall
87. Carpenter's Hall
88. The York County Colonial Court House
97. Franklin Court
98. General Taylor House
99. Congress Hall
100. Old City Hall
101. Pemberton House
102. Washington Crossing Historic Park
103. Morristown National Historical Park
104. Ford Mansion
105. The Wick House
106. Brandywine Battlefield Park
107. Fort Mifflin
108. Red Bank Battlefield Park and Fort Mercer
109. Valley Forge National Historical Park

Exit 27 *(continued)*
111. Wallace House
113. Rockingham
125. Wheatlands
134. Hampton National Historic Site
137. Todd House
138. Bishop White House
140. Delaware Canal Mule-Drawn Barge
144. Strasburg Rail Road
146. Hopewell Village
147. Waterloo Village
148. Wheaton Village
149. Hagley Museum & Eleutherian Mills
150. Mercer Museum
166. Fort Delaware State Park

Exit 30
143. Ellicot City B&O Railroad Station Museum

Exit 33
136. Union Mill Homestead
153. Carroll County Farm Museum

Exit 35
15. Fort Necessity National Battlefield Park
    and the Mount Washington Tavern
41. Rose Hill Manor Park
110. Fort Frederick
135. Beall-Dawson House
156. Barbara Fritchie House and Museum
167. Harpers Ferry National Historical Park
171. Antietam National Battlefield Park
174. Gettysburg National Military Park
192. Blue Blazes Whiskey Still
196. Eisenhower National Historic Site

Exit 40
159. Clara Barton House

Exit 41
139. Chesapeake & Ohio Canal National
     Historical Park

Inside the Beltway

23. Arlington House
61. The Old Stone House
120. Octagon House
121. The White House
126. Decatur House
160. Ford's Theatre
161. Petersen House
164. Fort Marcy
188. Woodrow Wilson House
189. Frederick Douglass Home
190. Sewall-Belmont House
194. Dumbarton Oaks
202. Marine Corps Museum and Historical Center
206. Navy Memorial Museum
208. Arlington National Cemetery

This book offers the American history no school has time to teach—the story of the men and women who really made this country, the brave, funny and very human account of their individual lives. It is an enduring saga that fills all who become involved in it with enormous pride—that they, too, are a part of the continuing story.

When history is studied, it is the facts that are learned, not the spirit. Here is the spirit, captured in the stories of the soldiers, politicians, farmers, tavern keepers, housewives and educators who made history happen. To understand their past it helps to walk in their footsteps: visit the homes where they lived, the churches where they worshipped, the taverns where they relaxed, the stores where they shopped and, all too often, the battlefields where they died.

One-Day Trips Through History meets a genuine need because most history books in mentioning significant sites give no indication when, or even if, the public can explore a particular spot. And travel books rarely provide the historical background that leads to an appreciation of these sites.

Those of us who live in the Middle Atlantic region are particularly fortunate because we can literally re-live the history of the United States from its earliest days. Names that are part of our American heritage—Jamestown, Valley Forge, Yorktown, Gettysburg, Appomatox—are here.

A family's experience can be as varied as "acting" on a jury in a treason trial at St. Mary's, riding on the prototype of today's railroad, the "Tom Thumb," practicing 18th-century domestic skills at the Old Stone House, barging up the C&O Canal or enjoying warm ginger-bread made from Mary Washington's own recipe at Kenmore. The excursions are as colorful and varied as our historical past. They are also instructive, for these sites have much to teach us.

Just how rewarding these trips will be depends to a large extent on an understanding of the significance of the particular site or event. It isn't enough to trudge along the Antietam battlefield trail or stand on the ramparts of Fort Monroe. One must view each trip as a time tunnel to the past, be drawn into the spell of an earlier time. Knowing the historical background provides the key.

Armies of the colonies and England marched across the Middle Atlantic area. Later brother fought brother in the Civil War. Here are the cities and roads they fortified and the rivers they crossed. Many of the book's excursions mark sites that played a strategic role in knitting a group of disparate colonies into a nation. These historic sites sustained the people's spirits when the country was challenged from within. To travel from Morristown to Yorktown or from Bull Run to Appomattox establishes a kinship with those who were there before.

Many feel that it is the diminishing of our sense of history that contributed to the spiritual crises of the 1970s. We benefit from the sense of historical continuity that this book provides. We need to feel related to those who forged our past and will create our future. We also need to look more closely at the historical buildings that serve as tangible reminders of earlier times.

In these pages there is all one needs to know about how, when and why any particular historic site should be explored. The outstanding advantage of these excursions is that they can be made in a day, providing an inexpensive mini-vacation. With the help of the geographic cross reference they can be turned into a weekend family adventure.

Many of these historic sites are under the jurisdiction of the federal or state government so the only cost for a fun-filled, educational day's outing is the gas required to get there. The list of annual events at the back of the book will also alert readers to special activities that add additional allure to some of the attractions.

There are four different ways to begin exploring these historical sites. The most organized is the chronological. Children can be given a thorough picture of our country's development by choosing one or more outings from each time period. A visit to the Pamunkey Indian Reservation, with its reproduced tribal village, will give a representative look at the Indians that Europeans encountered when they reached the New World. But expanding this visit to include a stop at the nearby Mattaponi Reservation continuing to the Kecoughtan Village and including the Moyaone, Lenape and Susquehannock sites broadens one's perception of the diversity of these first Americans.

Or, one can always resort to the random approach, as each selection is written so that it can be used independently. A visit to Sherwood Forest, an exploration of Independence National Historical Park, a look at the old trains at Strasburg Rail Road, a trip to retrace events of the War of 1812 or going to listen to the walls talk at the Nelson House in Yorktown are historically diverse and exciting options for a day's trip.

The third method, a mixing of different periods because of their geographical proximity, will appeal to the practical, economy-minded traveler. In the area around Frederick, Maryland, for instance, one spans the years from the colonial Children's Touch and See Museum at Rose Hill Manor Park, to the Revolutionary War's Fort Frederick. Moving ahead to the Civil War period there is the Barbara Fritchie House and Museum. Lastly the Roaring Twenties is evoked at the Blue Blazes Whiskey Still in Catoctin Mountain Park. This one-day trip covers 200 years of American history.

The fourth approach follows the calendar, exploring why we have our national holidays. Learning the meaning and background personalizes the celebration. It also heightens one's appreciation to be at a historic site on the same date that history was made there.

Beginning in January, there is the birthday of Robert E. Lee, one of the most brilliant of America's military men. He was born on January 19, 1807. Choose that day to visit his Boyhood Home in Alexandria, Virginia, or one of the Civil War battlefields so closely associated with General Lee. Linking this month's celebration with February is Arlington House, a link between the Lees and that earlier great American family, the Washingtons.

February is the perfect time to visit one or all of the eight homes in the area associated with the Washington family. Or the sites associated with the many aspects of George Washington's personality can be explored: his gristmill, the church where he worshipped, the head-quarters and battlefields from which he planned and fought the American Revolution and his beloved Mount Vernon where he is buried.

Maryland Day celebrations in March commemorate the founding of the colony by the Calverts. This is an excellent time to discover the many diverse attractions at St. Mary's City.

On April 14, 1865, John Wilkes Booth assassinated Abraham Lincoln at Ford's Theatre. Retracing the dramatic events of that night and Booth's flight provides an excursion with all the suspense of an adventure serial.

During May there is the yearly re-enactment of the Battle of New Market or the solemn Memorial Day ceremony at the Tomb of the Unknown Soldier. Flag Day is in June and the celebration at Fort McHenry can be combined with a visit to the Mary Pickersgill House where the story of the flag that inspired our national anthem comes to life.

The yearly commemoration of the signing of the Declaration of Independence on July 4th provides an added impetus to those considering a visit to any one of the 10 homes of the signers.

Hoover Days in August offer the only chance to explore the inside of the camp built by Herbert Hoover in the Shenandoah Valley.

September is believed to be the month when the new-fangled horseless engine, Tom Thumb, raced his four-footed competitor. It's fun to ride behind the reproduced Tom Thumb and hear the old stories about its early runs.

October is the annual month for the Revolutionary encampment at Gunston Hall, a real colonial gem. Another distinguished house from this period—Berkeley Plantation—was the location of America's first Thanksgiving and there is a big celebration held on the first Sunday in November. Holidays in history end with a grand finale as many historic homes from all eras recreate Christmas from years past.

These historic trips will renew and restore one's pride in being an American!

Prehistory

The small man, standing barely five feet tall, faces the huge elephant-like mastodon. He is armed with only a stick, to which is attached a sharpened stone. He is an American Ice Age Man and he lived over 11,000 years ago, right in this area.

Early people, called Paleoindians by archeologists, were hunters. They crossed a land bridge of 1,400 miles that connected Asia with North America. Their survival depended on bravely attacking great roaming herds of gigantic mammals which they killed for food and clothing. The harsh and rigorous existence of these hunters required courageous strength to kill these massive creatures with skillfully made spears and stone tools, and the determination to track the beasts on their prolonged migrations.

As the giant glaciers of the Ice Age melted over a period of hundreds of years the hunters followed their food supply south, settling along the new waterways. The melting ice in the Susquehanna River overflowed its banks to form the Chesapeake Bay.

The weather continued to moderate. Large animals began moving northward again and eventually became extinct, thus ending what is known as the Paleoindian Period.

Animals with which we are more familiar—such as deer, turkey and rabbits—then moved into this region. The Archaic Indians hunted these smaller animals. They had gradually improved the Clovis-point spears, which today verify the presence of hunters from the Paleoindian Period. Unlike those first spears, with only a few rough longitudinal flakes struck from each flat face, the Archaic Indians had developed a spear called the "atlatl." It allowed for greater distance and more strength of thrust. Other tools helped to enrich the Indians' food supply and to build their communities; fishing gear and axes were used for the first time.

Gathering also became a principal source of food. This was the job of the women in the tribe. Even as they moved from one camp to another the women would use their digging sticks to obtain food. There was, however, some danger involved in discovering which plants could be eaten. The women developed a carefully graduated testing system. One of them would put a small piece of the leaf, root, berry, flower or pod in her mouth and hold it for a short time. If there were no uncomfortable symptoms a small amount would be swallowed. If the woman still experienced no ill effects, a new source of food would be added to the diet of the group. Women also accompanied the men on their hunts so that they could butcher and preserve the meat.

When they began to plant their own food, the age which we call the Archaic Period ended and a new stage began. By this time—Early Woodland Period—the basic problem of survival had been solved, giving early men the chance to develop in other ways.

Several important social changes took place during the Early Woodland Period. The family unit was enlarged to encompass the clan, and religious ceremonies assumed greater importance for the new group. Travel on the rivers brought one clan in contact with another and objects were traded.

During the Middle Woodland Period which followed, there were two noteworthy accomplishments: the bow and arrow was introduced, and ceramic making became more sophisticated.

An increase in deaths among infants also reinforced reverence for established traditions. It was an Indian superstition that because infants' heads were becoming too large due to the increased amount of information they were amassing, deaths increased. Therefore, changes were suspect and made only very slowly. Every event in the life of a clan member was circumscribed by the past. Consequently, the shamans, or priests, gained considerable power as the guardians of the old ways.

The Late Woodland Period was the final stage of prehistoric man in this area. By this time individual clans had established their own protected villages. The plentiful supply of fish and game, augmented by the cultivation of additional crops, made travel away from the tribal region unnecessary. Territory began to be fiercely protected. Conflicts between tribes began to occur when hunting parties from one clan strayed into another clan's territory.

It was at this stage of development that the first Europeans arrived to settle the North American continent.

1. Thunderbird Museum and Archeological Park

The opportunity to explore a major archeological dig can teach far more than any diagram or museum display. Even the word "dig" takes on new meaning when the work is actually observed. "Carve" is a more accurate word to use, as the surrounding soil is removed very carefully to expose each artifact. Significant features of its placement in the soil and any surrounding objects have much to tell the trained eye.

A slide show at the Thunderbird Museum briefly explains the archeologist's work, showing the information that can be read from the soil levels, the techniques of dating artifacts and some of the conclusions that have been reached as a result of work done right here in the Shenandoah Valley. Viewing this show will certainly provide a more insightful appreciation of this little-known period of prehistory.

The 86-acre Thunderbird Archeological Park is of major importance because it contains artifacts from three areas of the Thunderbird Site, where much of the excavation was done. The museum has interpretive exhibits of the Thunderbird Site base camp. This is the only known North American base camp of the Paleoindian Period that has been uncovered in its original undisturbed location uncluttered with artifacts of later groups. Also included in the museum display are exhibits of the hunting and butchering camp the archeologists uncovered a mile up river from the base camp.

Completing the full range of prehistory in the East are exhibits from the Archaic and Woodland Periods. Any overview of history would be incomplete if it did not include mention of this revealing glimpse of our first neighbors.

Excavation within Thunderbird Archeological Park is done from Memorial Day weekend to Labor Day. Two sites may be visited—the Corral Site and the Lanier Site. At the Corral Site there are indications of Indian occupation from before 1000 B.C. and again from about 1100 to 1400 A.D. From this later period a small farming village of the Late Woodland Period is being excavated.

The Lanier Site, near the ancient bed of the South Fork of the Shenandoah River, gives indication of settlement as early as 7000 to 8000 B.C.

Thunderbird Museum and Archeological Park is open daily from 10:00 to 5:00 mid-March to mid-November. Admission is charged.

Directions: Take Beltway Exit 9 (Route I-66) to Front Royal, Virginia. Thunderbird is seven miles south of Front Royal. Take Route 340 south, then go right on Route 737 for the museum and park grounds.

2. St. Clement's Island Interpretive Center— Potomac Museum

How can archeologists tell when they pick up a stone that it is indeed a valuable prehistoric artifact? Potomac Museum's special Hands-on-Discovery Room provides the opportunity to actually feel an ancient projectile point so that even the novice can easily tell the difference between a rock and a crudely made projectile point. The secret is that in nature only a single side of the rock is sharpened—by water erosion, by roughly breaking from a larger piece or in a myriad of other ways. An artifact, though, is a stone that is sharpened on two sides, not by nature, but by man. A genuine sense of excitement is inevitable when visitors experience for themselves this clue to the past.

The museum's displays are divided into four periods—Paleoindian, Archaic, Woodland and Historic. The exhibits will help clarify these distinctions. Some of the fluted projectiles in the museum's collection indicate that man lived in this area over 10,000 years ago, while the remains of oyster feasts held by Archaic Indians on Breton Bay reinforce the idea that these nomadic hunters once camped along this waterway. Artifacts from the different eras provide evidence of the levels of development.

The museum is open Monday through Friday from 9:00 to 4:00 and on weekends from 12:30 to 4:30.

Directions: From the Beltway take Exit 7 (Route 5) towards Leonard-town, Maryland. From Route 5 take Route 242 to Colton Point. At the water bear left. The museum is on the left overlooking the Potomac River and St. Clement's Island.

3. Island Field Museum

There's a macabre fascination about the 125 exposed skeletons in the cemetery that's part of the Island Field Museum. These glass-covered remains may repel some but will certainly intrigue others. The sight resembles a pictorial representation of Dante's *Inferno*.

There is much that can be learned from this prehistoric Middle Woodland Burial Site. Burials took place here over 1,000 years ago. It is amazing that the graves were uncovered in their original position, called "in situ" by archeologists. Like the ancient Egyptians, these

Indians buried a representative sampling of their personal belongings with them. These artifacts—spears, fish hooks, pipes, cups, pendants and knives—provide a gauge of tribal development.

To explain the work being done at Island Field Museum there is a slide presentation for visitors. Learning about prehistoric man provides a strong feeling of continuity with those who lived and died in this region so long before us.

Island Field Museum is open March through November, Tuesday through Saturday from 10:00 to 4:30 and on Sunday from 1:30 to 4:30. There is no admission charge.

Directions: From the Beltway take Exit 19 (Route 50) to Route 404 towards Denton. At Denton take Route 313 north for two miles to Route 317. Follow Route 317 to Burrsville. Pick up Route 14 and continue on that to Route 113. From Route 113 take either Route 19 or Route 120 to South Bowers and the Island Field Museum. Be careful to note that there is no bridge linking Bowers and South Bowers.

OF NOTE: Some places are important not for what remains of them but for what once existed. Piscataway Park (see Indian Epoch: Moyaone) has no prehistoric artifacts to beguile visitors, but the simple fact that five separate prehistoric peoples once lived on this spot makes it significant.

Beginning as early as the Archaic Period, man camped here beside the Potomac River. The first group known to have stopped at this site were the Marcey Creek People. Next, between 100 B.C. and 300 A.D., the Pope's Creek People lived here. The very different techniques used by the two groups to make their pottery indicate to archeologists that they represented different biological groups, not just a cultural evolution from one to the next.

During the Middle Woodland Period two groups lived here; first the Accokeek Group, who began simple farming, then the Mockley People.

The last prehistoric group was the Potomac Creek People of the Algonquin Indians. As they evolved into the Piscataway Tribe they crossed the line into the Historic Period; they are covered in the Indian Epoch chapter.

OF NOTE: Everyone knows the Smithsonian Institution has one of the most outstanding museum collections in the world, but not everyone knows what it contains in specific areas. Consequently, when pursuing a topic of interest like the Prehistoric Period, the resources of the Smithsonian may be overlooked.

At the Museum of Natural History in the Hall of Prehistoric People of North America the Smithsonian uses a step by step approach to the study of the life-style of early man. The techniques used by archeologists to obtain information on people that lived thousands of years ago are illustrated and explained. For example, the process of carbon dating is explained so that the visitor can understand how archeologists work.

One exhibit of particular interest deals with Washingtonians of 500 years ago who quarried quartzite around what is now Piney Branch Road. Stone quarried here was used to make arrowheads, spears and knives.

The museum has an extensive collection of prehistoric artifacts.

The Indian Epoch

Throughout history the American Indian has been misnamed, mistreated and misplaced. Columbus reached the New World and called the inhabitants "Los Indios," believing he had landed on an island off Asia. Even if Columbus has realized the enormity of his conquest, he would have incorrectly identified the natives. They were different peoples who fought constantly to retain their tribal autonomy.

Though these Indian tribes were of diverse cultures, they did share certain fundamental ideas which were radically opposed to European ideas. A major difference which was to cause discord and eventually war concerned the right of land ownership. For the Indians, land and its produce, like air and water, were free for the use of the group. The idea of an individual owning land and forbidding others the use of that land or passage across it was foreign to Indian thinking.

The first North American Indians to come in contact with the European settlers were the Indians of Virginia and Maryland. The tribes of Virginia were loosely linked in the Powhatan Confederation and those in Maryland in the Piscataway Empire. All were of the Algonquin family. Their language is part of our daily life—Patuxent, Potomac, Portoback, Piscataway. But how much do we really know about the once powerful groups who lived in this area?

The first settlers were befriended by the Algonquins of the Atlantic Coast. The Indians taught them new methods of hunting, fishing and farming and how to construct the smaller boats used on inland waterways. They also introduced new foods to the Europeans: corn, potatoes, tomatoes, beans and squash.

But this harmony did not endure and conflict arose, primarily caused by the settlers' demands for Indian land. The intrusion by the whites into Indian homelands exposed them to reprisals such as horse thefts, torture and even cannibalism and human sacrifice. Though these practices had long been a part of Indian tribal warfare, they angered and repelled the Europeans.

While it is certainly true that were it not for the intrusion of the whites into Indian territory the conflict would not have occurred, it is also true that many Indian leaders invited the whites to battle with them against neighboring tribes and thus to participate in the destruction of rival Indian groups. Another factor that fueled the conflict was the warlike nature of the Indian male, associated with tribal rituals of bravery and manhood.

In the year 1587 a colony was established by the English on Roanoke Island in North Carolina by Sir Walter Raleigh. Ninety-one men, 17 women and nine children, including Virginia Dare, the first child born of English parents in America, were left in the New World to establish a settlement. This colony was not fated to endure. When supply ships returned four years later with new settlers they found no trace of what has since been called the "Lost Colony."

In 1607 the first permanent English settlement was established at Jamestown, Virginia. This area was under the control of Powhatan, a strong chief, who headed a confederation of some 200 villages. This network of 30 Algonquin-speaking tribes with roughly 12,000 Indians extended across most of Tidewater Virginia.

The Jamestown colonists dealt with Powhatan as they would with a European prince. They negotiated treaties of alliance for trade and defense purposes and cemented relations through marriage. Pocahontas, Powhatan's daughter, was converted to the Christian faith and later married John Rolfe. Folklore often imbues the story of Pocahontas' heroic rescue of Captain John Smith with romantic implications, but at this time she was just a young girl of 11 while Smith was a fatherly figure of 27.

Powhatan recognized the advantage of trade with the English. He was in his sixties when the settlers arrived and at his death in 1618 the harmony that had existed between the two groups ended. The friction caused by the colonists' desire to plant more land with the highly profitable tobacco, thus reducing the Indians' hunting grounds, caused resentment. Also, the efforts begun in 1620 to Christianize the Indian children led to mistrust. These two factors prompted Opechancanough, Powhatan's brother, to lead a surprise attack on the English which killed 350 colonists. Nine years of warfare followed this massacre.

Due to these wars, by 1669 the Indians in this area were reduced from approximately 15,000 to about 3,500, about a quarter of the population of 1607. These Indians were dispersed with remnant Indian groups re-establishing themselves on the eastern shore of the Chesapeake Bay. A few small groups remained in Virginia. Their descendants, the Pamunkeys, Mataponis and Chickahominys, reside there today.

In 1608 Captain John Smith left the Jamestown settlement in hopes of finding gold among the tribes in the north. On his journey up the Potomac River he stopped at a Piscataway village on Accokeek Creek which he named "Moyaone." It was one of the main towns of the Piscataway Empire, which covered the western part of Tidewater

Maryland. It is believed that the Piscataways lived in the Maryland area from the 14th century A.D.

In 1622 Maryland settlers attempted to massacre the Piscataway tribe at Moyaone. Conditions between the Indians and the whites continued to deteriorate and in 1623 the village was burned. The Piscataways were also suffering from repeated raids by the Senecas from the north and so they abandoned this location.

Another Piscataway site in Maryland that was deserted by the tribe in fear of Susquehannock raids was St. Mary's. It was at this location in 1634 that the first Maryland settlement was made by English colonists.

4. Jamestown Festival Park

If a picture is worth a thousand words, a reconstruction is worth a million. Wandering among the reconstructed houses inside James Fort at Jamestown Festival Park makes it easy to imagine the settlers' fear of the local Indians. Their roughly built homes indicate the harsh conditions and primitive life they experienced in the New World, and make an interesting comparison with the homes of their Indian neighbors.

At Jamestown Festival Park they have built and furnished an Indian lodge in the style of the local Powhatans. Costumed guides explain to visitors the tools, utensils and cooking methods typically used by area Indians. For example, the Indians were more adept with a "fire stick" than the British newcomers, making it unnecessary for the Indians to keep the fire going continuously. Many a colonial kitchen burned to the ground because the fire was only banked at night. This is why the kitchen—or the out-kitchen, as it was called—was separated from the living quarters.

Seeing the inside of a lodge, filled with the items used in the Indians' daily life, brings home the reality of their spartan existence. The only furnishings were ledges that extended along both long sides of the dwelling. These were draped with animal skins to provide some comfort and warmth while sleeping. Woven mats provided insulation from the cold ground. During cold weather the fire was kept going at night for heat. Twenty or more people of different sexes and ages all lived together in structures of this type.

Outside the lodge is a Ceremonial Indian Dance Circle. Harvesting, changes of season, hunting parties and forages against other tribes all were the focus of ritual dances.

Jamestown Festival Park's New World Pavilion contains a collection of authentic artifacts of the Indian era, including a dugout canoe and various spears, pipes, hammerstones and examples of Indian pottery. Pictorial displays provide information on the daily life of Indians in this area.

Adjacent to the Festival Park is Jamestown Colonial Historical Park (see Colonial Period: First Settlements), the original site of James Fort and early pottery kilns. The National Park Service sponsors a continuing series of interpretive programs and movies at the Visitor Center.

Jamestown Festival Park is open daily, except Christmas and New Year's, from 9:00 to 5:00. Admission is charged.

Directions: From the Beltway take Exit 4 (I-95) to Route 64 into the Williamsburg area. Then take Route 31 to Jamestown Festival Park.

5. Pamunkey Indian Reservation

Ten thousand years before the birth of Christ the Pamunkey Indians were working the soil of an area long since established as the Commonwealth of Virginia. When many of their neighboring Powhatans fled, leaving their homeland to the victorious English, the Pamunkey stayed. They remain there today.

Residents of the Pamunkey Indian Reservation, near West Point, Virginia, worked for years developing their interpretive museum. It provides visitors with a clear picture of the tribe's history.

Displays trace the tribe's origins in prehistoric Paleoindian days. The advances in both tools and agriculture during the Woodland Period become obvious as one sees specific examples of implements as they developed from archaic to modern. The museum shows, in detail, the gradually increasing sophistication in seven separate areas: cutting, hammering, chopping, grinding, piercing, scraping and tying.

Another exhibit traces the changing styles of Indian pottery, from the primitive beauty of Woodland work through the decades to the designs of the 1980s. It is noteworthy that the '40s and '50s produced a garishly colored inauthentic-looking design, whereas the 1980 pieces resemble very early works in form, clay color and texture. Some fine examples of recent work are available at the Trading Post Gift Shop. In addition to the pottery, the shop offers Indian jewelry and souvenirs designed to appeal to young visitors.

Adjacent to the museum and Trading Post work continues on the reconstruction of a 16th-century Pamunkey village. There is a completed wigwam, which was designed to house six to eight people. Two structures are finished and others are in progress. Most tribal villages had between 15 and 30 buildings. Observing the half-finished work reveals how the Indians used the available materials found in their area.

The museum is open for a nominal charge seven days a week from 9:00 to 5:00.

Directions: Take Beltway Exit 4 (I-95) to the outskirts of Richmond. Then take Route 360 north for approximately 15 miles to Route 30 south. There will be signs for the Reservation. From Route 30, turn on Route 633 and go eight miles to the Pamunkey Indian Reservation. Signs will direct you to the museum. This Reservation is almost directly across Route 30 from the Mattaponi Reservation.

6. Mattaponi Indian Reservation

Side by side, two tribes exist, the Mattaponi and the Pamunkey, both survivors of the powerful Powhatan Confederation. But neither are powerful any longer.

These two tribes have adopted contrasting approaches to preserving the past. At the Pamunkey Reservation the interpretive, educational, step-by-step displays are used to good advantage. But the Mattaponi Museum, operated by Chief Thundercloud, Jacob Custalow, is not a typical museum with annotated arrangements all separated and collated. Here, the collection of an entire people is jumbled together in a one-room display. Stuffed birds and local wildlife overlap ceremonial drums. Fossils dating from archaic man rest beside modern newspaper clippings on political figures who have met with Chief Thundercloud and his father before him, Chief Hoskinowanaah. It may well appeal to young boys more than the well-ordered, carefully marked cases across the road.

Jacob Custalow, though elected to office, is descended from a long line of tribal chiefs. He runs the museum and provides fascinating stories and legends that give life to the eclectic collection.

The artifacts span the entire history of the Mattaponi and the Powhatan Confederation. There is a headdress worn by Powhatan, a necklace that once belonged to Pocahontas and a tomahawk of Opechancanough's that reminds visitors of the more brutal past.

Opechancanough (pronounced Ope-can-canoe) is a tribal hero to the Mattaponi Indians, who consider him a member of their tribe. Some historians dispute this, claiming instead he came from the West Indies. The Mattaponi revere him as one of the few Indians to perceive the eventual catastrophe of English domination. The museum includes several items that once belonged to Opechancanough.

One unusual item is a "mercy" tomahawk, used by the medicine men for those they could not heal. Several medicine bags, in which powerful amulets were carried, are on display. There is also a replica of the execution club, a snake-like club used for ritual killings. This is modeled on the club Powhatan raised to kill John Smith before Pocahontas' timely intervention.

Children, as well as adults, seem to enjoy the opportunity to talk to a real Indian Chief and learn first hand about the culture of the Mattaponi. It is unfortunate that Hollywood-produced stereotypes have infiltrated the "real thing." So many children expect to see teepees and feathered warbonnets that even though they were not a part of the culture of the Algonquin Indians, they are now a part of the museum's collection.

The museum is open seven days a week from 9:00 to 5:00. There is a small admission charge. Call 804–769–2229 to be sure Chief Thunder-cloud will be on hand to provide his own unique tour of the many and varied artifacts. Or write him in care of the Mattaponi Indian Reservation, West Point, RFD #1, Virginia.

Directions: Take Beltway Exit 4 (I-95) to the outskirts of Richmond. Then take Route 360 north for approximately 15 miles to Route 30 south. From Route 30, turn on Route 633. This Reservation is almost directly across Route 30 from the Pamunkey Indian Reservation.

An alternate route to these Indian reservations is to take Beltway Exit 7 (Branch Avenue, Route 5) to Route 301 south. Continue to Port Royal and then take Route 17 south to Tappahannock. Go right on Route 360 for about 20 miles to Route 30 south. From Route 30 make a left on Route 640 and another left on Route 625 for the Mattaponi Indian Reservation.

7. Kecoughtan Indian Village

Mosquitoes were messengers of the gods, according to Algonquin lore. They, like all natural phenomena, had a purpose. The mosquito's message was that one should never become too satisfied or complacent about the bounty of nature. That philosophy certainly gives a new perspective to a summer nuisance.

Indians living at Kecoughtan might well have thought they were reminded more frequently than necessary, as their marshy location made them particularly vulnerable to mosquitoes. Many local tribes actually migrated inland during the summer months to escape the voracious insects, heat and humidity in the Tidewater area.

All this should be kept in mind when planning a visit to the recreated Kecoughtan Indian Village in Hampton, Virginia. Although the village is sprayed regularly for mosquitoes, visitors may still want to liberally apply a mosquito repellant before exploring. The village is worth seeing because it provides a wider depiction of tribal life than is found at any other site within a day's drive.

There are seven structures, built by the Syms-Eaton Museum, for visitors to investigate. The standard dwelling for these Indians of the Powhatan Confederation was the wigwam. The wigwam of the Kecoughtan was built like a quonset hut, and should not be confused with the stereotypical teepee of the Plains Indian. Large wigwams served as lodges for extended family groups; only the chief had his own wigwam.

Two other interesting structures often omitted in reconstructions are found at Kecoughtan—the sweathouse and the scarecrow hut. The sweathouse was the Indian equivalent of the modern sauna. It was used by the medicine men to cure various ailments. The scarecrow hut was, as the name implies, a precursor of the scarecrow used in fields today. A child would sit within the hut and rattle a gourd to keep birds away from the ripening crop.

Another interesting addition to the village is the temple. Here the villagers worshipped an idol of their God Okee. Though not permitted inside, the Indians would leave beads, shells, tobacco and other offerings to priests in the temple. The temple was also a mausoleum for the chiefs and religious leaders of the tribe.

The Kecoughtan Village may be toured without charge. It is open seven days a week, from 10:00 to 5:00 except Sunday when the hours are 12:00 to 5:00. Tours are scheduled daily. When inclement weather or other conditions prevent a tour of the Village a slide presentation is given.

Directions: Take Beltway Exit 4 (I-95) to Route 64. Follow Route 64 to Hampton then take the Coliseum exit north toward Hampton. The Syms-Eaton Museum is directly across the highway from the Visitor Information Center for Hampton Tours. You can park at the center and use the highway crossover to walk to the Museum and Kecoughtan Indian Village.

8. Moyaone

Although nothing remains but the ghosts from the past, those tracing the path of the Indians of Maryland should visit Piscataway Park as it figured so prominently in the history of the Piscataway Empire.

When Captain John Smith stopped at this Indian town in 1608, it was already over 300 years old. This was one of the principal towns of the Piscataway Empire. Smith, trying to map his route, called the town "Moyaone."

Archeological work at this location uncovered the burial sites of the early inhabitants of this town. In the 1970s at the request of Chief Turkey Tayak, the surviving Piscataway leader, the burial sites were recovered. Chief Turkey Tayak is now buried here with his ancestors.

When the digging was begun at what was called the Accokeek Creek Site, archeologists discovered that this was the location of five early prehistoric groups. It is unfortunate that the few artifacts that remained at this significant site were stolen, so that now nothing of these early people remains except the land and the river. It is a sad reminder of just how fragile our historical links can be.

Directions: From the Beltway take Exit 3 south on Indian Head Highway and go about 10 miles. Then turn right on Bryan Point Road and follow it until it ends at Piscataway Park.

9. Indian Steps Museum

The Susquehannocks, tall and powerful, could have been the model for the strong, silent Indian. The tribes along the Chesapeake feared these larger, more warlike, Indians from the north. Even John Smith, when he encountered the Susquehannocks on his voyage up the inland waterways, was impressed and alarmed by their obvious strength and fearless demeanor.

Yet these warriors were also great fishermen. More than 100 years before the white man encroached on Indian land these braves were fishing the Susquehanna River for shad. The Indian Steps Museum takes its name from the footholds the Indians carved in the rocks along the shore just south of the museum.

Although this area was the home ground of the Susquehannocks, other tribes did navigate the river on hunting trips. The river banks were the site of many inter-tribal battles. An extensive collection of artifacts belonging to these long ago warriors has been recovered.

These artifacts are embedded in the walls of the Indian Steps Museum in intricate patterns that are based on Indian drawings. They are much like the Indian picture writing found on pottery, with many birds, animals, snakes and Indian figures represented. In addition to this amazing wall collection of artifacts, there are numerous exhibits of fossils, some dating back to 10,000 years before Christ. The museum has a highly regarded collection of Indian and prehistoric relics.

Indian Steps Museum is open from April through October daily, except Monday, unless Monday is a holiday. Hours are 10:00 to 4:00, except Sundays and holidays when the hours are 11:00 to 6:00. There are usually special programs on Sunday afternoons. To find out about them call (717) 757-2874 or write to the museum at 1146 E. Poplar Street, York, PA. 17403. There is no fixed admission but donations are encouraged.

Picnic tables are available and it is an enjoyable place to spend a little extra time. There are several hiking trails. Along the trails the abundant bird and animal life can be spotted as well as some of the nearly 70 species of trees. There is a giant Holly that was growing here before the Pilgrims landed at Plymouth Rock.

Directions: From the Beltway take Exit 27 (I-95) to the Baltimore Beltway, Route 695. Take that to Route 83 north. At York take Route 425 to Newbridgeville and Craley. From Route 425 make a left on Route 616 for Indian Steps Museum. It is just outside a small town called Airville on the Susquehanna River.

10. Susquehannock Ceremonial Site

One hundred and seventy feet above the valley floor in Deer Creek State Park massive stone indentations form seats used by the Susquehannock Indians for their tribal meetings.

On the rocky promontory above Deer Creek tribal leaders would take their place in the King and Queen Seats, presiding over ceremonies designed to propitiate the gods.

The cliffs offer an imposing vista and it is easy to appreciate why the Indians, with their reverence for nature, believed this was a place of much "medicine" or magic. Legend suggests that the Susquehannocks sought these ceremonial seats in order to absorb some of the majesty of the setting and reinforce their own tribal leadership.

The seats can be reached by a rather steep climb from the picnic area or by the road that winds most of the way up the incline leaving only a short easy walk to the King and Queen Seats. It is fascinating to sit in these mammoth natural chairs and imagine the Indians who once held elaborate festivities and rituals on this very site.

Rocks State Park, which is part of the larger Deer Creek State Park, is open from 9:00 to sunset daily at no charge.

Directions: Take Beltway Exit 22 (Baltimore-Washington Parkway) to the Baltimore Beltway, Route 695. Go left toward Bel Aire. From Route 695 take Route 1 until it crosses Route 24. Deer Creek State Park is eight miles northwest of Bel Aire off Route 24.

11. Lenape Land

It's all a question of perspective. Called by the colonists "Delawares" because they inhabited that colony, the Delaware Indians titled themselves "Lenni Lenape," meaning "real men." Some of their fellow Algonquins spoke respectfully of them as "grandfather" to indicate that they were the parent tribe of other Algonquin groups. But among the more warlike tribes they were called "women," being considered weak and ineffectual in their dealings with the white intruders.

Though the Lenni Lenape were for the most part peaceful and friendly, they could react to provocation. For example, in the early 1630s a Dutch trading post where Europeans and Indians had met harmoniously was the scene of a misunderstanding that led to the Indians killing all members of the settlement.

This was the exception. The relationship of the Indians of Delaware with William Penn was particularly good. Penn was even adopted by the tribes as "Brother Onas." Despite Penn's fair treatment of the Indians in this area, they, like other Algonquin tribes to the south, began to move west in the 18th century. Most of the descendants of the Lenni Lenape now live in Kansas and Oklahoma.

But some still inhabit the old region and a Lenape association has recreated a small Indian village representative of those that once dotted the Delaware valley. Authentically built wigwams covered with reed mats or cat-tail thatch face the Neshaminy Creek. A sweat lodge is being constructed and there is a museum room.

In the museum is a model of a Lenape village, a representation of a wigwam interior and a collection of Indian artifacts. Some of the stone pieces date back to 3000 B.C. Demonstrations will also show interested visitors how the Lenni Lenape Indians made their clay pottery, wove baskets, braided their cornhusk mats and made arrowhead weapons. An audio-visual presentation will complete this view of an earlier time and people.

Visits to the Lenape Indian Village must be arranged in advance; call (215) 766-0666 or write Lenape Land, Park Avenue, New Britain PA 18901.

Directions: Take Beltway Exit 27 (I-95) north to Philadelphia, and follow Route 76 and 276 around Philadelphia, exiting on Route 611 north. Pick up Route 152 for Chalfont and make a right turn on Park Avenue for Lenape Land.

OF NOTE: One additional resource for the Indian Epoch should be mentioned. The Hall of Eskimo and Indian Culture in the Smithsonian's Museum of Natural History has numerous displays depicting the life-styles of different Indian tribes.

Only a few deal with local Indians. One interesting legend pictured involves Win-di-go, a man-eating giant. This creature was thought to roam the Maryland and Virginia forests during the winter months. Mothers would tell stories about Win-di-go to keep their young children from wandering too far from the village. The museum also has a collection of Iroquoian masks, which were thought to have the power to cast out demons of sickness. Lastly, a diorama of Captain John Smith meeting the Powhatan Indians is included.

Most of the exhibits deal with western Indian tribes, but it is a fascinating collection representing all the major American Indian groups. Hunting, warfare, clothing, weaving, pottery, rituals and agricultural pursuits are all covered.

Colonial Period

First Settlements

Imagine what it must have been like for the first English settlers leaving their homes for the wilderness of the New World. It was Christmas, 1606, an occasion for festive gatherings and the renewing of family bonds. These men, however, were severing all bonds, heading into an unknown future. Few would ever see England again.

What motivated them? Why did they risk so much? They were all men who hoped to better their lot, many of whom dreamed of finding gold and becoming rich. The London Company, which outfitted their three ships—the *Susan Constant*, *Godspeed* and *Discovery*—also believed that gold was available in the New World, and that exploration of the area might reveal a shorter route to the South Seas. The voyage itself was arduous and long, and made under difficult and cramped conditions. Both the Company and the adventurers must have been haunted by thoughts of an earlier group of Englishmen who had attempted a settlement at Roanoke and had vanished without a trace in 1587. The uncertainty of the voyage ended after four months when the three ships entered the Chesapeake Bay on April 26, 1607.

The Englishmen explored the banks of the James River for 11 days before picking Jamestown as the site of their settlement. Although marshy, the location had excellent anchorage and could easily be protected.

Spurred on by threats from the London Company to abandon them if they did not find riches, the original settlers of Jamestown did not spend any time preparing shelters or planting crops. All their efforts were directed towards finding gold.

By summer's end more than half the original group had died of dysentery or malaria. Discouraged, the settlers faced the cold winter housed only in tents and woefully short of food.

John Smith was responsible for the survival of the group. He supervised the building of crude log cabins which were enclosed by a fence stockade—the first James Fort.

He also traded with the local Powhatan Indians for much-needed food. As the Indians were reluctant to sacrifice food which was essential for their own welfare, Smith had to expand his efforts and visit tribes on nearby waterways and upriver. His explorations provided information on the Indian population in the area and allowed him to estimate that within 60 miles of Jamestown there were roughly 5,000 Indians.

The food John Smith obtained from the Indians literally made the difference between life and death. By early spring of 1608 the brave band that had left England were gaunt scarecrows, but still alive.

Despite these heroic efforts, had new supplies not arrived when they did, Jamestown might well have been another "Lost Colony."

The English supply ship also brought 100 new settlers. Renewed efforts were undertaken to make Jamestown more habitable; crops were planted and prospects improved. A summer fire that destroyed all their buildings was actually a benefit because it forced the settlers to erect more durable structures. Having shivered through one long winter they recognized that a little extra effort would be worthwhile.

In the fall of 1608 another English ship brought 70 additional settlers, including the colony's first two women. It was also in the fall that John Smith was chosen as council President, a position tantamount to being the colony's Governor. This development seems rather ironic because Smith had been excessively quarrelsome on the voyage over, and was, in fact, kept in irons for much of the journey. He was sentenced to be executed in the West Indies and the gallows constructed before he was reprieved. The group would later be grateful for their charity towards Smith; he certainly proved his worth under difficult circumstances.

John Smith returned to England in 1609, after being badly burnt when a spark ignited his powder bag. Smith's absence was sorely noted. The winter of 1609-10 was called the "starving time," and Jamestown was decimated by this famine. The colonists were reduced to eating mice, snakes, dogs, cats and horses—hides and all. Only 65 settlers were left when spring finally came. They were determined to return to England and when Sir Thomas Gates arrived demanded he immediately set sail for their return trip.

Jamestown was abandoned and the colonists were sailing out of the James River when they sighted ships approaching. It was the new governor, Lord De la Ware, with 150 new settlers, food and supplies. He had arrived just in time to save the colony. The 65 survivors reluctantly returned and Jamestown was saved.

Twenty-seven years after the arrival of the Jamestown expedition the ships *Ark* and *Dove* sailed from England. Lord Baltimore had been granted land along the Chesapeake Bay above Virginia, to establish the Maryland colony as a haven for persecuted Catholics.

The 322 settlers bound for Maryland spent four rough months crossing the Atlantic. Violent storms separated the two ships and each feared the other lost; when they finally sighted each other there was great rejoicing.

First landfall was St. Clement's Island on March 3, 1634. The English were met by 500 armed bowmen from a local Piscataway tribe. Governor Leonard Calvert learned that the Indians owed allegiance to the "Emperor of the Piscataways." He took the *Dove* down to Moyaone on Accokeek Creek to obtain the Indian leader's permission to settle. The "Tayac," or Indian ruler, did not encourage the English to settle in his domain, but neither did he forbid it.

Satisfied with his meeting with the Piscataway Emperor, Calvert returned to St. Clement's. He negotiated the purchase of land that was to become St. Mary's City from the Yoacomico Indians, a tribe which was planning to relocate anyway because they feared Susquehannock raids.

The settlers were able to make use of Indian huts as temporary shelters until they could build more substantial homes. As they had arrived in March they luckily were able to take advantage of the spring planting season. This, combined with the harvest from the abandoned Indian fields and the substantial amount of supplies they had brought with them, prevented the cruel starvation which had caused the death of so many early Virginia settlers.

Somewhat later Father White, spiritual leader of the Maryland colony, returned to Moyaone and converted the Emperor to Christianity. He also baptized the Emperor's only daughter, Kittamagund. She returned with Father White to St. Mary's. The Indian girl, now called Betty, was raised and educated by Margaret Brent, one of the first women's activists in America. Betty married Margaret Brent's brother, Captain Giles Brent.

Their son, Giles Brent, Jr., inherited the land that George Washington was later to buy and call River Farm. In July 1675, Giles, Jr. was involved in the series of events that precipitated the last major Indian war on English settlements in this region. Giles, Jr. and his cronies, seeking to avenge the death of an Englishman named Henn, attacked the wrong Indian tribe. The resultant Susquehannock War led directly to the colonial insurrection known as Bacon's Rebellion, which left Jamestown a burnt ruin.

12. Jamestown Colonial Historical Park

The 10-year-old blushed and shuffled her feet when asked by the costumed gentlemen if she had just arrived from England to find a husband. Though the question clearly embarrassed her, it is part of the atmosphere of Colonial Jamestown; all visitors taking the Living

History exploratory walk are greeted as if they had just stepped off a ship from 17th-century England.

Costumed people conduct walking tours around the foundations of this early "James Cittie." They fill newcomers in on all local news but may expect the latest word on activities back "home." They even talk like the 17th-century characters they create, which may amuse their 20th-century audience.

These colonists are enthusiastic about the opportunities offered in Virginia for advancement. They will tell you that tobacco provides the quickest route to wealth and position and that more and more farmers are acquiring land outside the city area on which to establish tobacco fields.

Although nothing remains from this early time except the foundations of the buildings and the Old Church Tower built in 1639, the knowledgeable guides make all the streets come alive. Those walking the path on their own can substitute for the guides taped messages which will provide pertinent information and local color.

Every visit to Jamestown should begin with the 15-minute orientation film shown at the Visitor Center. This film fills in the background of the first Virginia settlement. A tour of the museum room should follow, where artifacts uncovered from this colonial site are displayed. Efforts by archeologists to add to this collection have been hampered because the first James Fort is now under the James River.

Some fine pottery and glassware are offered in the museum shop, but before leaving stop by the Glasshouse where the glass pieces are produced, and the Jamestown potter located near the fort site. Jamestown was the first colonial town to produce "factory-made" items to export back to England. This 1608 industry is again in operation at the Glasshouse, where colonial methods are used to produce glassware. Even the green color remains as it was in the 17th century because the sand used in the process is from this area and contains iron oxide.

One last experience will offer a sobering picture of the natural environment which confronted the first settlers. Be sure to take the five-mile loop drive which winds through 1,500 acres of marsh and woodland that has remained basically unchanged since the early 1600s.

Jamestown Colonial Historical Park is open daily, except Christmas, from 9:00 to 4:30, and slightly later during the summer months. There is a per car admission fee.

Immediately before entering Jamestown Colonial Historical Park is Jamestown Festival Park (see Indian Epoch chapter). Here are reconstructed replicas of the three ships—the *Susan Constant*, *Godspeed* and *Discovery*—that brought the first settlers. James Fort has also been rebuilt with 18 structures laid out to duplicate the original.

Costumed personnel are available on one of the ships and in the fort to provide additional information about the difficulties these intrepid Englishmen surmounted.

In the New World Pavilion there are artifacts and displays related to the early colonial period.

Jamestown Festival Park is open from 9:00 to 5:00 daily except Christmas Day and New Year's Day. Admission is charged.

Directions: From the Beltway take Exit 4 (I-95) to Route 64. Take Route 64 to the Williamsburg area. Then take Route 31 to Jamestown Colonial Historical Park.

13. St. Clement's Island

It's fun to take the short boat ride from Colton Point to St. Clement's Island. Wandering the scenic trails and watching the waterfowl would be sufficient reason to explore St. Clement's; but the island is also historically significant.

This is where the English first landed in Maryland, not at St. Mary's City. In March 1634 the *Ark* and *Dove* sailed up the Potomac River and anchored off this island.

It had been a rough crossing and the *Dove* was lost in a storm for weeks. Once on land, the settlers were quick to offer a mass of thanksgiving for their safe arrival, which was celebrated by Father Andrew White.

Though St. Clement's was much larger than the 40 acres it covers today because of erosion, the settlers nevertheless felt that they needed more land and that an island settlement would present too many difficulties. Before moving to their new settlement, Governor Leonard Calvert issued a proclamation formally taking possession of Terre Mariae, reiterating the promise of freedom of religion for Catholics and Protestants.

The island is under the auspices of the St. Clement's Island Interpretive Center—Potomac Museum and there are displays which depict various aspects of early Maryland history. Facing out towards open water is the Great Cross of St. Clement's, which commemorates the first mass.

To check boat times call (301) 769-2222 or write to St. Clement's Island, Colton's Point, MD 20626.

Directions: From the Beltway take Exit 7 (Route 5) to Leonardtown. From Route 5 take Route 242 to Colton's Point.

The *Maryland Dove* sails for St. Mary's where she is a permanent exhibit. She is a replica of Lord Baltimore's ship *Dove* that brought Maryland's first settlers in 1634.

14. St. Mary's City

It's 350 years ago and "You Are There" in 17th-century Maryland. The action is so lively that the innkeeper seems remiss in not filling everyone's mug. Visitors join the sheriff or tavern keeper in a quick game of hazards, a dice toss game that caused many a colonial to gamble away his tobacco crop. The tavern is also a good place to hear the latest news—such as word of a massacre just two day's ride up country.

The tavern, or "ordinary," is just one of the focal spots for the afternoon historical dramas that are part of the Living History Show presented on summer weekends.

Another active site is Dan Clocker's farm. He and his wife recreate the struggle for existence faced by a young farm couple. Mary Clocker may even enlist the help of some visiting children in grinding the corn for evening supper or show the youngsters how to decorate a maypole for a special celebration.

The replica of the *Dove*, a square-rigged pinnace which served as the supply ship for the first settlers, is the scene of more activity. Visitors can climb aboard and explore this small ship. It is hard to imagine that it carried the necessities to support 140 settlers. There is a stone marker in back of Trinity Church which indicates the exact spot where settlers from the *Ark* and *Dove* disembarked after their short journey from St. Clement's Island.

All this activity takes place on the grounds of the Reconstructed State House of 1676, the second floor of which also has a number of exhibits on Maryland history. St. Mary's was the capital of Maryland until 1694 when the seat of government was moved to Annapolis.

To obtain more information on the Living History Show call (301) 862-1634 or write the St. Mary's City Commission, St. Mary's City, MD 20686.

Directions: From the Beltway take Exit 7 (Route 5) to St. Mary's City.

George Washington and The Washington Family Homes

George Washington, always larger than life, actually towered over his contemporaries. It is hard for us to imagine the "Father of our Country" as an awkward young man, but ladies once laughed behind their fans and were reluctant to dance with him because of his oversized feet. And he had virtually no talent for small talk. The few girls he fell in love with were totally uninterested in his proposals.

One of the true loves of his life was Sally Fairfax, the wife of a good friend and neighbor. Their relationship was always honorable and never evoked the usual neighborhood gossip. Sally helped George overcome his shy, inarticulate manner.

Though thwarted in his attempts to wed until the rather late age of 23, family was always important to Washington.

Born at Pope's Creek Plantation on February 22, 1732 to Augustine and Mary Ball Washington, George was named not after the English king but his mother's guardian. By the age of six, he had a sister, Betty, and three brothers: Sam, John and Charlie. He also had two half-brothers, Lawrence and Augustine, who were studying in England.

When George was 11 his father died suddenly of a severe gout attack. His half-brothers each inherited one of the Washington family homes. The eldest son, Lawrence, inherited Eppewasson, renaming it Mount Vernon, in honor of his commanding officer Admiral Vernon. Augustine settled at Pope's Creek, which his son renamed Wakefield. George was left Ferry Farm, on the Rappahannock River near Fredericksburg. His mother and the younger children also lived there.

Young Washington enjoyed exploring Fredericksburg. It was his first experience with town life. A chance observance of some surveying work being done outside town sparked the idea of pursuing that line of work. He found some rusting equipment his father had stored away, and in 1747, at the age of fifteen-and-a-half, he was paid for his first job.

A fortuitous opportunity presented itself when young George was given the chance to help survey Lord Thomas Fairfax's 15,000 acres beyond the Blue Ridge Mountains. This foray into Indian territory was an exciting adventure for the 16-year-old Washington. He often talked of watching painted warriors dance around the camp bonfire.

Washington's career as a surveyor was off to a good start. In three years he was made the official surveyor of Culpeper County.

But family matters did not go as well. His favorite brother, Lawrence, was suffering from a series of debilitating illnesses. Although Washington abandoned his own responsibilities to accompany his brother to the Caribbean in hopes of improving his failing health, it was to no avail. They returned to Virginia, where Lawrence died at the age of 34. Less than a month later Lawrence's infant daughter also died. These double tragedies meant that George inherited the family home, Mount Vernon.

Before dying Lawrence insured that his brother would follow his lead, taking his place in the Ohio Company, the House of Burgesses and the Virginia Militia.

During the French and Indian War, Major George Washington served as aide-de-camp to General Braddock. His heroic action in the Battle of Fort Duquesne began the Washington legends.

Washington, his clothes bullet ridden, with three horses shot from beneath him and so feverish he could barely remain in the saddle, continued to regroup the British forces in the face of the advancing French. When General Braddock was shot and the troops were in full flight, Washington was one of the three officers who carried the dying General back behind the lines. Still not giving in to his own condition, Washington returned to the battlefield, riding all night to get the wounded to wagons and safety. Though the British lost the battle, Washington's actions were so noble that the public cheered. Having a new hero salved the sting of defeat. His conduct during this crisis was a major factor in his later appointment as commander of the American Revolutionary forces.

Washington, having experienced success on the battlefield, was also to finally succeed in winning a wife. He married the wealthy widow, Martha Custis on January 6, 1759. He unofficially adopted her two young children Jack Parke Custis, age four, and Patsy, age two. It is ironic that Washington, paterfamilias to a whole country, never realized his own deep wish to have a child of his own.

The next 15 years were probably the happiest of Washington's life. He had his new family and was able to supervise the growth of his beloved Mount Vernon. He bought four additional farms in the area, increasing his acreage from 2,126 to 8,000 acres. His interest in the details of the estate overwhelmed his overseer.

As relations between England and the colonies disintegrated,

Washington was forced to leave Mount Vernon. He attended the Second Continental Congress in Philadelphia. His absence was greatly extended when he was appointed Commander-in-Chief of the colonial forces. For six long years Washington struggled against the British. He had to fight the Continental Congress as well for supplies, munitions and pay for his troops. In October 1781 the British finally surrendered at Yorktown.

Family misfortune conspired to blight what would otherwise have been a jubilant victory. His 24-year-old step-son, Jack, ill from exposure and fatigue, died immediately after the Battle of Yorktown. He requested his father take care of his family.

Washington again unofficially adopted Jack's two youngest children, George Washington Parke Custis and Eleanor (Nellie) Custis. He returned to Mount Vernon for Christmas with his new young family.

Every time Washington relaxed and began enjoying the life of a gentleman farmer he was interrupted by his country's call to service. This time he learned that Congress had unanimously elected him President of the United States.

Though Washington was inaugurated in New York, Congress moved to Philadelphia while the new capital was constructed. The new Federal City, situated between the north and the south, was laid out across the Potomac from Alexandria. In his honor the 10-mile square city was named Washington, but he always referred to it as the Federal City.

After two terms Washington relinquished the Presidency to John Adams and returned for the last time to Mount Vernon. Three years after his final homecoming, on Saturday, December 15, 1799, Washington died. His final wishes were followed and he was buried on the Mount Vernon grounds.

Eight houses of the Washington family survive and are restored to permit visitors a glimpse of the life-style of the different generations of our country's first "First Family." The houses are open to the public and easily accessible, none being more than two hours from the Beltway.

The nation's largest George Washington Birthday Parade winds through the historic streets of Alexandria, Virginia on February 16.

15. Fort Necessity National Battlefield Park and The Mount Washington Tavern

Here at this spot just over the Pennsylvania state line, George Washington would be both defamed and proclaimed. He would be accused of assassination and hailed as a hero. Here he fought his first battle, the only one in which he would ever have to surrender, and he eventually acquired this very same land to add to his immense holdings on the frontier. It would be Washington's men who fired the first shots here in a conflict that would lead to the Seven Year's War in Europe. The experience Washington gained during the French and Indian War, as it was called in the colonies, resulted in his being named Commander-in-Chief of the Revolutionary forces.

At the age of 21, George Washington was sent by Virginia Governor Robert Dinwiddie to lead an expedition into the Ohio Valley to warn the French against intruding into what the English viewed as their territory. Young Washington was chosen because of his surveying background in the area and because his older brother, Lawrence, was a major stockholder along with Governor Dinwiddie in the Ohio Company of Virginia. This venture, begun in 1747, brought the English and French into direct competition for the rich fur trade and land in the Ohio Valley.

Washington first traveled to Fort LeBouef in November of 1753 on a diplomatic mission to convince the French to withdraw. Failing this, a military force was assembled, and volunteers were promised land in the Ohio Valley. Troops were under the command of Colonel Joshua Fry and Lieutenant Colonel Washington, who at Fry's death early in the mission was put in charge and promoted to colonel.

Leaving the Winchester headquarters in April 1754 (see Colonial Plantations: Abram's Delight for additional information on George Washington's Office and Museum), Washington, with 40 men, moved ahead past Cumberland, then called Wills Creek, to Great Meadows. Four days after they arrived in the area, having marched 50 miles through a forested area that had to be cleared to permit the wagons to pass, they were sent word by the Indians of a company of 50 French soldiers seven-and-a-half miles away.

Surprising the French at dawn, Washington, in the first military skirmish of his career, was the victor. The French leader, Ensign Jumonville, and nine others in his party were killed; within 15 minutes the French surrendered. One member of the French party escaped to walk barefooted back to Fort Duquesne (now Pittsburgh) and reported that Washington had failed to cease fire when the French called out that they were on a diplomatic, rather than a military, mission.

Neither Washington, nor any of his men, had heard any such appeal. The yells of the Indians, the cries of the wounded and the noise of the battle may well have obscured the plea, if indeed, it was made. This brief encounter was the start of the war that ended with the English acquiring full claim to all the French land in North America.

Washington returned to Great Meadows after the Jumonville incident and built a fort "of necessity," knowing that the French would not let the loss of their men go unchallenged. Little more than a month later, in early July 1754, a large French force commanded by Jumonville's stepbrother attacked Fort Necessity. Greatly outnumbered, Washington's force held them off for eight hours before surrendering. Included in the terms Washington signed was the statement that he had assassinated Jumonville. This crucial word was incorrectly translated and Washington believed the statement read that Jumonville was killed in action. This signed statement by George Washington was used to discredit the English in Europe.

The Visitor Center at Fort Necessity runs a slide program on the dramatic events in this opening chapter of the French and Indian War. The location of Jumonville Glen is marked and Fort Necessity has been reconstructed. The fort itself is unbelievably small, making it difficult to believe that it is indeed the exact size of the fortification Washington fought so hard to defend on July 3, 1754. But extensive archeological excavation proved that this was indeed the size of the original fort.

A year later General Edward Braddock would follow the trail Washington had blazed up past Fort Necessity. When Braddock was mortally wounded at the Battle of the Monongahela (sometimes called the Battle of Fort Duquesne) on July 9, 1755, George Washington was instrumental in removing the suffering Braddock from the battlefield. Four days later Washington read the burial service at Braddock's grave, just a mile west of Fort Necessity. A monument commemorates the site.

In 1770 George Washington returned to survey this area. He had purchased 234.5 acres around Great Meadows from the Commonwealth of Pennsylvania for $120.00 in 1769. This was only one small portion of the 32,000 acres of frontier land Washington owned. As early as 1784, Washington recommended the land as an excellent spot for an inn, a claim he would repeat several times before he died. It was not until 1827 or 1828, though, that the Mount Washington Tavern was built along the National Road which ran in front of this property. Today the tavern is part of Fort Necessity National Battlefield Park. It has been restored to appear as it did when it was one of the most famous and lively inns on the National Road. Outside there is a genuine Conestoga Wagon, one of only 150 that have survived. The public rooms, parlor, kitchen and upstairs bedrooms have been decorated as they would have been during the tavern's heyday. In the dining room area is a display providing a wealth of information about the National Road and its many inns.

Fort Necessity National Battlefield Park is open daily during daylight hours and the Visitor Center and Tavern are open from 9:00 to 5:00 with extended hours during the summer. There is no admission charge.

Directions: From the Beltway take Exit 35 (I-270) to Frederick. Continue on Route 70 until the Route 40 junction. Follow Route 40 west to Cumberland, where it picks up Route 48. Then at Keysers Ridge pick up Route 40 west towards Uniontown. Fort Necessity National Battlefield Park is on the right at Farmington.

16. George Washington Birthplace National Monument

The date of George Washington's birthday has been treated rather capriciously by succeeding generations of his fellow countrymen. To be historically accurate, he was born about 10:00 a.m. on February 11, 1732 at Pope's Creek Plantation in Virginia. But when he was 20, England and her colonies belatedly adopted the Gregorian calendar, which corrected an 11-day error. This moved Washington's birthday to February 22. The new Federal holiday bill celebrates his birthday on the third Monday of February, regardless of the date.

Washington's birthplace, at least, has never been in doubt. Pope's Creek Plantation was a modest farm built by his father at the cost of 5,000 pounds of tobacco and 1 pound sterling. The house was later inherited by his half-brother, Augustine, and then his nephew, William Augustine, who renamed it Wakefield.

The Washington family moved from this plantation when George was three. After his father's death he did return for long visits with his half-brother.

A memorial house stands near the site of the original home whose foundations are marked by an oyster shell outline. The way of life young George experienced is evident in its 200-year old furnishings, the out-kitchen and herb garden. There is also a working colonial farm with livestock and crops much as little George would have seen.

Both birth and death are commemorated here. A monument honors Washington's birthplace, while not far away lie the Washington Family Burial Grounds. Washington's father, grandfather, great-grandfather and half-brother, Butler, are buried here. Only two of the gravestones are original; the others, which are marked by memorial tablets, were erected later.

The trail at the colonial farm winds through a cedar grove and down to the water. George may have used a similar trail himself, since he enjoyed fishing in Pope's Creek, hunting in the marsh and wood-lands and seeing the great ships from England as they loaded tobacco at the farm's wharf.

The George Washington Birthplace National Monument is open daily, except December 25 and January 1. Hours are 9:00 to 5:00. Admission is free.

Directions: From the Beltway take Exit 7 (Route 5) to Route 301. Continue on Route 301 to Route 3. This working colonial farm is 1.7 miles off Route 3 on Route 204. The turn-off is clearly marked.

17. Epping Forest

George Washington once said, "All that I am I owe to my mother."

Mary Ball Washington's life-long efforts to direct her children's lives were a reflection of her own childhood insecurities. She was only three when her father died; when she was 11 her mother died. Later when her husband also died and left her with young children, she realized from her own experience how important it was for her to become deeply involved in all their activities. It was the absence from her own life of this pivotal figure that made her the woman she was.

Mary Ball was born at Epping Forest in 1708. She left at age 11 to live with her guardian, Colonel George Eskridge, at Sandy Point Estate. As she matured and became a belle of local society she was known as "the Rose of Epping Forest."

The west side of the small, two-story frame house where Mary Ball spent her early childhood remains substantially as it was at the time. The handcrafted woodwork, English brick fireplaces and indoor overhead transoms are all of special architectural interest. The east wing of the house was added in 1842.

Four of Epping Forest's original dependencies have survived. The ice house, painstakingly constructed of 15,000 handmade bricks, the laundry house with the original hinges and weatherboarding and the smokehouse and carriage house all date from the 1700s.

Epping Forest is open April through November from 9:00 to 5:00. Epping Forest Antique Shoppe is located on the plantation and is open year round.

Directions: Take Beltway Exit 4 (I-95) to Fredericksburg. From Fredericksburg take Route 3 south approximately 75 miles through Montross and Warsaw. Epping Forest is on Route 3 on the right 18 miles from Warsaw.

18. Mount Vernon

Figuratively the clock stopped at Mount Vernon at 10:20 p.m. on December 14, 1799, the night of George Washington's death. Time seems to have stood still since then, and Mount Vernon is presented today as it was during the lifetime of the General, President and gentleman farmer who owned this great estate.

The task of reassembling the furnishings and household goods of the Washington family was an expensive and complicated assignment, but one which the Mount Vernon Ladies Association accepted as a challenge. Martha Washington, after her husband's death, frequently gave admiring visitors various household items as souvenirs. And then, a lot of the furniture from Mount Vernon was used by her granddaughter, Nellie Custis Lewis, to furnish her new plantation, Woodlawn. The china, silverware and other pieces were inherited by another grandchild, George Washington Parke Custis, and were used at Arlington House.

Fortunately, the appraisers of Washington's estate left a room-by-room inventory which has been the basis for the restoration of the house by the Mount Vernon Ladies Association. Approximately 40 percent of the furnishings on exhibition are original and the remaining pieces have been carefully selected to match the description in the inventory.

Many of the Washington family pieces provide a link with the significant events of their busy lives. There is the little table used for their wedding breakfast at Martha's Pamunkey River Plantation (actually White House on the Pamunkey). The trunk Martha took to Valley Forge is in the bedroom. Hanging on the wall is the key to the Bastille, presented to Washington by the Marquis de Lafayette.

Though the house is beautifully decorated and fascinating to explore, Washington's presence can be felt most hauntingly on a stroll around the grounds. The view from the porch across the Potomac to the Maryland countryside has been protected so that it remains the same delightful vista he so enjoyed. And the path down to the wharf should not be missed; Washington himself often used it when taking a small boat four miles downriver to visit his friend, George Mason, at Gunston Hall.

The Mount Vernon outbuildings are also worth seeing. Seven of the nine buildings have survived from Washinton's time—the kitchen, gardener's house, storehouse, spinning room, stables, smokehouse, and washhouse. The greenhouse burned in 1835 and was rebuilt, as was the little coach house, which was too run down to restore.

In the spring and summer the formal flower garden with its intricate boxwood pattern and the informal herbal kitchen garden show a stunning array of the plants known to have been grown at Mount Vernon during George Washington's time.

Washington's long years of service to his country left him little time to enjoy his beloved home. Despite his stated wish to be buried at Mount Vernon he was almost denied that by his countrymen. They wanted to honor him by burying him beneath the rotunda in the capitol. After 25 years of debate it was finally decided to allow him his final resting place at Mount Vernon. Both Martha and George are buried here, as are 25 other Washington family members.

Mount Vernon is open daily 9:00 to 5:00 from March through October; other months it closes at 4:00. Admission is charged.

Directions: From the Beltway take Virginia Exit 1, the Mount Vernon Parkway, south to Mount Vernon.

19. River Farm

In today's modern political climate the manner in which George Washington acquired River Farm might well raise an eyebrow. But rather than profit from public service our Founding Fathers all too often bankrupted themselves to establish and finance the new nation. No one questioned Washington's propriety.

It seems Washington had tried to purchase River Farm earlier from the owner, William Clifton. The deal fell through when Clifton decided to retain 500 acres and the manor house. Then deteriorating financial circumstances forced Clifton into court, and commissioners were appointed to arbitrate his affairs. Washington was one of the arbitrators. When the court placed the entire estate up for sale Washington purchased it for $2,884.80.

Like so many of the Virginia plantation aristocracy, Washington was land poor. The situation became almost tragic when he was forced to borrow $600 in order to attend his own inauguration in New York.

River Farm was one of four farms George Washington added to his Mount Vernon estate. The grounds reflect his agricultural concerns. As early as 1766, Washington began a system of crop rotation to avoid the ill effects of repeated tobacco cultivation of the same fields. He introduced a Kentucky coffee bean tree to this region. The Oswego Tea that colonials were forced to drink after the Boston Tea Party prompted many to search for an alternative beverage.

Also on the grounds is the first generation descendant of one of the large walnut trees Washington carefully nurtured and enjoyed. The manor house was given rent free to Washington's personal secretary, Tobias Lear, for the length of his life.

River Farm serves as the headquarters of the American Horticultural Society. Visitors are welcome. Call (703) 768-5700 or write to the Society in River Farm, VA 22121. Plan to visit during the week between 8:30 and 5:00. In the spring and at Christmas the Society holds an open house.

Directions: Take Beltway Exit 1 (the Mount Vernon Parkway) south. Turn left on the Arcturus-Herbert Spring exit to East Boulevard. Turn left for the entrance to River Farm at 7931 East Boulevard.

20. Mary Washington House

Highhanded, manipulative, bossy, opinionated, stubborn . . . *this* is Mary Washington? Yes, despite early portrayal of her as a self-effacing southern lady, Mary Washington was a highly protective mother and exerted a strong influence on all her children, particularly her oldest son, George.

When George was 15 his older step-brother, Lawrence, arranged for him to go to sea with the British navy. Excited at the idea of this great adventure, George couldn't wait to set sail. His mother, however, had his bags taken off the ship. When a disappointed George returned to Fredericksburg there was a gift waiting. It was a knife inscribed "Always obey your superiors."

Mary Washington did not approve years later when George got involved in the American Revolution. Her disapproval increased when, fearing for her safety on the rural Ferry Farm plantation, George moved her into the city of Fredericksburg.

His mother didn't want to move. She disliked the noise of the city and objected to the water. In fact, she sent a servant back to the old farm daily to bring fresh well water.

Her new house was a tailor's cottage on Charles Street in Fredericksburg that George enlarged. Some of the furnishings in the house today belonged to Mary Washington. Other pieces are similar to those mentioned in the wills of Augustine and Mary Washington.

Mary Washington was a widow for 46 years and spent the last 17 in this house. George Washington visited his mother on March 12, 1789 before continuing his journey to New York for his inauguration as President. He was never to see her again. She died at the age of 81 on August 25, 1789. There is a monument over her grave near Meditation Rock on land that was once part of the Kenmore estate.

The Mary Washington House is open daily, except December 24, 25, 31 and January 1. Hours are 9:00 to 5:00. A nominal admission is charged.

Directions: Take Beltway Exit 4 (I-95) to Fredericksburg. Follow signs to the Bicentennial Visitor Center. Continue four blocks to Amelia Street, then up to Charles Street. Turn right on Charles Street. The Mary Washington House is at 1200 Charles Street.

21. Kenmore

Many families maintain the tradition of handing down favorite recipes from one generation to the next. Grandmother's chocolate cake and Aunt Margaret's spaghetti sauce both form a bond that helps to keep the memory of past generations alive. This custom is followed at Kenmore. In the cheerful outkitchen they prepare Mary Washington's gingerbread, once enjoyed by her children Betty Washington Lewis and George. Guests sit at brightly covered tables and sip tea while sampling the delicious gingerbread. It really is a taste of the past.

This Georgian mansion was built in 1752 by Colonel Fielding Lewis when he married George Washington's younger sister, Betty. It is far more luxurious than most rural homes.

The list of *The 100 Most Beautiful Rooms in America* compiled by Helen Comstock includes the Great Room at Kenmore, the most distinctive feature of which is the ornamental plasterwork. The ceilings are considered the finest example of this art to be found in the United States. The carved plaster design over the mantel includes themes from *Aesops Fables*. With his mother only a few blocks away and his younger brother running a tavern in Fredericksburg, Washington was a frequent guest. Kenmore was like a second home to him.

The furniture has been selected to match closely items listed in an early Lewis inventory.

The garden has been completely restored. The Garden Club of Virginia has created an 18th-century formal boxwood garden, flanked on each side by matching gazebos. The garden path once led to Mary Washington's house a few blocks away.

Kenmore is open daily, except December 24, 25, 31 and January 1. November through March it is open 9:00 to 4:00; the rest of the year it stays open until 5:00. Admission is charged.

Directions: Take Exit 4 (I-95) to Fredericksburg. Follow Bicentennial Visitor Center signs into town, then turn left off William Street onto Washington Avenue. Kenmore is on the right.

22. Woodlawn Plantation

It was both fitting and appropriate that on George Washington's last birthday the youngest of his family was to begin her new life. Washington escorted his favorite stepdaughter, Nellie, to the altar and watched with pride the joining of his family with that of his sister's. Eleanor (Nellie) Parke Custis married Lawrence Lewis.

As their wedding gift Washington gave them 2,000 acres of Mount Vernon land, including one of his four farms, a grist mill (now restored) and a distillery. On this land they built Woodlawn.

The house was designed to resemble Kenmore and was furnished with pieces from Mount Vernon. From the river entrance Nellie could see the cupola of her girlhood home. A poignant suggestion of the grief she felt at Washington's death is evident in the placing of his bust on a pedestal which raised it to his exact height.

Nellie Custis' harpsichord and music are still in the Music Room. A taped rendition of her favorites recorded at Woodlawn evokes her presence.

Children will enjoy the collection of old-fashioned toys and games in the Touch and Try Room. On nice days the stilts and hoops can be used on the lawn. During cold weather youngsters may busy themselves with the dollhouse and quill pens. Mothers will be happy to learn the pens have been modernized to the extent that washable ink is used. Wooden block puzzles, games like cup and ball and dancing dolls are all here to intrigue the young.

Woodlawn is open from 9:30 to 4:30 except Christmas Day. Admission is charged. Frank Lloyd Wright's Pope-Leighey House has been moved onto the grounds and can also be visited.

Directions: From Beltway take Virginia Exit 1 (U.S. 1) south for 14 miles to the Woodlawn entrance on the right.

23. Arlington House

The story of Washington throwing a silver dollar across the Potomac has become an accepted part of American folklore. As in the children's game "Rumor," each retelling brought changes: the Rappahannock became the Potomac, the Spanish doubloon became a dollar, and the story became suspect. But it was included in a book that George Washington Parke Custis wrote about his famous foster father after Washington's death.

George Washington raised Custis after his father—Washington's step-son, Jack Custis—died at the very end of the American Revolution. As the principal male heir after Washington's death, Custis inherited the Mount Vernon china, silver, portraits and many other valuable pieces. He built Arlington House with the idea of making it a "treasury of Washington heirlooms."

In 1804 Custis married Mary Lee Fitzhugh and they entertained at Arlington House many of the notable figures of the time who came to pay tribute to the Washington legend. A frequent guest was the young Robert E. Lee.

After graduating from West Point, Lee married Mary Anna Randolph Custis, the only surviving Custis child. The marriage on June 30, 1831 was celebrated in the family parlor at Arlington House.

Mary Anna stayed in her girlhood home and raised their seven children. Lee's military career left him little time to spend with her. After the Civil War the estate was confiscated by the Federal government, and the Washington family possessions scattered. A Supreme Court decision returned the house to Robert E. Lee's son, but in 1883 he sold it back to the Federal government.

George Washington Parke Custis links two great American families, the Washingtons and the Lees, and through them two epic periods of United States history. Arlington House symbolizes that link.

A part of Arlington National Cemetery (see Recent History: Arlington National Cemetery), it is open to the public at no charge, from 9:30 to 4:00 during the winter months, and during other seasons until 6:00. Maps of the house with details of the rooms and furnishings permit visitors to explore at their own pace. The view from the center hall was described by Lafayette as "the finest in the world."

Directions: Arlington House is directly across the Potomac from Washington via the Arlington Memorial Bridge.

Colonial Agriculture

Communism in America's first settlement at Jamestown? Libelous? What else is it when the proceeds of each individual's labor are put in a common pot to repay the collective debt to the London Company? Well, it could also be called a failure. The communal system was totally unsatisfactory and in 1611 each settler was given three acres for his own use and profit.

Agriculture was the basis of the colonial economy; tobacco was actually the "coin of the realm." A horse cost roughly 500 pounds of tobacco, while a slave cost 5,000 pounds. A fair-sized house could also be built for that. The farm house where Washington was born cost his father 5,000 pounds of tobacco. A man could even use tobacco notes to gamble, but he was risking the rewards of back-breaking labor.

It required roughly 113 10-hour days of hard work to produce a tobacco crop. A hard working planter would grow about 1,500 to 2,000 pounds of tobacco a year on three or four cultivated acres. This works out to 5,000 plants an acre yielding about 500 pounds of tobacco per acre. The average size of a farm was 150 to 200 acres, but one man with his family's help could only cultivate four acres successfully.

The middle class planters were the largest group in the colonies. They were able to produce enough food on their farms to feed their families plus grow enough tobacco to acquire essential manufactured goods. However, it was a constant struggle to prevent a downward spiral into debt that would reduce their status to that of tenant farmer.

Everybody in the family worked except the very young—those under seven were exempt from field work. Frequent childbearing was one of the few ways for a family to obtain additional workers. This rough life, combined with yearly pregnancies, meant that few women lived through middle age. Serial monogamy was the rule, and it was not uncommon for a man to marry three times, thus siring three families.

Subsistence crops were an important element for all middle class planters. Corn was a major food crop. It averaged about 15 or 20 bushels for each acre planted. Planters tried to grow at least 15 bushels of corn for each member of the family. This meant cultivating one acre per person.

Corn was a good crop to grow because not only did it provide food, but the leaves, husks and stalks also could be fed to the livestock or even stuffed in a mattress for more comfortable sleeping.

Wheat, which provided flour for bread, was another important crop. Farmers took their wheat to a mill, paying part of their crop for the convenience of having it ground.

Also important to the livelihood of the family was the kitchen garden. This was the woman's responsibility. A wide variety of leafy green vegetables, root crops and an assortment of peas, beans and melons were grown. Herbs were another significant part of the kitchen garden. They served three purposes: as a spice to add variety to diet, as medicinal aids and for cosmetics.

There was never any leisure time on the farms. Although work in the fields was curtailed in the winter, buildings and fences needed repair. Wood had to be cut to heat the house. New fields needed clearing and farm implements had to be repaired. The livestock also needed tending.

For the women there was never a respite. Most colonial farm women bore at least 10 children, with about half dying in infancy. The continuing job of food preservation and preparation was awesome. The meals were simple but still the result of long labor. A typical dinner would be meat, cornbread and a vegetable.

Women generally tended the kitchen garden with their children's help. Being well versed in the uses of different herbs, they doctored the family as best they could with homemade remedies.

Life on these small farms was hard. Many historians feel that families were not overly affectionate because the mortality rate was so high that life was a tenuous thing. The church usually provided the only respite from this grinding and unending fight to survive.

24. The National Colonial Farm

If George Washington stepped out on the porch of Mount Vernon today he would see exactly the same view he saw over 200 years ago; this is a startling victory for history over commercial development.

An 18th-century freeholder's farm has been recreated across the Potomac River. The National Colonial Farm is a living historical farm museum, where costumed workers till the fields and prepare food in the old colonial kitchen.

Visitors are often entranced by the Colonial Herb Garden. Be sure to have one of the staff explain the medicinal, culinary and cosmetic uses of the different herbs. The herb garden contains colonial favorites such as tansy, camomile, sweet woodruff, rue, costmary, borage, and beebalm. Introduced to the New England colonists by the Oswego Indians, beebalm made a tea that, though less palatable than English varieties, was still patriotically consumed by colonists after the Boston Tea Party.

Guides encourage visitors to smell, touch and taste different herbs, something that should never be done unsupervised. For those anxious to try the herbs and spices they discover, the farm has an Herb Shop in the new Gatehouse where many of the herbs grown on the farm are sold.

Just a few steps from the Herb Garden is the Outkitchen. It was kept separate from the house because of the fire danger from the cooking fireplace. Handmade kitchen implements carved from gourds—cups, ladles and even a biscuit cutter—can be seen. Watching the women work with the old-fashioned oven, it is easy to see how the entire day could be spent in the kitchen preparing food.

As on all farms there are animals. Only historic varieties common in the 1700s are kept. The colonial practice of letting the animals forage at will and fencing the garden has been reversed. Modern day visitors would not be entirely comfortable with rambunctious, roaming turkeys, bulls and rams.

The newly planted orchard of apple, plum and pear trees and the grape arbor will provide fruit for juice and wine making. The colonists did not drink a lot of water so it was necessary to prepare substitute beverages. Crops on the farm include tobacco, the cash crop then and now for farmers in this area. Also grown is corn, a basic part of the 18th-century diet, and wheat, the source of flour.

Exploring the adjacent nature trail will be even more meaningful if one remembers that this is the location of the early Accokeek Creek Site (see Prehistory chapter) as well as the Moyaone Village (see Indian Epoch chapter).

The farm is open Tuesday through Sunday from 10:00 to 5:00. Admission is charged. Most weekends The National Colonial Farm has special craft demonstrations. For additional information call (301) 283-2113 or write the Farm at 3400 Bryan Point Road, Accokeek, MD 20607.

Directions: From the Beltway take Exit 3 (Indian Head Highway) south for 10 miles. At the light for Bryan Point Road turn right and continue for four miles to the end of the road.

25. The Godiah Spray Plantation

There's a new soap opera that won't be appearing on television screens. It is running instead at the Godiah Spray Plantation in St. Mary's,

Maryland. This continuing 10-year saga of life on a 1660 farm is possible because of a rare account book kept by Robert Cole during the first decades of life at St. Mary's settlement.

This record book provides a detailed account of what crops were planted and how much they yielded, what livestock were kept, what farm implements were purchased and what were made. It also provides personal details of the family's life: births, marriages, travels and deaths.

According to the Cole account book, tobacco, corn and the family kitchen garden were planted. The livestock on the farm consisted of 33 cattle, 29 hogs, several horses and some dunghill fowl, now called chickens. Sheep and goats were not found on most early farms because they were too easily killed by roving wolves.

Each year visitors will observe changes as the account for that year is recreated. This innovative approach will encourage annual visits to see the growth and changes in the family and farm.

Life on a pre-industrial farm was so difficult, so precarious and involved such back-breaking physical labor that it is hard to imagine what it was like unless it is actually experienced. The next best approach is to watch while the work is done with these old methods. The plantation also accurately portrays how the family was housed. There are four principal buildings on this working exhibit: the plantation house, freedman's cottage and the old and new barns.

Two architectural styles are employed. The plantation house and the old barn use rural English design. The new barn and freedman's cottage employ the fundamental adaptations colonial builders quickly made to these old world techniques. The new style was easier to build, quicker to raise and sturdier.

This living history program recreating life on the Godiah Spray Plantation is ongoing through the summer months. For additional information call (301) 862-1634 or write St. Mary's City Commission, St. Mary's City, MD 20686.

Directions: From the Beltway take Exit 7 (Route 5) to St. Mary's. Once in St. Mary's turn right on Rosecroft Road. The farm is located on Milburn Creek off Rosecroft Road, just 1 mile from the Reconstructed State House of 1676.

26. Turkey Run Farm

At Turkey Run Farm one may step into the life of the ordinary farmer in prerevolutionary America. This opportunity is unique, since usually only large plantations are preserved and restored. Thus 20th-century visitors get a distorted view of life in colonial times—we don't see how the majority of people actually lived.

But at Turkey Run Farm the "wife" (staff members portray an 18th-century family) complains about the crude wooden cabin. It was built in such a hurry to provide protection from the elements that the logs were not stripped and the mud mortar is crumbling where the logs meet. Though there is cross ventilation in the summer, it makes for a cold winter. The woman of the house is also unhappy because there's been no time to add a wooden floor, though her husband keeps promising he'll get around to it. She's tired of trying to smooth down the dirt floor with a hand-bound straw broom.

Visitors can experience the chill of evening for themselves. Special programs held at regular intervals provide an evening of 18th-century entertainment and conversation. The possibility of war with England may be considered, some musical relaxation on a fife or dulcimer enjoyed, or perhaps a sewing bee experienced.

When the weather permits, the man of the family can be found in the fields planting, hoeing or harvesting the crops. Tobacco is grown in hopes of raising a little money. Subsistence crops are also raised: beans, pumpkins, squash, corn and melons. Various foods are dried, smoked or salted to make the lean wintertime a little easier.

Visitors can watch the never-ending tasks that made up life on a colonial dirt farm. Soap had to be made from hog fat and cloth from sheep's wool. Animal skins were tanned to make shoes; buttons were made from bone or deer antlers. Water was fetched daily from a nearby stream and gourds hollowed out for serving bowls and utensils.

Turkey Run Farm operates at no charge from Wednesday through Sunday from 10:00 to 4:30. To find out about upcoming events, call (703) 442-7557 or write to Turkey Run Farm at 6310 Old Georgetown Pike, McLean, VA 22101.

Directions: Take Exit 14 from the Beltway (George Washington Memorial Parkway) toward McLean. Take Route 123 off the Parkway to Old Georgetown Pike, Route 193. Turn right at the Turkey Run Farm sign.

27. The Colonial Pennsylvania Plantation

Reading about history is one thing, reliving it is another. At The Colonial Pennsylvania Plantation, a 1770s "museum in the making," active involvement is encouraged. Visitors are urged to share in the ongoing colonial work when they stop by. Whether it's cutting curd for cheese, carding wool, dripping candles, playing a game of quoits or deciding where to plant next year's crops, there are plenty of opportunities to be directly involved.

The plantation buildings have been standing since the 18th century. The house is not a museum but appears as it would in the 1700s. Visitors may be surprised to see the brightly painted furniture and colorful quilts since it is more common to see the faded originals in most restored homes.

This plantation offers the opportunity to compare the colonial farming practices of Maryland and Virginia with those of southeastern Pennsylvania. There were a number of circumstances which made them different, the major one being that tobacco was not grown in Pennsylvania. In the north the crops were wheat, corn, buckwheat, potatoes, rye and oats. These were used to feed the family and the livestock. Because crop rotation was practiced in this area clover and grass were alternately sown. In the damp areas flax for linen was grown.

Farming in this area was more directly affected by the American Revolution than in the agricultural south. Troops crossed through this region frequently. Fences were destroyed, livestock and fodder confiscated and food sacrificed both willingly and unwillingly to the men on both sides. Many farms worked shorthanded as the able-bodied men joined the local militia, though this part of Pennsylvania was primarily Quaker and many did not believe in fighting.

Other features at the farm include the horses, cows, sheep, sows, boar and fowl which might have been found on colonial farms. There is also a stillroom for general storage; a root cellar to aid in preservation of foodstuffs; a springhouse (the 18th-century equivalent of the refrigerator); a barn; a wagon barn; and an old stone cabin. The important kitchen garden and orchard haven't been forgotten either.

The Colonial Pennsylvania Plantation is located at Ridley Creek State Park in Edgemont, Pennsylvania. It is open from April through October on Saturdays and Sundays from 10:00 to 4:00. Additional information on seasonal activities can be obtained by calling (215) 353-1777 or writing to the Plantation at P.O. Box 385, Edgemont, PA 19028.

Directions: From the Beltway take Exit 27 (I-95) north to Route 41 to Newport, the exit just prior to the Wilmington area. Follow Route 41 to U.S. 1. Go right on Route 1 past the Franklin Mint to Route 352. Go left on Route 352 and then right at the sign for Ridley Creek State Park.

28. Peter Wentz Farmstead

On October 4, 1777, George Washington, following his usual custom of stopping at the best house in the area, spent the night before the Battle of Germantown at the Peter Wentz Farmstead. One look at his bedroom may provide a small clue as to why the American forces were defeated. Washington certainly couldn't have had a good night's sleep in the bedroom garishly painted red with white polka dots.

The living room and entire downstairs hall is in this same loud pattern. But even this is relatively mild compared to some rooms. An upstairs bedroom looks like the painter ran amok; the room has black painted dots with red diamond stripes and red tadpole designs. Visitors just can't believe this pop art effect with spots, stripes and squiggles was used in the colonial period—but some sections are left unrestored to convince the skeptical.

The theme at this working farm is "as it was" in 1777, so instead of fading period pieces everything is freshly painted and restored.

Peter Wentz was a German immigrant and although the house, built in 1758, was of the English Georgian style so popular with the gentry in Philadelphia and in Virginia, it does incorporate some traditional German touches. These include the tile roof over the bee-hive oven, the two five-plate stoves and the bright colors throughout the house.

It is not just the house that is "as it was;" the barns, fields, orchard and kitchen garden have all been returned to their 1777 appearance.

Saturday afternoons there is a colonial craft program at the farm. Using authentic tools and methods, a wide variety of old-fashioned skills are demonstrated: spinning, quilting, basket weaving, broom making, crewel work, candle making, *scherenschnitte* (scissor cutting), wood carving and many others. Call ahead for detailed information at (215) 584-5104 or write to P.O. Box 240, Worcester, PA 19490.

The farm is open Tuesday through Saturday from 10:00 to 4:00 and on Sunday from 1:00 to 4:00. It is closed on Mondays, Christmas and Thanksgiving. There is no admission charged but donations are gratefully accepted. A Visitor Center with costumed hostesses provides an audio-visual presentation to orient 20th-century guests to life in 1777.

Directions: Take Beltway Exit 27 (I-95) to Wilmington, then north on U.S. Route 202 (Concord Pike) to PA Route 363 at Valley Forge. Go north on 363 to PA Route 73 (Skipjack Pike). Continue east one block on Route 73 to the first intersection then left to the Peter Wentz Farmstead.

Colonial Plantations

Plantations all had to have names for accurate record keeping, but what a variety of names there were. Some simply reflected the owner's name or family home back in England, others were more imaginative and gave some indication of the struggle necessary to obtain this land. For example, I Looked Many Places None I Liked Plantation; I Have Been A Great While At Plantation; Aha, the Cow Pasture Plantation; Penny Come Quick Plantation; or Long Looked For, Come At Last Plantation.

But whether the name was elaborate or simple, the physical layouts were similar. Each plantation had a main house. In Virginia the English Georgian style was sometimes copied, or the Palladian style, as at Thomas Jefferson's Monticello. Maryland houses often followed the Georgian five-part plan. That is, they had a central section with narrow side passages called hyphens. Smaller buildings were attached on each side; usually the kitchen, with house servant rooms above, was on one side and the chapel, with a school room above, was on the other.

The main house would have a large central hall with two entryways, one the approach, or carriage, entrance and the other overlooking the river and garden area. There would be a library, study, withdrawing room, ladies' parlor and dining room. The bedrooms were upstairs.

Plantations were planned to be self-sufficient. Food was grown on the grounds and most of the clothes and other necessities were provided by skilled workers. Down from the main house there would be two rows of dependencies used as workrooms.

The shoemaker, cooper, carpenter and tanner each had his own building. There would also have been a saw pit, stable and barn area. The noisier and smellier occupations were farther from the house.

Women's work buildings included the springhouse, weaving and spinning house, laundry, storehouse, soap making house, dovecote and chicken run. Women were also in charge of the herb and kitchen gardens.

Even on the large plantations the owner personally supervised his estate, though there was an overseer as well. The planter's wife also personally ran the household.

Unlike their European counterparts, plantation owners were compelled to exhibit resourcefulness. To hold and improve their position they had to direct their agricultural empire tirelessly. This prevented them from leading the leisurely life of the English aristocracy.

The large estates were located on the water to permit the shipping of the cash crop, tobacco, directly to England. One of the high spots of plantation life was the arrival at the wharf of a ship to pick up the year's tobacco harvest. This ship would bring news from London as well as from those plantations it had already visited. A representative of a London merchant, known as a "factor," would take orders for the goods required from London. Planters ordered furniture, farm implements, horses and guns; their ladies, after being apprised of the latest fashions, ordered clothes. No money changed hands; the tobacco sent on board by the planter paid for the order. If the tobacco did not cover the order the merchant gave credit. Many planters went deeply into debt to support an increasingly lavish 18th-century life-style. It is thought that by the time of the Revolution, colonial Virginians were 2,000,000 British pounds sterling in debt. Some families stayed indebted for as much as 150 years.

An expensive part of this lavish life-style was the fabled plantation hospitality. The isolation of many of these estates encouraged long visits by relatives, friends and often by travelers who had acquaintances in common with the planter. After 1751 when the ballroom was added to the Governor's Palace in Williamsburg, many of the plantations also added ballrooms. Large balls in the spring became a colonial custom to break the monotony of winter's enforced isolation.

By 1785 when Virginia abolished the English rule of primogeniture, whereby the elder son inherited the entire estate, the dissolution of the plantations had already begun. Wartime losses during the Revolution, soil exhaustion and the indebted state of many planters also contributed to the end of the plantation era.

29. Gunston Hall

When George Mason, near the end of his life, looked back at the historic epoch the fledgling country had passed through, he remarked, "We seem to have been treading on enchanted ground." Gunston Hall, Mason's plantation home, provokes that same reaction.

The men who built the nation also built beautiful homes, and Mason's was no exception. Although the exterior is unassuming, the interior is opulently designed. It was described as "a cottage on the outside, a palace inside."

George Mason began building Gunston Hall in 1755. He asked his brother, who was in England, to engage the services of a good carpenter. William Buckland, a 21-year-old carpenter, had just completed his apprenticeship as a joiner and woodcarver. He came to America as Mason's indentured servant. Buckland's work would become so popular he was called the "taste maker" of the period.

Severely afflicted by gout, Mason preferred to serve the Revolutionary cause through his writings. He was called the "pen of the revolution" after drafting the Non-Importation Resolutions (1769), the Fairfax Resolves (1774), the Virginia Declaration of Rights (1776) and the first Constitution of Virginia (1776). Although he did serve for a brief time in 1759 in the House of Burgesses, he refused to serve in other elected and appointed offices.

George Washington, Mason's neighbor, would often row down the four miles from Mount Vernon to Gunston Hall. Mason had worked with Washington's brothers in the Ohio Company. He was a sage advisor to many of the early patriots. Jefferson called him the "wisest man of his generation."

Mason was meticulous in his supervision of the construction of Gunston Hall. Concern for details included personally watching as the lime and sand was mixed for mortar. Mason insisted on two batches, one for inside and one for outside work. Mortar was often infested with cockroaches and they were in effect built into the house. Mason noted that he had seen brick homes "so infested with these devils that a man had better live in a barne . . ."

Gunston Hall is far from that. The interior woodwork is unrivaled in any colonial mansion. The Palladian Room, based on the 16th-century Italian style made popular by Andrea Palladio, with richly carved pilastered door, window and niche frames, is considered Buckland's masterpiece.

Also lovely is the Chinese Chippendale dining room. This was a popular architectural motif in London at the time. It is the first known application of chinoiserie—or Chinese—architectural style in the colonies. The upstairs has bedrooms for the nine surviving children. The master bedroom is downstairs.

The house is furnished with many Mason family pieces. They are predominantly in the American Chippendale style. Mason would not have any furniture in his home made in England after 1769, in accord with his own Non-Importation Resolution.

At one time there were approximately 500 people working this plantation. The outbuildings resembled a small town. There was even a busy wharf from which Mason shipped his tobacco and wheat. The estate was virtually self-sustaining. A number of the old dependencies, such as the kitchen, wellhead and smokehouse, have been reconstructed on their original sites. Also added were a dairy, wash house and kitchen garden.

Almost equaling the lavish interior is the lovely garden with its boxwood alley planted by Mason. It is flanked on either side by summerhouses which overlook the Potomac River. There is also an adjacent deer park with a nature trail that circles to the river and back.

At Gunston Hall there is a Visitor Center with exhibits from the 18th century and a 20-minute orientation film on George Mason and Gunston Hall.

Gunston Hall is open daily, except Christmas, from 9:30 to 5:00. Admission is charged.

Directions: Take Beltway Exit 1 south on U.S. 1. Proceed east off U.S. 1 on Route 242 to the plantation entrance.

30. Carter's Grove

There are many levels of good taste and while it is certainly true that the Carter Burwell family had one of the most beautiful plantation homes in the south, the ladies in the family did not always display the same discerning eye for excellence in their private lives.

This lapse of judgment on the part of two young ladies of the extended Carter clan was demonstrated when they rejected the suits of two of Virginia's finest and most famous gentlemen. One of the rooms at Carter's Grove is called the Refusal Room because, as the popular story goes, it was here that George Washington asked Mary Cary, a Carter relative, to marry him and was turned down. Thomas Jefferson proposed here also to his "Fair Belinda," Rebecca Burwell, and he, too, was refused. If these two young patriots had married and settled down at this time it might have affected the course of American history.

One of the young ladies seemed to regret her decision later. When Washington returned to Williamsburg at the head of the Continental Army for the final battle of Yorktown, Mary Cary, now married to a member of the local gentry, ran weeping from the parade ground.

The interior woodwork is the chief distinction of Carter's Grove. Carter Burwell, who built the house in 1750, brought Richard Bayliss, another carpenter, and his family from England to Virginia just so that Bayliss could create the interior design. The Georgian masterpiece he created has not always been treated with the respect it deserves. When British Colonel Banastre Tarleton was headquartered here in 1781 he rode his horse up the staircase, slashing the stair rails with his sabre. The deep scars are still visible.

Carter's Grove is a working plantation, demonstrating farm operations and crafts of an 18th-century tobacco plantation. Ongoing archeological work uncovered the site of Martin's Hundred Fort, which was built shortly after 1619. Archeological excavations are now uncovering significant artifacts from this earlier period.

Carter's Grove is open daily from 10:00 to 5:00 from mid-March to the Sunday after Thanksgiving. Admission is charged.

Directions: Take Beltway Exit 4 (I-95) to the Richmond area. Follow Route 64 to the Williamsburg area. Carter's Grove is six miles east of Williamsburg off Route 60.

31. Shirley Plantation

Hospitality is one thing, but a silver drinking cup for a horse is certainly something else again! But Nestor—a racehorse owned by the Carter family—was a special horse and he only got a drink when he won. After a victorious run he would celebrate with wine from "his" cup, reversing the normal tradition of presenting the loving cup to the owner.

Shirley Plantation was noted for its lavish entertainment and was even built with hospitality in mind. A carved pineapple—symbol of hospitality—decorates the roof. Washington, Jefferson, the Harrisons and the Byrds all enjoyed the friendly atmosphere at Shirley. Today it is occupied by the 10th generation of Carters and visitors are still made welcome.

Construction on the Carter plantation house was begun in 1742 by John Carter, but later generations completed the work. There are some striking departures from traditional designs of the time. The mansion was built in a square pattern, rather than the popular Georgian style with hyphen and wings. Its most unusual feature is the free hanging staircase. But unlike the curved style so popular, this staircase is square and rises with no visible means of support. Carved walnut forms the railing and the underside of each tread shows a graceful scroll.

It was in the parlor at Shirley that Anne Hill Carter married Governor "Light Horse" Harry Lee, the Revolutionary War hero. Their son, Robert E. Lee, would spend several years here.

Approaching Shirley visitors observe the Queen Anne forecourt, with its formal arrangement of dependencies. It is the only example of this style in Virginia. These outbuildings include a two-story kitchen,

The most unusual feature of Shirley Plantation in Virginia
is its free hanging staircase.

smokehouse, dovecote, stable and barns. As a working farm the plantation still produces corn, barley, wheat and soy beans.

The old fashioned shrubs, boxwood and seasonal flowers form an appealing garden, and the grounds slope down to the James River.

Shirley Plantation is open daily except Christmas Day from 9:00 to 5:00. Admission is charged.

Directions: Take Beltway Exit 4 (I-95) to I-64 east in Richmond. Continue to the Larburnum exit, turn right on Larburnum until Route 5. Take a left on Route 5. Shirley Plantation is located off Route 5.

32. Castle Hill

Some men take their responsibilities very seriously. But when Peter Jefferson asked his close friend and neighbor, Dr. Thomas Walker, to be his son's guardian, he never realized what a heavy responsibility Walker was asked to bear.

During the American Revolution, Dr. Walker saved his young ward from capture and imprisonment by the British. It was on June 4, 1781 that a young American stopped at Castle Hill with word that the British were heading for Monticello to arrest Thomas Jefferson. This warning served to alert Dr. Walker, who was also on the British arrest list. When Colonel Tarleton arrived at Castle Hill to capture Walker, he was met not with protest but with southern hospitality. In order to give Thomas Jefferson time to escape, Walker served the enemy a lavish country breakfast complete with mint juleps. Colonel Tarleton relaxed to such an extent that he had his orderly in to show Dr. Walker the tallest British soldier in America. The mark notched on the door jamb to measure his stature indicates an impressive six feet, nine-and-a-quarter inches. By the time Tarleton and his men left Castle Hill for Monticello, Jefferson was far away.

The original house Walker built in 1765 was enlarged by his granddaughter, Judith Walker, the wife of Senator William Cabell Rives. In 1824 she significantly increased the estate with an addition in the American Federal Period. This new section faces the formal garden planted by the Rives from cuttings obtained at the Tuilleries Garden while Rives was ambassador to France.

The combination of the simple clapboard colonial section and the more elaborate Federal section makes Castle Hill particularly interesting. The outbuildings of this 18th-century colonial plantation have also been restored.

Castle Hill is open daily March through November from 10:00 to 5:00. Admission is charged.

Directions: Take Beltway Exit 8 (Route 29-211) south past Warrenton to Culpeper. Take Route 15 through Orange to Gordonsville. From there, take Route 231 south. Castle Hill is eight miles farther on the right.

33. Smith's Fort Plantation House

Smith's Fort Plantation House is also called the Rolfe House. Both names are misleading, however, since neither John Smith nor John Rolfe ever lived here. But both men are associated with this land.

In 1614, Chief Powhatan gave John Rolfe this tribal property, across the James River from Jamestown, at Rolfe's marriage to Pocahontas. Though Indian land, it had been commandeered by the English five years earlier. Captain John Smith had built a fort on the high ground overlooking the river, giving the settlers protection from hostile Indians and the marauding Spanish from the south. There is a trail here which leads to the Smith's Fort foundations. They comprise the oldest remaining fort site in English America. James Fort, though built earlier than Smith's, now rests beneath the James River.

Rolfe was able to use this wedding gift to experiment with various tobacco varieties. It was here that he grew the West Indian blend that would make tobacco the cash crop of the southern colonies.

After his parents died, young Thomas Rolfe deeded the land to his English friends, the Warrens. They were the ones to build the plantation house in 1652. It is noted for the fine woodwork and period furniture. There is a small English garden on the grounds.

Smith's Fort Plantation is open daily from Garden Week in April through September from 10:00 to 5:00. Admission is charged.

Directions: Take Beltway Exit 4 (I-95) to Richmond, then follow Route 295 to connect with Route 64 to Williamsburg. Take Colonial Parkway to Jamestown and then the ferry that leaves from the Glass House. The ferry runs on the half hour (10:00-7:30) June 1 through September 15. Otherwise it runs on the hour, 6:30-12:30. The plantation is on Route 31 just on the other side of the James River.

34. Scotchtown

As Robert Burns once said, "The best laid schemes of mice and men often go astray." This certainly was the case with the scheme of Charles

Chiswell, who wanted to establish a Scottish town in Virginia with himself as laird. His plan was dashed when an epidemic killed his workmen and his dream.

The 960-acre estate and manor house were sold at auction to Patrick Henry in 1770 or 1771. The Henrys with their six children lived at Scotchtown during the Revolutionary period. Patrick Henry's involvement in the patriot cause left him with little time to spend at home. He established his family here and made this his home for the next seven years.

For the first three years he was active in Virginia affairs, attending the sessions of the House of Burgesses in Williamsburg and the First Virginia Convention. But on August 29, 1774, he left to serve in the First Continental Congress in Philadelphia. He broke his journey at Mount Vernon and resumed the five-day trip with George Washington.

After only a brief time back at Scotchtown he left again on March 23, 1775 to attend the Second Virginia Convention at St. John's Church in Richmond. It was here that he made the spellbinding speech which ended, "Give me liberty or give me death!"

When Henry left next in June of 1776 to attend the Fifth Virginia Convention in Williamsburg, he was elected the first Governor of Virginia. He served three one-year terms, living in the Governor's Palace in Williamsburg the second and third terms. During his first term the palace was renovated. In 1778 Patrick Henry sold Scotchtown to Wilson Miles Cary.

The manor house has been restored and furnished in 18th-century style. Also reconstructed are the law office, kitchen and guest cottage. The dry well is completely rebuilt, while the wellhouse dairy is only partially rebuilt.

Scotchtown is open daily April through October from 10:00 to 4:30 and on Sunday from 1:30 to 4:30. Admission is charged.

Directions: Take Beltway Exit 4 (I-95) south to Route 54 at Ashland. Go through Ashland to Route 671. Turn right on 671 and bear right at Route 685. Scotchtown is off Route 685, 10 miles northwest of Ashland.

35. Red Hill Plantation

Patrick Henry had seven different homes during his lifetime but his favorite was the last, Red Hill Plantation. He called this 2,920-acre estate the "garden spot of the world." He retired here in 1793, an aging and sickly 57, refusing high appointments in both the Washington and Adams administrations.

Patrick Henry particularly enjoyed the restful garden at Red Hill. It has been restored and its focal point is still the large 400-year-old osage orange tree. The tree is listed in the American Forestry Hall of Fame, and is the world's largest osage orange, 54 feet high with a span of 90 feet. It provides a genuine link with this towering figure from America's past, for he spent many afternoons sitting beneath its branches. When Henry died on June 6, 1799, he was buried, at his request, at the bottom of the sloping garden. His gravestone reads, "His fame his best epitaph."

Though the main house was destroyed by fire, it has been rebuilt to reflect the five years spent here by the Henrys. All of the dependencies have also been restored to provide a complete picture of plantation life. The overseer's cottage that Patrick Henry used as a law office has remained intact through the years.

At the entrance to Red Hill Plantation is the Patrick Henry Museum which contains personal belongings as well as family possessions. The major events in Patrick Henry's life are memorialized.

Red Hill Plantation is open daily 9:00 to 5:00 from November through March; for the remainder of the year hours are 9:00 to 4:00. Admission is charged.

Directions: Take Beltway Exit 8 (Route 29–211) south to Lynchburg. Then continue south on Route 501 to Brookneal. Follow Route 40 east, then Route 600 to Red Hill Plantation.

36. Weston Manor

What young bride wouldn't be thrilled with the gift of a 13-room house overlooking the Appomattox River, built on a site where an Indian Queen once entertained English explorers from Jamestown? They just don't give presents like that anymore!

Built in 1735 for an Eppes family wedding present, this three-story white frame house is not pretentious. But it is noteworthy as one of only two houses still standing in America built in the Early Georgian frame style.

One feature that always intrigues visitors is the "funeral door." Most colonial homes had this special door made large enough to permit a coffin to be carried through, since at that time funerals were held in the home.

Another oddity was the cannonball embedded in the ceiling of a room facing the river. During the Civil War the house was shelled by a Northern gunboat from the river below. One of the cannonballs entered through a dining room window and was for years embedded in the ceiling. It was removed, disarmed by a demolition crew from nearby Fort Lee, and is still on display.

General Philip Sheridan made his headquarters at Weston Manor during the later part of the Civil War. It is thought that it was also temporarily used as a hospital when General Ulysses S. Grant occupied this part of Virginia.

Weston Manor is open by appointment. To plan a visit call (804) 458-5536 or (804) 458-9642. Or write to the Historic Hopewell Foundation, P.O. Box 851, Hopewell, VA 23860. Admission is charged.

Directions: Take Beltway Exit 4 (I-95) to Richmond. Continue on I-95 to Exit 6A and follow Route 10 to Hopewell. Weston Manor is located near the Hopewell Yacht Club off 21st Avenue on the Appomattox River. See Weston Manor direction sign on 21st Avenue.

37. Abram's Delight

The names given these early homes often reflect very clearly the owners' pride and love for what they have been able to achieve—often at bargain prices—in this land of opportunity.

Abraham Hollingsworth gave the Shawnee Indians a cow, a calf and a piece of red cloth for the 582 acres he called "A Delight to Behold." Beside a spring he built a log cabin and a mill. The Hollingsworth family prospered not by farming but by industry. They had the area's first flour mill, then added a flax-seed-oil mill. Technically this was not a colonial plantation; but it is representative of the Shenandoah Valley colonial estates.

In 1754 the Hollingsworths built a two-story native limestone house, the oldest house still standing in Winchester. The walls were two-and-a-half feet thick. The house was quite grand for its time and location. The interior is still plain by comparison with Virginia plantation standards. The house is furnished with 18th-century pieces, many of which belonged to the Hollingsworth family.

In the basement there is an unusual colonial candle wheel which held 200 candles for dipping. There is also an old spinning wheel with Issac Hollingsworth's initials and an iron fireback with the Fairfax crest. Fairfax crest.

A gracious touch at this country estate is the small formal boxwood garden characteristic of the late 17th and early 18th centuries. It is a nice mixture of boxwood and old brick.

Abram's Delight can be visited daily from 10:00 to 5:00. Admission is charged.

In addition to Abram's Delight this area has another historically significant spot—George Washington's Office-Museum.

Washington first came to this area in 1748 as a 16-year-old surveyor for Lord Fairfax. Both Washington and Lord Fairfax were frequent guests at Abram's Delight. Washington returned as a colonel in the Virginia Regiment in September 1755, using a log cabin as his office until December 1756. His military post was to oversee the building of a chain of forts along the 300-mile frontier. The French, having allied with the Indians, were threatening the British territory in the Ohio Valley. Savage Indian attacks had caused loss of life among the British settlers and Governor Dinwiddie of Virginia was anxious to protect them.

The log cabin in which Washington worked is now the center room of George Washington's Office-Museum. The museum has a collection of colonial relics and Washington memorabilia. It is open May through October daily from 10:00 to 5:00 and on Sunday from 1:00 to 5:00. Admission is charged.

Directions: From the Beltway take Exit 10 (Route 7) west to Winchester, Virginia. Abram's Delight is at 1340 Pleasant Valley Road. George Washington's Office-Museum is located at the corner of Cork and Braddock Streets.

38. Montpelier

Is it possible to be too wealthy? Thomas Snowdon found out that it certainly was if he wanted to remain a participating member of his Quaker Meeting. When he married Ann Ridgely in 1774, their combined fortune was so excessive that he was forbidden to take part in the Friends service. Only after he freed 100 slaves was he again allowed to attend meetings.

The Snowdon family home, Montpelier, reflects not only their wealth but their religious nature. The doors were designed in the shape of a cross with the bottom panels representing open Bible pages.

The English boxwood garden, considered one of the finest in America, was also laid out in the form of a cross. A boxwood-lined allee, or path, leads to the belvedere, or summer house. It is original and is the only one in Maryland to survive from the 18th century. It may be one of only two from this early period still in existence in America.

Montpelier was built on the main road connecting the northern and southern colonies. The Snowdons kept open house for a steady stream of distinguished travelers. George Washington often stopped here as he went back and forth to Philadelphia. Martha Washington stayed here before heading to New York to see her husband inaugurated as first President. Another First Lady, Abigail Adams, enjoyed the Snowdon hospitality before joining John Adams in the White House.

Maryland does not have the number of plantation houses still open to the public that Virginia offers visitors, but Montpelier is considered one of the most beautiful Georgian houses in America. It provides an interesting comparison with its Virginia counterparts.

Montpelier is open in the spring from April to mid-June, then again the Saturday after Labor Day until the end of November on weekends only. Hours are from 11:00 to 3:00 on Saturday and 12:00 to 4:00 on Sunday. Call the Friends of Montpelier at (301) 779-2011 to tour by appointment at other times. Or write to 12828 Laurel-Bowie Road, Laurel, MD 20811.

Directions: Take Beltway Exit 22 (the Baltimore-Washington Parkway) to the Laurel exit on Route 197. Signs at the community of Montpelier will direct visitors to historic Montpelier.

39. Sotterly

Sotterly has all the ingredients of a Hollywood melodrama, which is singularly appropriate as it is located in Hollywood, Maryland. One parlor has a secret passage to a bedroom upstairs; it's fun to speculate on the purpose of that. In that same parlor during an evening of gambling the dissolute heir to the estate gambled it away—George Plater V actually lost the entire estate on a roll of the dice.

It would be hard to find a more theatrical setting than Sotterly. The house stands at the top of a ridge commanding a superb view of the Patuxent River. It resembles Mount Vernon, with a columned facade on the river side.

The interior carving was done by an indentured servant, Richard Boulton, who did the Chinese Chippendale staircase with a trellis effect, one of the few of that style to survive from the colonial period. The dining room chairs repeat this Chinese trellis motif. The Great Hall, or drawing room, with its matching shell alcoves on either side of the fireplace, was included in Helen Comstock's *100 Most Beautiful Rooms in America*. This room is still lit only by candles, retaining its colonial atmosphere.

Sotterly is a working plantation. From the house on the hill a "rolling road" runs down to the water. Hogsheads of tobacco were rolled along this road to waiting ships. Sotterly was a port of entry into the colony and the wharf was a very busy place. Alongside the road is the only remaining slave cabin. It was originally just one of a row of such houses.

The southern ambience is never stronger than in the spring when the smell of magnolias and lilacs fill the air. The garden is delightful when the orchard is in bloom and the spring bulbs flowering.

Sotterly is open daily from June to September from 11:00 to 5:00. It can be visited in April, May, October and November by appointment. Call (301) 373-2280 or (301) 373-2179, or write Box 67, Hollywood, MD 20636. Admission is charged.

Directions: Take Beltway Exit 7 (Route 5) south. Bear left on Route 235 to Hollywood. Make a left at Route 245 and continue 3 miles to Sotterly.

40. Mount Clare

Charles Carroll, the barrister who owned Mount Clare plantation, shared a very popular name with a number of other gentlemen. And it might have been a dangerous one, had another Charles Carroll—signer of the treasonous Declaration of Independence—not distinguished himself by adding "of Carrollton" after his signature.

The Mount Clare Carrolls spent the winter season in Annapolis and the summer at Mount Clare, Baltimore's only pre-Revolutionary plantation house. Charles Carroll's thriving legal practice was in Annapolis, where he was also actively involved in politics. In addition he managed an iron furnace and gristmill. At Mount Clare he bred race horses and was involved in agricultural research. Ten varieties of grass seed were imported from England, as were various vegetables, to test their adaptability to the Maryland soil.

Charles Carroll the Barrister was instrumental in the drafting of Maryland's Declaration of Rights and the state constitution. After his death in 1783, his widow continued to live at Mount Clare. Her interest in gardening prompted her to supply George Washington with a number of rare trees and plants for Mount Vernon.

A nephew inherited the estate and donated some of the family property to the Baltimore & Ohio Railroad. America's first railroad station, Mount Clare, was built here (see Era Between the Wars: Transportation—Baltimore & Ohio Railroad Museum).

Mount Clare is open daily, except Mondays, Easter, Thanksgiving, December 24-25 and January 1. Hours are 11:00 to 4:00 and Sunday from 1:00 to 4:00. Admission is charged.

Directions: Take Beltway Exit 22 (Baltimore-Washington Parkway), then go north on Route 1. Go north on Monroe Street to Carroll Park. The Mount Clare entrance is on the left at the corner of Monroe Street and Washington Blvd.

41. Rose Hill Manor Park

A variety of diversions are available at the Rose Hill Manor Park. There are three museums on the grounds—the Children's Touch and See Museum, the Frederick County Farm Museum and the Robert Renneburger Carriage Museum.

History is experienced at the Rose Hill Manor Children's Museum. This rural Georgian residence was built in 1790 for John Grahame, husband of Anne Johnson, daughter of Maryland's first governor, Thomas Johnson. After his retirement Governor Johnson spent the last nine years of his life, from 1810 to 1819, at this gracious manor house. It was Thomas Johnson who had the honor and distinction of nominating George Washington as Commander-in-Chief of the Continental Army.

Costumed guides conduct leisurely tours with plenty of time for visitors to add a few stitches to an old-fashioned quilt or throw the shuttle of the loom to get a feeling for 19th-century weaving. Turning the handles of a variety of kitchen utensils from the chopper to the cherry pitter gives a real feeling for the past. There are clothes to be tried on and a rocking chair to be ridden.

The house contains three main exhibits, including an antique toy collection, a textile exhibit and the 19th-century kitchen exhibit. More than 300 items are part of the manor house Children's Museum. It provides a unique opportunity to get in "touch" with one's heritage.

All senses are delighted as visitors move on to the 19th-century flower and herb garden behind the house. The herbs provide a potpourri of smells and taste. During the summer months the vegetables are tempting.

This 43-acre park also has a log cabin, built more than 150 years ago, that provides a glimpse of the simpler life-style of the earliest settlers. The trades are represented at the blacksmith shop.

The Frederick County Farm Museum houses hundreds of farm implements in a restored barn. These old-fashioned tools and tractors tell the agricultural history of this area.

To complete the picture, the Robert Renneburger Carriage Museum has 20 restored carriages and sleighs. This view of transportation in the 19th century completes the visitors' glimpse of life at Rose Hill Manor in the 1800s.

Rose Hill Manor Park is open at no charge Monday through Saturday from 10:00 to 4:00 and Sunday from 1:00 to 4:00, April through October. During March, November and December it opens for weekends only.

Directions: From the Beltway take Exit 35 (Route 270) to the Frederick, Maryland area. Then follow Route 15 north to Exit 8. Turn onto Motter Avenue, then left onto 14th Street. Make another left onto North Market Street to 1611 North Market Street; make a left into Rose Hill Manor Park.

42. Pennsbury Manor

What was a good real estate deal in 1683? Does it seem reasonable to purchase several thousand acres of prime real estate overlooking the Delaware River in exchange for 350 fathoms (a fathom equals six feet) of white wampum, a score (that's a set of 20) each of blankets, guns, coats, shirts and stockings, 40 axes, 40 pairs of scissors, 200 knives and a handful of fishhooks?

That was what William Penn paid the Delaware Indians and both sides thought it was a fair exchange. Penn even met formally with Chief Tammany at Shackamaxon (now Philadelphia) to cement their friendship.

Though Pennsbury Manor was a grand house by colonial standards, William Penn could have chosen the life of a courtier at the Royal Court in England. As a Quaker, he chose instead a simpler life. He may have been served better if it had also been a quieter life, as he was imprisoned for speaking out against the Church of England. King Charles II, repaying a debt to Penn's father, granted him a huge tract of land in the New World. William Penn called it "Sylvania" meaning wooded; the King added "Penn."

It was 1682 when William Penn arrived in his colony. He found others had reached this area earlier. Already settled were a diverse mixture of Swedes, Dutch and English. Penn decreed religious and political freedom for all.

Pennsbury Manor has been completely restored using information from the original documents of William Penn, in-ground archeological excavations and 17th-century English tradition. The 43-acre site is the only extant residence of William Penn and interprets the accomplishments and domestic life of William Penn and late 17th-century Pennsylvania. Visitors can see 21 buildings which include the Manor House, Bake and Brew House, Barge House (with replica of a period

English river barge), Plantation Office, Barn, Joyner's Shop, Blacksmith Shop and other support buildings.

Pennsbury Manor is open 9:00 to 5:00 Tuesday through Saturday and Sunday from 12:00 to 5:00; in winter it closes at 4:30. Admission is charged.

Directions: Take Beltway Exit 27 (I-95) north of Philadelphia. Travel east on Route 413 to Route 13. Go north on Route 13 to Green Lane (first traffic light on Radcliffe Street which follows the Delaware River). Proceed through Tullytown. Turn right at large Pennsbury Manor directional sign and follow this road to Pennsbury Manor.

43. Landingford Plantation

Some historical sites merit attention not because of the contributions of the owner but because of their connection with the larger figures from America's past. At Landingford Plantation is the last remaining house in Pennsylvania that William Penn is known to have visited.

This original house was built in 1683 by Caleb Pusey. Pusey came to the Pennsylvania area to work as a mill manager for William Penn. Chester Mills, a sawmill and gristmill, was built in this area by Penn and his partners, Pusey and Samuel Carpenter. They brought a prefabricated mill over with them.

Pusey's modest two-story house has been carefully restored and furnished with pieces reflecting the life-style of the middle class in the 17th century. A colonial herb garden has been planted outside and beyond that a vegetable and flower garden.

Also on the plantation grounds is a 1790 log cabin where Caleb Pusey's great-granddaughter and her husband William Pennock lived. Another building is the 1849 schoolhouse, built by a later textile miller, John Price Crozer. It houses a museum that displays artifacts found on the plantation by the Archaeological Society of Delaware.

The plantation is open 1:00 to 4:30 Saturday and Sunday in May, September and October, and Tuesday through Sunday from 1:00 to 4:30 in June, July and August. A nominal admission is charged.

Directions: Take Beltway Exit 27 (I-95) to Upland, Pennsylvania. Exit at Kerlin Street and follow signs.

44. John Dickinson Mansion

How strange that the man known to this day as "the Penman of the Revolution" because of the many articulate papers he wrote listing the colonists' rights and complaints and opposing the Stamp Act and the Townshend Acts should refuse to sign the one document that enumerated all of the colonial grievances against the British crown. John Dickinson lost a great deal of his popularity after he refused to sign the Declaration of Independence. Some even accused him of turning Loyalist, a rumor quickly scotched when he served in the Continental Army, reaching the rank of brigadier general.

Although he was the author of the Articles of Confederation and one of the framers of the U.S. Constitution, he never achieved prominence outside of Pennsylvania and Delaware once he left the Second Continental Congress arguing for delay in hopes that England would even yet modify her stand.

John Dickinson's popularity in these two states remained undiminished. He served as chief executive of Delaware from 1781 to 1782, then that same year (1782) was elected Governor of Pennsylvania, serving until 1785—a governmental transition unequaled.

John Dickinson's boyhood home, built by his father in 1740 outside Dover, Delaware, has been restored. This plantation house overlooks the St. Jones River and provides an excellent sample of plantation architecture in Delaware.

A fire in 1804 did cause considerable damage to the interior and some early Dickinson family pieces were lost. But the house has been carefully restored and some of the furnishings are original.

The John Dickinson Mansion and out-buildings are open Tuesday through Saturday from 10:00 to 4:30 and on Sunday from 12:30 to 4:30. The house is closed on Mondays and holidays. There is no admission charge.

Directions: Take Beltway Exit 19 (Route 50) over Bay Bridge, continue north on Route 301 when it splits from Route 50. Make a right on Route 300 and another right on Route 44 to Dover. From Dover go south on Route 113 to Route 68 and Kitts Hummuck Road, which will lead directly to the John Dickinson Mansion.

45. Daniel Boone Homestead

Whether it's east or west, the frontier is that part of the country that borders the inhabited or settled area. Daniel Boone, though associated with the western advance of America, was born on the eastern frontier in what is now Berks County, Pennsylvania.

His family had come from Devonshire, England in 1717 and settled in the primitive outlying reaches of the Pennsylvania colony. Daniel Boone was the sixth son among 11 children. Formal schooling was not available in this outpost but young Daniel did learn to hunt and shoot. He was given a rifle on his 10th birthday and rapidly became quite a marksman. His father was a blacksmith, so Daniel learned the art of rifle and musket repair at a young age.

In 1750, when Daniel Boone was 16, his family moved south. Like so many frontier families, the Boones hoped to find better soil. They ultimately settled in the Yadkin Valley of North Carolina. This served as home base for Boone as he journeyed farther into the west. He married a valley girl and returned to North Carolina after each of his western adventures. When he finally moved his family into the Kentucky region which he had been exploring, his wife and daughter were the first non-Indian women in Kentucky.

The Daniel Boone Homestead in Pennsylvania has been restored and is now a museum representing not only the Boone family but also the Pennsylvania pioneer—those intrepid settlers who extended America's borders all along the colonial boundaries. A visit to the Daniel Boone Homestead will present a vivid picture of life on the Pennsylvania frontier in the 18th century. The house is furnished as it would have been by the Boone family, who depended not only on farming but also on Squire Boone, Daniel's father, for his skills as a blacksmith and a weaver.

At the homestead a blacksmith shop, stone smokehouse, bank barn and log cabin are also restored. The area around the homestead is a game sanctuary. Deer, raccoon, pheasants, quail and rabbits are often sighted. The lake and stone dam provide excellent fishing.

The Daniel Boone Homestead is open 8:30 to 5:00 Tuesday through Saturday and 12:00 to 5:00 on Sunday. It closes at 4:30 during the winter months. The homestead is closed on major holidays. A small admission is charged.

Directions: Take Beltway Exit 27 (I-95) to Philadelphia and pick up Route 76 to Exit 23, Route 100, for Pottstown. At Pottstown go west on Route 422. The Daniel Boone Homestead is on the right, at Baumstown.

Colonial Churches

Two colonies—Maryland and Pennsylvania—were founded by proprietors who placed the right to worship in the church of their choice above all else. Most settlers came to America to improve their economic lot rather than to practice religious freedom. It is estimated that in the years before the Revolution only about one person out of eight in the New England area belonged to a church, in the Middle Colonies one in 17 and in the South one in 20.

These figures do not mean that most were unbelievers, but instead reflect other factors. Citizens of isolated settlements were often too far from a church to attend services. Many others considered formal church affiliation unnecessary; they felt it was sufficient to read the Bible within their own home.

A widespread policy of religious toleration eliminated much of the political element of church attendance—it was less vital to have the protection of the group. Religious troubles did still occur, however, as evidenced by the disruption of the government in Maryland as Protestant vied with Catholic for control.

Religion in the colonies, as elsewhere during this period, contained a strong superstitious element. The unsettling wilderness, importation of black slave labor and hostile Indians confirmed for some the impression that this was a place in which God would do battle with the Devil.

Many colonists believed in the direct intervention of God. This personal God was accepted by those of all social classes, regardless of the degree of education. Supernatural intervention was held accountable for unusual weather phenomena; hurricanes, drought, comets, earthquakes and floods were all assumed to be direct warnings from God. On the other hand, good crops, success in battle and good health were seen as signs of God's favor.

Of the organized churches in colonial America, the oldest was the Anglican, or the Church of England. Begun in Jamestown, it was strongest in the south where, prior to the Revolution, more than half of the 480 churches were Anglican. The philosophy of these worldly parishioners can be summed up in this 1676 epitaph for William Sherwood of Jamestown:

A Great Sinner
Waiting for
A Joyful Resurrection

Anglicans had confidence that God would forgive their sins and they would be saved. The southern colonists enjoyed drinking, singing, dancing, horse racing, cock fighting and rich apparel. Sunday was not a day of penance but of service and sociability.

The largest denomination in colonial America was comprised of the New England-based Congregationalists, who were descendants of the early Puritan settlers. Second were the Presbyterians, located mainly in the Middle Colonies; third were the Baptists, who had founded Rhode Island and expanded from there. The Church of England was fourth largest, with the Methodists fifth, and the sixth and least numerous of the major sects, were the Quakers.

Despite the fact that Maryland was established by the Calverts to offer persecuted Catholics a refuge, there were only 50 Catholic churches in America at the time of the Revolution, almost all of which were located in Maryland.

Although ministers, or priests in Maryland, were the first professional men in the colonies, their position of leadership and influence soon declined. By the 1700s many pastors had to sue their congregations for their pay. In the southern Anglican area, since clergy had to travel to London to be ordained, positions were filled primarily by English pastors who had not succeeded in England. Conditions deteriorated so that in 1624 the Virginia legislature passed laws forbidding the clergy to drink excessively, to gamble or to engage in other excesses.

Things were equally bad in Maryland, where in June 1747 a woman in Patapsco was only fined a penny for flogging the minister, since the court decided he deserved it.

The Great Awakening of the 1740s brought a religious revival. The nondenominational character of this five-year revival led to a great many conversions. It also increased the respectability of the clergy.

Ultimately the colonial religious experience led those who would write the laws of the new country to establish freedom of religious worship.

46. Bruton Parish Church

Philadelphia was not the only town with a Liberty Bell. Williamsburg also had one which was presented to Bruton Parish Church in 1761. It too rang out to celebrate momentous events in colonial history.

On June 1, 1774, when it became known that Parliament had closed the port of Boston, the bell called members of the parish and House of Burgesses to a day of fasting, humiliation and prayer. From that day's events came the call to the First Virginia Convention.

The bell rang once again to announce the repeal of the Stamp Act. On May 15, 1776, it rang out for Virginia's first act of sovereignty, six weeks before the Liberty Bell in Philadelphia would peel out a similar message.

Construction on Bruton Parish Church was begun in 1711 when it became obvious that the small church that had served the middle plantation area would not accommodate the congregation of Virginia's new capital.

This church has been in continuous use from 1715 to the present. It was quite fashionable to attend Bruton Parish Church during colonial times. Plantation owners and their wives from the large estates along the York and James Rivers came into town by coach for services.

Prominent political figures often served as vestrymen, including George Washington, Henry Tyler, and America's first Professor of Law, George Wythe. In the galleries set aside for college students sat Thomas Jefferson, James Monroe, John Tyler, Edmond Randolph, John Marshall and Winfield Scott. Although the interior of the church was simple, it did have a special box in front of the pulpit for the Royal Governor.

It was the rector of Bruton Parish Church, Reverend W.A.R. Goodwin, who in 1905 began the crusade to restore the city of Williamsburg to its colonial glory. He interested John D. Rockefeller in this project and the rest is history. Visitors leaving the church will see his grave along with those of two Royal Governors and numerous important figures of colonial days.

Bruton Parish Church is open daily at no charge. Special candlelight organ concerts are held here; check Colonial Williamsburg Visitor Center for times.

Directions: Take Beltway Exit 4 (I-95) to the Richmond By-pass, Route 295. Follow this to Route 64 east, which will lead into Williamsburg. Bruton Parish Church is on the corner of Duke of Gloucester Street and Palace Green.

47. St. John's Church— Richmond

Somehow one doesn't relate Patrick Henry's fiery speech which ended with the words "Give me liberty or give me death!" with the solemnity of a church setting. But it was to St. John's Church that the Second Virginia Convention retreated when the Royal Governor, Lord Dunsmore, indicated his displeasure with the rebellious legislators.

On summer weekends costumed actors portray such colonial leaders as George Washington, Thomas Jefferson, George Mason, George Wythe, Richard Henry Lee, Benjamin Harrison, Peyton Randolph and Archibald Cary. Again their impassioned words ring out, bringing history to life.

This old church was chosen for the meeting of the Second Virginia Convention because they needed the largest public building in Richmond. Benedict Arnold would choose this same church for a similar reason during the Revolution when he needed a large building to serve as a barracks for his soldiers while occupying Richmond.

St. John's has been repaired and enlarged since colonial times but the pews, glass windows, pulpit and sounding board have all survived from the 18th century.

Directions: From the Beltway take Exit 4 (I-95) to Richmond St. John's Church is at 24th and Broad Streets.

48. Christ Church

Washington was not only " . . . first in war, first in peace and first in the hearts of his countrymen." He was also first to pay for his family pew when Christ Church was built in Alexandria, Virginia.

Washington was one of the original vestrymen of this new parish. In 1774 he purchased pew 15 for 36 pounds, 10 shillings or roughly 20 dollars.

Established in 1765, Fairfax Parish included Alexandria and Mount Vernon. James Wren, a descendant of the great English architect Sir Christopher Wren, did much of the interior work of Christ Church, including the inscribed panels on either side of the pulpit. Many feel that Wren also contributed to the church's design.

There are several historical events which make Christ Church unique. At Martha Washington's death, her grandson George Washington Parke Custis gave the Washington family Bible to Christ

Church. It is a custom frequently observed by incumbent Presidents to attend Christ Church on the Sunday closest to Washington's birthday. President Roosevelt and Winston Churchill worshipped here in 1942.

This is also the Lee family church, where General Robert E. Lee, as well as two of his daughters, were confirmed.

The church is open to visitors daily. The regular schedule of Sunday services includes Holy Eucharist at 8:00 a.m., Morning Prayer & Sermon at 9:15 a.m., Adult Forum at 10:10 a.m., Morning Prayer & Sermon at 11:15 a.m. and Holy Eucharist at 5:00 p.m.

Directions: Take Virginia Exit 1 (U.S. 1) into Alexandria to Columbus Street and the entrance to Christ Church.

49. St. John's Church— Hampton

The Anglican parishioners of Elizabeth City Parish got off to a rather unchristian beginning. When famine and disease struck the settlers of Jamestown, they recalled the plentiful goods given to them by the Kecoughtan Indians they had encountered in a village to the south.

The Jamestown community sent out a party in 1610 comprised of soldiers to build and man a fort and a group of settlers to establish themselves near the Indians. The murder of an Englishman by the Indians of another tribe was the provocation for the white men to overwhelm the small Indian village and take control of the lower peninsula area.

The present church is the fourth one in the parish. It was built in 1728 in its cruciform shape. A belfry was added in 1762. The British inflicted heavy damage on the church both during the Revolution and in the War of 1812.

After the Revolution this now Episcopal church suffered from its close ties with England. Involvement in church activities diminished. It was not until 1825 that a renewed interest developed. At that time the church was repaired, vestry elected and the name St. John's chosen.

The interior of the 1825 church was destroyed during the Civil War by a fire which was deliberately set by local citizens to keep the town from falling into Union hands. The church was restored after the war. Throughout its troubled existence the parish was able to retain the communion silver made in 1618 for the church in Smith's Hundred but given to Elizabeth City Parish Church after an Indian massacre had destroyed Smith's Hundred, wiping out church, congregation and settlement.

Religious services are still celebrated on Sundays and on Thursday at 10:00 a.m. Visitors are always welcome. A taped historical interpretation is in the church. A small museum in the Parish House contains exhibits of parish history.

Directions: Take Beltway Exit 4 (I-95) to Richmond, then Route 64 to Hampton. Stop at the Hampton Tourist Information Center at 413 West Mercury Blvd., right off Route 64, for maps of the Hampton area.

50. St. Ignatius Church

The suppression of the Catholic minority in Maryland is one of the terrible ironies of colonial history. Maryland was a colony founded by the family of Sir George Calvert, First Lord Baltimore, to provide a sanctuary for the persecuted Catholics of England as well as other victims of religious persecution. The Calverts believed in religious freedom for all. But it was this tolerance for those of other faiths that ultimately led to the Catholics again being a minority group and again being forbidden to practice their religion in the colony they founded.

The first Catholic service in Maryland was held on St. Clement's Island (see First Settlements: St. Clement's Island). Once established at St. Mary's City, the Catholic congregation met in an Indian hut abandoned by the Yoacomico Indians. The first chapel of St. Ignatius, named for Ignatius Loyola, the founder of the Jesuit Order, was built at St. Mary's in 1641.

In 1704 Catholics were forbidden to practice their religion in Maryland after 70 years of religious freedom. Royal Governor Seymour banned services at St. Ignatius. The parishioners took the bricks from their damaged chapel down river to St. Inigoes Manor land. Since the law permitted worship in private homes they held services in the improved Manor House.

In 1745 a small wooden church was built adjacent to the Manor House. In 1785, when religious toleration was again the policy in the new state of Maryland, the present St. Ignatius Church was built.

In the cemetery are buried the Jesuit fathers who were the missionaries of the American Catholic Church.

There are no regular services held at St. Ignatius but visitors are welcome. Special services are held on Maryland Day and the Feast of St. Ignatius Loyala. St. Ignatius Church is open 9:00 to 4:30 daily.

Directions: From the Beltway take Exit 7 (Route 5) to St. Inigoes.

51. Ephrata Cloister

One would think that life in the wilderness of this new country was austere and arduous enough to satisfy the strictures of any religion. But the sect founded in 1732 by Conrad Beissel went even further.

This community of recluses was reminded of their religious vows in all their daily contacts. The narrow halls of their buildings symbolized the straight and narrow path they were to walk; the life of humility was taught each time they had to stoop to go through a door; their white clothes emphasized anonymity; and board benches with wooden blocks for pillows were all their sleeping cells contained. It was a hard life of rigid self-denial and pious simplicity.

The community had three orders—a brotherhood and sisterhood, each practicing celibacy, and a married order. The Bethania, or brothers' house, was torn down in 1908. Still standing is the Saron, or sisters' house.

In all there are 11 sturdy 18th-century buildings that were part of this religious commune. In addition to the Saron, the chapel or Saal, the Almonry, the alms and bake house, Beissel's log house, a householder's cabin, three cottages and the 1837 Academy remain. The larger buildings are excellent examples of medieval German architecture.

At its height the community had approximately 300 members. They engaged in farming, fruit growing, basketry, bookmaking, carpentry, printing and milling. From 1743 they printed a series of books and religious tracts, along with hand-illuminated hymnals and wall inscriptions. During the Revolutionary War 500 wounded soldiers from the Battle of Brandywine (September 1777) were brought here and nursed.

By 1800 the celibate orders were no longer able to attract members. In 1814 the householders of the sect were absorbed into the Seventh Day German Baptists.

Today during the summer months the Ephrata Cloister Associates present a musical drama called "The Vorspiel," which depicts life at Ephrata Cloister in the 1700s. This historical drama is held in an outdoor amphitheatre on Saturday evenings at 7:30 with tours preceding it.

Ephrata Cloister is open for tours 10:00 to 4:30 Tuesday through Saturday and from 1:00 to 4:00 on Sunday. Admission is charged. For more information call (717) 733-6600 or write the Cloister at 632 Main Street, Ephrata, PA 17822.

Directions: Take Beltway Exit 22 (the Baltimore-Washington Parkway) to the Baltimore Beltway. Go northwest toward Towson, then take I-83 north around York. Follow Route 30 east to Lancaster, Pennsylvania. At Lancaster take Route 222 north to Ephrata Cloister.

Other Churches of the Colonial Period

Virginia:

St. Luke's Church—This Anglican church is often called America's oldest existing Protestant church. Its old brick structure (circa 1632) with stepped gables and buttresses embellished by the original traceried windows is a link to the Gothic churches of Europe. It is located on Route 10, four miles south of Smithfield.

Christ Church—Viewed by many experts as "the most perfect example of colonial church architecture now remaining in Virginia," Christ Church was built in 1732 with money provided by Robert Carter, whose later descendants would number eight Governors of Virginia, three signers of the Declaration of Independence and two Presidents, the Harrisons. His condition for building the church was that it be erected on the site of a former small wooden chapel and that his parents' graves remain in the chancel. The 25 high back pews are the only original ones to be found in Virginia's colonial churches. The Carter pew has brass rods, from which a damask curtain once hung to provide even greater privacy and to cut down on the chill in the unheated church. Christ Church is a National Historical Landmark. It is located on Route 646 just past Kilmarnock.

Yeocomico Church—This church, built in 1706 on the site of a 1655 wooden chapel, was one of the original outposts of Christianity in the New World. The congregation included members of the Washington family, the Lees and the Carters. Yeocomico Church is built in the form of a cross with Georgian windows. There is a sundial in the yard dated 1717. This church near the Hague, off Route 606, is also a National Historic Landmark.

Nomini Church—This colonial church was built in 1704. George Washington often worshipped here when visiting his brother John Augustine Washington and his nephew Bushrod Washington, who would later inherit Mount Vernon. Only two of the original walls remain standing from the colonial period as Nomini Church was burned during the War of 1812. It was rebuilt utilizing these two brick walls from the first church. Nomini Church is on Route 202 in Mt. Holly.

Pohick Church—This is the only church remaining from the colonial Truro Parish, which was divided in 1765 to found the Fairfax

Parish. Pohick Church was built between 1769 and 1773 under the watchful eye of a committee which included two well-known vestrymen, George Washington and George Mason. Although the Washington family did switch their attendance to Christ Church in Alexandria, Pohick Church is still called the "Parish Church of Mount Vernon." It is located 10 miles south of Alexandria on U.S. 1.

St. Peter's Church—This church achieved notice as the one in which Martha Custis and George Washington were not married. Martha was christened here and was a regular member of the congregation as this was the closest church to her Pamunkey Plantation. The Reverend from the church performed the service on January 6, 1759, but at her estate rather than at St. Peter's. The church was desecrated during the Civil War, when it was used as a stable by Federal troops who carved their initials on the wooden entrance. St. Peter's Church is located in New Kent, between Richmond and Williamsburg.

Grace Episcopal Church—In 1696 the York-Hampton Parish began building a church of marl rock from the York River. Located in the growing village of Yorktown, it served many of the colonial patriots, including the Nelson family. During the American Revolution British General Cornwallis stored ammunition within the church. The British burned the church in the War of 1812, but it was rebuilt and used as a hospital during the Civil War. Six generations of the Nelson family are buried outside the church, including Thomas Nelson, Jr., signer of the Declaration of Independence. Located on Waterstreet in Historic Yorktown, it is open daily from 9:00 to 5:00.

Maryland:

St. Francis Xavier Church—Erected in 1766, this is the oldest Catholic church built by Englishmen in America. This was the third church to be built on this spot, the first small wooden chapel having been completed in 1662 and the second in 1704. This second church was closed when the Protestant majority in Maryland outlawed Catholic services. The present church is the oldest Catholic church in continuous use in English America. It is located in Newtown, off Route 243.

Emanuel Protestant Episcopal Church—This church was built in 1768 and was the site of the convention held in 1780 which changed the name "Church of England" to "Protestant Episcopal Church" for the American branch. It is located in Chestertown on the corner of High and Cross Streets.

Wye Chapel—This small church built within a grove of trees remains the way it was when consecrated in 1721. It has the traditional raised pulpit with sounding board. It is located off Route 662 south of Wye Mills.

Old Trinity Church—This Dorchester County church was built before 1680 and has been faithfully restored. The colonial box pews, high pulpit and sounding board have all been rebuilt. The church contains a silver chalice that was a gift of Queen Anne. Old Trinity Church is on Route 16 less than 10 miles from Church Creek.

All Hallows Church—Reflecting the colonial practice of doing business with tobacco, this church cost 80,000 pounds of tobacco when it was built in 1756. It also contains a gift from Queen Anne, a Bible dated 1701—London. Above the altar is a stained glass arch. All Hallows Church is at Market and Church Streets in Snow Hill.

St. James Church—This church, built between 1763 and 1765, has stained glass windows which reflect various aspects of colonial life, particularly the emphasis on tobacco growing. It is also noteworthy for the tombstones of the Birckhead family dated 1666, the oldest in Maryland. It is located on Route 2 just prior to the intersection with Route 258 at Tracys Landing.

Middleham Chapel—Eighty thousand pounds of tobacco appears to be the going rate for churches in the 1700s. That was the cost of this chapel built in 1748. A bell from an earlier church is dated 1699. Queen Anne made a contribution of a communion service to this parish. Middleham Chapel is located on Route 2 just south of Lusby.

Durham Church—The original church was built in 1732, rebuilt in 1791 and restored to its colonial appearance in the 1930s. George Washington attended services here as did General William Smallwood. Durham Church is located in Ironsides.

Pennsylvania:

Christ Church—This beautiful church was finished in 1754, and during the days of the Continental Congress many of the members attended services here. George Washington, John Adams, Benjamin Franklin and many other patriots made up the congregation. The church is located on Second Street in the historic district of Philadelphia. The Christ Church Burial Grounds on Fifth Street contain the graves of seven signers of the Declaration of Independence.

Arch Street Friends Meeting House—This is the oldest Quaker meeting house in Philadelphia. The Royal Proprietor, William Penn, established this colony to provide a place for the Quakers to practice their religion without persecution. The land was given to the Quakers by William Penn in 1693 but they didn't build this simple meeting house until 1804. A 15-minute film on the Quaker faith is shown here. The Meeting House is located at Fourth and Arch Streets in the historic district of Philadelphia.

Free Quaker Meeting House—During the Revolution a group of Quakers dissented from the pacifist opinion of the main body of the church. They separated and were called the "Fighting Quakers." When barred from the main meeting house they built their own down the street at Fifth and Arch. Tours of the meeting house are available and a 10-minute slide show is shown in the basement.

Gloria Dei Church (Old Swedes')—Forty-three years before the first English colonists arrived the Swedes settled in the Philadelphia area. Gloria Dei is one of the oldest houses of worship in the state. It was dedicated in 1700, at a ceremony attended by William Penn and John Markham, his deputy governor. Originally a Lutheran church, it affiliated with the Episcopal Diocese in 1845. The tall white spires are still an inspirational sight. The baptismal font and altar carvings were brought over from Gothenburg, Sweden in 1642. Models of the *Key of Kalmar* and the *Flying Griffin*, the ships that brought the first Swedish settlers to America, are suspended from the ceiling. The nautical past is also represented by the heads of two brightly painted wooden angels which hang beneath the organ. They once served as a ship's figurehead. The sacristy contains a 1608 Bible that belonged to Queen Christina. This fascinating old church is located in the Southwark section of Philadelphia at Delaware and Christian Streets.

Colonial Towns

If the goal of all new settlers was to farm their own land, what caused the development of towns? Simply that they were necessary. As settlements grew, towns developed as centers of trade which supplied the necessities farmers could not grow or produce for themselves. Since many of these items came from Europe, towns generally grew around ports and served as centers for shipping.

By the time of the American Revolution the largest colonial towns were already all over 100 years old. Philadelphia, with 40,000 inhabitants, was second only to London as the largest English-speaking city in the world. Also in the top five were New York with 25,000 people, Boston with 16,000, Charlestown at 12,000 and Newport with 11,000.

Only Philadelphia and Charlestown were laid out by city planners. The others just grew from irregular roadways. Of these two, Philadelphia was the most advanced. It was one of the first towns to pave its roads. Boston's method of putting gutters on the side of the street rather than having a shallow trench down the middle was also rapidly incorporated. This latter method was often disastrous for poor drivers, who were constantly getting their wagon wheels stuck in the trench. Charlestown, on the other hand, had dirt roads long after the Revolution.

Baltimore is a good example of the growth of one of the smaller colonial towns. It developed because in 1729 planters north of Annapolis wanted a convenient tobacco inspection site. The town was originally 60 lots of one acre each. By 1752 the population of the entire city of Baltimore was still only 250. There were 25 homes, two taverns and one church. Baltimore was noteworthy because it was America's only walled city. It is uncertain whether the city dwellers were trying to protect themselves from marauding Indians or the foraging of pigs and geese from the surrounding pastures.

The towns were the hotbeds of the Revolution. The merchants and lawyers would frequently meet in the taverns and exchange complaints. The harsh restrictions imposed by George III hit them the hardest of all the colonists. These articulate colonials were able to express the anger felt not only by them but also by the more isolated farmers.

Though many of the colonial lawyers were trained in England, they were also the ones who wrote the script of the Revolution. However, the architect of the Declaration of Independence, Thomas Jefferson, received his legal training with George Wythe in Williamsburg, Virginia.

Communication between the colonies was made easier by the improvement of inland roads. By 1732 there was enough travel to warrant the publication of a small book giving the mileage between major colonial towns.

The mail service was the main beneficiary of the improved roads. By 1692 post riders were traveling from one colony to another. In 1763 a road linked not only the British colonies but also extended all the way down to Spanish St. Augustine in Florida.

This improved communication helped the patriot cause. Committees of Correspondence insured that British actions against the citizens in one area were known by all. Thus were formed the links that would forge a nation.

52. Hammond-Harwood House

In 1773 young Matthias Hammond was a lucky man. His new home near the center of Maryland's capital city, Annapolis, was being built by America's noted architect, William Buckland. He was engaged to marry a pretty young lady and was even able to afford a shopping spree in Philadelphia to furnish their new showplace.

Unfortunately, while he was in Philadelphia his luck ran out. His fickle fiancée eloped with another man. Hammond could not bear to set foot in his beautiful new home, so he left his growing Annapolis law practice and moved to the country. He died a bachelor at an early age.

The house survived and is considered Buckland's finest work. Architects see it as the high point of the formal Georgian five-part design. It is fortunate that the entire house remains unaltered and the details can be appreciated as they were 200 years ago. The delicate carved woodwork should be most closely observed when exploring the Hammond-Harwood House.

The house now serves as a museum for 18th-century decorative arts. It is open daily, except Monday. Admission is charged.

Directions: Take Beltway Exit 9 (John Hanson Highway, Route 40) to the Historic Annapolis exit. From State Circle take Maryland Avenue to King George Street. The Hammond-Harwood House is on the right corner.

53. Peyton Randolph House

Lost in flames when the British burned Washington during the War of 1812 was the entire book collection of the Library of Congress. Thomas Jefferson, a life-long collector, then gave his personal library to the Federal government. Jefferson's collection, in turn, had grown from the library he purchased from his cousin Peyton Randolph's estate. So the nucleus of the present Library of Congress collection was once to be found in the library of the Randolph's home in Williamsburg.

The Randolphs were a distinguished Virginia family. John Randolph was the only colonial gentleman to be knighted. He was an influential member of the House of Burgesses. His son, Peyton, followed his father into the House of Burgesses and also served as Speaker of the House. Peyton Randolph presided over the assembly during the critical decade of debates that led to the Revolution.

The Randolphs began their Williamsburg home in 1715. They followed the not uncommon practice of buying the house next door and linking the two with a middle section. The paneled rooms are the finest in Williamsburg.

The French enjoyed the hospitality of this gracious house on two occasions. During the Siege of Yorktown it served as the Count de Rochambeau's headquarters, while George Washington stayed at the nearby Wythe House.

Lafayette stayed at the Randolph house when he returned to America to celebrate the festivities commemorating the victory at Yorktown.

The Peyton Randolph House is one of the Colonial Williamsburg exhibition homes and is open daily from 9:00 to 5:00. Admission is charged.

Directions: Take Beltway Exit 4 (I-95) to the Richmond By-pass, Route 295. Follow this to Route 64 east, which will lead into Williamsburg. Signs will provide directions to the Visitor Center where maps of Colonial Williamsburg can be obtained, plus information on tours and special programs.

54. Brush-Everard House

The garden of the Brush-Everard House has a tendency to upstage the home. The dwarf boxwoods that form the hedge are the oldest in Williamsburg and the yard is paved with the original bricks. The small goldfish pond is an unusual feature in a colonial garden.

This Williamsburg home was the home of a tradesman. The furnishings are on a modest level, definitely middle-class as compared to the homes of the wealthy Wythes and Randolphs.

The library reflects the reading taste of Thomas Jefferson. It was compiled from a list prepared by Jefferson in 1771 to aid a Virginia planter in acquiring suitable books for his library. Looking at the titles of some of the 300 books tells a lot about the cultural and intellectual life of colonial Virginians.

The Brush-Everard House is another of the exhibition homes in Colonial Williamsburg and is open daily from 9:00 to 5:00.

Directions: Take Beltway Exit 4 (I-95) to the Richmond By-pass, Route 295. Follow this to Route 64 east, which will lead into Williamsburg. Signs will provide directions to the Visitor Center where maps of Colonial Williamsburg can be obtained, plus information on tours and special programs.

55. James Geddy House, Shop and Foundry

Most restored houses reflect the life-style of the rich merchants or the plantation aristocracy, and few examples of middle-class homes have been considered worth preserving.

As a restoration of an entire town, Williamsburg does offer an intriguing cross section of both. The Geddy home is a perfect example of the "middling class."

James Geddy, a silversmith, was one of three artisans elected to the Common Council. He also served on a "committee to represent the city" in advancing the patriot cause.

The Geddy family built this two-story L-shaped house after 1750. The shape, the dormerless roof and the balcony over the front porch were all unusual features at that time. The house is original but the

Norfolk's Adam Thoroughgood House, the oldest standing brick house in America, is one of the features of the Norfolk Tour.

attached shop and outbuildings have been reconstructed on the old foundations.

The James Geddy House, Shop and Foundry are part of Colonial Williamsburg and are open to the public daily from 9:00 to 5:00.

Directions: Take Beltway Exit 4 (I-95) to the Richmond By-pass, Route 295. Follow this to Route 64 east, which will lead into Williamsburg. Signs will provide directions to the Visitor Center where maps of Colonial Williamsburg can be obtained, plus information on tours and special programs.

56. Adam Thoroughgood House

"Early to rise and early to bed makes a man healthy, wealthy and dead." This humorous variation of the old proverb never had more application than in the life of Adam Thoroughgood.

Adam Thoroughgood came to Virginia in 1621 as an indentured servant. He worked hard during his indentureship and, when it ended in 1624, he was a man of property.

He married a young girl of 15 and built a lovely brick home in the British style. It is well that he enjoyed his early success because he died at the young age of 35.

His wife, still a young woman at Thoroughgood's death, went on to marry two more times. She was a wealthy widow, having inherited the manor house and surrounding land.

The house is one of the oldest still standing in Virginia. It was built sometime between 1627 and 1670. Costumed guides show visitors through the house, which is furnished to recreate the year 1636.

The house is open 10:00 to 5:00 Tuesday through Saturday and 12:00 to 5:00 on Sunday. Admission is charged.

Directions: Take Beltway Exit 4 (I-95) south to Richmond. Then take Route 64 to Norfolk. Exit on Northhampton Boulevard. The Adam Thoroughgood House is off Route 225. It is part of the drive yourself "Norfolk Tour" and signs direct drivers to the house.

57. Moses Myers House

People are always curious about millionaires, and especially so about the life-style of the extremely rich. That is why it is interesting to see this 18th-century home built by one of Norfolk's "merchant princes."

The Moses Myers House was built after the American Revolution and so is technically not in the colonial period. But Moses Myers was the embodiment of the 18th-century millionare and his elegant townhouse captures the style of the period.

Three-fourths of the furniture is original. Costumed guides will explain the provenance of different pieces. For example, there is a set of chairs once owned by Marie Antionette. Also intriguing is the collection of 18th-century musical instruments and manuscripts.

The library and parlor contain authentic Adam fireplaces with irons and fenders. The parlor fireplace is reproduced in the American wing of the Metropolitan Museum in New York.

The dining room is considered by many to be one of the most beautiful in the south. Distinguished guests who have enjoyed the hospitalty of the house include Lafayette, President James Monroe, Henry Clay, Daniel Webster, Stephen Decatur, General Winfield Scott and President Theodore Roosevelt and his Cabinet.

The colonial rose garden has also been restored. The Moses Myers House is open from 10:00 to 5:00 Tuesday through Saturday and from 12:00 to 5:00 on Sunday.

Directions: Take Beltway Exit 4 (I-95) to Route 64. Follow Route 64 to Norfolk. This house is on the "Norfolk Tour" and is located off St. Paul's Boulevard, Route 460.

58. Willoughby-Baylor House

Reversing normal practice, in this townhouse the town is in the house. That is, the Early Norfolk Room of the Willoughby-Baylor House features a doll-size replica of Norfolk in the 1790s showing the development of the city. This is only one item in the collection focusing on Norfolk's history.

Another unique item is the only surviving symbol of colonial municipal regalia. A full-size replica of the Norfolk mace, presented to the town council by Lieutenant Governor Dinwiddie in 1754, is also part of the city's history collection.

When this house was built by William Willoughby in 1794 there were only 20 brick homes in town. An inventory taken at Willoughby's death in 1800 has made it possible to furnish the townhouse as he did.

The Willoughby-Baylor House is open Tuesday through Saturday from 10:00 to 5:00 and Sunday from 12:00 to 5:00. Admission is charged.

Directions: From the Beltway, take Exit 4 (I-95) to Route 64, then Route 64 to Norfolk. The house is located one block from the Moses Myers House near downtown Norfolk. Part of the "Norfolk Tour," the Willoughby-Baylor House is off Route 460 at St. Paul's Boulevard.

59. Ramsay House

In these days of soaring real estate prices, William Ramsay's solution to moving may be particularly appealing. In 1749, anxious to get settled on his recently purchased lot in the new town of Alexandria, he just shipped his house down the river and hauled it to its new location. His instant home was the first in Alexandria.

Ramsay situated his portable home so that it overlooked the Potomac River. He could keep his eye on river traffic and be first on hand when trading ships arrived. This enterprising approach made him a highly successful merchant.

A popular figure in the town, he was Alexandria's first postmaster. At an early Alexandria celebration he was made honorary Lord Mayor of the city. His son would later be elected Mayor of Alexandria. William Ramsay was also town overseer, census taker and a member of the committee of safety. He was a life-long friend of George Washington.

The Ramsay House now serves as Alexandria's Visitor Center. After exploring the house and gardens visitors can view a 13-minute film on the city. Free parking passes and walking tour maps are available at Ramsay House, as are hotel and restaurant guides and an annual calendar of events.

The Ramsay House is located at 221 King Street and is open daily except for Thanksgiving, Christmas and New Year's Day at no charge from 9:00 to 5:00.

Directions: Take Virginia Exit 1 (U.S. 1) north into Alexandria. Turn right on Franklin Street, left on Washington and right onto King street. The Ramsay House Visitor Center is located at the intersection of King and Fairfax Streets.

60. Carlyle House

Let's not let the history books get away with calling the Battle of Lexington and Concord the beginning of the American Revolution. The roots of the struggle go back much farther. One contributing factor in the breach between England and her colonies was the idea of taxing the colonists to support British expenditures in the New World. This idea was introduced at Carlyle House.

General Braddock, leader of the British forces, was headquartered here when he arrived in 1755 to handle the problem of French expansion and alliance with the Indians. At a council meeting with five colonial governors the suggestion was made that the colonists be taxed to pay for military expenses incurred by England in fighting the French and Indian War. The plan for "taxation without representation" was not adopted until England issued the Stamp Acts 10 years later in 1765. These acts became one of the pivotal areas of dispute between England and the Colonies.

Carlyle House, intended to resemble a Scottish manor house, was one of the first homes built in Alexandria. In fact, construction began before the town ordinances were written. That is why it is the only house in Alexandria that is not built in line with the street.

Carlyle built his home between 1751 and 1753 for his bride, Sara Fairfax. It has been restored and furnished to reflect their life-style. A number of pieces likely to have belonged to the Carlyle family were recovered when archeologists uncovered five 18th- and 19th-century privy shafts. These shafts were sometimes used like modern apartment trash chutes, except that they were never emptied. Many items were found intact—a pitcher, flower pot, glass, wooden African doll complete with brass hoop earring, a clay pipe bowl and many more.

These items are just part of the constantly changing exhibits at Carlyle House arranged to reflect different aspects of life in the 18th century.

Also intriguing is the architectural exhibit room. The original floorbeams, fireplace openings and plasterwork are left untouched in one area. Another section of the room shows how the early 18th-century work was adapted in the 19th century. Finally, one can see how the room was ultimately restored to its original state in the 20th century.

Carlyle House is open 10:00 to 5:00 Tuesday through Saturday and 12:00 to 5:00 on Sunday. Admission is charged.

Directions: Take Virginia Exit 1 (U.S. 1) north into Alexandria. Carlyle House is at 121 North Fairfax Street.

61. The Old Stone House

Proverbs are often true and if "experience is the best teacher" then The Old Stone House is the place to take young girls to learn what it was really like to live in colonial America. Their free, one-day apprentice program for girls 10 to 14 teaches more than many books because it actively involves the girls in the chores that would have been part of their daily life if they had lived in the 18th century.

Outfitted in colonial dresses, the girls are shown how to prepare a meal over an open fire using old-fashioned utensils. Other domestic activities attempted are spinning and quilting. Advance reservations are required for this popular program; call 426-6851 or write to The Old Stone House at 3051 M Street, N.W., Washington, D.C. 20007.

The house is also worth exploring. It is the only pre-Revolutionary building in the District of Columbia and reflects the dual nature of Georgetown both then and now—it was used as a home and a business.

The 60 acres called "Georgetown" after George III were divided into 80 lots. Christopher Layman's lot was on the main street. He started this stone house in 1764, living above the ground floor carpentry shop. Layman sold not only his own work but also that of enterprising carpenters who°wanted to display their work in this growing port city. Layman's death in 1765 left the burden of finishing the house to his wife. She remarried and sold the house to Cassandra Chew, a prosperous businesswoman who added to the north wing.

The shop has been restored, as have five family rooms, providing a glimpse of middle-class life in Georgetown in the 1700s. On the ground floor, in addition to the shop, is the kitchen. On the second floor are the dining area, family parlor and one bedroom. On the third floor are the family bedrooms. The small yard has a seasonal garden.

The Old Stone House is open at no charge from 9:30 to 5:00 daily.

Directions: The Old Stone House is located at 3051 M Street, N.W. in Washington, D.C.

62. Betsy Ross House

Did Betsy Ross really live in this Philadelphia townhouse? Did she make the first American flag? The Philadelphia Historical Commission disputes both of these claims.

There is evidence to support the legends. Betsy Ross did upholstery work for Independence Hall and for various civic leaders, including

Benjamin Franklin. She made flags for the Pennsylvania navy. Many believe that she did make the first American flag. The house on Arch Street which bears her name has a restored upholstery shop, where colonial methods and equipment are demonstrated.

Even if Betsy Ross never lived in this house it would be worth a visit. It is an excellent example of in-town living in the largest and most advanced colonial town. Like other town homes, it has a basement kitchen and the typical winding staircase. The house is furnished with many pieces that belonged to Betsy Ross.

It was common in the 18th century for both men and women to have a series of matrimonial partners because life expectancy was much shorter than it is today. Betsy Ross had three husbands. The first two died during the Revolutionary War. She is buried with her third husband, John Claypoole, in the Atwater Kent Park next to the Betsy Ross House.

The house can be visited daily, except Thanksgiving, Christmas and New Year's Day. Hours are 9:00 to 6:00 from May to October and 9:00 to 5:00 from November to April. There is no admission charged.

Directions: Take Beltway Exit 27 (I-95) north to Philadelphia. The Betsy Ross House is located just a few blocks from Independence Park at 239 Arch Street.

63. John Bartram's House and Gardens

There's a tendency to imagine that during the arduous task of establishing a new country the arts and sciences were ignored in America. But while they didn't flourish, they did, in fact, exist.

It was as early as 1728 that the Quaker farmer John Bartram bought a 102-acre farm complete with a small stone house. He started to develop a garden, but unlike most backyard hobbyists he took his seriously. He had been fascinated by plants since he was a young boy and though he had little formal education he taught himself Latin so he could understand botanical books.

His interest in the plants of America was shared by many Englishmen. A prosperous London wool merchant, Peter Collinson, contracted with John Bartram to provide an assortment of plants from the New World. Though they never met, Collinson and Bartram corresponded for 35 years and their letters provide a fascinating record of Bartram's expeditions throughout the American wilderness and the concurrent growth of his garden. On his plant quest Bartram went north as far as New York, south to Florida and west to the Ohio River. He returned each time to his Pennsylvania farm and planted the seeds, roots and cuttings he gathered. As his collection grew so did his fame, until in 1765 George III appointed him a Royal Botanist.

The famous Swedish botanist, Carl Linnaeus, who developed a system for classifying plants, called Bartram "the greatest natural botanist in the world."

Fortunately for the continuity of his work, one of his 11 children, William, followed in his father's footsteps. Bartram called him "my little botanist." At an early age William began accompanying his father on his trips. He not only toured the Florida area with his father but also went back at a later age alone and spent four years exploring the deep south.

William returned to the Schuykill farm and spent the rest of his life writing and maintaining America's first Botanic Garden. George Washington and Thomas Jefferson both expressed an interest in the burgeoning collection.

Visitors today can explore the same garden and tour the large stone house that John Bartram built around the original portion he acquired in 1728. He labored on the house and garden himself and above an attic window there is a date stone that says "John–Ann Bartram 1731."

The historic house and garden of John Bartram is open 10:00 to 4:00 Tuesday through Sunday from April through October and Tuesday through Friday from November to March.

Directions: Take Beltway Exit 27 (I-95) north to Philadelphia. Exit from I-95 at University Ave. The John Bartram House and Gardens is at 54th Street and Lindbergh Boulevard in Philadelphia.

64. Corbit-Sharp House

The mistress of the Corbit home would have much preferred the Brick Hotel, which was just across the street, in its present incarnation as an art museum. Back in 1860 when Mrs. Corbit lived in Odessa, Delaware, there was considerable rowdy behavior at the hotel. So incensed was this Quaker matron at the carrying on she began a campaign that resulted in the hotel losing its liquor license.

The Corbit-Sharp House was built between 1772 and 1774 by William Corbit and it has been faithfully restored using inventories kept since the 18th century by various family members. The family has also contributed to the present decor. There are small samplers done by William Corbit's granddaughter in the 1820s.

Much of the furniture is original to the house. The grandfather clock was listed in Corbit's records as costing $60.00 in 1772. It was made by Duncan Beard, a Scotchman who settled one mile outside Odessa in 1767. The dining room also has a desk made by Delaware valley craftsmen between 1775 and 1790.

When the house was restored in 1938 an old-fashioned boxwood parterre garden was added. Also on the grounds is a smokehouse, the only outbuilding remaining from the 18th century.

The Corbit-Sharp house is open Tuesday through Saturday from 10:00 to 4:30, Sunday from 1:00 to 4:30. It is closed on Mondays and holidays. Admission is charged.

Directions: Take Beltway Exit 19 (Route 50–301). After crossing the Bay Bridge follow Route 301 to Odessa, Delaware. The Corbit-Sharp House is on Main Street.

65. Wilson-Warner House

It may seem unusual to name an American town after a Ukranian city. In the case of Odessa, Delaware, it was not because the townspeople were emigrants but rather a reflection of the similar functions of the two towns. Odessa was the great grain port of Russia and this town the principal grain market of the region. Six large granaries stored the harvests from 1820 until 1840. The town shipped 400,000 bushels of grain annually.

One of the town's prosperous merchants was David Wilson, brother-in-law of William Corbit. Wilson built his home in Odessa in 1769. He had a general store on Main Street. Older, smaller and more simple than the Corbit House, this is more typical of Delaware architecture. Like the Corbit House, it too is painstakingly decorated with period pieces from the colonial era.

On the grounds is a "skinning shack" built in the early 18th century and moved here during restoration. Also, a stone stable built by David Wilson in the late 1700s or early 1800s still stands.

The Wilson-Warner House is open Tuesday through Saturday from 10:00 until 4:30 and on Sunday from 1:00 until 4:30, and closed on Mondays and holidays. Admission is charged.

Directions: Take Beltway Exit 19 (Route 50–301); after crossing the Bay Bridge follow Route 301 to Odessa, Delaware. The Wilson-Warner House is on Main Street in Odessa.

Colonial Business

The colonies indeed proved to be a land of opportunity. Many of those who came as indentured servants or worked as apprentices went on to enjoy success and even fame. There was no stigma attached to humble beginnings. Three of the signers of the Declaration of Independence worked as apprentices. While a young man, Benjamin Franklin was a printer's apprentice. Roger Sherman of Connecticut worked for a shoemaker and George Walton of Georgia was a carpenter. The "taste maker" of the colonies, William Buckland, came to Virginia as George Mason's indentured servant. He went on to become America's most noted architect.

The men who first came to America performed all tasks; they planted, built, panned for gold, fought the Indians and explored the wilderness. But as time passed, towns grew and specialization began.

New towns created new jobs—the early lamplighters, town criers, bell ringers, chimney sweeps and inspectors. The inspectors were respected community members who insured that certain standards were maintained in agricultural produce and in building safety. One of the most important inspectors checked the tobacco harvest to be sure that it was of high quality.

These men were often called viewers. The gutter viewer made sure roof gutters did not spill rain or snow on pedestrians. The egg viewer checked for bad merchandise. There was also a chimney viewer, weight viewer, tide viewer, fence viewer and a scrutineer, now called election judge.

Public service functions were filled by policemen called leatherheads, street cleaners, who were known as whitewings because of their white uniforms, and volunteer fire fighters.

The most respected colonial professionals were the landed gentry with their large plantations and the lawyers and merchants. Many distinguished colonists also were inn or tavern keepers. John Adams, the second President, owned an inn and George Washington's youngest brother, Charles, had a tavern in Fredericksburg, Virginia.

On the plantations most of the necessary work was done on the estate but in towns small enterprises served the general population. The term "maker" was added to any number of jobs—candlemaker, wigmaker, clockmaker, sleighbellmaker—and even such short-lived jobs as the paper collar maker and mantuamaker.

Another job suffix was "wright," which meant skilled workman. There were millwrights, plowwrights, tilewrights, timberwrights, bookwrights and, of course, playwrights.

The traders and peddlers were "mongers." There were cheesemongers, fishmongers, coalmongers, poultrymongers and fellmongers, who sold animal pelts.

There were a great deal of "smiths," a word indicating all those who worked with metal: brasssmith, silversmith, goldsmith, scissorsmith, toolsmith, coachsmith and swordsmith.

Finally "man" and "woman" were added to a long list of jobs: clipperman, codman, stallman and cat food man (a person who fed city cats in areas where they were needed to catch mice and rats). There was even a secondhand meat man, who sold restaurant table scraps. There were applewomen, herdswomen, woodswomen, shopwomen, leechwomen, lacewomen and many more.

Most of the jobs in the colonies were individual trades, but there were a few early American industries: iron ore smelting, charcoal burning to produce carbon blocks and glassmaking. There were also paper mills and those jobs connected with transportation, such as building the roads and bridges that would connect the diverse colonies.

66. George Washington's Gristmill Historical State Park

George Washington ran this gristmill for three decades. Of course, he didn't personally run it, but hired a miller. His first employee became so fond of the products of the distillery associated with the mill that he turned into a drunken sot. Though the miller had seven children, Washington was forced to fire him.

This is the second mill Washington owned. The one at Mount Vernon was not operating efficiently when Washington inherited the estate from his sister-in-law. So in 1770 Washington had this three-and-a-half story stone millhouse constructed. Associated with the mill was the distillery that so tempted the early miller, a cooper's shop and a stable.

All of these activities are represented at George Washington's Gristmill Historical State Park. There is much to see, and the displays provide modern visitors with an insightful look at the ingenuity of our forebears.

A taped message from the miller's wife clearly explains what

On the ground floor of George Washington's Gristmill one can view the massive waterwheel head on.

happened when grain was brought by customers to be ground. The "merchant trade" had wheat ground into flour while the "country trade" relied more on ground corn. Each customer's grain was tagged and ground separately, for each wanted to be sure he received his own batch. The presence of the early machinery allows visitors to visualize how it once operated.

An intriguing feature of the mill is that the three floors above the ground level each permit a different perspective of the large waterwheel. On the ground floor is a "cog pit" where the wheel can be seen head on, but on the upper levels visitors look down and watch as the stream water turns the massive wheel.

The cooper's art is represented in exhibits and diagrams. Once wheat was ground into flour it was stored in barrels, which is why cooper's often were associated with mills.

On the top floor of the mill there is a display of early American tools: the mallet, axe, froe club, sashsaw and hand adze.

In 1799 George Washington rented this mill to his nephew Lawrence Lewis, but he still kept an eye on its operation. His mill was the last place Washington visited before his death. It was a snowy day and he caught a cold from which he never recovered.

The George Washington Gristmill Historical State Park is open daily Memorial Day to Labor Day from 10:00 to 6:00. In the spring and fall it is open on weekends. There is a small admission charged.

Directions: From the Beltway take Virginia Exit 1 (U.S. 1) south seven miles. Near the Woodlawn Plantation entrance turn left on the Mount Vernon Memorial Parkway (Route 235). The mill is about one-fourth mile beyond on the left.

67. Stabler-Leadbeater Apothecary Shop Museum

Passerbys noticing two red-filled jars in the window of an apothecary shop in the 18th century would quickly cover their faces and hastily leave town. These jars served as a warning to travelers when the town was suffering through an epidemic. Normally apothecary jars contained red and green colored water, providing a visual sign for the unlettered that this was a shop where medicine could be purchased.

In Alexandria the Stabler-Leadbeater Apothecary Shop served the community for 141 years from 1792 until 1933. When it closed it was the second oldest apothecary shop in the United States and the oldest in Virginia.

Though closed for business, it remains as it was when George Washington was a steady customer. He even picked up his mail here and Martha would frequently send a messenger for a quart of "your finest caster oil." A tape recorded story of this old apothecary shop now informs visitors of its history.

The shop has the largest and most complete collection of apothecary jars in their original setting in the country. There is also an exhibit of early medical implements and patent medicines. The tiles built into the counter have an interesting background. It is said that one tile was used for mixing medicinal powder for people, while another was used to prepare medicine for horses.

There is no admission to this old shop. Donations and sales at the Antique Shop help support the museum. Hours are 10:00 to 4:30 Monday through Saturday. Closed at lunchtime.

Directions: Take Virginia Beltway Exit 1 (U.S. 1) into Alexandria. The Stabler-Leadbeater Apothecary Shop Museum is in Historic Alexandria at 107 S. Fairfax Street.

68. Hugh Mercer Apothecary Shop

Anyone who has ever left either their home or shop with others in charge for even so short a period as a few days can appreciate the significance of the absolute fidelity of the Hugh Mercer Apothecary Shop. The door was closed when Dr. Mercer went off to serve the Revolutionary cause and the shop remains just as it was in the 18th century. Though only a few of the items actually belonged to Mercer, all of the furnishings and equipment are of the period and could have been found in Dr. Mercer's shop.

Hugh Mercer, a Brigadier General in the Continental Army, was killed at the Battle of Princeton. But in his shop the clock stopped and visitors see it as it may have looked when he shut the door behind him in 1776.

On Washington's frequent visits to Fredericksburg he used the shop's adjoining sitting room and library as his office. Mercer and Washington became acquainted while serving in the French and Indian War.

Dr. Mercer's experiences during the war were quite dramatic. He was wounded in battle and narrowly escaped capture by Indians. He wandered lost in the mountains for 10 days before he finally regained the British lines. He was later promoted to Colonel and appointed Commandant of Fort Pitt, later Pittsburgh.

Visitors to the Hugh Mercer Apothecary Shop will gain some insight into the practice of medicine in the 18th century. On the ancient showcases are gold-labeled bottles and handblown glass apothecary jars painted from the inside. Silver-plated pills and faded prescriptions rest beside a yellow-leaved ledger recalling a life that was never resumed.

The Hugh Mercer Apothecary Shop in Fredericksburg is open daily from 9:00 to 5:00. There is a small admission charged.

Directions: Take Beltway Exit 4 (I-95) south to Fredericksburg. Follow Bicentennial Visitor Center signs into town. The Hugh Mercer Apothecary Shop is located at 1020 Caroline Street, just two blocks from the Visitor Center.

69. Batsto Historic Area

What's a "batsto?" Many of the settlers in this part of New Jersey were Scandinavian, and when they saw the steam rising from the hot iron they called it "baatsto" which actually meant steam bath.

The word stuck and this branch of a chain of ironworks in southern New Jersey was called Batsto Furnace. It was built in 1766 and was such a crucial industry for this young country that men working here were exempt from military service. The Batsto Furnace was almost captured by the British in 1778 but was saved by Pulaski's Legion.

In 1779 a lumbering concern was added at Batsto. A glass factory was opened in 1846. There were at one time nearly 1,000 people living and working in this industrial community.

Batsto has been restored as a Historic Area. There is the Iron-master's Mansion on the hill, a number of ironworker's cabins, a gristmill, sawmill, general store, blacksmith shop and assorted barns and sheds. Tours of these historic buildings can be arranged at the Visitor Center.

Batsto Historic Area is only open during the summer months, hours 10:00 to 5:00. The Ironmaster's House can be toured year-round. Additional information can be obtained by calling (609) 561-3262. Or write to Wharton State Forest, RD 4, Hammonton, NJ 08037.

Directions: Take Beltway Exit 27 (I-95) north to the New Jersey Turnpike. Make a left on the Atlantic City Expressway, then a right on Route 54 and another right on Route 542 to the Batsto Historic Area.

70. Bethlehem Historic District

On Christmas Eve 1741 a new Bethlehem was christened. The members of a Moravian sect called Unitas Fratrum were meeting in their new Pennsylvania settlement for a religious service. Count Zinzendorf, their leader, called this new town Bethlehem.

The group settled in this sparsely populated region, hoping to serve the spiritual needs of the isolated German settlers and also to convert the Indians to Christianity.

There are two interesting sections of Bethlehem to explore: the Historic Industrial Quarter and the old Moravian community buildings. In the Industrial section is the 1762 Waterworks, which provided the first municipal water system in the colonies, the 1764 Springhouse with exhibits of old agricultural tools, and the Tannery. At the Tannery costumed guides explain the process of converting animal skins to leather while demonstrating the old equipment. Also open is the 1868 Gristmill and the 1768 Sun Inn.

Also significant historically are the buildings in the old Moravian community. The Moravian Museum is in the 1741 Gemein Haus, the oldest building in Bethlehem. Exhibits show various aspects of 18th-century life in this community. Other old buildings include the Old Chapel built in 1751, the Sisters House, dating from 1747, and the Widows House which dates from 1768.

Directions: Take Beltway Exit 27 (I-95) north to Philadelphia. Make connections with the Northeast Extension of the Pennsylvania Turnpike north of Philadelphia. Bethlehem is located on Route 22.

Colonial Taverns

Talk about paying for your drink with bits and pieces—that was literally the preferred currency during the colonial period, referring as it did to pieces of the gold doubloon. The doubloon was the Spanish dollar, available throughout the English colonies as a result of extensive Spanish trading for British goods. Gold pieces were routinely divided into eight sections, or pieces of eight. Each piece was called a "bit" and was worth twelve-and-a-half cents, hence the expression, "two bits, four bits, six bits, a dollar." A tankard of ale cost half a bit, or six-and-a-half cents; if the patron had two tankards it would cost a whole bit and the piece would not have to be broken. It would take a thirsty customer to drink two tankards.

Another method of payment was the barter technique. Drinks could be purchased with farm goods. A quart of rum was worth one-and-a-half pounds of butter. Tobacco notes were also accepted by tavern keepers.

Of course, since Americans were then English colonists, English currency was also used—the pence, shilling and pound. With inflation creating a constant fluctuation of monetary values, it can only be roughly estimated that in the 1740s a pence was worth a penny. There were 12 pence, or cents, to a shilling and 20 shillings to a pound.

The menu prices charged by inns and taverns were set by the court. For example, in 1791 the court of Bath County, Virginia established the following prices: six pence for a night's lodging, four pence for a gallon of corn whiskey, four shillings for a quart of rum, 12.5 pence for a cold supper and 21 pence for a hot dinner.

Taverns were the social and civic centers of most towns. From 1619 taverns operated in America, providing food, shelter, lodging and a meeting place for the community. Jamestown had a lively tavern during the 92 years that city served as Virginia's capital. Popular taverns like the Raleigh in Williamsburg, City Tavern in Philadelphia, the Rising Sun in Fredericksburg and Gadsby's Tavern in Alexandria were centers of patriot activity.

Taverns played a considerable role in events leading up to the Revolution, serving as a patriot "underground." George Washington made his headquarters in a tavern while fighting the British in New York. He later appointed Samuel Fraunces, the tavern keeper, to be his household steward during his terms as President. The second President, John Adams, owned a tavern during the 1780s. It was quite a respectable colonial occupation.

In the country taverns were much simpler, many even crude. Often they were called "Ordinaries" because the food would likely be similar to a family's ordinary fare. Travelers needed these rest stops, although gentlemen usually were able to find a nearby plantation to the owners of which they were either related, acquainted or carried letters of introduction. The ferry taverns sometimes slept as many as 13 in one room. It was quite common, even in city taverns like the Raleigh, to find yourself sharing a bed with one or more strangers.

71. Raleigh Tavern

"Jollity, the offspring of wisdom and good living," the motto carved over the mantel at the Raleigh Tavern in Williamsburg, Virginia, could well have served as the watchword of the 18th-century gentleman. The fire of patriotism was fueled by many a drink.

If Williamsburg was the focal point of rebellion in the colony, then the Raleigh was the hub. It was here that the radical Burgesses met when they were dismissed by the Royal Governor for disloyalty and sedition.

Taverns such as the Raleigh could be compared to clubs today. Colonial leaders wined, dined, gambled and slept here. The Raleigh's public room, the Apollo, was used for many fine receptions. Thomas Jefferson danced here one night with his "Fair Belinda," as he noted in his diary. Citizens gathered at the Apollo to celebrate the signing of the Treaty of Paris ending the American Revolution. In 1824 Lafayette attended a party at the Raleigh during festivities to mark the victory at Yorktown.

The tavern was destroyed by fire in 1859 but it has been faithfully reconstructed on its original foundation. Sketches of the exterior and information on the insurance claim gave a clear picture of the colonial structure.

Raleigh Tavern has been restored, but only the Raleigh Tavern Bakery still serves the public. A baker using 200-year-old methods prepares gingerbread men and other delicacies for visitors. Three other taverns have been restored in Colonial Williamsburg: Wetherburn Tavern, King's Arms Tavern and Christiana Campbell's Tavern. The last two are again open for business, preparing 18th-century fare for visitors. Colonial Williamsburg is open from 9:00 to 5:00 daily.

Directions: Take Beltway Exit 4 (I–95) south to the Richmond Bypass, Route 295. Follow this to Route 64 east, which will lead into Williamsburg. Raleigh's Tavern is located on Duke of Gloucester Street in Colonial Williamsburg.

72. Rising Sun Tavern

History has so venerated the Washington family that it is hard for us to look back and visualize George's younger brother owning a tavern that was a "hotbed of sedition."

But in Fredericksburg at the Washington Tavern, later called the Rising Sun Tavern, the Revolutionary leaders of Virginia often met to consolidate their position and plan anti-British action. George Washington, Thomas Jefferson, Patrick Henry, George Mason, Hugh Mercer, John Marshall and the Lees all frequented this tavern.

Rising Sun Tavern was the social center of the community, and its activities were diverse. It not only served as a stage coach stop and post office but colonial balls were also held here. It, of course, provided the food, lodging and drink expected of an 18th-century tavern.

The tavern has luckily remained structurally unaltered, though it has been restored and refurnished. It is a typical story-and-a-half frame building with a gabled roof.

Part of the original wooden bar was uncovered during restoration and it has been rebuilt. The Tap Room has a large collection of English and American pewter. At the gaming tables there is a "man-sized" checkers set made from a whale's backbone.

Rising Sun Tavern is open daily. Hours in January to February are 10:00 to 4:00; March hours are 9:00 to 4:00. April through October the tavern is open from 9:00 to 5:00 and November and December from 9:00 to 4:00. Admission is charged and hot spiced tea served.

Directions: From the Beltway take Exit 4 (I–95) south to Fredericksburg. Rising Sun Tavern is at 1306 Caroline Street.

73. Historic Michie Tavern Museum

Despite the colonial desire to be "with it" and keep up with the latest fashions in Europe, when Miss Jefferson and her French boyfriend

Historic Michie Tavern was a meeting place where local gentlemen relaxed. Now a museum, its exhibits depict colonial life in Virginia before the Revolutionary War.

demonstrated the waltz at Michie Tavern it so scandalized a colonial matron that she berated Martha for her wanton behavior. The young girl fled the ballroom in tears. It would be a while before this European import was received with favor.

Although balls were held in taverns such as Michie Tavern, taverns were used most often as a meeting place for area gentlemen to relax and air their grievances.

It is appropriate that a number of the American Revolutionary leaders met at Michie Tavern, since "Scotch John Michie" was himself a rebel. He had opposed the move to unite Scotland with England in the commonwealth. He narrowly escaped death, and his earlobes were cut off when he was exiled from England.

He bought land and a large clapboard house, which became Michie Tavern, from Major Henry, whose 10-year-old son, Patrick, would also mature into an outspoken opponent of English ties.

The original tavern furniture is intact. There is a colonial variation on the hideaway Murphy bed and Chippendale chests and tables so shiny that they appear to be varnished. They have been rubbed with a mixture of beeswax and turpentine daily since 1735.

There are various dependencies outside the tavern—a smokehouse, springhouse, gristmill, blacksmith shop and the necessary. There is no refinement in the necessary, just four holes. On the wall, by a rope suspended from the ceiling, is a message: "If ye fall into the hole, do not call proprietor, use rope to pull ye out."

Patrons are still served colonial fare at the Ordinary. This converted log cabin was once used as a slave house.

There are exhibits in the Michie Tavern Museum that provide a comprehensive picture of colonial life in Virginia before the Revolution. Michie Tavern is open daily from 9:00 to 5:00. Admission is charged. The Ordinary is open for lunch from 11:30 to 3:00.

Directions: Take Beltway Exit 8 (Route 28–211) to Charlottesville. Historic Michie Tavern Museum is one mile from Monticello on Route 53.

74. Gadsby's Tavern Museum

George Washington himself may be gone but his birthday ball at Gadsby's Tavern is a tradition still observed faithfully today. Considering that the ball was instituted in 1787, that's what could be called a long run. George Washington enjoyed a dance here on his last birthday in 1799. It was a big day for him because earlier his step-daughter, Nellie Custis, had married his nephew, Lawrence Lewis, at Mount Vernon.

Gadsby's Tavern has been called the "finest tavern in the colonies built before 1800." There are two buildings, the early 1770 tavern and the hotel built in 1792. Today the two are joined by a passageway.

There were actually four taverns on this property. The oldest was Mason's Ordinary, built in 1752. This early tavern, or inn, provided food, lodging and stabling for horses. In 1796, John Gadsby leased the City Hotel (1792), which became known as Gadsby's Tavern. It became a popular spot with the Alexandria populace. Noted figures who enjoyed the tavern's hospitality included the Marquis de Lafayette, John Paul Jones, Baron de Kalb, Aaron Burr, George Mason, Francis Scott Key and Henry Clay.

The tavern has been restored to its colonial appearance and both the 1770 and 1792 buildings are open. Another addition built in 1878 cannot be toured. Restoration has yielded artifacts that have provided details on the china pattern, silverware and glassware once used.

Visitors can even peer down into the 18th-century ice-house. Large chunks of ice from the Potomac River were lowered from Cameron Street through a chute and packed in straw. Wines could then be chilled before serving.

Directions: Take Virginia Beltway Exit 1 (U.S. 1) to Alexandria. Gadsby's Tavern Museum is at 134 North Royal Street.

75. London Town Publik House and Gardens

From London Town to London, this bustling town on the South River was one of the favored departure points for Englishmen returning home. In its heyday, the town was home to numerous merchants and lawyers and had busy streets lined by tobacco warehouses, shops, inns and other businesses.

London Town was also a major ferry crossing for travelers going north and south. Most of these travelers availed themselves of the hospitality of the largest inn, London Town Publik House. Records kept by George Washington, Thomas Jefferson and Francis Scott Key all mention making the South River ferry crossing.

The Publik House also served as a post house and source of news for the community. The innkeeper had a variety of jobs, in addition to housing and feeding those who stopped. For example, William Brown, innkeeper from 1753 to 1793, was also the ferry keeper, operated a cabinet making business and owned an upriver plantation.

The London Town Publik House still has the original brick, exterior doors and much of its glass. The all-header brick pattern of the exterior walls is similar to that used in the Paca House and other Annapolis landmarks. The house is furnished simply with sturdy furniture designed to withstand heavy use. The Publik House was designated a National Historic Landmark in 1970.

Eight acres have been planted to enhance the natural landscape around the Publik House. The garden path offers beautiful vistas of the South River. In the spring the daffodils, azaleas, camellias, magnolias, rhododendron and wild flowers are delightful. Day lilies bloom in abundance during the summer months.

There is a 1720 log tobacco barn which has been moved onto the grounds. Tobacco made London Town a bustling port but the relocation of the tobacco inspection station combined with the growth of nearby Annapolis forced London Town into decline by mid-century.

The London Town Publik House and Gardens is open Tuesday through Saturday from 10:00 to 4:00 and on Sunday from 12:00 to 4:00. Admission is charged.

Directions: Take Beltway Exit 19 (Route 50) east. Exit south on Route 424 to Davidsonville, then go east on Route 214. Turn left on Stepneys Lane, one block past the traffic signal at Route 2. Follow Stepneys Lane to Mayo Road, proceed straight across the intersection onto Londontown Road, and follow Londontown Road until it terminates at the London Town Publik House and Gardens in Maryland.

76. George Washington House 1760

Here is a tavern that really served the law—it was sold to pay for William Wirt's legal education. Young Wirt went on to have a distinguished career. He was the attorney who prosecuted Aaron Burr for treason. Wirt also served as Attorney General longer than anyone before or since, under both President James Monroe and President John Quincy Adams. He tried to cap his career with an unsuccessful bid for the presidency in 1832.

It was William Wirt's father, Jacob, who built George Washington House 1760 as part of a commercial and entertainment complex in this thriving port city. Garrison's Landing, as Bladensburg was first called, was one of the major colonial seaports in terms of total tonnage. The tavern, located on the Post Road connecting the northern and southern colonies, was an immediate success.

After Jacob Wirt's death in 1774 his widow married Peter Carnes. The new tavern keeper was one of the earliest hot-air balloon enthusiasts. In 1784 he launched a series of unmanned balloon ascents that are the first known to have occurred in the United States. Also a first was his manned ascent in Baltimore on June 24, 1784.

The George Washington House 1760 also figured in two later historical events. During the War of 1812 artillery emplacements were positioned on the grounds of the tavern by the British at the Battle of Bladensburg, August 24, 1814. The British defeated the smaller American force and moved on to Washington, where they burned the White House and the Capitol.

On May 14, 1894, Jacob Coxey and his army of unemployed, or his "living petition," marched to Washington from Ohio to protest economic conditions and descended on the tavern. Coxey and his family were given rooms inside, while his followers pitched tents on the grounds. When Coxey reached Washington, he was arrested for trespassing while giving a speech on the Capitol steps.

The George Washington House 1760 is rich in history and has been painstakingly restored. The tavern also houses the George Washington

House Museum. There are 15 dioramas depicting significant events and personalities in Maryland history. The museum has artifacts from the Piscataway Indians; includes exhibits on the first settlement at St. Mary's and has a depiction of the Battle of Bladensburg.

The museum and tavern are open Wednesday through Saturday from 9:30 to 2:30. A small admission is charged.

Directions: From the Beltway take Exit 25 south on Route 1 (and Alt. Route 1) to Bladensburg, Maryland. George Washington House 1760 is a half mile north of Peace Cross near the intersection of Route 450.

77. City Tavern

If billboards and commercials had been a part of 18th-century life, then Philadelphia's City Tavern would have featured John Adams' testimonial that this tavern was "the most genial one in America."

From its opening in 1774 through the next 80 tumultuous years in America's burgeoning statehood, this tavern served the men who made the nation. It was a favorite meeting spot for revolutionaries and businessmen during this period. Many significant revolutionary activities were either planned or celebrated here. Paul Revere brought news on May 20, 1774 that the port of Boston was closed and a large group gathered here and agreed to send a message of sympathy to the people of Boston.

During the American Revolution, the tavern was used by General Washington as his headquarters. Colonial officers lodged here, including Horatio Gates, Benedict Arnold and the Marquis de Lafayette. The British also enjoyed the hospitality of City Tavern during their occupation of Philadelphia. Many Tory balls were held here during 1777 and 1778.

The tavern has been restored and is part of Independence National Historical Park. The walls have the white-washed effect popular during the 1770s. The bench-like tables and Chippendale chairs are also representative of an 18th-century tavern. The first innkeeper, Daniel Smith, was an Englishman who wanted the place to resemble a London tavern.

The menu reflects not only colonial but also modern tastes. Eighteenth-century fare is combined with other selections to offer an enjoyable interlude in the midst of colonial exploring.

Directions: Take Beltway Exit 27 (I–95) north to Philadelphia. Follow signs for downtown Philadelphia. City Tavern is located on Second Street between Chestnut and Walnut Streets.

78. A Man Full of Trouble Tavern

Many a man full of drink fulfilled the prophetic name of A Man Full of Trouble Tavern in Philadelphia. This tavern is even older than City Tavern, going back as it does to the 1750s. It did indeed serve some troublemakers, determined to wreak havoc on British domination in Pennsylvania.

This historic old tavern has been restored to its condition in 1759. On the first floor is the tap room. The second floor has bedrooms and sitting rooms furnished with period pieces, including a set of Windsor chairs which belonged to John Jay. American pewter and English Delftware reflect the frequent mixing of colonial and English styles.

Costumed hostesses guide visitors through this old tavern. It is open daily, except Monday, from April through December; the hours are 1:00 to 4:00. Other months it is open from 1:00 to 4:00 on the weekends only. Admission is charged.

Directions: Take Beltway Exit 27 (I-95) north to Philadelphia. Follow signs for downtown Philadelphia. A Man Full of Trouble Tavern is located at Dock and Spruce Streets.

79. Golden Plough Tavern

It is not uncommon even today to have a court that moves around the state hearing cases, but it is strange to have the legislative branch move from town to town.

War creates exigencies, and in the fall of 1777 the Continental Congress was driven from Philadelphia by British occupation. The legislators first moved to Lancaster. Then they decided it would be more prudent to have the Susquehanna River between the British troops and their meeting site. They crossed the river and convened in York, Pennsylvania.

Colonial leaders met in the Golden Plough Tavern in York. The legislators included John Adams, John Hancock, Thomas Paine, Samuel Adams, Philip Livingston, Francis Lightfoot Lee, Charles Carroll and Gouverneur Morris.

The Golden Plough Tavern is the oldest building in York. It was built in 1741 by Martin Eichelberger to suggest the buildings of his early home in Germany's Black Forest. In fact, this tavern is one of the few buildings in the United States built in this medieval style. The tavern is half brick and half large hand-hewn timber with a pitched roof.

The Golden Plough Tavern is only one of a number of restored buildings in Historic York. Other restorations and museum exhibits in the area depict the Center Square as it was in the 1830s. The Golden Plough Tavern is attached to the home of the Revolutionary General, Horatio Gates.

Historic York is open daily from 10:00 to 5:00, Sundays from 1:00 to 5:00.

Directions: Take Beltway Exit 27 (I-95) north, then around the Baltimore Beltway to Route 83 for York. The Golden Plough Tavern is on West Market Street in York.

80. Red Rose Inn

A ceremonial ritual more attuned to the English courtly days of knighthood than to Quaker Pennsylvania is still being observed at Red Rose Inn.

Each year on the first Saturday after Labor Day a single red rose is paid to a descendant of William Penn as rent. This tradition stems from the early deed that stipulated a yearly rent of one red rose be paid on demand for this land.

Red Rose Inn was on a colonial road that connected Baltimore and Philadelphia. It was only a primitive trail during the 1740s, used by horseback riders and an occasional wagon. The trail crossed a path used by the Delaware Indians as they headed westward to hunt. The inn was an active spot for news of the colonies and for trading.

Travelers still enjoy stopping at this colonial inn for lunch or dinner. It is surrounded by a sunken garden and a field of roses. Star Roses, a commercial nursery, is located in the area and the fields have literally hundreds of varieties. It is a beautiful place to visit during the summer months.

Directions: From the Beltway take Exit 22 (the Baltimore-Washington Parkway) north through the Harbor Tunnel to I-95. Follow I-95 to Delaware then exit on Route 141 north to Newport. Continue north on this road as it becomes Route 41. When you reach U.S. 1 at Avondale, turn off on U.S. 1. The Red Rose Inn is on Route 1 just past West Grove, Pennsylvania.

81. The Indian King Tavern

In a real-life American version of "The Student Prince," the niece of this Haddonfield, New Jersey tavern keeper did succeed where the original heroine failed. Young Dolly Payne, after attracting the admiring attention of the eager soldiers and legislators who frequented her uncle's tavern, did succeed in becoming America's First Lady—Dolly Madison.

The Indian King Tavern served as the meeting place for the New Jersey legislature during the Revolutionary War. Like the Continental Congress, they had been forced to shift their meetings as the British consolidated their hold on New Jersey. It was at a meeting here on September 20, 1977 that the term 'state' was substituted for 'colony' in all future references.

There are stories that claim British loyalists were imprisoned in an empty wine cellar of the tavern. Later tales indicate that this was also a stop on the Underground Railroad during the 1800s.

The Indian King Tavern, built in 1750, is a part of the Haddonfield Historic Walking Tour. It is open Tuesday through Saturday from 10:00 to 5:00. There is a small admission charged.

Directions: From the Beltway take Exit 27 (I-95) north to the Delaware Memorial Bridge. Follow Route 295 north to Route 70. Bear left and continue to the Haddonfield exit. Signs will indicate the restored historic area.

Other Taverns of the Colonial Period

Hollingsworth Tavern—Talk about fence straddling! This tavern keeper served both George Washington and the British General Howe within a two-day period. The tavern is located near the colonial port, Head of Elk, and served ships arriving from England. During the Revolution soldiers from the south came ashore at this port. Directions: Take Beltway Exit 27 (I-95) to the Baltimore Beltway. From there take Route 40 north to Elkton, Maryland. The tavern is on West Main Street.

Rodgers Tavern—Built near Perryville in 1696 when a ferry began operating across the Susquehanna River connecting post roads, this imposing three-story tavern was operated by Colonel John Rodgers, who commanded a militia company during the American Revolution.

Now restored and refurnished, it serves as a museum. Directions: Take Beltway Exit 25 (Route 1) across the Susquehannock Toll Bridge to Perrysville, Maryland.

Old Ferry Inn, Washington Crossing State Park—On December 25, 1776, George Washington's Christmas meal was not the relaxed, convivial family dinner he would have enjoyed. He hurriedly ate at this 18th-century tavern while he and his staff were busy with last minute preparations for their nighttime crossing of the cold, icy Delaware River. Washington and 2,400 men surprised the Hessians, giving the Continental Army their first victory.

The Old Ferry Inn is a two-story brick structure with a basement kitchen. Furnished with period pieces, it is open daily from 9:30 to 5:00. Food is still served. Directions: Take Beltway Exit 27 (I-95) up through Pennsylvania, exiting at Route 32 just before crossing into New Jersey. Signs will direct visitors to Washington Crossing State Park in Washington Crossing, Pennsylvania.

Colonial Government

There are a great many myths and fallacies in the standard portrayal of America's past. It is a common belief that the first democratic representative legislature met in Jamestown, Virginia in 1619. This belief is far from accurate. Democratic representation was not the colonists' objective; they were Englishmen and there was nothing democratic about the English system of government at that time. What the colonists really wanted were the rights of free Englishmen under British common law.

The London Company kept Jamestown under martial law for the first five years. There was a communal economy with no individual rights of property. By 1618, company directors had decided this system was not feasible and had made substantial reforms. The colonists were given common law rights as well as the power to elect two Burgesses from each plantation to a legislative body that would make laws for the colony. This legislative body, composed of 22 leading planters from 11 boroughs, or plantations, met with the Governor and Council for the first time from July 30 to August 4, 1619 in the Memorial Church at Jamestown (see First Settlements: Jamestown Colonial Historical Park).

From 1624, when the London Company broke its colonial connections, to 1638, the Burgesses were left with no legal status. Royal Governors called them to meetings at their whim. Colonists made numerous attempts to have the King establish the right of the colony to an elected Assembly that met regularly. This King Charles I did in 1638, marking a victory for limited self-government in the colonies.

This new legislature was hardly representative since it served only the wealthy tobacco planters and the merchants. That the wealthy used their power is illustrated in the manner in which taxes were levied by the Assembly. The poll tax passed in 1629 required everyone to pay five pounds of tobacco. The farmer with only a few acres paid as much as the plantation owner with thousands of acres.

The outcry against this was loud and long. In 1645 the tax was changed to reflect the amount of property and number of servants a person owned. This democratic shift was shortlived. It was repealed and in 1648 the poll tax again benefited the large plantation class. From this, the Assembly gained the name "planter's parliament."

Events in England were leading to a more active interest and involvement in colonial trade. At the same time, the colonists were anxious for self-determination. The years from 1677 to 1698 were a time of expanding royal control. The Royal Governor kept the House of Burgesses on a tight rein, disbanding them whenever he was displeased with their actions.

Dissatisfaction with autocratic King James was spreading not only in the colonies but also in England. In the late 1680s the Glorious Revolution removed King James from the throne. The change brought reforms in the relationship between the mother country and the colonies. The right of the colonial legislative bodies to issue laws was affirmed, and they were assured of permanent status; no longer were they to be disbanded at the whim of Royal Governors. Finally, they were, henceforth, to be bicameral bodies.

Charles I granted Maryland as a Royal proprietoryship to Cecilius Calvert, who held the hereditary title of Lord Baltimore. The Maryland colony was established to provide religious freedom. So, unlike Virginia which belonged to a company of merchants (the London Company), Maryland belonged to a family (the Calverts).

As Royal Proprietors the Calverts were empowered to govern the inhabitants on their land. It was a return to feudal Middle Age customs, when the landowners had sole power over their serfs.

On February 26, 1635, the first General Assembly, composed of all free adult males, met in St. Mary's to pass laws for the Maryland colony. When these measures were forwarded to London, Lord Baltimore refused to acknowledge their right to make laws. He reminded the colonists that under the terms of the Royal Charter only he or his representative, the Governor, could make laws. The Governor could convene an Assembly if he so desired, but merely to approve his laws. A meeting was not held again until 1638.

The Puritan revolt in England caused problems in Maryland. Governor Calvert fled the colony and Maryland had no effective government for two years. In 1646 Calvert, aided by the Governor of Virginia, regained control. At his death the following year a Protestant Governor was chosen. This was an effort to appease the Protestant settlers and enable the Calvert family to retain the Royal Charter. It was at this time, in 1649, that Lord Baltimore issued the Toleration Act giving complete religious freedom to all Christians.

From 1649 to 1661 Maryland suffered turbulent times with one religious group or another vying for political control. Government chaos was the result. At the request of the Protestant settlers, Maryland became a royal province in 1649. Thus the King rather than the Calverts, as proprietors, controlled its administration.

127

82. Governor's Palace

A man's home may be his castle but few want to pay the cost of building a castle or a palace for someone else. The problem of spiralling costs for government buildings is not new. In 1706 the Virginia Burgesses set aside 3,000 pounds to build a home for the Royal Governor in the new capital at Williamsburg. A popular story concerning this "home" is that when it was finished in 1720 it had cost so much more than originally allotted to build that the public protested loudly. The people complained that they had ended up building a palace, and that is what it has been called ever since—the Governor's Palace.

The first of the seven Governors who would live in this palace was Alexander Spotswood. He spent a considerable amount of his own fortune embellishing his new home.

The castellated walls of this Georgian mansion provide the formality thought appropriate for the King's representative. The gardens, too, reflect European formal tradition; but the outbuildings are distinctly Virginia plantation style.

At the Governor's Palace, now a part of Colonial Williamsburg, the passive spectator has been changed into an active participant. Visitors are part of living history and their role changes as they move through the rooms. Roles shift from that of being a tradesman petitioning the Governor, to servant, to invited guest and even to a relative of the distinguished representative of the King. The illusion of the past comes to life and is appreciated more fully because it is personalized.

The gardens recreate many of the intricate details of English gardens of the time. A holly maze copies Hampton Court. The twelve yaupons, a fast growing holly of this area, were called the "Twelve Apostles" and could be found on many English estates. Geometrically designed hedges, topiary work and a greensward open enough for a garden game also remind visitors of England.

The last Royal Governor, the Earl of Dunsmore, fled the Palace one June morning in 1775. He recognized the beginnings of colonial revolt. This ended one phase of English rule in Virginia. The first two elected Governors of Virginia, Patrick Henry and Thomas Jefferson, would also live in this Palace.

Colonial Williamsburg is open daily from 9:00 to 5:00.

Directions: Take Beltway Exit 4 (I-95) to the Richmond By-pass, Route 295. Follow this to Route 64 east, which will lead into Williamsburg. Signs will provide directions to the Visitor Center where maps of Colonial Williamsburg can be obtained, plus information on tours and special programs.

83. Capitol

The idea of legislators being fired up over an issue is not unusual; but the Jamestown legislators carried it too far. The State House in Jamestown was burnt to the ground on two separate occasions. After the second experience the legislators decided it was time to move. The capital was shifted inland to a small village outside the College of William and Mary.

The burned out Burgesses were so determined to prevent this disaster from occurring in their new chamber that it was built without chimneys. The use of fire, candles, or tobacco was forbidden. The building eventually became so cold and damp that the papers actually began to mildew.

In 1723 the needed chimneys were added. Candles were also permitted and the Burgesses allowed to smoke their "noxious weed." It looked like they just couldn't win. On January 30, 1747, the Virginia legislature was again burned out of business when the building was completely gutted by fire. It was rebuilt, but after the government moved to Richmond the legislative building was a victim of fire for the fourth time in 1832.

The first capitol has been reconstructed at Colonial Williamsburg. The original design, begun in 1701, was supervised by Henry Cary. He erected a Renaissance building, without the elaborate facade it would have had in England. The H-shaped building was well planned to serve the needs of the Virginia government. One wing was for the House of Burgesses and the other for the General Court. The second floor had the Council Chamber as well as committee rooms for the Burgesses. The Conference Room on the second floor linked the two wings and both Burgesses and Councilors met there for morning prayer.

Almost every Virginian of note would meet within these walls in the 18th century. A great deal of American history took place here. George Washington was lauded for his heroic action in the French and Indian War. Patrick Henry made his famous Caesar-Brutus speech and was accused by some of treason. The Virginia Declaration of Rights by George Mason was passed in 1776 and Patrick Henry was elected first Governor of the Commonwealth of Virginia.

Colonial Williamsburg is open year round, with many special events occurring in the evening. There are Candlelight Tours of the Capitol. Admission is charged to tour the Capitol. Hours are 9:00 to 5:00 daily.

Directions: Take Beltway Exit 4 (I-95) to the Richmond By-pass, Route 295. Follow this to Route 64 east, which will lead into Williamsburg. Maps of colonial Williamsburg and information on tours and special programs can be obtained at the Visitor Center.

84. Reconstructed State House of 1676

For the first 41 years of Maryland's history the legislators were quite literally a roving band forced to meet infrequently at taverns, the fort, the church and in private homes. It wasn't until 1676 that the first Maryland State House was built in St. Mary's City.

It was to have only a brief period of usefulness as it was decided in 1694 that St. Mary's was too isolated, and the capital was moved to the middle plantation area, in Annapolis.

The State House was used by the Church of England as a parish church until 1829 when it was torn down. The Reconstructed State House was not built on the original site because the burial grounds of Trinity Church had encroached on this early location. A marker commemorates the actual spot and the replica is built a short distance away.

Visitors can explore the Assembly chambers where Maryland legislators could meet and—to their chagrin—merely advise the Lord Proprietor. The upstairs area is where the Calverts once kept all the town guns. They didn't want firearms falling into Protestant hands. It is now an exhibit area with a display showing the development of St. Mary's City from its early settlement to the present (see Colonial Period: First Settlements).

Directions: From the Beltway, take Exit 7 (Route 5) to St. Mary's City.

85. State House

In 1696 the colonial equivalent of the St. Mary's Chamber of Commerce launched an all out campaign to retain the privilege of serving as Maryland's capital. The Royal Governor had announced he was moving the capital to a site on the Severn River. Governor Nicholson complained that St. Mary's City was too remote, was served by poor roads and that there were too many rivers to cross to reach the town.

St. Mary's community leaders in return offered numerous suggestions and inducements to offset the complaints. Suggested was a day coach or caravan service provided by the city when the Assembly was in session. They also promised to keep a dozen horses always available for post riders. These attempts to persuade Governor Nicholson failed and the capital was moved to Annapolis.

The town was named in honor of Princess Anne. The new State House was called the Stadt House, to honor the Dutch born King

William. It was erected in 1697 but suffered the same fate as the Virginia Assembly. It burnt to the ground in 1706. The State House was rebuilt following the same plans and stood until mid-1772 when it was called "an emblem of public poverty." The former crumbling edifice was then considerably redesigned. In recent years it has been substantially restored to its colonial appearance.

Significant historical events occurring here include the first meeting of the Continental Congress, the resignation in 1783 by General George Washington as commander-in-chief of the American Revolutionary forces, and, in January 1784, the ratification of the Treaty of Paris by the new Congress of the United States.

Directions: From the Beltway take Exit 19 (John Hanson Highway) to Annapolis. Continue into Annapolis and the State House at State Circle.

86. Independence Hall

The single most historic room in all of the United States is the Assembly Room of Independence Hall. In this room delegates met to debate and sign the Declaration of Independence and to write the Constitution of the United States.

Designed by Alexander Hamilton after funds were appropriated for a State House in 1729, it would be 19 years before Independence Hall was completed. It served as the government meeting rooms for the Pennsylvania colony. The ground floor had a large Assembly Room. The room had a door (unlike the other large chamber) because the legislative body often met in secret session.

The Assembly Room has been restored to look as it did when the Second Continental Congress met there. The individual tables that served each colonial delegation are placed in a semi-circle before the table where the Declaration of Independence was signed. Few pieces in the room are original. Thomas Jefferson's walking stick has been placed on a table which is believed to have been the Virginia delegation's. Elsewhere in the hall the original inkstand used by the delegates to sign the Declaration of Independence is on display.

After Lord Cornwallis surrendered to Washington at Yorktown, the captured colors of the British army were brought to Philadelphia and presented in this room to the state delegations on November 3, 1781.

There is also a chamber on the first floor which was used by the Supreme Court of the Province. The court room was in the English tradition and graphically illustrates the term "standing trial." The defendent was forced to stand throughout the trial in a spiked cage-like dock. If considered dangerous, the defendant would be placed in handcuffs by a blacksmith. Should the defendant then be declared innocent, he would have to pay to have the iron cuffs sawed off. Trials were enjoyed by town residents, who watched the proceedings, groaning or applauding at each decision.

Upstairs is the Long Gallery, the largest room in colonial Philadelphia. This was the scene of many balls and banquets. On September 16, 1774, the 500 members of the First Continental Congress gathered here for a sit-down dinner. Also on this floor was the office of William Penn, the proprietor of the colony. Another room was used by the legislature of Pennsylvania while the Continental Congress met in their Assembly Room below.

It was in 1824 that the State House was given the name Independence Hall. Lafayette was in the city celebrating the American victory in the Revolution. When touring the State House he said, "that is the hall of independence," and so it has been called ever since.

The Park Service provides free tours of Independence Hall, a part of Independence National Historical Park. Visitors may be surprised to discover that one of the landmarks of the hall has been moved. The one-ton Liberty Bell is now in a pavilion directly opposite the hall. This bell was made in England in 1753 to commemorate the colony's Charter of Privileges. It cracked after arriving by ship and was recast twice by Pass and Stow, local artisans. Their efforts were successful and the bell hung in the State House steeple for many years. In 1835 John Marshall, Chief Justice of the Supreme Court, died while visiting Philadelphia. The bell was rung for 36 continuous hours and finally cracked. Repairs were attempted in 1846 and it was tested on George Washington's birthday. After three hours it cracked again. From that time on it became a symbol. Visitors can touch this tangible reminder of the turbulent events in our country's history.

Before touring Independence Hall visitors should stop at the Visitor Center where a 28-minute film directed by John Huston literally introduces the great leaders who met in Philadelphia in 1774 and 1776. Actors portraying these giants explain the events that took place here. All of the historic buildings at the park are open at no charge daily from 9:00 to 5:00.

Directions: Take Beltway Exit 27 (I-95) north to Philadelphia. Follow it into the city where it will become Front Street. Turn left on Walnut or Chestnut Street for Independence National Historical Park.

87. Carpenters' Hall

A political statement was made in 1774 when the First Continental Congress voted to meet in Carpenters' Hall instead of the State House, which was just two blocks up the street.

The moderates wanted to meet in the formal, official government offices of the colony. They hoped to exert more influence at the State House. Joseph Galloway, Speaker of the Pennsylvania Assembly, had aspirations of leading the Congress. All of these plans were circumvented when the delegates met at City Tavern on September 5, 1774 and headed as a group to inspect Carpenters' Hall.

Not even quite finished, Capenters' Hall was built by the craftsmen's guild. It was a handsomely proportioned two-story building. On the ground floor there were two meeting rooms divided by a long hall. The delegates to the First Continental Congress inspected the East Room. It was a small, bright chamber with rows of commodious hickory armchairs.

The delegates were well pleased and voted, with the moderates objecting, to meet for their deliberations in this room. Peyton Randolph was then chosen to chair the meeting.

The next major point of dispute was how to count the delegates' vote: by colony, one vote for each; or by poll, counting heads with a majority winning. There was no real correlation between population of the colony and the number of delegates. Massachusetts with a large population had four members, New Jersey had far fewer residents but one more delegate. Virginia had seven delegates and there were fears that Pennsylvania and Maryland would send additional members to vote on major issues. John Jay of New York proposed that the Congress give each colony one vote as a temporary working arrangement but not as a precedent.

These events are brought to mind when exploring Carpenters' Hall. The East Room is restored to duplicate the appeal of the room when the delegates met there over 200 years ago.

The hall also contains modern exhibits of the carpenter's guild, which is the oldest trade organization in the United States.

Carpenters' Hall is part of Independence National Historical Park in Philadelphia. The hall is open 9:00 to 5:00 daily at no charge.

Directions: Take Beltway Exit 27 (I-95) north to Philadelphia. Follow it into the city where it will become Front Street. Turn left on Walnut or Chestnut Street for Independence National Historical Park.

88. The York County Colony Court House

The idea of turning back the clock or stopping the clock is a recurring theme at many historical restorations. The York County Colonial Court House carries this concept one step further. They have retained the tall case-clock that marked the time during the momentous debates that forged one country from 13 separate colonies.

It was to this court house in York that the Continental Congress fled in 1777 when they evacuated Philadelphia to the superior British forces. Here in York they wrote the Articles of Confederation, adopted as our country's first constitution. As part of America's Bicentennial Celebration a sound and light reenactment of the dramatic debates that resulted in eventual unity are brought to life. A deeper realization of the difficulty of sacrificing individual sovereignty and an awareness of the magnitude of the accomplishment comes while watching this three-screen dramatic narrative..

Another excellent display illustrates the interdependence of the three documents crucial to the foundation of our country—the Declaration of Independence, the Articles of Confederation and the Constitution.

The court house has been restored to reflect the days when colonial leaders met here to draft the Articles of Confederation. There is a collection of personal memorabilia from numerous Revolutionary giants—Hancock, Adams, Paine, and foreign allies like Lafayette and Von Steuben.

This is a relatively new addition to historical preservations and sheds light on yet another page of American history.

Call (717) 846-1977 for York County Colonial Court House times of operation. Or write the York County Bicentennial Commission, Inc., P.O. Box 1776, York, PA 17405.

Directions: From the Beltway take Exit 27 (I-95) to the Baltimore Beltway. Proceed to Route 83 north to York, Pennsylvania. The York County Colonial Court House is located at Market and Pershing Avenue.

The Declaration of Independence

If the colonials couldn't obtain their rights as Englishmen then they were determined to obtain them as Americans. The denial of their rights led them to sever ties with England and create their own laws. The concepts of equality and freedom expressed in the Declaration of Independence were the motivating force that inspired many of the early colonists. But few had previously envisioned freedom to the degree encompassed by this Declaration. Social and political reform, spurred in part by this document, would occur more slowly throughout Europe, Asia and Africa. The Declaration of Independence is therefore one of the most important documents in American and world history.

The First Continental Congress met in Philadelphia in September 1774. This first attempt to get delegates from all 13 colonies together was for the purpose of making a consolidated appeal to King George to listen to their grievances. They hoped their united plea would persuade the king to make policies more equitable to the colonial economy.

Rather than adopting a conciliatory stand, by the end of 1775 King George was considering sending a larger army to the colonies. Fights had already erupted between British Redcoats and irate colonists; yet the laws became even more dictatorial.

In April 1775 the first shots of the Revolution were fired at Lexington and Concord. In May, Ethan Allen and his Green Mountain Boys captured Fort Ticonderoga on Lake Champlain acquiring needed muskets for colonial forces. By the time the Second Continental Congress met in June they were confronted with a situation already out of control. The delegates chose George Washington as Commander-in-Chief of the Continental troops. But the Congress still did not formally sever ties with England.

Early in 1776 Thomas Paine published a pamphlet called *Common Sense* arguing the case for independence. It was highly influential, selling more than 120,000 copies in less than three months. Even the Prince of Wales was discovered by the Queen Mother reading it.

When the Second Continental Congress reconvened in Philadelphia on June 6, 1776, Richard Henry Lee proposed that the colonies declare their independence. John Adams seconded the motion, but it was not unanimously received. Many—especially those from the middle colonies—still felt that the differences with England could be reconciled. It was decided to postpone the vote until July and a committee of five was chosen to draw up the document that would declare the colonists' intentions.

Committee members included Benjamin Franklin of Pennsylvania, John Adams of Massachusetts, Thomas Jefferson of Virginia, Roger Sherman of Connecticut and Robert Livingston of New York. Jefferson was picked to draft the document. Livingston, who was not in favor of the proposed document, returned to New York and did not rejoin the Congress. Franklin already had too many other obligations and Adams was too unpopular. Sherman was not adept at writing. Besides, Jefferson had already demonstrated a facility with words and a capacity to lead others.

Working each night after the regular session, Jefferson prepared the statement. He incorporated the ideas expressed by his fellow Virginian, George Mason, in his "Declaration of Rights." Both Adams and Franklin were delighted when shown the proposed declaration. It was presented to the Congress on July 1, 1776.

No vote was taken the first day although the delegates met for nine hours. By the end of the second day 12 colonies voted and all favored independence. Only New York abstained. The New York delegation was concerned about their fate with General Burgoyne's army about to occupy New York.

On the third day the text of the declaration itself was read. The Preamble was accepted with much approval and only minor changes. The 27 charges against George III were agreed upon after discussion and corrections. When the last charge was read in which Jefferson accused King George of taking away the liberty of distant people and carrying them from their homeland to be slaves, the delegates from South Carolina and Georgia balked. Their economy was based on slavery and they refused to vote in favor of a document which condemned slavery.

It was necessary for the 13 colonies to act unanimously. With the tenuous nature of the new country they could not afford to have any colony stand apart. It would be a base for English troops and a wedge to defeat all the Americans' hopes.

Reluctantly the other delegates agreed to drop the last charge condemning slavery. It was Thursday, July 4, 1776 when the delegates voted to adopt the Declaration of Independence. Contrary to popular thinking, it was not signed until August 2. The delay, necessary to permit the printer to strike a formal copy, gave the delegates time to ponder their action. As they signed, each knew that if the British succeeded in crushing their revolution their signature on this document would be evidence of treason.

Their concern was well advised. Of the 56 patriots who signed the Declaration of Independence, nine died of wounds suffered during the war. Seventeen lost everything they owned. The houses of 12 signers were burnt to the ground. Five were captured and imprisoned. In many cases wives and children of patriots were killed, jailed or left destitute. Despite these considerable hardships and tragedies, not one signer defected to the British cause. Their honor, like their new country, remained intact.

89. George Wythe House

It is ironic that perhaps the finest legal mind of his day should die by poisoning and his alleged murderer go free because of a legal technicality. George Sweeney, Wythe's nephew, was in dire financial straits and all the evidence indicates he poisoned his uncle for the inheritance. The only testimony that could prove the charge came from Wythe's Negro slave and was inadmissible under Virginia law. Though suffering an agonizing death, Wythe lived long enough to alter his will and disinherit Sweeney. George Wythe is buried at St. John's Churchyard in Richmond.

Wythe's life began in 1726 in Elizabeth City County, Virginia. He attended the College of William and Mary and was admitted to the bar at the age of 20. By 1754, Wythe was established in Williamsburg. He served as a member of the Virginia House of Burgesses and assumed the job of Attorney General when Peyton Randolph was sent to England. One of the young law students studying under George Wythe was Thomas Jefferson, who always considered Wythe his mentor and friend.

Although Wythe was a close friend and advisor to several of the Royal Governors, he sided with the Patriot cause. He drafted the Virginia "Resolution of Remonstrance" to protest the Stamp Act. Wythe was a member of the Continental Congress and the first Virginia delegate to sign the Declaration of Independence.

After Virginia became a state Wythe served as a judge on the new high court of chancery. As one of the foremost legal minds in the colonies it was not surprising that he was asked to become the first professor of law at an American college. He began teaching at William and Mary College in 1779 and continued until 1790 when he left to establish a law school in Richmond.

The George Wythe House on the west side of Palace Green in Williamsburg has been completely restored. As there was no record of the furnishings of Wythe's house, records by his contemporaries were used. Both English and American pieces reflect the popular taste in the 18th century.

The Wythe house served as Washington's headquarters before the siege of Yorktown. Rochambeau used it after Lord Cornwallis' surrender.

The house, outbuildings and garden are a miniature plantation set down in the heart of this colonial town. The yard not only contains a kitchen and herb garden but also a decorative garden with tree box topiary. One of the Wythe outbuildings is used to demonstrate the colonial craft of basketmaking.

The George Wythe House is one of the Exhibition Homes of Colonial Williamsburg. Admission tickets are available at the Williamsburg Visitor Center. The house is open daily.

Directions: Take Beltway Exit 4 (I-95) to the Richmond By-pass, Route 295. Follow this to Route 64 east, which will lead into Williamsburg. Signs will direct you to the Visitor Center where maps of Colonial Williamsburg can be obtained, plus information on tours and special programs.

90. Stratford Hall

The only two brothers to sign the Declaration of Independence were the Lees of Virginia—Richard Henry and Francis Lightfoot. Their's was one of the most illustrious families in Virginia and both had played an active role as members of Virginia's House of Burgesses.

It was Richard Henry Lee who actually proposed the resolution for independence from England at the Second Continental Congress. It is likely he would have been asked to draft the resolution had he not been called back to Virginia during the debate. It is perhaps best, as he was considered an orator while Jefferson was noted as a superior writer.

Richard Henry Lee was an activist. He had established the first association in the colonies to boycott English goods, the Westmoreland Association. At the First Continental Congress his efforts in this direction led to the Continental Association, the first step toward a union of the colonies.

The father of these distinguished patriots, Thomas Lee, had held the highest office in the Virginia colony as President of the King's Council. In 1720 he built the family estate, Stratford Hall, on the cliffs overlooking the Potomac River.

The house remains as it was 250 years ago. It is an architectural anomaly in colonial America because it is the only house to utilize the Italian device of having the major living areas on the second floor.

The Great Hall at Stratford is considered one of the most beautiful rooms in America. The hall, 28 feet square, forms the center of an "H" with windows on both sides. The house is furnished with lovely period pieces from the 18th century.

Stratford Hall is still a working farm. Cattle still graze in the meadows, fields are planted with crops grown during the colonial period, and the spacious gardens have been restored. The numerous outbuildings which made this, as many plantations were, a town in itself have also been rebuilt. The school house, law office, stables, coach house and mill all present different faces of colonial life. The kitchen has a fireplace large enough to roast an entire bull. It was frequently necessary to feed large groups as the Lee family entertained lavishly.

The family continued to make contributions to American history. Thomas Lee's great-nephew Light Horse Harry Lee was a military hero of the Revolutionary War, then went on to serve three terms as Governor of Virginia. His son, born at Stratford Hall, was Robert Edward Lee who would lead the Confederate forces in the Civil War.

Stratford Hall is open daily, except Christmas Day, from 9:00 to 4:30.

Directions: Take Exit 7 (Route 5) wouth to Route 301. Follow Route 301 to Route 3. Go left on Route 3 to Lerty and make a left on Route 214 to Stratford Hall.

91. Monticello

Thomas Jefferson died at the age of 83 on July 4, 1825, just a few hours before his old friend, John Adams. Jefferson had written his own epitaph. He wanted his tombstone at Monticello to read:

Here lies buried
Thomas Jefferson
Author of the Declaration of Independence,
of the Statute of Virginia for Religious Freedom,
and Father of the University of Virginia.

Actually, no stone would have been large enough to encompass all Jefferson's accomplishments. They included serving as Governor of

Virginia, Minister to France, Secretary of State under Washington, Vice-President under Adams and then President for two terms.

Jefferson once wrote from France, "All my wishes end where I hope my days will end ... at Monticello." This home in Virginia was a beacon throughout his life. He was constantly involved in its design, redesign and embellishment.

The land was originally acquired by his father, Peter Jefferson, in 1735. Jefferson inherited it at his father's death in 1759. It wasn't until 1768 that he began leveling the top of an 857-foot mountain so that he could build his home.

To make this location accessible he designed four roundabouts, or paths, connected by oblique roads. Construction began after this preparatory work was completed and would continue until 1809. Jefferson actually moved to Monticello on November 26, 1770 when his home, Shadwell, burned to the ground. He moved into the only completed building, a one-room brick cottage which would eventually become the end of the south terrace.

Jefferson designed Monticello with two wings flanking a center block. He concealed the outbuildings by placing them beneath long terraces, each ending with a pavilion. The south terrace terminates with the aforementioned cottage, known as the "honeymoon cottage," and the other with Jefferson's office, later used by his son-in-law Colonel Thomas Mann Randolph.

One of Monticello's dominant features is the dome over the west front. The octagonal room beneath was often called the ballroom, but Jefferson referred to it as the sky room. The house reflects the Palladian style popularized by the Italian architect Andrea Palladio. Jefferson owned several books on architecture which served as his guides in designing the house. Monticello has 35 rooms but the steep, narrow steps and fire regulations prevent visitors from viewing the entire house.

Jefferson had an inventive mind and a number of the features at Monticello reflect this. One is the seven-day clock in the Entrance Hall. The clock is operated by a system of cannonball weights which indicates the day of the week. Jefferson built a special ladder to reach the clock for winding. The skylights throughout the house were among the first to be used in an American home. He also designed the bedrooms with the beds in alcoves to conserve space.

Monticello was one of the first houses in America to have double windows on the first floor. Jefferson installed them in the dining room for insulation. The windows across the west front are triple sash windows, which can be opened to the size of a doorway for improved ventilation. After his good friend, James Madison, fell out one day, stout wooded grills were added.

The gardens at Monticello also reflect Jefferson's love for agriculture. He started the gardens in 1767 before construction on the house had even begun. The vegetable garden is currently being restored to reflect Jefferson's plans, and his orchard will be recreated with the planting of 280 fruit trees. Today there are goldfish in the fish pond he once enjoyed.

Archeological excavations along "Mulberry Row," Monticello's industrial street, are uncovering original building foundations and a wealth of interesting artifacts. An exhibit beneath the main house describes the scope of the excavations to visitors.

Monticello is open daily, except Christmas Day, from 8:00 to 5:00 March through October and 9:00 to 4:30 the rest of the year. Admission is charged.

Directions: Take Beltway Exit 8 (Route 29) to Charlottesville. Once in Charlottesville, take the Route 250 By-pass to I-64 east and follow the signs to Monticello.

92. Nelson House

Never think that walls can't talk, for at the Nelson House in Yorktown, Virginia there is a marvelous free program called "If These Walls Could Talk." The program has a cast of two who, by assuming the roles of prominent Nelson family members and retainers, recreate the tumultuous days of our country's past through one family's story. This Living History Theater brings the Nelson family and their patriotic activities dramatically to life.

Thomas Nelson, Jr. was educated at Cambridge and became a member of the Royal Governor's Council when he returned to Virginia. But he quickly found his political sympathies were with the Virginia colonists. He was chosen as one of the Virginia delegates to the Continental Congress and thus was one of the signers of the Declaration of Independence.

During the American Revolution, Nelson served as a Brigadier General in the Virginia militia, leaving the service only when chosen to succeed Jefferson as wartime Governor of Virginia in 1781.

When the British invaded Virginia he joined General Washington in the final siege of Yorktown. In his absence the British Commander, Lord Cornwallis, had chosen Nelson's house as his headquarters, but this did not deter Nelson. He directed the American fire at his own home. To this day two cannon balls remain in the east wall. Many feel that it was from this house that Cornwallis wrote Washington proposing a cessation of hostilities.

The war proved costly to Nelson. He used his own money to outfit and provision troops during the Virginia campaign. Despite the reversal in the Nelson family fortunes, the house was the scene of a lavish gala in 1824 to entertain Lafayette when he returned to celebrate the victory at Yorktown. These events as well as later episodes all are included in the dramatic performance of the Living History Theater.

The Nelson House with its lovely formal English garden is open daily from 10:00 to 4:00 from mid-june to Labor Day. The Living History drama "If These Walls Could Talk" and another production about the Nelsons called "Where Two Chimneys Rise" are presented during the summer months. For additional information call (804) 898-8248 or write to the Colonial National Historical Park, P.O. Box 210, Yorktown, VA 23690.

Directions: Take Beltway Exit 4 (I-95) to Richmond then take Route 64 to the colonial area. The Nelson House is on Nelson Street in Historic Yorktown.

93. Berkeley

Only two homes in America boast the distinction of being both the home of a signer of the Declaration of Independence and the ancestral home of two Presidents of the United States—the Adams home in Braintree, Massachusetts and Berkeley, the James River plantation of the Harrison family.

Berkeley's history goes back to the early days of colonial settlement in Virginia. It was in 1619 that King James I granted this land to the Berkeley Company. On December 4, 1619, the first 38 settlers arrived at Berkeley Hundred, as it was called then, on the small 40-ton ship *Margaret*. The settlers, following the proprietors' instructions, celebrated the day of arrival as a day of Thanksgiving. Thus Virginia inaugurated its own Thanksgiving a year before the Pilgrims arrived at Plymouth.

The house itself was built in 1726 by Benjamin Harrison. It is considered the oldest three-story brick house in Virginia. Built in the Georgian style, it is flanked by two outbuildings. The kitchen was connected to the main house by an underground "whistling tunnel." It was so named because the slaves had to whistle while carrying food through the passageway to show they weren't sampling any of the dishes.

At his father's death, young Benjamin Harrison inherited the estate. As a leading member of the community he was elected to the Continental Congress. He signed the Declaration of Independence

142

representing Virginia. From there he served the Revolutionary cause with distinction as a Colonel. Later he was Governor of Virginia for three terms.

Leading colonial figures enjoyed the hospitality of Berkeley. The first 10 presidents from Washington to Buchanan were entertained at this Virginia plantation. This notable family was to make further contributions to the American political scene.

Colonel Benjamin Harrison's younger son, William Henry, became well known as an Indian fighter, earning the nickname "Old Tippecanoe." He introduced direct campaigning for the presidency. He produced the first campaign publicity, starting the use of buttons, banners and slogans. Harrison's campaign souvenir was a commemorative handkerchief that showed a good deal of imaginative reinterpretation of the facts of Harrison's background. Attempting to appeal to the common man, it shows his birthplace as a log cabin instead of the lovely Berkeley Plantation. Also, Harrison is shown plowing the field, an unlikely activity for the scion of this distinguished family with hundreds of slaves available to do the manual labor.

Harrison was elected as the ninth President and came back to Berkeley to write his inaugural address. It was the longest address ever delivered, running over two hours. The Washington weather was uncomfortable and wet. Harrison caught pneumonia and died within 30 days. His neighbor and Vice-President, John Tyler, assumed the presidency, thus setting another precedent for the smooth transition of power.

Later his grandson, another Benjamin Harrison, would be elected the 23rd President of the United States.

Though the house today is completely restored to its 18th-century condition and furnished with period pieces, it did not survive the country's turbulent past unscathed. In 1781 Benedict Arnold's troops plundered the house and grounds.. During the Civil War General McClellan used the house as his headquarters after the Battle of Malvern Hill.

In fact, the entire Union Army of 140,000 men was camped on the grounds, with the U.S. Navy anchored in the James River off Berkeley's dock. Lincoln came to Berkeley twice while McClellan was here. He inspected the Union Army massed on the rolling grounds of Berkeley. Jeb Stuart took a shot at McClellan from the river and the cannonball is still embedded in the window of one of the flanking outbuildings. The present owner of Berkeley is the son of a drummer boy who served with McClellan's army here.

Berkeley is open daily from 8:00 to 5:00. Admission is charged. In addition to escorted tours of the manor house, there is a slide presentation reviewing Berkeley's historic moments. Visitor are then encouraged to enjoy the beautiful gardens.

The five terraces leading down to the river were dug by hand before the Revolutionary War. Young boxwood plants can be purchased as a living reminder of these ancient shrubs planted by Benjamin Harrison, the builder of Berkeley. At the river is a stage model of the good ship *Margaret*. On the first Sunday of November a re-enactment of the first Thanksgiving is held.

Directions: Take Beltway Exit 4 (I-95) to Richmond. From Richmond take Route 5 towards Williamsburg. Berkeley is located off Route 5 halfway to Williamsburg. Signs will indicate the turnoff for the plantation.

94. Chase Lloyd House

Maryland's decision to vote for independence had all the elements of a tense dramatic play. One man, Samuel Chase, remained in Annapolis while the rest of the Congressional delegates attended the meetings in Philadelphia. Chase argued the case for severing the ties with England before the Maryland provincial Assembly. His perseverance finally paid off and he rode to Philadelphia with fresh instructions giving the Maryland delegation the go-ahead to vote for independence. Covering the 150 miles in two days just in time for the great debate on the question on July 1, 1776, Chase arrived with one of the crucial votes only one day ahead of the final vote. He signed the Declaration of Independence as one of the four Maryland repesentatives.

Chase was one of Maryland's more radical patriots. He was a member of the Sons of Liberty. His outspoken espousal of revolution prompted the Mayor of Annapolis to call him "an inflaming son of discord." He served in Congress for two years but was dropped due to questionable business practices.

In 1769 he started construction on a great house in Annapolis. He had long envisioned such a residence; but before he could complete his house he suffered business reverses and in 1771 sold the mansion to Edward Lloyd IV. Lloyd enlisted the noted architect William Buckland to design and decorate the house. The combined talent of Buckland and the wealth of Lloyd resulted in one of the finest 18th-century interiors in the country.

The main hall is a particularly fine example of architectural excellence. The entrance hall is separated from the staircase by freestanding Ionic columns. The stairs rise to a large Palladian window and then divide into flanking stairs rising on each side to the second floor. It is a particularly felicitous combination of form, light and sculpture.

After selling his dream house Chase's financial affairs continued downhill and he went bankrupt in 1789. He continued to practice law and in 1796 was appointed by President Washington as an Associate Justice of the Supreme Court. He was impeached in 1805 but was not convicted. He died in 1811.

The Chase Lloyd House is open from 2:00 to 4:00 daily except Sundays and Wednesdays. Although open to the public the house is used as a home for elderly ladies. For additional information call (301) 263-2723 or write Historic Annapolis, Inc., 194 Prince Street, Annapolis, MD 21401.

Directions: Take Exit 19 (Route 50) to the John Hanson Highway and the Historic Annapolis exit. Continue into Annapolis to State Circle, then take Maryland Avenue to King George Street. The Chase Lloyd House is on the left corner.

95. William Paca House and Gardens

Some were called upon to die for their country but others, like Fielding Lewis, Thomas Nelson, Jr. and William Paca, also suffered for the cause. All of these patriots bankrupted themselves to pay the cost of the American Revolution.

William Paca is sometimes called Maryland's Thomas Jefferson. Though he studied law in London, he adopted the Revolutionary cause when he returned to Maryland. Paca served in both Continental Congresses and signed the Declaration of Independence. He then went on to help draft the Maryland Constitution.

After the war William Paca served as Governor of Maryland from 1782 to 1785. In 1789 Washington appointed him U.S. District Judge, a position he held until his death in 1799.

His Georgian-style Annapolis home was begun in 1763. It took two years to build. Though it was later used as an adjunct of the Carvel Hall Hotel, restoration work has returned it to its colonial appearance. Furnishings reflect the period some 10 years prior to the American Revolution.

Restoring this house was a formidable task. Twenty layers of wallpaper had to be removed before Paca's decorated plaster overmantle was again visible. Research revealed the sky blue color that Paca had used for the parlor walls and hall woodwork. Visitors are dazzled by this surprisingly bright color.

145

Attention to detail is also evident in the restoration of the Paca Garden. It has five terraces that fall to water level. On each side of the central walk are rectangular parterres, each enclosed by hedges to that they form a single unit. There is a rose parterre, one dedicated to boxwoods with topiary designs and others with seasonal flowers.

At the bottom is a pond with a Chinese Chippendale bridge. This was built to match the one in Charles Wilson Peale's portrait of William Paca. Beyond the pond is an octagonal garden pavilion with a silver dome also placed as it was in the portrait of Paca.

The William Paca House and Gardens are open Tuesday through Saturday, 10:00 to 4:00.

Directions: Take Beltway Exit 19 (Route 50) to the Historic Annapolis exit. Continue to State Circle and take Maryland Avenue down one block to Prince George Street. Turn right—the Paca House is on the left.

96. Carroll Mansion

At the end of his life Charles Carroll was a living relic of the American Revolution. In his last five years he was the sole surviving signer of the Declaration of Independence. Though in his nineties, Carroll was still active. He received a constant stream of visitors, all interested in hearing first hand about the momentous events of the young country's past.

Charles Carroll's home was a great estate, Doughoregan Manor, near Ellicott City, Maryland; but for the last 15 years of his life he moved in with his youngest daughter, Mary, each fall. He spent the winter months in Mary's Baltimore townhouse. Her husband, Richard Caton, had purchased this spacious house in 1818 for $20,000. When Caton suffered financial reverses in 1824, Carroll bought the house and deeded it to his daughter and grandchildren to save it from Caton's creditors.

The Carroll Mansion is considered Baltimore's finest townhouse of this early period. Nine of the rooms have been decorated to suggest their appearance when Charles Carroll was in residence with the Catons. Several rooms also have taped conversations to augment their visual displays.

The ground floor reflects the common practice of using the street floor for business purposes. In what is called the Counting Room a tape brings to life the figures of Richard Caton and a visitor. These two young men discuss Charles Carroll's career and the early days of

Considered Baltimore's finest townhouse of the Colonial
Period, Carroll Mansion was the home of Charles Carroll,
a signer of the Declaration of Independence.

Baltimore. When Carroll was a young boy, Baltimore only had a dozen
houses, but by 1800 it was the third largest city in America.

The elegant winding stairs lead to a formal room on the second floor.
The Grand Salon is decorated in the "Empire" fashion popular in 1810.
The furniture, called antique even then, was based on classical designs
of Greece and Rome. The gracious dining room is enhanced by taped
dinner table talk that one might have enjoyed in 1825. The music room
also has a tape of period music using the old-fashioned pianoforte and
pipe organ, duplicating the musicales once enjoyed in this room.

On the third floor is Charles Carroll's bedroom, where he died on
November 14, 1832. The room is furnished with objects that are listed
in Carroll's estate inventory although they are not the original pieces.
One interesting piece is the Mexican chair, the forerunner of the
modern lounge chair.

The Carroll Mansion at 800 East Lombard Street in downtown
Baltimore may be explored on a free self-guided basis. Each room has
a carefully itemized listing on each important piece in the room. The

Carroll Mansion is open from 10:00 to 4:00 Tuesday through Sunday. It is closed on all major holidays.

Directions: Take Beltway Exit 22 (the Baltimore-Washington Parkway) into Baltimore, turn right on Pratt Street and continue down to the 800 block. Turn left just past the Star Spangled Banner House at Albemarle Street. Continue up one block to East Lombard Street and the Carroll Mansion.

97. Franklin Court

Imagination, innovation, the latest in modern museum technology—Franklin Court is as inventive as Benjamin Franklin himself. It is a new and marvelous addition to historic Philadelphia.

The best approach to touring Franklin Court is to start at the bottom and work up. It is the bottom quite literally because the museum is underground, reached by a winding, slanted passage. Once in the museum see the movie first; it is called "Portrait of a Family" and gives a personal view of Benjamin Franklin. It's interesting to learn how little formal schooling Franklin received—only two years. But his inquiring mind prompted him to develop his intellect on his own. Another fascinating detail is that Franklin spent 10 years in England representing the colonial cause. Just prior to his return his wife, Deborah, died. He would later leave his family again for eight more years to serve in France.

After getting acquainted, so to speak, visitors can find out what some of his contemporaries and later great figures, both in America and Europe, thought about Mr. Franklin. The Franklin Exchange lists 22 Americans and 26 Europeans who can be telephoned for their insights into this complex figure. The Americans include John Adams, Henry Steele Commanger, Jefferson Davis, Ralph Waldo Emerson, Thomas Jefferson, Harry Truman, Mark Twain and, of course, George Washington. Some of the Europeans are Lord Byron, Charles Darwin, David Hume. Immanuel Kant, John Keats, Lafayette, D. H. Lawrence and even George Sand.

There is also a chance to check Franklin's own witty remarks on a variety of topics. Franklin's views on women, virtue, money, government and ethics all still seem apt and fresh.

"Franklin on the World Stage" presents miniature figures in a sound and light show which depicts Franklin before the House of Commons in England in 1766, at the Court of Versailles in 1778 and at the Constitutional Convention in 1787.

After viewing the museum movie the significance of the restoration of Franklin Court is felt by all. Unfortunately, there was not enough hard evidence to support a reconstruction of Franklin's own home. The uncovered foundations are still visible through giant peepholes.

The courtyard of Franklin Court has been restored to create a colonial "pleasure garden." This, however, is only part of the historic reconstruction. There are also five Market Square houses, three of which were owned by Franklin. Each represents a different facet of his life.

The center house at 318 Market Square reflects Franklin the builder, Through a new technique visitors are able to "read" an original wall the way historical architects do. The 18th-century plaster, wallpaper, chair rails, chimney and joists can all be seen. One innovation Franklin employed to meet regulations he made as the founder of the country's first volunteer fire department was to design the house so that the joists of one room did not meet those of another. This prevented fires from spreading.

Another house focuses on Franklin the printer. An 18th-century press prints park bulletins, menus and handbills. Books are bound on the premises as well.

At 322 Market Square the office of Franklin's grandson Benjamin Franklin Bache is restored. *The Philadelphia Aurora* was published from this office.

A fourth house is a post office, as Franklin was the first Postmaster General of the United Colonies. Stamps are available and letters can be cancelled with the postmark Franklin made famous, "B Free Franklin." Upstairs is a Postal Museum sure to interest stamp collectors. It contains rare stamps, a saddle mail pouch from a Pony Express rider, early mail boxes and other unusual memorabilia.

The last house serves as a park sales outlet.

Franklin Court is on Market Street between Third and Fourth Street. It is open daily from 9:00 to 5:00 at no charge as part of Independence National Historical Park. This historic site provides a glimpse of the many aspects of this remarkable American patriot.

Directions: Take Beltway Exit 27 (I-95) north to Philadelphia. Follow it into the city where it will become Front Street. Turn left on Walnut or Chestnut Street for Independence National Historical Park.

98. George Taylor House

Even more profitable than marrying the boss's daughter is marrying his widow. When young George Taylor arrived in Philadelphia at age 20 from Northern Ireland, his first job as a "redemptioner" was in an iron foundry. He was working to pay back his passage. But shortly after the death of his employer he married the widow and took over the management of the furnace.

Taylor was to be very successful in the iron business. The iron forge at which he spent most of his career was Durham Furnace, an 8,511-acre iron plantation. To get an idea of what such an operation was like, visit Hopewell Village (see Era Between the Wars: Industries.) It recreates life on one of the 18th-century iron plantations.

During the American Revolution, George Taylor served as a Colonel in the Army. He also was a delegate to the Continental Congress and signed the Declaration of Independence as a representative of Pennsylvania.

In 1767 he bought the land for this house in Catasauqua, Pennsylvania. It was part of a 10,000-acre tract that William Penn had deeded to his daughter in 1736. This lovely stone house was the first one that Taylor had ever planned and built for himself. His hopes for a leisurely life with his family in their new home were dealt a blow when his wife, Anne, died the same year the house was finished.

The George Taylor House is furnished to suggest its original appearance. Used as a summer residence, it was more elegantly designed than most houses in the Lehigh Valley. There is a formal walled garden in the park surrounding the house.

The house is open June through October from 1:00 to 4:00 on Saturday and Sunday.

Directions: Take Beltway Exit 27 (I-95) to Philadelphia. Then take Route 76 along the outskirts of city; go right on Route 276 to the Route 9 exit. Follow Route 9 to Allentown, then take a right on Route 22 to the Fullerton exit. Go north on 3rd Street to Bridge Street, then est on Bridge Street, crossing the river to Lehigh Street. Take a right on Lehigh Street to Popular Street and a left on Poplar Street to Front Street and the George Taylor House.

OF NOTE: Graff House, which is part of Independence National Historical Park, is where Thomas Jefferson wrote the Delcaration of Independence. The house belonged to Jacob Graff, Jr., a Philadelphia bricklayer. Jefferson worked after the regular sessions of the Continental Congress in his rented second floor parlor, one of two rooms he rented from Graff during the summer of 1776. The house is restored and is open at no charge. There is an audio-visual presentation to further acquaint visitors with the events that occurred there.

OF NOTE: The only engrossed copy of the Declaration of Independence that was signed by all the delegates on August 2, 1776 is on display in the Exhibition Hall of the National Archives Building in Washington, D.C.

Revolutionary War Years

The "shot heard round the world" still echoes. The gallant fortitude of the men of the Continental Army—not only on the battlefields but through the cold winters at Morristown and Valley Forge—inspires each new generation of Americans.

It was on April 19, 1775 that Paul Revere hurried to the home where patriots Sam Adams and John Hancock were in hiding from the British. He brought word that there were 600 Redcoats marching on Lexington. The town's 70-member Minuteman Brigade, so called because they could be called out at a moment's notice, formed ranks on the village green. Their ranking officer, Captain John Parker, said, "If they mean to have a war let it begin here."

Seventeen Minutemen were cut down in the first minutes of the skirmish, as the British easily overwhelmed the small force and proceeded to Concord to confiscate military supplies. But when they attempted to return to Boston the Redcoats fell under fire from a countryside swarming with militia. Lacking uniforms, training and even experienced leadership, this farmer's army killed 73 British soldiers, wounded 174 and was responsible for the disappearance of 26 others. Only reinforcements from Boston saved the British from a total debacle. The British were confounded to find that the rebels would dare to fire on the King's troops. The Americans had shown that they would stand up to the British as they would do again and again through the long struggle to defeat their former countrymen.

The British had not meant to start a war, just to continue their policy of isolated incidents, but when they fired on this small band of colonials it *was* war. It would be more than a year before independence was formally declared, but it was a year filled with skirmishes and confrontations. The first step had been taken.

It was only a matter of months after the skirmish in Massachusetts that the Second Continental Congress, meeting in Philadelphia, chose George Washington as Commander-in-Chief of the Continental Army.

Washington is often depicted as reluctant to lead, anxious only to do his duty and return as quickly as possible to Mount Vernon. But it should be noted that he attended the Second Continental Congress, which was a political gathering, in the uniform of a Colonel of the Virginia militia. He was the only delegate in uniform. His wearing of a uniform at that time in the turbulent state of colonial affairs was of marked significance. He may not have been as unwilling to command the army as history often implies.

The colonists were reluctant rebels; and while rebelling against the British crown they remained loyal to many British principles—trial by jury, free assembly, free petition and free speech. In a sense, the patriots were fighting to maintain the status quo, to defend their rights as Englishmen. George III, in denying them rights they considered their due, forced their hand. In their view, they could restore their rights only by creating a new country. At the same time they broadened the scope of those rights and secured them from the whim of a king.

In attempting to wrest their independence from England the Americans faced sizeable obstacles. They had to raise, equip and train an army to meet one of the best and most often tested military forces in the world. England's population was three times that of the colonies; her finances enabled her to hire foreign troops to assist her own, and England had the largest navy of any colonial power.

The colonists also had to contend with a divided country, since not all citizens wanted to sever their ties with England. Their problems were compounded by inadequate financial support and woeful shortages of ammunition. The army itself was a constantly changing group. Men would be trained only to leave when their enlistment expired. It was not until half way through the war that the standard term of enlistment became three years rather than one.

When Washington crossed the Delaware to attack the Hessians at Trenton on Christmas night 1776, it was a now or never proposition. At least 1,400 men of the Continental Army were scheduled to end their duty on December 31. Washington would be virtually without men. It could mean the end of hope for the Revolution.

Washington's action at Trenton and at the Battle of Princeton thwarted the early objective of Britain in this conflict—that of dividing America in half geographically with its military force. General Cornwallis felt that from a secure New York the British would be able to subdue New England and the South bit by bit.

The last attempt to realize this goal was the Battle of Saratoga, one of the most crucial encounters of the war. The American ability to stand firm resulted in the surrender of General Burgoyne's entire army. It was a major defeat for the British and a significant turning point of the war.

There were two results of the Battle of Saratoga. The King sent peace commissioners to meet with Congress—but not to grant independence, and the Americans would settle for nothing less. Also, this victory convinced France to enter the war. The French had not wanted to squander money and men on a losing cause, but once the odds indicated the possibility of an American victory. France sent much needed men and ships. Other European powers also aided the new country as a means of weakening England.

The war would last six more years. But it was the government rather than the army which proved weak. Congress had so little power that it could not raise money to pay or supply the army. Soldiers risked their lives and served without regular pay and often without adequate food or clothes. Isolated mutinies occurred. It was a sad commentary that American troops marched on the newly formed American government before the war was even won.

In the last days of the war—after a long southern campaign in which the British under Cornwallis had lost a third of their army despite victories at Savannah in December 1778, Charleston in May 1780 and the capture of all major points in South Carolina—the British turned at last to the sea. This led to the final confrontation of the war. Washington was now able to cut off Cornwallis' escape by sea with the help of Admiral De Grasse and the French fleet.

The British army was trapped at Yorktown. On October 17, 1781 Lord Cornwallis and the 8,000 men of the British army surrendered. Two years later the Treaty of Paris was signed, formally declaring the United States a free and independent country.

99. Congress Hall

On March 4, 1797, the new nation's leaders assembled in the House of Representatives' chamber in Congress Hall to watch the inauguration of John Adams as the second President of the United States. George Washington was on hand to facilitate the nation's first transfer of executive power. After Adams took the oath of office and Washington became a private citizen again, Washington motioned for Thomas Jefferson, who was now the Vice-President, to precede him from the room. Jefferson hesitated, then stepped in front of George Washington; thus did the nation achieve the transfer of power with dignity and smooth precision.

The still young Federal government was to meet in Philadelphia, called by some the "capital of the New World," for 10 years while the new Federal City was built. The legislative branch used the Philadelphia Court House, which is now called Congress Hall, for its sessions.

The "lower house" met on the lower, first floor chambers. A large dais was added for the Speaker of the House and rows of mahogany desks were built by a Philadelphia cabinetmaker. The county commissioners added a gallery for the spectators interested in watching the Federal government in session.

The upstairs was also refitted for the Senate chambers. The Senators each had their own desks with comfortable leather armchairs. The Vice-President, who presided over the sessions, sat beneath a canopy in almost a "kingly" splendor.

Also on the upper floor are restored committee and conference rooms and the office of the Secretary of the Senate.

During the time Congress met here three new states were added to the Union—Vermont in 1791, Kentucky in 1892 and Tennessee in 1796. On May 14, 1800, Congress adjourned to reconvene in the new capital. Philadelphia was no longer the center of the new country.

Congress Hall is part of Independence National Historical Park and is open at no charge from 9:00 to 5:00 daily.

Directions: Take Beltway Exit 27 (I-95) north to Philadelphia. Follow it into the city where it will become Front Street. Turn left on Walnut or Chestnut Street for Independence National Historical Park.

100. Old City Hall

The lights are dim in the courtroom of Old City Hall and candles illuminate the room, restored to look as it did in 1791 when the Supreme Court met here for the first time. Called upon to define the law, but with no power to enforce it, the Supreme Court had initial problems in achieving the respect of the states. The first cases heard by the Court were unresolved, the Justices unable to reach a decision.

In Chisholm vs Georgia, the court was asked to rule on whether a citizen of one state, in this case South Carolina, could bring a suit against another state, Georgia. The court ruled that it could even though Georgia did not even send a lawyer to argue its position. The Eleventh Amendment to the Constitution reversed this ruling.

These early days of trials and errors are portrayed in the sound and light audio-visual presentation at Old City Hall. The development of the American judicial system is imaginatively traced in this brief program.

The upstairs floor has an exhibit on the life-styles in Philadelphia from 1774 to 1800. One display has a slide show that might have been viewed through the window of an early American home. The constant activity on the street and the interaction of the people as they go about their daily lives is captured in this vignette. Other displays reflect the entertainment of the 18th century, the activities on the dock, the shopkeeper and the public services provided in the city.

Just outside Old City Hall is a reminder of one of those public services—a colonial watch box. These were used as the city's watchmen made their rounds, keeping their eyes open for fire. The watch boxes contained buckets of water. Each house also had to have two buckets of water ready in case the watch sounded the alarm.

Old City Hall is part of Independence National Historical Park and is open daily from 9:00 to 5:00 at no charge.

Directions: Take Beltway Exit 27 (I-95) north to Philadelphia. Follow it into the city where it becomes Front Street. Turn left on Walnut or Chestnut Street for Independence National Historical Park.

101. Pemberton House

Standing on the gun deck of an 18th-century frigate and hearing the sound of water lapping against the boat reinforces the illusion that one has stepped into a time machine. But it is just one of the effective means employed by the Pemberton House to bring to life the early days of the American Navy.

A series of lighted maps trace the course of the important naval confrontations of the American Revolution. Visitors can even try their hand at maneuvering for a sea battle in the 1700s. A series of switches enable the operator to move a ship's sails and rudder to position her for battle. A light indicates a successful effort. This is a popular feature with young visitors.

Lighted maps and dioramas also trace the major land battles of the Revolution. Models of early militia uniforms reflect the development of the American army. Early battle flags and weapons are also included in the exhibits. In fact, one of the flags is from the First Regiment, the lone infantry regiment from 1784 to 1790.

The Pemberton House collection at Independence National Historical Park depicts the military side of this historic period.

Just across the cobbled path from Pemberton House is New Hall, which houses the Museum of Marine Corps History, completing the military picture. Displays tell the story of Marine action from 1775 to 1783. There is a Memorial Room with an Honor Roll of Marine deaths which rests on sand from Iwo Jima.

Both Pemberton House and New Hall are open daily from 9:00 to 5:00.

Directions: Take Beltway Exit 27 (I-95) north to Philadelphia. Follow it into the city where it will become Front Street. Turn left on Walnut or Chestnut Street for Independence National Historical Park.

102. Washington Crossing Historic Park

The German word for enemy is "feind," and that's exactly what the unexpected Americans were to the celebrating Hessian soldiers on December 25, 1776. The surprise appearance of 2,500 determined Continental soldiers in the early hours of the snowy morning after Christmas night festivities provided the needed edge for an American victory.

The Hessian commander had even received a message warning him of possible attack but he had stuffed it, unread, into his pocket. He was contemptuous of the ragged, farmer army. Colonel Rall's careless action was to cost his men the battle and him his life.

The plans for this brilliantly timed attack were formulated by Washington and his staff in the kitchen of the Thompson-Neely House, which is now restored and part of Washington Crossing Historic Park in Pennsylvania. This house was used as the headquarters for various officers of the Continental Army. General William Alexander, Lord Stirling, was the ranking officer. Also billeted here was a Washington relative, Captain William Washington, and a fellow Virginian, James Monroe, who would go on to become the fifth President. So momentous were the events that transpired here, that the house is now called the House of Decision.

It was here Washington completed plans to cross the Delaware in a three-pronged attack. Time was running out on the enlistment of his troops. Washington had no more options left if he were going to save the patriot cause.

The Hessians provided an easy target but Washington's army was almost defeated before the attack began—not by men but by the elements. The Delaware River was so icy the boats could not cross. Washington was determined, so fighting the cold, a blinding snow storm, the ice and time the 2,500 men finally reached the New Jersey shore. Only Washington's men made it across; the other two divisions did not succeed.

At the Memorial Building in the park there is a copy of the painting by Emanuel Leutze of Washington Crossing the Delaware. History buffs will enjoy finding flaws in this famous picture. The boat is all wrong, the ice looks like Antarctica and Washington would not have been foolish enough to stand while negotiating such a difficult crossing. Outside there is a reconstruction of four Durham boats, which were used to row the men across the river.

After reviewing the plan Washington and his staff ate a hurried Christmas dinner at the Ferry Inn (see Colonial Taverns), also part of the park.

The area on the New Jersey side is Washington Crossing State Park. The spot where Washington and his men came ashore is called Washington Grove and it is preserved in its natural state. Each year on Christmas Day this famous crossing is reenacted. The modern crossers, however, have been known to resort to the bridge when the Delaware becomes too icy.

After Washington surprised the Hessians, he offered the more than 1,000 men whose enlistment expired a $10.00 bonus to extend their duty long enough to defeat the British at Princeton. He then headed with this depleted army to Morristown for the winter of 1777.

The historic buildings at Washington Crossing Historic Park are open Monday through Saturday from 10:00 to 4:30 and Sunday from 12:00 to 4:30.

Directions: Take Beltway Exit 27 (I-95) up through Pennsylvania. Exit at New Hope just before crossing into Delaware. Go north to PA 532 and east to PA 32. Signs will direct visitors to the various attractions at the park.

103. Morristown National Historical Park

The Revolutionary battles tested the soldiers' mettle and the officers' acumen, but the Revolutionary winters tested the army's endurance. Washington's troops spent two winters in the north at Morristown, New Jersey. Both times this defensible position was chosen to closely contain Howe's army 30 miles away in New York.

Washington picked Morristown for the first time in January 1777 when his army was severely depleted after the New Jersey campaign. Despite Continental victories at Trenton and Princeton, many of the soldiers saw no reason to stay with the army, as their enlistments were up, so half the force returned to their homes.

Morristown offered a number of advantages. Protected by large swamps to the east and beyond these, Watchung Mountain, it could be secured from surprise attack. Also, the posted watch could alert Washington to British moves on Philadelphia. Another plus was the regiments already stationed at Morristown. Tested at Ticonderoga, they helped to fill the ranks which were so woefully short.

Though the alert patrols prevented any British military action, the army did suffer a devastating attack—not by men but by disease. A virulent smallpox epidemic struck. Washington resorted to the still questionable technique of inoculation, first secretly treating the soldiers and then, when results were positive, extending inoculation to the civilian population of Morristown.

While the army wintered at Morristown, Congress finally authorized raising 88 battalions which the Continental army desperately needed to meet the British in equal combat. By spring the army was greatly reinforced. When Howe moved from New York into New Jersey, Washington advanced with his army and the British decided against battle. They returned to New York and sailed south. The Americans followed by land, leaving a small unit to guard the supplies and fortifications. Washington's troops would return to winter here two years later.

As the winter of 1779 approached, Washington again found himself needing a defensible position to watch the British who were quartered in New York. He returned to Morristown.

Washington made his headquarters at the Ford Mansion and General St. Clair of the Pennsylvania Line moved into the Wick House. Both of these homes are at Morristown National Historical Park. The junior officers lived with the men in Jockey Hollow, a major part of the Park.

The men built huts, destroying 900 acres of woods in the area. Washington issued strict orders about the way huts were to be constructed. He had learned at Valley Forge that disease could destroy his men more effectively than the British. When the huts for the 13,000 men were complete, Jockey Hollow became, for a short time, the sixth largest city in the United States.

The winter of 1779–80 was the worst of the century. Twenty-eight blizzards brought freezing temperatures, winds that tore through the roughly made huts, deep snow that buried those trying to make their way outside and impassable roads. In early January the weather was so bad that no supplies could reach the men for four days. The starving troops were reduced to eating tree bark, company dogs, leather cartridge boxes and in some cases their shoes. But despite this incredible hardship only 86 men died at Morristown. Two attempted mutinies during this winter dramatically demonstrated the need of more support from Congress. Only Washington's strong leadership held the men together.

But the army endured. When they could, they drilled in front of their huts. Spring brought improved weather and the news that France was sending six warships and 6,000 soldiers to aid the American cause.

When the British moved into New Jersey in June the role of Morristown in the American Revolution ended. It was a testimonial of courage over conditions and conviction over convenience—indeed, over the lowest level of expectation. The winters were the real testing ground of the American Revolution.

The Soldier Huts of the Jockey Hollow Encampment may still be seen on a visit to Morristown National Historical Park, which is open at no charge 9:00 to 5:00 daily. Also see the Grand Parade Grounds, the position of the Pennsylvania Line and the site of Fort Nonsense. During the summer months uniformed guides give talks and demonstrations and answer questions about the events at Morristown. A good place to begin exploring is the Visitor Center on Jockey Hollow Road.

Directions: Take Beltway Exit 27 (I-95) north of Philadelphia until I-95 ends. Continue north on Route 1 until it intersects with I-287. Go west on I-287 to Exit 26B Bernardsville. Go north on Route 202, Mt. Kemble Avenue to Temple Wick Road. Go left on Temple Wick Road to the parking lot at the Visitor Center.

104. Ford Mansion

Washington was genuinely concerned for the officers of the Continental Army. He called his staff his "family." This care did not go unnoticed or unrewarded. When patriot Colonel Jacob Ford became ill during the New Jersey fighting in 1776, he returned home and died. General Washington, learning of his death, ordered a military funeral with full honors. His widow appreciated this compliment to her husband. When Washington came to winter quarters in Morristown the second time, she offered him the use of her mansion. Thus the finest house in town, in fact, one of the largest houses in all the colonies, was made available for winter quarters and staff meetings.

For almost seven months during the blizzards of 1779 and 1780, Washington lived and worked here. It was the military capital of the nation. Meetings went on constantly though the snow was four feet high around the house and the temperature hovered near zero day after day.

Though Mrs. Ford was highly grateful, she wasn't foolish. The Main Hall of the Mansion, which is restored to reflect the era in which Washington was in residence, is sparsely furnished and the walls bare. The army had a tendency to pilfer needed, or just wanted, items and Mrs. Ford stored all her valuable pieces. The restoration of the house reflects her concern.

The Ford family remained in residence, though they kept only two rooms on the ground floor for their own use. Mrs. Ford moved all her treasured possessions into her room, where she and her daughter ate, slept and entertained. This explains the crowded look of the room.

The three boys of the family slept together in another bedroom. The oldest boy joined the local militia and was wounded at the Battle of Springfield in June 1780. Washington often inquired after him.

The kitchen was frequently chaotic since at least nine separate meals were prepared daily by Washington's mess staff and Mrs. Ford's servants. It got so bad that Washington had a log kitchen constructed next to this one.

The two unheated rooms normally allocated to the house servants were pressed into service by 20 servants assisting Washington and his staff.

One of Washington's aides quartered in the house, Alexander Hamilton, would go on to achieve prominence as the Secretary of the Treasury. Hamilton found diversion to warm his winter while in Morristown. He met and courted Betsy Schuyler, whom he married in December 1780.

There is a Guest Room that was used by numerous aides when no dignitaries were visiting. Don Juan de Miralles, the first Spanish minister to the rebellious new country, stayed here and unfortunately died while a guest of the Washingtons. Lafayette was a guest at Ford Mansion as well.

The bedroom used by the Washingtons is also upstairs. Martha had joined her husband and spent most of her time in this room sewing, reading and entertaining. As in most of the house, 80 percent of the furnishings are original and many pieces in the room were used by the Washingtons.

Back downstairs are Washington's private office, conference room and dining room. The main meal of the day began at 3:00 and usually lasted two hours, though only three courses were served. It was a time to informally discuss military matters.

Behind the house is a museum with artifacts from the Revolutionary period. The Ford Mansion and museum are part of Morristown National Historical Park and are open for a small charge from 9:00 to 5:00 except major holidays.

Directions: Follow directions for Morristown National Historical Park except continue on Route 287 to Exit 32A, Morris Avenue East. Turn left on Lafayette Avenue for the parking area serving the Ford Mansion; signs may refer to the house as Washington's Headquarters. To reach the house from the Wick House proceed around the park tour road to Western Avenue. Then turn right on Route 24, then around the green and left on Route 202 and right on Morris Avenue East.

105. The Wick House

Having one's house requisitioned for use by Revolutionary officers brought its hardships and perils. Local legend says that when soldiers of the Pennsylvania Line mutinied, Temple Wick hid her horse so it wouldn't be commandeered for the march to Philadelphia to demand supplies and back pay. This forceful march did convince Congress that more had to be done if they expected Washington to maintain an army in the field.

Temple Wick's father also felt the burden of housing officers of the Continental Army. His livestock were taken to feed the starving men and his fence burned to provide fleeting warmth.

General Arthur St. Clair and the staff of the Pennsylvania Line, formerly Anthony Wayne's command, lived in the Wicks' house while their men suffered through the "hard winter" in soldiers' huts on the Wicks' 1,400-acre farm.

The house, available for touring, was known as Wick Hall as it was more substantial than most farms in the area. It also was architecturally different from local structures, resembling instead the New England "Cape Cod" style with which Wick was familiar from his earlier home on Long Island.

Built in 1750, the house has a central chimney with three fireplaces and a large kitchen-like room called the "keeping room." This was the heart of the house; around the largest fireplace family chores and entertaining were done. One of the pieces in the room is a large chair with a high back to contain the heat, called a settle. This is where the term "settle down" originated.

Henry Wick was certainly well-off for a farmer. His dining room and parlor are well appointed. The simple, homemade furniture was functional but still attractive. A collection of pewterware, which was called "poor man's silver," is displayed in the cupboard. The dining table is formal Queen Anne although the chairs are of the style "Country Queen Anne."

General St. Clair used the spare bedroom, or spinning room. A folding camp bed and camp chest used in the Revolutionary War suggest his presence. When the house was used by the officers of the Pennsylvania Line some of the General's staff slept in the dining room.

Two other bedrooms are restored. In the master bedroom is the large "klass" used to store linens and found in most farmhouses in the middle colonies. The German word "klass" is the forerunner of the English closet.

Temple Wick, the 21-year-old daughter of the family, was the only one of five children still at home when the house was used by the Revolutionary soldiers and her bedroom is also restored. After exploring the house, stop and see the adjacent garden. Vegetables, spices and herbs are identified as to their use.

The Wick House is part of Morristown National Historical Park and is open 9:00 to 5:00 daily, except Thanksgiving, Christmas and New Year's Day.

Directions: For the Wick House follow directions for Morristown National Historical Park. The Wick House is directly behind the Visitor Center on Jockey Hollow Road.

106. Brandywine Battlefield Park

Washington could certainly be excused for thinking that 'intelligence' wasn't the correct word for the information he was receiving as the American and British troops positioned themselves for battle along Brandywine Creek.

General Howe, who had landed at Head of Elk in Maryland with 15,000 British and Hessian troops had moved up into Pennsylvania toward the capital at Philadelphia. Washington first heard that Howe had divided his force. Washington sent a division, part of his 14,000-man force, under General Nathaniel Greene to attack the British. A second report followed indicating that Greene now confronted the entire British force. Washington then ordered General Greene to retreat to the other side of the Brandywine. A third intelligence report came in to headquarters. The British had indeed split their force. Washington just shook his head and laughed, believing instead the second message. Unfortunately, he guessed wrong. This error may well have cost the American army the comfortable winter quarters in Philadelphia enjoyed by the British, consigning them instead to the misery of Valley Forge.

By the afternoon of September 11, 1777 the troops of General Howe met the American force on Osborne's Hill and at Chadd's Ford. The Americans valiantly tried to hold their ground, but misinformation, ammunition shortages, plus the great numbers and experience of the British troops prevailed. By night the Americans retreated to Chester. Howe tried to cut off their escape but was repulsed by cavalry under General Pulaski.

British casualties were slightly under 600, while American losses reached about 1,000. The Americans also lost 11 cannons, a devastating blow to the ill-equipped army.

Visitors to Brandywine Battlefield Park should start at the Visitor Center, where displays and maps will explain the course of the battle in detail. It will also place the Battle of Brandywine in context with the total picture of the Revolutionary War.

Within the park are the restored headquarters of General Washington and the quarters of his aide, General Marquis de Lafayette. Though both houses belonged to Quakers, who were pacifists, they still were sympathetic to the revolutionary cause.

Washington used the spacious house of Benjamin Ring, which was close to Chadd's Ford where the British were expected to attempt crossing the Brandywine. The house was large enough to permit Washington to meet here with his staff. There is a group of life-size figures representing Washington and Sullivan getting reports on British troop movements.

Regrettably, this is not the original house but a careful reconstruction furnished to look as it did in August of 1777.

Only three-tenths of a mile away, in the more modest farmhouse of Gideon Gilpin, the Marquis de Lafayette made his headquarters. The house is furnished with period pieces, though not the furniture which was there when Lafayette used the house. A report filed by Gilpin for damages after the Battle of Brandywine does give an idea of the appearance of the farm. Listed as lost were such items as 10 cows, 48 sheep, 28 swine, a yoke of oxen, 12 tons of hay, 230 bushels of wheat, 50 pounds of bacon, a history book, a clock and a gun. Gilpin received permission to operate a tavern from his home to help recover from his losses.

These two historic headquarters are open during the summer months from 9:00 to 5:00, except Sunday when the hours are noon to 5:00. From October to May the park is open on Saturday from 10:00 to 4:30 and Sunday 12:00 to 4:30. There is no admission charged.

Directions: Take Beltway Exit 27 (I-95) north to the Wilmington area. Exit on U.S. 202, continue on Route 202 to U.S. 1, go left a short distance to the Brandywine Battlefield Park.

107. Fort Mifflin

The Alamo of the Revolution—Fort Mifflin! Four hundred and fifty men withstood 40 days of bombardment from the 94 ships of the British fleet. General Howe's garrison in Philadelphia needed munitions and supplies before they could pursue Washington's army. Fort Mifflin and Fort Mercer straddling the Delaware River blocked their progress.

River traffic was halted by a chevaux-de-frise. This was an obstacle more frequently used to repel cavalry charges. It was simply tree trunks chained together with spiked protrusions.

The British, stuck beneath the forts, began firing on October 11, 1777. After four days the guns were firing every half hour. Except for a brief time on October 22, when British guns turned to aid the Hessian land attack on Fort Mercer, the guns remained on the more vulnerable, low Fort Mifflin. Howe began calling this obstacle to his plans "that cursed little mud fort."

The men manning the fort could be excused if they felt it was "cursed." By November 7 only 115 of the 320 men left could still man the guns. The men tried to rebuild the fort walls at night but the constant bombardment was reducing the fort to rubble.

By November 13 three of the fort's four blockhouses were destroyed. Only 11 cannon could still be fired. By November 15 the British were firing 1,000 shots every 20 minutes. The chevaux-de-frise was released either by accident or treachery and it fell to the bottom of the river allowing the British to fire point-blank at the already crumbling fort.

By the afternoon of November 15 the fort was out of ammunition. When night came those of the fort's defenders who were still able to walk left. There were only 40 men able to walk away from this siege. Some estimates of the American casualties ran as high as 400. The British lost only seven lives.

But the British did lose valuable time. When Howe's supply ships finally managed to destroy this small fort, the American army under Washington was beyond his reach and a major confrontation was avoided.

This ended Fort Mifflin's usefulness during the American Revolution. It was rebuilt in the 1800s during the Adams administration. Enlarged during the Civil War, it was used as a prison garrison for deserters, Confederate soldiers, bounty jumpers and political prisoners. The fort conducted executions on what is now the Sunday drill grounds.

Fort Mifflin, which stands on Mud Island, still has its original moat and some Revolutionary walls. The enlisted men's barracks, underground bomb-proof vaults and fortifications have been restored.

On Sunday afternoons in addition to fort tours, there are militia guard drills and living history programs. A working blacksmith is often on hand to demonstrate how old weapons were made. A museum completes the historical picture of events at Fort Mifflin.

Fort Mifflin is open daily during the summer from 12:00 to 4:00. From Labor Day to Memorial Day it is only open on Sundays. Admission is charged.

Directions: Take Beltway Exit 27 (I-95) north to the outskirts of Philadelphia; follow International Airport signs for Overseas

Terminal. Fort Mifflin is behind the airport. Turn on Island Avenue, then south on Magazine Lane.

108. Red Bank Battlefield Park and Fort Mercer

Little remains of Fort Mercer, one of the twin bulwarks that stood in General Howe's way as he attempted to supply his Philadelphia garrison and pursue the American army under George Washington.

Visitors to Red Bank Battlefield Park can walk the high bluff on which Fort Mercer once stood. Remains of the earthen ramparts on the river side and a dry ditch on the land side reveal the fort's first and second lines of defense.

Fort Mercer was manned by 400 Rhode Islanders and local farmers. They had 14 cannons with which to repulse the attack on October 22, 1977, made by 2,000 Hessian troops under the command of Colonel von Donop. The Hessians approached by land from Haddenfield, New Jersey. The Americans retreated to the inner redoubt behind a hastily built wall completed just in time to be utilized in this engagement.

The Hessians believed the Americans had abandoned the fort, as their gunfire was not returned. They crossed the dry ditch and prepared to scale the walls. As they did the Americans opened fire and cut them down in a lethal volley.

When the Germans retreated they left 400 dead and wounded in the ditch. Of the fort's defenders, 14 were killed. According to a memorial column at the Park, the Hessians lost 600 men and 33 officers including those taken prisoner.

Also at the park is a collection of relics related to the fort. Included is a part of one of the old chevaux-de-frise mentioned in the defense of Fort Mifflin. The logs that made up this barrier are roughly 300 years old; a portion of the chain that linked them is still attached.

Red Bank Battlefield Park is open daily at no charge.

Directions: Take Beltway Exit 27 (I-95) to the Delaware Memorial Bridge, cross the river and continue up Route 295 to exit for National Park, New Jersey. At the town of National Park take Hessian Avenue to the Red Bank Battlefield Park.

109. Valley Forge National Historical Park

Valley Forge was a battle of wills not bullets, a crucible requiring more bravery than that necessary to stand up to a cavalry charge and more faith than any general had a right to expect.

The enemy at Valley Forge was not the English or Hessian soldiers, but something worse. The inadequately clothed men fought the bitter cold. They fought hunger with few rations. They fought disease and despair. From this valley of trial the Continental Army emerged as a disciplined, trained, fighting force. It was a transformation that marked a turn in the direction of the war.

What forged this army into the well-ordered martial ranks that broke camp six months after they had repaired to Valley Forge? The answer is an inspiring chapter in American history.

Why Valley Forge? Washington was unable to deflect General Howe's advance to capture the patriot capital in Philadelphia at the Battle of Brandywine in September 1777. At the end of the fall campaign both sides positioned themselves for the weather-enforced cessation of hostilities. On December 19, 1777, the 12,000 men of the Continental Army arrived at this site 18 miles northwest of Philadelphia. From here Washington could keep an eye on the British and prevent raiding parties striking into the Pennsylvania interior.

The tired, cold men hastily built 2,000 huts to provide some shelter from the elements. Before a week passed snow was six inches deep. Though the area around the open fields where they camped was heavily wooded when they arrived, most of the standing timber was cut for use in the camp. Washington, refusing to take shelter while his men froze, lived with them in a field tent. A field tent that belonged to Washington is on display at the Visitor Center. By Christmas, when the huts were at last complete, Washington moved into the fieldstone house he would use as headquarters. The house is approximately 80 percent original.

Two thousand men died that winter. Typhus, typhoid, dysentery and pneumonia all ravaged the cold, hungry men. But though they suffered, they were taken out onto the wind-swept plain called the "Grand Parade" and drilled by the Prussian General von Steuben.

Once on the elite General Staff of Frederick the Great of Prussia, von Steuben arrived in February. Despite the handicap of knowing little English, he went onto the field and worked with the men. He drafted a manual of drills in French and his aides translated each night so it could be used the next morning. Working from dawn to dusk, the men, many just farmers a short time ago, were soon executing smart drills and moving together as a company. One of von Steuben's most successful ploys was to form a 100-man select company and personally work with them so that they could show the others what he had in mind. Seeing is believing. It worked.

Nowadays at Valley Forge they still believe seeing is best. At the Muhlenberg Brigade huts, interpreters in Revolutionary War regalia demonstrate various aspects of the soldier's life daily from mid-June through late August and on weekends the rest of the year when staffing permits.

There are ten stops on the Encampment Tour Route within this 2,500 acre park. The best way to see everything and also appreciate the various spots along the route is to stop at the Visitor Center. The park is open at no charge from 8:30 to 5:00 daily, except Christmas Day. Displays and an audio-visual program will complete the picture of 1777-78. Tour maps can be obtained or taped tour dramatizations rented at the Visitor Center. The rental tapes are only available mid-April through October.

Other highspots include the National Memorial Arch commemorating the brave men who endured here, the forts that protected the army's winter quarters—Fort Washington and Fort Huntington—Artillery Park, where the cannons brought to Valley Forge were massed, and General Varnum's Headquarters.

Directions: Take Beltway Exit 27 (I-95) to Philadelphia. Before entering the city take Route 76 west to the Valley Forge exit. Proceed on Route 363 to the Visitor Center.

110. Fort Frederick

Prison labor is not a new idea; it was utilized during the American Revolution. Colonel Rawlings, the Commandant of Fort Frederick, received such a steady influx of British and German prisoners of war at this western Maryland fort that he was unable to feed or house them. He was forced to hire many of them out to local farmers as laborers.

Fort Frederick was reactivated in 1777 by the Continental Congress as a prison camp. It had been built in 1756 to protect the western boundaries during the French and Indian War.

On summer weekends costumed guides provide tours of the fort and demonstrate various facets of 18th-century military life. Visitors' first stop should be outside the fort at the Visitor Center where a historical orientation film is shown. Also outside the fortifications is the garrison garden which was used to supplement the inadequate government issue diet of salted meat, dry beans and bread.

The stone walls of the fort are a large square shape with diamond-shaped bastions in the four corners. While many of the forts built for the French and Indian War were of earth and timber, Fort Frederick's stone walls made it nearly impregnable and insured its survival.

The east and west barracks have been reconstructed and are open to visitors. The second floor of the east barracks has exhibits covering the history of this fort.

Fort Frederick is open during the summer months daily from 10:00 to 5:00 and on weekends in April, May and September. There are picnic facilities and the C&O Canal passes through the Fort Frederick Park Area.

Directions: Take Beltway Exit 35 (I-270) west of Hagerstown to Route 56. Take Route 56 to Fort Frederick State Park.

111. Wallace House

Yet another winter of the Revolutionary War is recaptured at the Wallace House. Here George Washington had his winter headquarters from February until June 3, 1779. The army bivouacked at nearby Camp Middlebrook.

It was another cold winter. Though not as cold as the preceding winter Washington had spent at Valley Forge, Martha Washington, who had accompanied the General to this New Jersey home, later commented that her strongest impression was of the bitter cold nights spent huddled under quilts and comforters.

Wallace House was not quite complete when Washington rented it for 1,000 dollars, but it would be the finest house in the area. The other officers who were billeted in the area and even some of the enlisted men were invited to dine at Wallace House so that Washington could get better acquainted with the men serving under him.

It was at the Wallace House that Monsieur Girard, the first Ambassador from France to the self-proclaimed free colonies, presented himself to Washington.

Washington became good friends with the pastor of the Dutch Reform Church, Jacob Hardenberg, whose parsonage was adjacent to the Wallace House. This old church home, moved across the street from the Wallace House in 1914, was built in 1751 and is also open to the public. Its unique feature is a smokehouse on the third floor, rather than on the ground floor as was common. With hungry armies in town, the third floor smokehouse proved to be a secure place to preserve meat and keep it from being pilfered.

Both the Wallace House and the Old Dutch Parsonage are open Wednesday, Thursday and Friday from 9:00 to 12:00 and from 1:00 to 6:00. On Saturdays they are open from 10:00 to 12:00 and from 1:00 to 6:00 and on Sunday from 1:00 to 6:00. They are closed Christmas, New Year's and Thanksgiving.

Directions: Take Beltway Exit 27 (I-95) to Route 206 north towards Princeton to Somerville. Both historic buildings are just south of Somerville, New Jersey, off Route 206 on Washington Place.

112. Smallwood's Retreat

The patriotic men who fought and governed during the first days of the young republic couldn't really be said to have a retreat because for them their homes were the scenes of constant meetings and live-in-guests.

Major General William Smallwood's home, though called Smallwood's Retreat, was the location of much political activity. Neighbors George Mason and George Washington from the Virginia side of the Potomac often met here to plan and discuss military as well as political strategy. Like Washington, Smallwood had been involved in the French and Indian War. He volunteered in the early days of the Revolutionary conflict, entering the Continental army with the rank of Colonel in 1776. By 1780 he was a Major General. Smallwood's troops, called the "Old Liners," covered Washington's retreat during the Battle of Brooklyn, saving it from annihilation. Smallwood was wounded during this engagement but he continued to command. He was formally commended for his bravery at the Battle of Camden by the U.S. Congress in 1780.

His service was not completed with the conclusion of the war. Returning to his Maryland home he involved himself in politics. He served as Governor of Maryland from 1785 to 1788. Towards the end of his life his house did become a retreat, as he returned here, contenting himself with the plantation administration. Smallwood died at his home on February 21, 1792, and is buried on the estate grounds.

After years of neglect Smallwood's Retreat has been authentically restored. The furniture covers the years 1600 to 1800. The house is open on weekends from March 1 to November 31 and during the week by appointment. Tours through the Retreat are conducted by hostesses in colonial costumes. For more information call (301) 743-7613 or write Smallwood State Park, P.O. Box 25, Rison, MD 20681.

Directions: Take Beltway Exit 3 (Route 210) south. Turn left on Route 227 and then right on Route 224. Continue on Route 224 for seven miles to Smallwood State Park entrance on the right.

113. Rockingham

It is one of the ironies of colonial history that George Washington, a man whose greatest love was his Mount Vernon home, should have been forced to spend so many years so far away from his Potomac estate.

After a series of military headquarters up and down the east coast, Rockingham, just outside Princeton, New Jersey, would be the last. Congress had abandoned Philadelphia because their sessions were so frequently interrupted by mutinous soldiers demanding back pay. The 1783 fall session of Congress met at Nassau Hall in Princeton. When General Washington was asked to attend the meetings, accommodations needed to be found for him and Mrs. Washington. Congress rented the Berrien house.

The widow, Mrs. John Berrien, with her six children grown up and on their own, had put the house up for sale. Her husband, a New Jersey judge who had built the house, came to an untimely end in 1776. After inviting a number of friends to witness the formal signing of his will, he drowned himself in the Millstone River in front of his guests.

Although the home no longer has the original furnishings, period pieces recreate Washington's bedroom and office. Martha Washington was suffering from a fever during her stay here and used the ground floor bedroom. Washington's upstairs office is called the Blue Room. Here he prepared the "farewell address to the troops," sending it to West Point to be distributed. The house is open to visitors at no charge.

Directions: Take Beltway Exit 27 (I-95) north of Philadelphia to the Trenton area, proceed north on Route 1. Make a right on Route 522 to Rocky Hill, New Jersey. Rockingham is off Route 518.

114. Yorktown Victory Center

It is singularly appropriate that here, where the American Revolution ended, a unique street has been created. At Yorktown Victory Center the entire Revolutionary period is encapsulated in a most engaging fashion.

Walking down "Liberty Street" provides an excellent review of the events that culminated on the nearby battlefield. This recreated colonial street with its colorful multi-media exhibits starts with the Tidewater Gazette, where events in Boston are being discussed and the Boston Tea Party and its aftermath are depicted. A 12-foot reproduction of the Declaration of Independence heralds the break with England. There is a replica of Washington's campaign tent and displays outlining the course of the war.

At the conclusion of Liberty Street a 28-minute award winning film "The Road to Yorktown," completes the exciting story of the Revolution. Though centuries have passed, one still feels an emotional jolt in watching the slow moving ranks of British soldiers surrender their arms.

Yorktown Victory Center, which is Virginia's gift to the nation, also has a museum with a constantly changing series of exhibits on the Revolutionary period.

Adjacent to the center is a recreated military encampment depicting those that surrounded Yorktown during the siege of 1781. Living history demonstrations of camp life are presented during the summer months.

Yorktown Victory Center is open daily from 9:00 to 5:00, except Christmas and New Year's. Admission is charged.

Directions: Take Beltway Exit 4 (I-95) south to Route 295, the Richmond By-pass, which will connect with Route 64. Take Route 64 to Williamsburg, then follow the Colonial Parkway to the well-marked turn for Yorktown Victory Center.

115. Yorktown Battlefield

The colonial triangle is: Jamestown, where the British first settled in 1607; Williamsburg, where the great issues that led to the formation of a new country were debated; and Yorktown, where independence was finally won. This country's early history is captured within a radius of a few miles, culminating at Yorktown Battlefield.

To appreciate the significance of the siege of Yorktown stop first at the National Park Service Visitor Center at Colonial National Historical Park. The free museum, movie and creative exhibits will provide additional insights and a broader perspective of this historic battlefield. The movie gives visitors an in-depth view of this final confrontation as well as a moving depiction of the surrender.

Downstairs is one of the National Park Service's marvelous reconstructions. The gun deck and captain's cabin of the British ship

Charon, have been rebuilt. The *Charon* was a 44-gun frigate destroyed by cannon fire during the siege of Yorktown.

Another fascinating exhibit is the field tent used by General Washington, as well as the Hessian colors that were surrendered to Washington on the battlefield at Yorktown.

Before heading on to the battlefield itself, climb to the Observation Deck of the Visitor Center. The entire battlefield can be seen and maps point out significant spots. It is a small area to encompass so much history.

In September of 1781 Lord Cornwallis with 7,500 men dug in at Yorktown to create a British naval port. The war in the south had not gone well for Cornwallis. He was concerned about the location of Washington's main force. There were conflicting reports, deliberately circulated, concerning the position of the Continental Army. Actually, it was marching on Yorktown and Cornwallis.

By September 28 more than 16,000 American and French soldiers were heading down the Virginia peninsula to trap the British General. As the British weakened, Cornwallis tried to escape across the York River, but failed. It was poetic justice that the winds of fortune should finally penalize the British as it had certainly devastated the Americans during the long winters. Cornwallis was foiled by squalls. On October 17th a red-coated drummer appeared on the British ramparts and beat a "parley." The guns stopped.

Representatives of the American, French and British forces met at the Moore House, now restored and part of the Battlefield tour, to discuss the surrender terms. It is hard to resist the pull of history standing in the redoubt on the field where Washington signed the surrender documents adding, "Done in the trenches before York Town."

Finally at two o'clock on October 19, 1781, the British marched, or so the story goes, to the tune of "The World Turned Upside Down." Wearing new uniforms, their guns at rest and colors cased, the troops passed through the lines of American and French soldiers along Surrender Road. Many of the British soldiers cried. Cornwallis pleaded illness and was not present. When his second-in-command, General O'Hara, attempted to present his sword to Rochambeau, he was referred to Washington. Realizing this was a slight, Washington passed him on to his second officer, General Lincoln.

That night the defeated British officers, again without Cornwallis, dined with their American counterparts. The British soldiers went into town and got drunk. Two days later they were marched off to prison camps in Maryland and Virginia. The war had been won but the fighting went on for more than a year in parts of the south and west. Two years would pass before the Treaty of Paris was finally signed formally ending the war and recognizing the new country.

Yorktown Battlefield at Colonial National Historical Park is open daily from 9:00 to 5:00 at no charge.

Directions: Take Beltway Exit 4 (I-95) to Route 295, which connects with Route 64. Take Route 64 to Williamsburg, then follow the Colonial Parkway to Yorktown.

OF NOTE: On the third floor of the Smithsonian's American History Museum (14th and Constitution Avenue), the oldest American man-of-war in existence, the Continental gondola *Philadelphia*, is displayed. Fighting the British on Lake Champlain, the Americans frustrated English efforts to isolate New England by occupying central New York The fifteen small boats of the Lake Champlain fleet that Benedict Arnold had built saved the cause of the American Revolution in the early days of the war. Arnold would betray this cause just four years later.

The *Philadelphia* was sunk by the British on Lake Champlain in 1776. It was not discovered until 1935, when the white pine mast could be seen standing upright barely ten feet below the surface at Valcour Bay.

Also on display is a Headquarters Tent used by General Washington in the field. Some of Washington's own equipment furnishes the tent. Washington's uniform, dress sword and field chest are part of the American Revolution exhibit.

War of 1812

Sea captains in the British Navy were "lords of all they surveyed" but it was an uneasy sovereignty. One of their responsibilities was to maintain a large enough crew to man their ships. The hard life of a British seaman did not encourage volunteers, so captains resorted to impressing men on streets, in taverns and on British merchant ships. When even these methods failed to muster sufficient men they turned to foreign ships—frequently American—and began seizing U.S. seamen for duty in the British navy.

This unpopular practice mocked American sovereignty and was one of the factors which led to the "second war for independence" in 1812. Impressment was not new in 1812; in fact, in 1807 the British had fired on the U.S.F. *Chesapeake*, boarded her and seized four seamen. Reaction ran high but President Jefferson first tried economic rather than military action. An embargo forbade commerce with both England and France, which was also guilty of ignoring the neutral rights of the United States. The hope was that the loss of trade would force the European countries to respect American sovereignty. Unhappily, its principal effect was to ruin the economy of the New England port cities. There was even talk of secession by the impoverished New Englanders.

To make matters worse, impressment continued. When James Madison was inaugurated as the fifth President in 1809, there was growing popular support for war. North, west and south were suffering economic depression in 1811 and 1812 as a result of the curtailment of trade.

The west was also threatened by renewed incitement by the British of the frontier Indians. To the "war hawks" of the west open conflict with England would provide a chance to rid Canada of the English and end this incessant provocation once and for all. Southerners also had their eye on expansion—the rich Florida land beckoned.

Conservatives argued that the American Navy could not hope to successfully challenge English superiority on the seas. It was ironic that the espoused cause, defense of the maritime rights of the North and East, was not supported in New England. It was the Southern and Western "war hawks" who forced Madison to declare war in June of 1812. There was a real question of whether the new government would be able to finance a war without bankrupting the country.

But it was finally a question of submission to continued humiliation, loss of national status and taking a minor position in international dealings, or fighting for the soverign rights of the country. The vote in Congress did not achieve a two-thirds majority in either house—the count was 79 to 49 in the House and 19 to 13 in the Senate in favor of declaring war on England.

Americans anticipated a four-pronged attack on the British in Canada. Though the war was envisioned as a land struggle, most of the significant encounters were to be on lakes or at sea. Military probes into Canada failed miserably, confounding those who felt, as Andrew Jackson did, that this would be a "mere military promenade."

Oliver Hazard Perry built a fleet on Lake Erie and won a stirring victory over the British fleet, forcing the English to abandon Detroit and giving the Americans their first real victory in this war. (Of Note: Perry's battle flag from the Lake Erie campaign with the motto "Don't Give Up The Ship" can be seen in Memorial Hall at the U.S. Naval Academy in Annapolis, Maryland.)

Another American victory at Plattsburg on Lake Champlain prevented the British army, now reinforced with troops no longer needed in Europe after the British victory over Napoleon, from advancing southward down the American coast. The British loss was most striking as their force was three times larger than the American contingent.

American victories at Plattsburg and at Fort McHenry, where the British were held at bay and failed to take Baltimore, convinced the British it would be too costly to continue the struggle. Unfortunately, victory at Baltimore came after the American capital was ignomiously burned by the British following the Battle of Bladensburg.

News of peace did not come soon enough to prevent the war's greatest battle, that of New Orleans, which occurred two weeks after the war was over. It was almost as if this last battle fought between American and British troops replayed the first instances of their conflict with one important difference—the Americans *won* the battle. Just like the Battle of Bunker Hill in the early days of the American Revolution, the British under Sir Edward Pakenham marched in the open while the Americans under Andrew Jackson fired from behind a barricade, this time of cotton bales. The results were the same as at Bunker Hill; the British were cut down in rows, suffering terrible losses. After two hours a third of the British force, some 2,000 men, had been killed or wounded; their General was slain and they were compelled to surrender. Only seven Americans died in the greatest American victory of the War of 1812.

The Treaty of Ghent was signed on Christmas Eve, 1814, and unanimously ratified by the Senate. But it did not even address the issues of the war. Impressment was not mentioned, no land changed hands, the protection of neutral rights at sea was not clarified; it simply restored the peace.

The War of 1812 can still be considered significant because it did establish the United States as a nation with the strength and the will to make her voice heard. Americans had gained confidence at home and respect abroad. American patriotism was enhanced by the stirring words of "The Star-Spangled Banner." Oliver Hazard Perry and Andrew Jackson joined with the heroes of the American Revolution to instill pride in the strength of America's fighting force.

The 1814 British Invasion Route

In August 1814 the British landed at Benedict, Maryland. They marched on the capital and burned the public buildings. While it is certainly not recommended that their example be followed, their route at least, can be. It took the British a week on foot to reach Washington, but by car it can be done in less than a day.

The landing of 4,000 British soldiers under General Robert Ross on August 19, 1814 at the small seaport town of Benedict in Charles County, Maryland was one of the easiest landings on a foreign shore in history.

News of this British invasion 45 miles from Washington was rushed to the White House, then just a grey stucco mansion. The government was confused as to the British objective. Would it be Baltimore or Washington?

Secretary of State James Monroe, unbeknownst to the rest of the government, decided to scout the British position to determine their strength and, if possible, the direction of their attack. Some feel Monroe was meddling and adding to the confusion, hoping for further military glory. Others feel his efforts were of considerable assistance to General Winder. He did bring news indicating his strong feelings that the British were heading for Washington.

After resting at Benedict the English land force, escorted along the Patuxent River by a small fleet under Admiral Sir George Cockburn, headed towards the port village of Nottingham. (For auto route take Route 231 from Benedict, then north on Route 381, right on Route 382 and right again on Tanyard Road to the village of Nottingham.)

The U.S.F. *Constellation* was not the only American ship bottled up by the stronger British fleet. The flotilla under Commodore Joshua Barney had been forced to remain inactive in the Patuxent River during the summer of 1814. Barney had made his headquarters at Nottingham, but now with Admiral Cockburn sailing up the river he had no choice—Barney had to salvage the guns and burn and scuttle his ships in the headwaters of the Patuxent River. Commodore Barney and his men set off for Washington to join forces with General Winder, contributing the guns and ammunition.

By August 22 the British were in Upper Marlboro. (For auto tour return to Route 382, join Route 301 and proceed north to Upper Marlboro.) General Ross, joined by Admiral Cockburn, made his headquarters at the home of the town's leading citizen, Dr. William Beane, who was taken hostage when the British retraced their route back to Benedict. His seizure by the British would prompt his good friend Francis Scott Key to try and negotiate with the British outside Baltimore, thus placing Key on a ship to witness the attack on Fort McHenry. This so moved Key that he wrote the words that have become our national anthem.

The Americans attempted to engage the British in battle while they were in Upper Marlboro but inadequate intelligence foiled their efforts. The next day's march on August 23 took the British force to Melwood (located on Route 4 at Woodyard Road; the Americans were camped in what is now Forrestville, farther down Route 4). The Americans believed they might face a night attack and retreated back to the capital, burning the bridges leading across the Anacosta River to Washington.

The British headed for Bladensburg, which was considered the best place to ford the river. Marching up what is now Kenilworth Avenue in the intense August heat, they arrived in the Bladensburg area at noon on August 24, 1814. After an all too brief rest, the battle commenced.

The American force under General Winder was not a regular army nor had it received military training as a group. The men had no uniforms and no standard equipment. General Winder did not even have a staff. The result was absolute confusion. In fact, while President Madison was inspecting the troops, trying to offer the men encouragement, he narrowly escaped walking into the main body of the British force. Madison left the battlefield and returned to Washington, where frantic residents were evacuating the city. Dolly Madison had collected many of the treasures of this fledgling country—the Declaration of Independence, Washington's portrait and other important documents. Then the Madisons also left the capital.

The Battle of Bladensburg was quickly over, the British routing the American force (see Colonial Period: Colonial Taverns—Indian Queen Tavern). Only Commodore Barney stood firm with his men. The troops under Winder ran when the British fired their new Congreve rockets, which made a frightful noise and looked like flaming fireworks.

177

Having made quick work of the opposition the British continued on to the capital. The British arrived so soon after the Americans had fled that the officers were able to enjoy the hot meal prepared by the White House staff for the Madisons and 40 invited guests. Not ideal guests themselves, the British not only ate and ran, but burned the house as they left. Most of the government buildings were destroyed as well as some private homes. It should be pointed out that the Americans had burned the British city of York in Canada earlier in the war.

The next day, after a violent tornado struck the city, the British began their return trip to Benedict and their ships. (They returned on what is now Route 202, the most direct route.)

In all the British force was on American soil for twelve days; they were victorious and the Americans were humiliated by their poor showing and the burning of their capital. But the forces of war would turn soon at Fort McHenry when the British tried to take Baltimore.

To obtain a map for this self-guided auto tour call (301) 952-3514 or write the Maryland National Capital Park and Planning Commission at 14741 Governor Oden Bowie Drive, Upper Marlboro, MD 20772.

116. Fort Washington

The present Fort Washington is the second fort to stand on this site. The first structure, originally called Fort Warburton, was started in 1808. Congress, constantly strapped for funds, had been reluctant to appropriate the money needed to protect the ports and harbors of the United States. As the impressment of seamen gained momentum in 1807 and after the British fired on the *Chesapeake*, needed funds were obtained to start a system of defensive forts. One of the main priorities was a fort that would protect the capital. Land opposite Mt. Vernon was obtained and work on a small fort completed by December 1809. Destined to stand for only five years, the fall of this first Fort Washington is no story of a gallant defense against superior odds. The British action against this fort during the War of 1812 was part of a subsidiary movement by a small naval force under Captain James Gordon, planned to provide an alternate route of retreat from Washington for the British should it be needed.

Gordon's force of two frigates, one rocket ship, three bomb vessels and a dispatch vessel had difficulties maneuvering on the Potomac, running aground on 22 occasions. But once they reached the fort they encountered no problems.

As soon as Gordon's ships opened fire on August 27, 1814, the commanding officer of Fort Washington, Captain Samuel Dyson, withdrew his men, blew up the powder magazine and retreated. This startling action was the result of Dyson's confusion over what was happening and his express orders not to let the fort fall into British hands. He had been ordered to destroy the fort if it came under a land attack. His precipitous action when fired on from the river cost him his commission.

Their success at Fort Washington permitted the British to sail up to Alexandria unmolested. The city surrendered without a fight as all her militia were diverted to Washington. Alexandria was occupied for three days while 22 ships were loaded with merchandise. Despite efforts of the United States Navy to block Gordon's retreat with his captured ships and plunder, he got away.

The delay caused by the Alexandria action did, however, break the momentum of the British advance. Their next attack would not fare as well. Efforts to capture Baltimore were thwarted at Fort McHenry.

Only 12 days after the fort was destroyed, James Monroe ordered the French engineer L'Enfant to reconstruct Fort Washington. So necessary was this work thought to be that L'Enfant was given a free hand and there was no suggestion of economy until the Treaty of Ghent was signed ending the war.

Work on the new fort was suspended in June 1815 when L'Enfant refused to rein his enthusiasm and modify his plans. Work commenced once more in the spring of 1816, and the fort was completed in October 1824. Manned as a river defense post, the fort was active until 1872. The Civil War saw the largest garrison in the fort, with a strength of nearly 350 men present at times. The fort appears today as it was in the mid-1800s.

Fort Washington is enclosed by high brick and stone walls. Entrance is across a drawbridge over a dry moat. The gateway entrance provides a panoramic view of the entire 833-foot fort. The fort was constructed so that guns could deliver a lethal bombardment from three levels: the water battery, which was begun by L'Enfant and is 60 feet below the main fort; the casement positions, which were bombproof gun positions; and finally the ramparts, two half-bastions overlooking the river from above and below the fort.

On the parade ground within the fort, visitors can see the officers' quarters, soldiers' barracks, powder magazine and guardroom.

Fort Washington is open daily from 7:30 until dark. The Old Fort is open from 8:30 to 8:00 from May until September and 8:30 to 5:00 the remainder of the year. Programs depicting life at the fort in the mid-1800s are offered on Sunday afternoon all year.

Directions: Take Beltway Exit 3 (Indian Head Highway, Route 210) south. Turn right on Fort Washington Road and continue to the fort.

117. Star Spangled Banner Flag House & 1812 War Military Museum

Speculation has it that the first American flag may actually have been made, not by Betsy Ross, but by a Philadelphia flag and banner maker, Rebecca Young. This widow did make the first flag of the Revolution under General Washington's direction. That flag, the Grand Union, was raised with the Continental Colors at Cambridge, Massachusetts on January 1, 1776.

Rebecca Young came to Baltimore in 1807 with her widowed daughter, Mary Pickersgill, and Mary's daughter. When Mary was asked in 1813 to make a flag for Fort McHenry, her mother and daughter provided help in this formidable undertaking.

For this was not going to be an ordinary flag but one that would, as Major Armistead, Commandant of Fort McHenry , requested, be seen by the enemy from a great distance. Mary had six weeks in which to work because the War of 1812 had been declared and Baltimore was in danger. She worked 10 hours every day, using 400 yards of wool bunting to sew the largest battle flag ever designed. It was 30' x 42' and on completion weighed 80 pounds. It took 11 men to raise this flag.

But it could be seen and was—by fearful Baltimore residents, by the British destroyers and by a worried Washington lawyer waiting from a truce ship outside the harbor, young Francis Scott Key. It was the sight of Mary's flag that inspired him to write our national anthem, *The Star Spangled Banner.*

Mary, her mother and 13-year old daughter, Caroline, made the flag in the upstairs bedroom of this Baltimore row house at 844 East Pratt Street. The house was built in 1793 and has been restored and furnished in the Federal period as if Mary Pickersgill was still in residence. A few of the decorative pieces actually belonged to her. In the parlor there is a portrait by Charles Willson Peale of her uncle, Colonel Flower, Commissary General on George Washington's staff. It was Flower who saved the Liberty Bell from the British. Mary's military connections and her mother's reputation as a flag maker secured for her the job of making the flag for the "Star Fort," as Ft. McHenry was called.

In the attic a loom as well as old spinning wheels are on display. But Mary bought the material for the Fort McHenry flag at the Fell's Point dry goods store owned by her brother-in-law, Captain Jesse Fearson. Mary would later be paid $405.90 for her work on this flag.

A copy of the receipted bill given to her by Major Armistead is just one of the exhibits in the 1812 War Military Museum that adjoins this old house. Also included in the collection is a replica of the flag made by Mary Pickersgill. There is a model of Dartmoor prison, where American seamen were imprisoned by the British before and during the War of 1812. Guns and military decoration from the War of 1812 are also on display. The museum has an audio-visual program on the war as it affected Baltimore. This provides a good introduction and leads to an interesting follow-up visit to Fort McHenry.

The house and museum at 844 East Pratt Street in downtown Baltimore are open from Tuesday through Saturday from 10:00 to 4:00 and Sunday from 1:00 to 4:00. There is a nominal admission charge.

Directions: Take Beltway Exit 22 (the Baltimore-Washington Parkway into downtown Baltimore. Go right on Pratt Street just past the Inner Harbor area to the 800 block. The Star Spangled Banner Flag House is on the left (corner of Pratt and Albemarle Streets) with a parking lot adjacent.

OF NOTE: The flag made by Mary Pickersgill that flew over Fort McHenry is on display at the Smithsonian Institution's Museum of History and Technology.

118. Fort McHenry National Monument & Historic Shrine

At Fort McHenry the oft-heard phrase "ghosts of the past" is used quite literally. There have been some "spirited" incidents a this old fort. On certain autumn weekends candlelight tours are conducted on Friday and Saturday evenings. These tours roam through the spookiest parts of the park while rangers tell visitors about some of the nocturnal activity.

There are stories about a shadowy figure seen on the Civil War battery walls, a psychic "presence" in a guardhouse cell and even a mischievous spirit who likes to rearrange furniture and switch the lights on and off. Thus far the spirit has refrained from blowing out candles, but who knows?

Park personnel who are susceptible to these incidents think it possibly could be Lieutenant Levi Clagett, who was killed by one of the bombs that didn't burst in the air but instead scored a direct hit on the gun position maintained by Clagett on September 13, 1814 during the Battle of Baltimore.

National Park Service

U.S. Marine Corps units perform at the Fort McHenry Tattoo Ceremony.

This 25-hour bombardment withstood and repulsed by Fort McHenry saved Baltimore from suffering a fate similar to the burning of Washington. In order to reach the city the British ships had to get past the guns of Fort McHenry. One thousand soldiers manned the fort on September 13-14, 1814 to defend the city against the English. The British ships anchored two miles off shore, so that their guns and the new Congreve rocket could hit the fort but the American shells would land short of the ships. The U.S. forces held their position, and although the British expended between 1,500 and 1,800 rounds in their attack, only four soldiers at Fort McHenry were killed, with 24 wounded. The successful defense of Fort McHenry inspired eyewitness Francis Scott Key to write our national anthem (see War of 1812: Star Spangled Banner Flag House).

Visitors at Fort McHenry are reminded of these momentous events in a 15-minute film presentation at the Visitor Center. The film ends with a dramatic touch: while *The Star Spangled Banner* is played the curtains part and the flag is visible flying over the fort.

The present fort was built between 1798 and 1803. During the

Revolutionary War, Fort Whetstone occupied this pivotal position protecting the approach to Baltimore. Fort McHenry is constructed in a star shape so that each point of the star is visible from the points on either side. This made a surprise attack almost impossible and increased the effectiveness of the fort's fire power coverage.

There are three types of buildings within the fort: the barracks, the powder magazine and the guardhouses. The fort underwent some modernization of the batteries during the Civil War but it never again came under attack after 1814.

Fort McHenry is open at no charge seven days a week, except Christmas and New Year's Day. Hours are 9:00 to 5:00, except during the summer when it is open until 8:00. There are picnic facilities and a pleasant mile walk along the sea wall.

Directions: Take Beltway Exit 22 (the Baltimore-Washington Parkway) into Baltimore; turn right on Pratt Street and proceed to Light Street Just before reaching the Inner Harbor area. From Light Street bear left on Key Highway one mile to Lawrence Street and turn right to Fort Avenue which will lead to the gates of Fort McHenry.

119. U.S.F. *Constellation*

Talk about chutzpah! When Congress declared war on the British in 1812 England had over 100 ships-of-the-line with more than 90 guns, almost 250 ships with 50 guns and 32 frigates carrying 38 guns plus smaller brigs, sloops, schooners and cutters. Against this the United States had three frigates with 44 guns—the *Constitution*, the *President* and the *United States*.

This fledgling navy was designed to out-sail the larger English ships. Their objective was to attack, maneuver and retreat. The *Constitution*, the best known frigate, was launched in October 1797. But the first official ship of the U.S. Navy was the *Constellation*, a smaller frigate, launched at Fell's Point in Baltimore in September 1797. There were three other frigates in the 32 to 38 gun class—the *Chesapeake*, the *Congress* and the *Essex*. The U.S. also had one corvette, two sloops and six brigs.

With such a small fighting force it is easy to see why the inability of any of these ships to be actively involved in the fighting of the War of 1812 would have been a severe blow to the Americans—but that is unfortunately what happened to the *Constellation*.

In Washington Captain Charles Steward supervised preparation of the *Constellation* for sea duty against the British in the War of 1812. Setting sail from the capital, Captain Steward headed the

Constellation around Annapolis and down the Chesapeake Bay toward open sea. Reaching the Yorktown area, he sighted strange sails. Unhappily for Steward they were the sails of seven ships under British Admiral Warren's second-in-command, Sir George Cockburn. The only option for Steward was to turn in toward Norfolk, where the *Constellation* stayed bottled up while the British plundered the Chesapeake Bay area throughout the war.

The *Constellation* would, however, sail again in the Civil War and as the flagship of the Atlantic Fleet during World War II.

This historic ship has the distinction of being the first U.S. ship to engage and defeat a man-of-war from the old country, the French frigate *L'Insurgente* in 1799. She is the oldest official ship still afloat. There is considerable debate concerning the degree of restoration. Some argue that the *Constellation* was so extensively rebuilt in 1853 she is no longer the original vessel. In any case, she is anchored at Baltimore's Inner Harbor and may be visited from mid-June to Labor Day from 10:00 to 8:00 daily. From Labor Day to mid-October and from mid-May to mid-June hours are 10:00 to 6:00. From mid-October to mid-May the *Constellation* is open 10:00 to 4:00. On Sundays and holidays hours are 10:00 to 5:00. Admission is charged.

Directions: Take Beltway Exit 22 (the Baltimore-Washington Parkway) into downtown Baltimore. Go right on Pratt Street to the Inner Harbor area and the U.S.F. *Constellation*.

120. Octagon House

In 1797 Colonel John Tayloe let a fellow Virginia planter, George Washington, persuade him to build the Tayloe townhouse in the new capital city rather than in Philadelphia.

Since the city was being laid out by L'Enfant with a pattern of circles, there were many irregular lots. But the Tayloe land was more of a challenge than most.

To fit this unusual size lot, a six-sided mansion was designed by William Thornton, the architect of the U.S. Capitol. It would subsequently be misnamed Octagon House due to an imprecise counting of the sides. The design cleverly solved the problem presented by the property lines by having round rooms with rectangular and triangular offshoots which served as closets. Walls, windows and doors were curved, utilizing shipbuilders art, to adapt the house to the lot.

It was to this architecturally unique but elegant townhouse two blocks west of the White House that President James Madison and his wife, Dolly, moved when they returned to Washington after the British burned their official residence during the War of 1812. The Madisons lived here for six months from September 1814 to March 1815. Madison used the circular rooms on the second floor as a study. In this study on February 17, 1815, he signed the Treaty of Ghent ending the War of 1812. Now called the Treaty Room, it has been restored and includes the table used by President Madison.

The Treaty Room is reached by a wide, oval staircase that is not only the architectural centerpiece of the house but also the focus of fanciful stories about a ghostly presence. The stories vary, but it seems Colonel Tayloe did not approve of one of his daughter's suitors. During a heated argument she fell over the stair railing (or, some even hint, was pushed) to her death. Reports have circulated about the sound of a young girl crying on the steps.

Octagon House is now the headquarters of the American Institute of Architects Foundation. There is no charge to explore this interesting townhouse but donations are welcome. It has been decorated with Federal pieces, some of which belonged to the Tayloe family, and the original Italian marble floors and ceiling molding in the Treaty Room can still be admired for their exquisite workmanship.

Octagon House is open Tuesday through Friday from 10:00 to 4:00 and on weekends from 1:00 to 4:00. The house is closed on major holidays.

Directions: Octagon House is located at 1799 New York Avenue, N.W., at 18th Street in downtown Washington.

Era Between the Wars

Presidential Homes

America has no royal family, no castles that have stood since the Middle Ages. The great diversity in the homes of the men we have chosen to hold the highest office in the country testifies to the opportunity for even the poorest to reach great heights.

In fact, it was sometimes incumbent on would-be office seekers to rusticize their origins. When William Henry Harrison campaigned for the presidency he depicted his birthplace as a log cabin—a far cry from the gracious splendor of his ancestral plantation, Berkeley.

But the homes of the American Presidents do reflect the diverse backgrounds of our nation's leaders. Our Presidents have been farmers, lawyers, tavern keepers, scholars, businessmen and soldiers. Their homes provide an insight into the private side of these public figures.

Patterns do emerge; of the first 10 Presidents six were of the Virginia landed aristocracy. Their homes were elegant plantations reflecting taste, intelligence and a mastery of vast domains. Some of these homes are represented in earlier sections—Mount Vernon, Monticello and Berkeley.

No section on presidential homes would be complete without including the one home they all, with the exception of George Washington, shared in common—the White House.

121. The White House

The most famous home in America is the focal point of government—the President not only lives there, he works there. The history and traditions of our democracy are reflected in the home of our Presidents. The White House also is a mark of the special nature of the American government: it is the only residence of a chief of state in the world that is open regularly to the public without charge.

In 1790 George Washington signed a measure to ceate a "Federal City" on the Potomac. However, he would not live to see John and Abigail Adams move into the President's home on November 1, 1800. Mrs. Adams felt the house needed a good deal of work just to make it livable. Even though she was a veteran of New England winters, she was accustomed to a snugger environment; the Adams's called this house their "chilly castle." They lived there for only four months before Thomas Jefferson replaced Adams.

Jefferson was certainly the right man at the right time. He was never happier than when remodeling. His own plantation, Monticello, was always being altered as he conceived new innovations. The job of running the country did not allow Jefferson to give full rein to his enthusiasm, so he hired a professional architect, Benjamin Henry Latrobe. An architect was certainly needed as the White House roof had been so poorly constructed that the Washington rains had caused the East Room ceiling to collapse. But gradually the house took shape.

Though Jefferson devoted time to the building's interior, being a widower he did not provide a woman's touch. When Dolly Madison moved in after the inauguration of 1809, she immediately began redecorating. Barely a year after she had the house decorated to her taste the British inconsiderately burned it to the ground during the War of 1812.

James Monroe was President when the house was again livable in 1817. The Monroe furnishings were purchased by the U.S. government in 1817. They were in the French Empire style.

Each successive administration has added something to and made changes in the White House as a result not only of taste and personal preference but also of the incredible wear and tear caused by the endless procession of guests and visitors that seem to perpetually populate the house.

It wasn't until Theodore Roosevelt's administration in 1902 that funds were appropriated to build executive offices and provide some separation between the President's living and working quarters. Work to expand the office space of the executive mansion continued off and on through 1934.

But problems with the house continued. Chandeliers trembled, upper floors sagged and swayed and plaster peeled and flaked away. In 1948 an architectural study indicated evidence of instability—the White House gave signs of collapsing. The Trumans moved across the street to Blair House and work began again on the house. Some people even suggested total demolition, beginning again with granite or marble. But the desecration of what many considered a national monument was forestalled. Extensive rebuilding was necessary, requiring 27 months to reinforce and rebuild the White House. The Trumans moved back in on March 27, 1952.

No perspective on presidential homes would be complete without visiting the country's "first house." The White House is open Tuesday through Saturday from 10:00 to 12:00. During the summer it stays open until 12:30. Though there is no charge, due to larger summer crowds advance tickets are required and must be picked up on the Mall in person the day of the tour.

Directions: The White House is located at 1600 Pennsylvania Avenue, N.W., Washington, D.C.

122. James Monroe Law Office–Museum and Memorial Library

A man for all seasons, a statesman for all occasions—this was James Monroe. But everybody, no matter what his stature, must start somewhere. Monroe started in this small law office in Fredericksburg, Virginia. He opened his law practice here in 1786 and went on to hold more high public offices than any other American statesman.

James Monroe served as a Senator from Virginia, American Minister to France, England and Spain, the Governor of Virginia for four terms, Secretary of State and Secretary of War and capped his career with two terms as President.

In Monroe's old office in this historic town visitors can see reminders of the many phases of Monroe's career in public service. James Monroe succeeded James Madison as the fifth President. His was the first presidential family to occupy the White House after the British burned it in 1814. When the Monroes moved in they decorated their official residence with furniture purchased while Monroe was Minister to France (1794–1796); when he left office the furniture went with him. Many of the pieces at this museum were part of these furnishings. Some *copies* are in the White House today. In 1932 Mrs. Herbert Hoover had some of the Louis XVI furniture duplicated.

One of the most interesting pieces is the desk on which President Monroe signed his annual message to Congress in 1823. This address contains what has become known as the Monroe Doctrine, which denied European countries the right to interfere in the Western Hemisphere, but did recognize existing European colonies. In 1906 a secret compartment was discovered in the desk which contained many letters, among them one from Alexander Hamilton and one from Benjamin Franklin.

The museum has an extensive collection of letters from Monroe and from many of his contemporaries as well. There is also a library associated with the museum that is accessible by appointment only to those doing research on James Monroe and the Monroe Doctrine.

One of the most popular features of the museum is the collection of outfits worn by the Monroes at official functions both at home and abroad. James Monroe wore a green velvet suit and Elizabeth Monroe an elegant gown when they were presented at the Court of Napoleon in France. Earlier dresses include one Mrs. Monroe wore in Fredericksburg with the stylish "butterfly bustle." Her jewelry, slippers and other ornaments are also displayed.

Visitors exit by way of a delightful walled garden. A bust of Monroe adds a focal point to this area. On special occasions Mrs. Monroe's mint juleps are still served in the garden.

The James Monroe Law Office-Museum is open daily from 9:00 to 5:00, except December 24, 25, 31 and January 1. The museum is located at 908 Charles Street. Admission is charged.

Directions: Take Beltway Exit 4 (I-95) to Fredericksburg, Route 3. Exist east and follow the signs to the James Monroe Museum.

123. Ash Lawn

Like a disproportionately large percentage of America's early leaders, James Monroe was a Virginian. He was a friend and associate of the many remarkable men from this southern area.

He served with distinction under General Washington in the American Revolution. In the famous painting of *Washington Crossing the Delaware* Monroe is the young man holding the flag behind Washington. When he returned to Virginia after the war, he studied law under Thomas Jefferson for three years.

Jefferson, always one for grandiose schemes, wanted to create "a society to our taste" around his own beloved Monticello. Monroe, ever eager to please his mentor, purchased in 1793 a substantial tract of land just two-and-a-half miles away. Before he could proceed further, President Washington appointed Monroe Minister to France. In his absence Jefferson and another good friend, James Madision, selected a site for the house and sent the Monticello gardeners over to begin the orchards.

It wasn't until 1799 that the Monroes moved to their Ash Lawn tobacco plantation, then called Highlands. The house was not as yet complete but they began the enjoyable task of decorating the eight rooms with the elegant Louis XVI furniture they had acquired while in France. The contrast between the simple exterior and the stylish decor prompted Monroe to dub it his "cabin-castle."

James Monroe and his family lived at Ash Lawn from 1799 to 1823. Because of its simple exterior and stylish interior Monroe called it his "cabin-castle."

Many of these pieces were later used at the White House, and some are now back at Ash Lawn. Only five rooms, the original one-story rear portion of the house, are standing today. There is an addition built by a later owner.

Although Monroe had hoped to retire to Ash Lawn, his 40 long years of public service left him so impoverished he could not afford to retain this estate and in 1826 regretfully sold it.

Ash Lawn is today the property of the College of William and Mary, alma mater of not only President Monroe, but also of Presidents Jefferson and Tyler. The atmosphere of a 19th-century working plantation has been retained. On this 535-acre estate there are delightful boxwood gardens, enhanced by peacocks that roam the grounds. Flowers, vegetables and herbs are also grown in abundance. Throughout the year special programs demonstrate cultural activities and traditional farm crafts of the Monroe era.

Ash Lawn is open daily 9:00 to 6:00 from March to October and from 10:00 to 5:00 November through February. It is closed Thanksgiving, Christmas and New Year's. Admission is charged.

Directions: Take Beltway Exit 9 to Route 66 west, then take Route 66 to Route 29 south to Charlottesville. On Route 29 look for signs for I-64 east to Richmond. Ash Lawn and Monticello are marked as an exit. Ash Lawn is on Route 795 just minutes from Monticello.

124. Sherwood Forest

John Tyler named his Virginia plantation Sherwood Forest, as he considered himself a political outlaw, a Robin Hood. It was a view shared by many members of his own party. When, as the country's 10th President, he vetoed a banking bill highly favored by the Whigs, he was thrown out of the party.

In the closing days of his administration, his wife threw a gala affair to mark the end of his presidency. Tyler was heard to remark that at least now no one could say he was a President without a party.

Invitations to the parties at Sherwood Forest were highly prized. This was the only James River plantation to have a ballroom. The 69-foot length of this room was designed to enable dancers to enjoy the popular Virginia Reel. Tyler also used to entertain guests in this room by playing his own violin compositions.

The ballroom connecting the office to the main house is matched on the other side by a long hall which connects with the kitchen. These lengthy additions make this the longest frame house in America.

In three centuries only three generations of Tylers have lived at Sherwood Forest. The present owner, Harrison Tyler, is the grandson of John Tyler. This makes the house very personal in its decor since most of the furniture and decorative pieces are original.

Tyler was the only President to support the Confederate cause. He even held a seat in the Confederate Congress in 1862 and died while serving at the winter session in Richmond. Due to Union activity in Virginia he was buried in Richmond. His wife and children fled to family protection in New York. Union troops broke into the house, and indentations still show on the great front door where their rifles split the wood. The northern troops ransacked the house, burning the furniture, books and papers. They piled hay in the main hallway and lit it, intending to burn the house; but when they left, a union gunboat captain saved the Tyler home.

One of the rooms at Sherwood Forest is believed to be haunted by the Grey Lady. The Grey Room, as it is now called, was once the family sitting room. Stairs lead up to the nursery and the children's nurse would bring the youngest child down to rock before the fire in the Grey Room. One night the child died. Since that time footsteps have been heard in the empty room and the sound of a non-existent rocker is sometimes heard late at night.

After being conducted on a tour of the house visitors will enjoy exploring the 1,600-acre estate with its 12-acre grounds. The Tyler estate is bordered by trees that have been there since the days when the Powhatan Indians occupied this land. There are over 80 varieties of century-old trees, almost half cultivated here by Tyler but not indigenous to Virginia.

Sherwood Forest is open daily, except Christmas Day, from 9:00 to 5:00. There is an admission charged. A reservation is necessary. Call (804) 829-5377 or write to Sherwood Forest, Charles City County, VA 23030.

Directions: From the Beltway take Exit 4 (I-95) to Richmond. From Richmond take Route 5 for 35 miles east to Sherwood Forest. Sherwood Forest is only 18 miles west of Williamsburg on Route 5, the John Tyler Memorial Highway.

125. Wheatlands

Although the phrase "amber waves of grain" conjures up the midwest for some, for one Pennsylvanian it meant home. James Buchanan, the only Pennsylvanian to become President, lived at an estate called Wheatlands.

Bought in 1848 for $6,750, the residence was named for the fields of waving grain surrounding this Lancaster estate. Buchanan was then in his fifties and would live at Wheatlands for the rest of his life, except during intervals when he served as Minister to England in 1853 and as President from 1857 to 1861.

Buchanan had made bids for the presidency earlier in 1844, 1848 and 1852. Wheatlands was the scene of many political strategy sessions. Buchanan finally gained the Democratic nomination in 1856 after being out of the country while President Pierce alienated party leaders and left a void in the ranks of contenders. Buchanan was 65 and had given up on ever winning the nod. As he said on August 20, 1856, "My aspirations for the presidency had all died four years ago . . ." But southern leaders were looking for a northerner who would accept direction. They believed Buchanan was their man. Buchanan was on the porch at Wheatlands when word was brought in June of 1856 that he had the nomination and from this porch he made his acceptance speech.

He had been a politician for 42 years, serving as both Representative and Senator from Pennsylvania. He was Jackson's Minister to Russia, Polk's Secretary of State and Pierce's Minister to Great Britain. But despite all this experience it is conceded by many historians that the job of President was just too much for him. In the growing division between North and South he was not strong enough to provide the wide leadership needed to head off disaster. It is uncertain if anyone could have succeeded.

At the end of his term Buchanan returned to Wheatlands a beaten old man trying to justify his administration. He had been backed by southern Senators who anticipated he would favor compromise, and one of the main failures of Buchanan's presidency was that he failed to get the South to moderate its obdurate stand. The country was consequently divided by the devastating Civil War.

Visitors to Wheatlands see the house as it was during the last years of Buchanan's life, 1848-68. His study still has the bookcase filled with references he often used and a bottle of his favorite Madera wine sits on the table.

The dining room is set with the Paris porcelain Buchanan used while in the White House. The large formal table was built specifically for Wheatlands and has never been removed. The wine rinsers, which enabled diners to rinse their glass when changing wines, are uncommon table accessories today.

Buchanan was a bachelor President and his niece, Harriet Lane, served as his White House hostess. When he returned to Wheatlands she remained in his household. In the parlor her music is on the piano that Buchanan gave to her. On the walls are signed portraits of Queen Victoria and Prince Albert representing Buchanan's days as Minister to England. The Prince of Wales visited the White House and was entertained by Buchanan and Miss Lane.

The authentic atmosphere of Wheatlands is heightened by the antebellum costumes worn by the hostesses. After exploring the many Buchanan family rooms, step out onto the veranda and enjoy the flower gardens and estate outbuildings. A large carriage house, still occupied, has Buchanan's Germantown wagon.

Wheatlands is open April 1 to November 30 from 10:00 to 4:30 daily. Admission is charged.

Directions: From the Beltway take Exit 27 (I-95) and pick up the Baltimore Beltway west. Then take Exit 24 (I-83). Proceed north on I-83 to York. Then take Route 30 to Lancaster. Wheatlands is located at 1120 Marietta Avenue, Route 23, in Lancaster. It is bounded by President Avenue, Harrisburg Avenue and Columbia Avenue.

Homes

The popular interest in antiques has long encompassed the old homes in which old furnishings are so often found. History buffs and avid collectors appreciate the careful restorations that provide a complete picture of life in an earlier era.

This revival of the past is even more significant when, as often happens, it recreates the home of some important figure from the pages of our history books.

Great men, great houses and great objects all combine to provide fascinating footnotes to events on the larger stage of history. Sometimes what makes a house worthy of consideration is not its style but that it survived. The fact that it still exists and that William Penn, Benjamin Franklin or George Taylor once lived and worked in it makes it significant. Even when the house hasn't itself survived, but enough records, inventories, diagrams or pictures remain to allow it to be authentically rebuilt, it becomes significant historically.

In the 47 years between the War of 1812 and the Civil War, America developed, expanded and grew. These houses represent that period of growth.

126. Decatur House

Local boy makes good! Born at the Maryland coastal village of Sinepuxent on January 5, 1779, Stephen Decatur came from a seafaring family. Young Decatur was in college when the American Navy was formed and immediately dropped out of school to enlist. His father also joined the fledgling organization and won first honors for his country by capturing the French ship *Le Croyable* and bringing her to Philadelphia as a prize ship.

Stephen Decatur brought even greater glory to the family name. During the War with the Barbary Pirates in 1804, he led a group of 74 volunteers into the harbor of Tripoli and burned the captured U.S. frigate *Philadelphia* before it could be used in battle against her sister ships. It was a courageous raid and Decatur a hero. Lord Nelson, of British naval fame, called it "the most daring act of the age."

In June of 1807 an incident occurred which would dramatically affect Decatur's life. Commodore Barron, commanding the *Chesapeake*, allowed the British officers of the *Leopard* to remove four American seamen from the U.S. vessel. This incident was one of the events that led to the War of 1812. Decatur, though reluctant to do so, was one of the nine officers who suspended Barron in the court-martial resulting from this incident so humiliating to the U.S. Navy. Barron's anger at Decatur for serving on the court-martial board was intensified when Decatur was given command of Barron's former ship, the *Chesapeake*. In 1820 Barron challenged Decatur to a duel. Feeling he was honor bound to accept, Decatur met Barron at the dueling ground in Bladensburg, Maryland. Both were wounded but Decatur died after being carried back to his Washington home. He was only 41.

Decatur had moved to Washington in January 1816 to serve on the Navy Board of Commissioners. With prize money won during the War of 1812, Decatur bought 19 lots on the President's Square around the White House. He first lived next door to the Madisons, who had been forced to abandon the White House after it was destroyed by fire.

To build his new home Decatur enlisted the noted architect Benjamin J. Latrobe, who had just finished redesigning the Capitol after the fire of 1814. Latrobe designed a three-story brick townhouse, with rear dependencies and a garden. This 170-year-old house is of particular significance because it is the only surviving residence designed by Latrobe. His drawings remain at the Library of Congress and have made it possible to preserve the original appearance despite additions by such distinguished subsequent owners as George M. Dallas, Vice-President under Polk, and three Secretaries of State—Henry Clay, Martin van Buren and Edward Livingston. Both France and Russia have also used the Decatur House as their legation.

Visitors to the house today will see reflected the elegant life-styles of the mansion's first and last residents. The first floor rooms are reminiscent of Decatur's short one-year residence in his new home (1819-20). The Victorian grandeur of the reception rooms on the second floor represent the Beale family years (1872-1957). Throughout its long history the Decatur House has hosted elegant parties for Presidents, Senators and diplomats. This tradition continues today as Decatur House is still used for government social functions.

Decatur House is open Tuesday through Friday from 10:00 until 2:00. On weekends and holidays it is open 12:00 to 4:00. Admission is charged.

Directions: Decatur House is located at 748 Jackson Place, N.W., on Lafayette Square across from the White House.

127. Lee-Fendall House

Sorting out the genealogy of the Lee-Fendall House is rather like exploring the interconnections of characters in a modern soap opera. It seems Philip Richard Fendall, who built the house in 1785, was the grandson of Philip Lee of Blenheim. Young Fendall had a penchant for Lee wives—he had three. His first wife was a Lee cousin, his second was the widow of one of the Lees at Stratford and the mother of Matilda, the first wife of "Light Horse" Harry Lee. Keeping it all in the family, Fendall's third wife was Harry Lee's sister, Mary.

All in all, 37 Lees lived in this Greek Revival-style house from 1785 to 1903. The furniture is mostly a collection of pieces donated or loaned by the various branches of the Lee clan.

The most historic room in the house is the dining room. "Light Horse" Harry Lee was dining here when the Mayor of Alexandria stopped by to inform them that Washington was to pass through Alexandria on his way to his inauguration in New York. Lee moved to a desk in the room and wrote the Farewell Address to Washington from the citizens of Alexandria. Ten years later in Philadelphia he wrote the famous Washington eulogy which contains the line "First in war, first in peace—first in the hearts of his countrymen."

Upstairs is a lady's bedroom where the last Lee born in this house was delivered in 1892. There is a delightful "swooning couch" where ladies who were indisposed could rest before the fire. Other interesting decorative additions are the pair of face screens, held or positioned by the ladies to prevent their wax make-up from running. Since smallpox was rampant during this early period, many ladies, and gentlemen, had badly pocked faces. Both resorted to wax to smooth the contours.

The house has a portrait of Harry Lee as a Major General, a rank he reached in 1794 when Washington sent him to Pennsylvania to dowse the Whiskey Rebellion.

The toys in the children's room span a number of Lee generations. One of the dolls, Minerva, was from the first Sears and Roebuck catalog. Other dolls and a rocking horse, called "Traveler," are even older.

Outside the house is a large garden, with a massive magnolia and old chestnut trees. A small rose garden and boxwood paths have also been added.

The Lee-Fendall House is open Tuesday through Saturday from 10:00 to 4:00 and Sunday 12:00 to 4:00. Admission is charged.

Directions: Take Virginia Beltway Exit 7 (U.S. 1) north into Alexandria, turn right on Oronoco Street. The Lee-Fendall House is at 429 N. Washington Street.

128. Chippokes Plantation

Chippokes Plantation is hard to pigeonhole, spanning as it does 350 years of American history. Structures on the grounds reflect 17th-, 18th-, 19th- and 20th-century architecture. Many familiar names are part of the story of this Virginia plantation.

The history of Chippokes goes back to 1612, when the land was patented by Captain William Powell and named after a minor Indian chief, Choupouke, who had befriended the settlers at Jamestown. The land came to the crown, in the person of Royal Governor Sir William Berkeley, at the death of Powell and his heirs. Berkeley's widow married Colonel Philip Ludwell and Chippokes was owned by three generations of that family before passing to John Paradise, a foreigner in whom Thomas Jefferson took a great interest.

The main house, a large antebellum mansion, was built in 1854, on the site of an earlier house. This is an excellent example of a pre-Civil War plantation house. Behind the mansion is the six-acre garden, with a background of magnolias, crepe myrtle and boxwoods. The flowers bloom from spring until autumn's frost.

The only other building open to the public is the brick kitchen built in the 18th century for use during the summer months so the main house wouldn't get overheated. Other plantation structures include slave quarters, barns, a carriage house, tobacco houses and another large home called "River House," built in the 1700s.

It isn't only the Chippokes buildings that reflect the passing centuries, but also the agricultural methods and crops which changed over the years. At Chippokes a model farm has been developed which demonstrates the numerous changes. In the 17th and 18th centuries, tobacco was grown as a cash crop and corn and other grains were grown for plantation use. The plantation orchard also provided apples for distillation into apple brandy. In the 19th century there was a shift from tobacco to peanuts. The model farm provides a look at the crops that have been grown in Virginia over the centuries: figs, cotton, sorghum, tobacco, peanuts, corn, soybeans, and loblolly pines for the lumber industry.

The Visitor Center gives a more complete picture of this diverse plantation. Maps of the model farm and of Chippokes' bike and hiking trails are available. There is a lovely trail along the James River.

The Chippokes Plantation is open year round; from Memorial Day to Labor Day there is a small charge per car for park use.

Directions: Take Beltway Exit 4 (I-95) to Route 295, the Richmond By-pass. Then take Route 64 to Williamsburg. Take the toll ferry at Jamestown across the James River. Continue on Route 31 to Surry. Chippokes Plantation is 3.5 miles east of Surry on Route 634.

129. Sully Plantation

Richard Bland Lee attempted to combine the best of both worlds, architecturally speaking, when he built this Virginia plantation house after the Revolutionary War. Begun in 1793, Sully Plantation reflects a combination of the Virginia style of Georgian colonial architecture that was his heritage and the Philadelphia touches he became acquainted with while serving as northern Virginia's first Congressman.

It is a harmonious blending of styles, more modest than many Tidewater plantations but still lavishly furnished. Its frame exterior resembles a Philadelphia townhouse, although if Lee had enlarged it as he originally intended the asymetrically placed hall would have been transformed into the more traditional central hall.

Richard Bland Lee's wife, Elizabeth Collins, was the daughter of a prominent Quaker merchant in Philadelphia. When the Lee family sold Sully in 1842, it was to another Quaker family from the north—the Haights. During the Civil War years the men of the family, despite their pacifist position, had to remain behind Union lines, while the women of the family ran Sully and protected it from the armies of both north and south.

The plantation house has been restored and is furnished with furniture of the Federal period. Several outbuildings have also been restored such as the kitchen-laundry, smokehouse and stone dairy.

Sully frequently hosts special events that bring to life the post-Revolutionary period. Sully Plantation is open Wednesday through Sunday 11:00 to 4:00 from March 15 through December 31. Admission is charged.

Directions: Take Beltway Exit 9 (Route 66) to Route 50 west for 5.5 miles to Route 28 (Sully Road). Bear right and proceed three-fourths of a mile to site.

130. Oatlands

If the word "plantation" conjures up a large mansion with a colonnaded porch framing the front and spacious grounds then Oatlands will fully live up to expectations. Built shortly after 1800 by George Carter, the great-grandson of Robert "King" Carter, it was the embodiment of gracious southern living.

The land had been acquired by the Carter family from Lord Fairfax in 1776 but the Carter family holdings were so vast that development was slow. Oatlands in the 1800s encompassed approximately 5,000 acres; now only 256 acres remain. But there is enough to recreate a by-gone era of hooped skirts, dashing men and mint juleps on the verandah.

The house was designed by George Carter from architectural guidelines set forth in a book by a London architect, George Chambers. His book, written in 1768, provided a blueprint for this post-colonial mansion. The house was built with material supplied on the grounds. The bricks were molded and fired at Oatlands and the wood cut from the surrounding forest. Both the interior and exterior ornamental work reflect the Greek Classical Revival influence.

George Carter died in 1846 and his family left the plantation at the start of the Civil War. Both sons served in the Confederate Army. Confederate troops were billeted at Oatlands for a few days. The original furniture disappeared during the economically depressed antebellum years. In the 1880s and 1890s the Carters took in summer boarders.

By the 1900s the house and gardens were in disrepair but new owners restored Oatlands, improving the house with the addition of a rear porch. The gardens that George Carter had laid out were recovered from their overgrown appearance and expanded with a gazebo and terraces. The boxwoods are well into their second hundred years' growth.

The magnolias are at their best in the spring when Oatlands also hosts a number of horse shows and races, reflecting the interest of earlier owners in the Virginia Hunt activity. Oatlands is open April through November from 10:00 to 5:00, Sundays from 1:00 to 5:00. Admission is charged.

Directions: Take Beltway Exit 10 (Route 7) west to Leesburg. Oatlands is 6 miles south of Leesburg on Route 15.

131. Morven Park

Architecture and art are in bountiful variety at the 1,200-acre Morven Park estate begun in 1781. The elegant white-columned mansion has evolved with a felicitous mixture of styles. From the Greek Revival entrance, visitors are ushered into a Renaissance Great Hall with walls covered by tapestries made in Flanders in the 16th century. The dining room is Jacobean and the drawing room French. The furnishings were collected by Governor and Mrs. Davis as they toured Europe and Asia and represent a mixture of styles and times.

Morven Park has been the home of two governors. In the 19th century it was the residence of Thomas Swann, Governor of Maryland; in the 20th century Virginia Governor Westmoreland Davis lived here.

Representing an era of luxurious living seldom encountered today, the estate is reached by a mile-long tree-lined drive that leads first to the Marguerite Davis Boxwood Gardens. Beyond the garden is the mansion.

Though the house is fascinating, there is still another incentive for visiting Morven Park. The Carriage Museum has a nationally famous collection of carriages and sleighs evoking an earlier period of transportation. Carriages include everything from carts, surreys and everyday phaetons to coaches used by the English nobility. There are more than 70 horse-drawn vehicles in the collection.

Once the interior of the house and museum have been explored visitors can enjoy the self-guided nature trails on the mansion grounds. They are particularly nice in the spring when the wild flowers are in bloom. The size of this great estate allows one to slip back to an earlier day far removed from hurtling cars and crowded freeways.

Morven Park is open weekends mid-October through May. Memorial Day through Labor Day it is open Tuesday through Saturday from 10:00 to 5:00 and on Sundays from 1:00 to 5:00. It is closed Mondays, except holidays. Admission is charged.

Directions: Take Beltway Exit 10 (Route 7) to Leesburg. Morven Park is in Leesburg on Old Waterford Road.

132. John Marshall House

Though John Marshall occasionally accepted government assignments that took him from his Richmond home, as in 1797 when he went to France, he stubbornly resisted efforts to enlist him in a permanent government position because of the ill health of his adored wife.

But in 1801 he did become the fourth Chief Justice of the Supreme Court, spending part of each of his 34-year tenure in Washington and part at his Richmond home. Under Marshall's direction the Supreme Court was transformed from the weak third branch of government it had been to that time to a strong court. He implemented the doctrine of judicial review.

Though Marshall delivered his decisions in Washington, he did much of the work at home in Richmond. He was extremely close to his invalid wife, Polly, and their 10 children.

The John Marshall House is the only surviving brick 18th-century house in Richmond. Marshall purchased the one-block site in 1786. During the two years the present house was being built the Marshalls lived in a two-story frame cottage on the grounds. The main house, completed in 1790, was lived in by John Marshall for 45 years until his death. It has been restored and contains much of the original Marshall furniture. It was sold to the city of Richmond by John Marshall's granddaughter and so came to the public directly from the family. It has the largest collection of Marshall memorabilia in existence.

The gardens have also been restored and a reproduction of the sundial John Marshall once enjoyed again decorates the yard.

The John Marshall House is open Wednesday through Saturday from 11:00 to 4:00. Admission is free.

Directions: Take Beltway Exit 4 (I-95) to Richmond. The John Marshall House is at 818 East Marshall Street.

133. Centre Hill Mansion

It is a wonder that Petersburg was not renamed "Bollingberg" after the Centre Hill family that owned most of the town land. It was actually named after an earlier settler who had established a trading post with the Indians during the first years of Virginia's settlement.

The Bolling family came to this area much later. They built Centre Hill Mansion in Petersburg during the Federal period in 1823, but it was extensively remodeled in the 1840s by the fifth generation of Bollings to settle in America.

In the 1840s a Greek Revival facade was added to the house, the kitchen moved inside and elaborate molding used to decorate the interior. To make arrival on the Appomattox River easier for guests, a two-block tunnel reached from the house to the river.

Towards the end of the Civil War, Robert Buckner Bolling left Centre Hill when Union troops occupied the city. General Hartsuff used Centre Hill as his headquarters and President Lincoln met here with his staff to discuss the progress of the war. The mansion did sustain some damage as a result of artillery barrages during the 10-month Siege of Petersburg, the longest battle of the Civil War.

New owners in the 1900s again remodeled Centre Hill. These changes parallel the Victorian era. A belvedere was added as were round radiators and fireplaces on the second floor. The evolution of architectural styles makes Centre Hill particularly interesting.

The furnishings, too, span the period from the 1820s through the early 1900s. Three Presidents—John Tyler, Abraham Lincoln and William Howard Taft—have enjoyed the hospitality of Centre Hill. It is now the official host center of Petersburg. It is open Monday through Saturday from 9:00 to 5:00, Sunday from 1:00 to 5:00.

Department of Tourism., Va.

Centre Hill Mansion in Petersburg was built in 1823. President Lincoln met here with his staff during the Civil War.

Directions: Take Beltway Exit 4 (I-95) past Richmond to Petersburg. Centre Hill is located in Centre Hill Court in the heart of downtown Petersburg.

134. Hampton National Historic Site

Not everyone who makes money from a war is a profiteer. Some amass riches while serving their country's needs. This was true of the Ridgely family of Maryland. On land the family acquired in 1745 a large iron ore deposit was discovered. Using this iron, the Ridgelys supplied cannon and munitions to the Revolutionary War cause. The money earned from the ironworks enabled the family to build one of the most ornate post-Revolutionary homes in America.

When Charles Ridgely died, his nephew became the master of Hampton. His position of wealth and influence led him to the Maryland General Assembly where he served first as Representative then as Senator. In 1815 he was elected Governor of Maryland.

The mansion house has been restored to its appearance during the Ridgely family's occupancy from 1788 to 1948. Most of the furnishings belonged to the Ridgely family, who made Hampton their home for 158 years. Baltimore painted furniture, Chinese porcelains, family portraits and other period pieces reflect the affluent life of this prominent Maryland family.

In addition to the mansion and 24 associated structures, there are a formal garden and an herb garden which have been restored on this 60-acre estate.

Hampton National Historic Site is open Tuesday through Saturday from 11:00 to 4:30 and Sunday 1:00 to 4:30, closed Monday and major holidays. Hampton is administered by the National Park Service. No admission is charged. There is also a Tea Room and Gift Shop.

Directions: Take Beltway Exit 27 (I-95) north to the Baltimore Beltway. Go left to Exit 27 off the Baltimore Beltway at Dulaney Valley Road. Continue on this to Hampton Lane and turn right for the Hampton National Historic Site.

135. Beall–Dawson House

It is a uniquely American preoccupation, this concern for where Washington, Jefferson, Lafayette and their many illustrious contemporaries ate or slept. Perhaps the egalitarian nature of the country and early tumultous events account for the string of houses, inns, taverns and farms which proudly boast such distinction. Somehow it's doubtful, even if George Washington had traveled to France, that American tourists today would see houses still carefully noting that Washington once stopped at that spot. But here in America we still remember the French hero, Lafayette.

Lafayette not only gallantly served the cause of independence during the American Revolution, he also paid this country the highest compliment by attempting to copy our sweeping reforms in his own troubled land. When Lafayette returned to America in 1824 to celebrate the victory at Yorktown, he was feted from Philadelphia to Williamsburg. He saw the New Year in that year at a stylish Rockville house owned by the Beall family.

Surrounded by extensive grounds, this Federal-style brick home has been restored to its 19th-century appearance. The furniture dates from 1815 to 1860 and has been collected from throughout the state of Maryland. The living room represents a mixture of styles including a magnificent "Hair Picture," a Duncan Phyfe sofa and Pier table. The dining room is in the Federal style with a recently acquired magnificent 1820 Sheraton dining table. The only significant original pieces in the house are the Chickering pianoforte and the Hepplewhite-style mahogany drop leaf table.

The Beall-Dawson house serves as the headquarters of the Montgomery County Historical Society. Its research library is now housed in a separate frame structure built in the late 1940s. The Society's exhibits and collection go back to early habitation of the Maryland area and include many artifacts from the colonial period.

An office used by Dr. Stonestreet when he practiced in the Rockville area in the 1850s is on the grounds. The office is furnished with medical instruments and apothecary accessories of a 19th-century medical practice.

The Beall-Dawson House at 103 West Montgomery Avenue in Rockville is open 12:00 to 4:00 Tuesday through Saturday and 2:00 to 5:00 the first Sunday of each month. Admission is charged.

Directions: Take Beltway Exit 35 (Route 270 north) to Route 28 exit. Take a left on Route 28 (Montgomery Avenue) to the Beall-Dawson House.

136. Union Mill Homestead

The Shriver homestead at Union Mills became a house, a business and a town that grew with one family through America's history. From 1797 to the present, six generations of Shrivers lived in this old homestead and developed this western Maryland area. Their careful records and fortunate habit of keeping household goods now provide a glimpse of rural America.

A four-room house was built just over the Pennsylvania line in Maryland by two brothers, Andrew and David Shriver. They called their home "Union Mill" to symbolize their harmonious relationship.

David, a bachelor, moved on to engineering work after the family business was well established. Andrew, with his 11 children, stayed at Union Mill. After campaigning for Jefferson's presidency in 1802 he was rewarded with the postmastership of the community. One corner of a first floor office still has the desk Andrew Shriver used to handle the mail in the early 1800s. As the family business activities expanded, along with the size of the clan, the house also grew to 23 rooms.

Two sons of Andrew Shriver, William and Andrew Jr., supported opposite sides in the War Between the States. William, who ran the mill and owned no slaves, supported the South. Six of his seven sons served in the Confederate Army. Andrew, although he did own slaves, supported the Union. He had two sons; one could be spared, and he fought for the North.

Within a 24-hour period before the Battle of Gettysburg troops from both armies were fed at the homestead. Jeb Stuart's cavalry ate pancakes from the large kitchen just as fast as they could be cooked. The following night General Barnes and his staff enjoyed dancing and games at Union Mill before the next day's battle.

After the Civil War the Shriver family again turned their attention to business. For a good part of the 19th century, travelers on the stage road from Baltimore to Gettysburg stopped at the homestead. Washinton Irving may have found inspiration for his comments on country inns from the night he spent at the Union Mill Homestead. The noted ornithologist, James Audobon, once watched Baltimore orioles building a nest in a willow tree outside the house.

Union Mill Homestead has not been restored; it has been retained. The great-great-grandson of the first Andrew Shriver said, "No one seems ever to have thrown anything away." This habit serves us well. In the parlor, for instance, visitors can see the entertainment preferences of several centuries—a rare barrel organ from the 1780s, an 1863 Steinway piano, an 1875 Swiss music box, an 1892 Edison-cylinder phonograph and, finally, a 1917 spring-driven Victrola. Living patterns are reflected in the changes in fireplaces, toys, kitchen appliances and other household items.

The family's water-powered gristmill has been restored directly across the street from the homestead.

Union Mill Homestead and gristmill is open June 1 to September 1, on Tuesday through Saturday from 10:00 to 5:00 and on Sunday from 12:00 to 5:00. During May and September it is open on weekends only. There is a small admission charged.

Directions: From the Beltway take Exit 33 (Route 185) north. Continue on Route 97; the house and mill are located off Route 97 in Westminster.

137. Todd House

On the very day popular Dolly Paine, from the King's Arm Tavern in Haddonfield, married the promising young Philadelphia attorney, John Todd, Jr., he bought this house.

They lived here from 1741 to 1743, and during this period Dolly had two children. But the great Philadelphia yellow fever epidemic brought tragedy to the Todd family. Even though Dolly left the city, one of her children still contracted the plague and died, as did her husband, who remained in the city. Fifty percent of the population fled from the city where 20 percent of the inhabitants had died. At the height of the plague people were dying at a rate of 100 a day.

When the cold weather killed the mosquitoes and the epidemic ended, Dolly returned to the city a widow with her two-year-old son. She had three choices: take in boarders as her own widowed mother had done, open a small shop or marry again. Being young and attractive, she took the last alternative. Aaron Burr introduced her to James Madison and after only a few months they married. Dolly would later become the country's First Lady.

Todd House is a good example of an "end of row" house, a style found only in Pennsylvania, New Jersey and Delaware. It is furnished from exact inventories, representing a middle-class Quaker house in the 18th century.

One of the indications of 18th-century frugality is the old-fashioned forerunner of the Xerox, a press-like device which created a copy of correspondence. Unfortunately, the copy came out backwards, so a mirror was placed on the desk to enable the copy to be read. This served a secondary function of doubling the candle power, by reflecting the flame.

The National Park Service provides free guided tours of the Todd House, a part of Independence National Historical Park. The house is open daily 9:00 to 4:30. Adjacent to the house is Harmony Court, a recreation of a formal colonial garden.

Directions: Take Beltway Exit 27 (I-95) north to Philadelphia. Follow it into the city where it will become Front Street. Turn left on Walnut or Chestnut Street for Independence National Historical Park.

138. Bishop White House

The Bishop William White's house has none of the Quaker sparseness of the Todd house. The house was built in 1786 while White was in

London being consecrated the first Protestant Episcopalian Bishop of Pennsylvania.

Built on eight levels, the top of the house is a loft; next is the boys' floor, where their initials are carved into the wood. The third floor is the girls' room, with White's bedroom and library just below. On the first floor are the formal rooms. Beneath that is the kitchen area, the scullery, the wine cellar and root cellar and finally the ice well.

This large house was filled by White's wife, their five children, a cook and coachmen. White also entertained a number of legislators, gentlemen whose acquaintance he made while serving as both Chaplain of the Continental Congress and of the United States Senate.

This upper class home is quite elegant, and is one of the first in America to use the decorative touch of wallpaper. The early paper was in small sections in very limited colors. The ceilings are 12 feet high, so there was a lot of wall space to cover.

The restoration was aided by an 1836 painting of Bishop White's study. The details have been so faithfully recreated that two half-smoked cigars have been added to duplicate those shown in the picture. Archeological research led to the discovery of silver and crockery in the drain under the house, permitting exact copies of the original pieces.

The Bishop White House is part of Independence National Historical Park and can be toured at no charge from 9:00 to 4:30 daily. As the number of visitors that can be accommodated on the tours is limited, tickets are required but can be obtained at no charge at the Visitor Center.

Directions: Take Beltway Exit 27 (I-95) north to Philadelphia. Follow it into the city where it will become Front Street. Turn left on Walnut or Chestnut Street for Independence National Historical Park. The Bishop White House is at 309 Walnut Street.

Transportation

After the American Revolution and the subsequent "second war for independence" in 1812, the American people finally had a chance to contemplate the magnitude of their achievement and to consolidate the strengths of the new nation.

Since the most abundant resource the United States had was land one of the principal occupations in the era between the wars was to build routes to the western territories. Roads, canals and railroads pushed resolutely forward through the mountains to the vast lands waiting to be tapped in the Northwest Territory.

The roads came first. The major highway to the west at the beginning of the 18th century was the Pennsylvania Road, now U.S. 30. Another important thoroughfare was the National Pike, or Cumberland Road, started in 1808. Conestoga wagons, loaded with all the worldly possessions of the pioneers, made the dangerous trip. It was a rugged life. The pioneers needed constant vigilance to protect themselves from Indians, to keep the animals on the road and to provide water, firewood and food to feed the family.

Water travel was smoother and offered the advantage of company along the way. But since goods could flow down stream and not up, canals were dug for easy movement both up and down by water. The first major canal was the Erie Canal, finished in 1825. This started a wave of canal building which peaked in 1828, when the Chesapeake & Ohio Canal was started on the same day that the first stone of the Baltimore & Ohio Railroad was formally laid.

The trains were faster and reached a greater number of destinations. They quickly superseded the canal system and many canals reverted to great grassy ditches.

139. Chesapeake & Ohio Canal National Historical Park

The outlook for transportation in America changed on July 4, 1828. In Baltimore, Charles Carroll was laying the first stone for the Baltimore

The *Canal Clipper*, a 19th-century mule-drawn packet barge, glides through history on the C&O Canal.

& Ohio Railroad, while outside Washington President John Quincy Adams turned over the ground to begin construction of the Chesapeake & Ohio Canal. The race to reach the west was on!

The C&O Canal was first envisioned by George Washington as a waterway connecting the Potomac and Ohio Rivers. He anticipated Georgetown becoming a major hub of commerce linking Pittsburgh with the capital. This plan was never realized as construction ended in Cumberland, just 185 miles from Washington. The simultaneous construction of the B&O Railroad made the canal obsolete.

However, the portion of the canal that was completed represents an engineering masterpiece, as it presented numerous construction complications. The major difficulty was the necessity of raising the water level 605 feet from the canal's origin in Georgetown to its final stop in Cumberland. A series of 74 locks enabled the barges to negotiate this gradual upgrade. This incline was not the only problem facing the builders. The canal spans 11 tributaries of the Potomac River, so Roman-style aqueducts were used to float the barges above the river level. As the canal moved into the mountain area of western Maryland a third difficulty complicated its progress. Great stone cliffs extended all the way down to the water. The only option was to tunnel. So the 3,100-foot Paw Paw Tunnel was dug through the mountains, enabling the barges to continue on their way.

The operation of the locks and other aspects of canal life can best be appreciated by riding the C&O Barge *Canal Clipper*. The barge workers are dressed in costume and recreate life along the canals in 1876, a time when 400 barges plied the C&O Canal. Ninety-eight percent of these were commercial and the other 2 percent were packet barges like the one currently operating.

The trip begins with the fascinating "locking through," a technique which raises the barge eight feet in five minutes. Just watching this complex operation makes one appreciate what an accomplishment it was to build the more than 4,000 miles of canals that once crosscrossed America.

The barge captain blows the great lock horn to inform the lock tender of the barge's presence. Maneuvering through the lock is done by pole and rudder. A mule team is harnessed after the barge is through the lock. Giant lock keys turn the hidden panels that permit the water to fill the lock. The barge is raised, the gate opened and the one-hour trip begins.

Maximum speed along the canal is four miles an hour. Someone has to walk with the mule team to keep the barge moving smoothly. Pay for this job, usually held by boys in their mid-teens, was four cents a day. Barges covered about 40 miles per day.

The trip is not only very educational, as the crew keeps passengers informed on the life they would have led in 1876, but it is also fun—various crew members play old-fashioned instruments such as the jews harp, fiddle, banjo and harmonica and encourage everyone to join in singing the old songs.

As in earlier days, there is an admission charged for this round trip ride, though it's not quite as low as it once was when it cost thirty-seven-and-a-half cents to go from Georgetown to Cumberland. Tickets are available at the Visitor Center for the barges that run Friday, Saturday and Sunday three times a day from April until mid-October. From mid-June until Labor Day they also run on Wednesday and Thursday.

Further information is available at the Great Falls Tavern Museum where the barge rides begin. This early stone lock house was built 14 miles from Washington in 1828. It very soon became a gathering place for travelers and was enlarged to provide overnight quarters as well as public rooms for dining, dancing and drinking. It was the only hotel built by the C&O Canal Company.

Activity at Great Falls Tavern increased during the Civil War when gold was discovered nearby. The brief spurt of prosperity didn't continue.

After the Civil War, when the canal boom was at its height, as many as 700 barges traveled through the locks daily. The railroads were luring away canal traffic and storm damage in 1889 further disrupted business. In 1924, less than 100 years after it opened, the Canal Company ended operation.

This old tavern now serves as a Visitor Center. There are displays and a movie on the canal. Great Falls Tavern is open at no charge year around. For more information call (301) 299-3613 or write to the C&O Canal National Historical Park, P.O. Box 4, Sharpsburg, MD 21782.

Directions: Take Beltway Exit 41 (the Cabin John Parkway) to Great Falls, Maryland.

140. Delaware Canal Mule-Drawn Barge

For those who feel that cost overruns, poor construction and time tables not met are something new, the story of the building of the Delaware Canal is revealing. Started in 1827, it was finished in 1832, but was so poorly built it could not be used until repaired. It would be 1840 before the canal was commercially operational. This ineptitude doubled the projected cost to over one million dollars, a cost overrun of $500,000. And, all this occurred in the early days of the railroad boom which would soon render canals obsolete anyway.

The Delaware Canal runs parallel to the Delaware River, starting at Easton and ending at Bristol, Pennsylvania. There was a difference of 165 feet between these two points and the canal had to compensate for this with a series of 25 lift locks. To accommodate the canal nine aqueducts and 106 bridges were constructed.

At peak periods in 1862 almost 3,000 boats traveled the canal. Barges still ply the canal today and visitors can compare the experience on the Delaware Canal with the Chesapeake & Ohio Canal.

Delaware has more development along the banks; there are houses and bridges to observe as one moves slowly along the canal. It adds a nice dimension to glide beneath the trestled bridges. As on the C&O Canal, the barges are pulled by mules and average about four miles an hour.

The barges leave from New Hope, Pennsylvania for a trip which lasts slightly less than an hour. During April and from mid-September to mid-November the barges run Wednesday, Saturday and Sunday. From May through mid-September they run daily. There is a charge for the barge rides. For additional information call (215) 862-2842 or write to P.O. Box 164, New Hope, PA 18938.

Directions: Take Beltway Exit 27 (I-95) north of Philadelphia. Just before crossing into New Jersey exit on Route 32 and continue to New Hope.

141. Chesapeake & Delaware Canal Waterwheel and Pumphouse Museum

Another of the many canals that crosscrossed the Eastern seaboard in the early days of American transportation was the Chesapeake & Delaware Canal. In 1661, when the Dutch map maker, Augustine Herman, was charting the Delmarva Peninsula, he proposed such a waterway, as only 14 miles separated the Chesapeake Bay from the Delaware River.

It was more than 100 years later, in 1764, before a canal survey team measured their way across this 14-mile stretch. This early team had the distinction of being the forerunner of all canal projects in what would become the United States. The uncertain nature of the colonial situation and the subsequent conflict intervened and work was not actually begun on the C&D Canal until 1804. Work stopped again two years later when money for the project ran out.

October 17, 1829 was the big day when the C&D Canal was finally operational. Covering only 13 miles, it started at Delaware City in the east and moved west to Chesapeake City, Maryland. It needed only four locks to cover this short distance. The only lock now remaining is the Delaware City lock.

At the other end one additional reminder of the early canal is the two-story grey stone pumphouse, located beside the project office from which the Army Engineers' Philadelphia District operates and maintains the waterway. This contains a wooden waterwheel that could lift 1,200,000 gallons of water into the lock every hour. Twelve buckets on the huge, 38-foot diameter wheel emptied the water on a continuous basis. This ingenious construction fascinated that master tinkerer, Henry Ford, and still intrigues visitors. The pumphouse is a National Historic Landmark and part of the Army Engineers' C&D Canal Museum which sheds further light on one of the earliest canal ventures. The museum contains working models of the pumphouse machinery and a lock.

Directions: Take Beltway Exit 19 (Route 50) across the Bay Bridge, then bear left on Route 301. Continue on Route 301 and take Route 213 to Chesapeake City.

142. Baltimore & Ohio Railroad Museum

September is the anniversary of the historic race between Tom and Bob. Doesn't ring a bell? Tom was the new guy in town—quite jazzy—while Bob was the old standby. Many cheered when they heard the news that the newfangled upstart, the iron horse "Tom Thumb," had been beaten by the old horse "Bob" at pulling a passenger car on parallel tracks.

Poor Bob may have won the race but his prize was not to be envied. Being somewhat vindictive, legend has it that Peter Cooper, who built the "Tom Thumb," acquired the victorious steed. Then he got even with Bob by consigning him to another of his successful ventures—his glue factory.

Until Peter Cooper's "Tom Thumb" made its first run in August 1830, the Baltimore & Ohio Railroad used horses to pull their railroad cars. American railroads had tried to use the English engines, but after the first and only run of the massive "Stourbridge Lion" on the wooden tracks of the Delaware and Hudson Company the railroad tracks were reduced to toothpicks.

Peter Cooper worked almost a year developing what he called the "Teakettle." Others later nicknamed it "Tom Thumb." Looking like a water heater bolted onto a farm wagon, the little engine used war surplus musket barrels for its pipes. Cooper built it on the site of what is now the B&O Railroad Museum.

On August 24, 1830, the "Tom Thumb" was ready for its first run. Traveling at the dizzying speed of 15 miles an hour, it delighted the dozen volunteers making the initial run. Early passengers scribbled notes to attest to the marvelous fact that the human brain could still function while traveling at this great speed.

On August 28, the directors of the railroad made the 13-mile run to Ellicott City. This ceremonial occasion was meticulously reported and, though often cited as the run on which the engine raced the horse, there is no mention of such a race in the earliest accounts of this trip. Also, the time of 26:22 minutes for the run between Relay and Baltimore could not have been bested even by the finest horse. Later in September, on another ceremonial occasion marking the 94th birthday of B&O founder and Declaration of Independence signer, Charles Carroll, the fan belt broke, slowing the train. It was probably on this run that the famous race between the iron horse and gallant grey actually occurred. The victory was short-lived. Within a very brief period the new marvel had ousted the horse drawn carriage from the rails. The era of the stream locomotive had arrived. Though in 1830 when the "Tom Thumb" was built there were only 50 miles of tracks in all of

America, the railroad's growth was assured with the success of the iron horse.

The exciting news is that visitors can still ride the "Tom Thumb." Once a month during the summer "the little engine that could" again pulls passengers in the open-sided "Directors Car" on the one-mile trip to Mount Clare Mansion. A fee shuttle bus runs back to the B&O Railroad Museum.

While at Mount Clare be sure to tour Baltimore's oldest house. (See Colonial Period: Homes.) This Georgian-style plantation was built in 1754 by Charles Carroll, the Barrister. It was Charles' nephew, James Carroll, who sold the B&O Railroad 10 acres to build the first railroad station—the price, $1.00.

Today that same $1.00 buys a ride on the "Tom Thumb." No reservations are accepted but the waiting is fun as the B&O Railroad Museum provides ample diversions. It's actually a great place to visit on a cold winter's day as well. Here is the world's largest collection of historic railroad equipment. On the 22 tracks of the ornate round-house turntable you can see some famous old engines—Pangborn Engines, the "Iron Mule of 1945," Imlay Coaches and an elegant car from the first "Royal Blue." Other early modes of transportation are also represented: Conestoga wagons and commercial vehicles like a fire engine and a 1937 Buick Hy-Rail car. The tools that built the iron road are a part of the collection.

It is appropriate that the museum should be housed in the Mt. Clare Station of Baltimore. This is literally the birthplace of the American railroad. It is the oldest depot in the United States and one of the oldest in the world. Passengers for the first scheduled train ride bought their tickets at Mt. Clare in August of 1830. It cost 75 cents for the 13-mile ride to Ellicott City. Today there is another B&O Railroad Station Museum at the other end of this historic run to Ellicott City.

The B&O Railroad Museum is open Wednesday through Sunday from 10:00 to 4:00. Admission is charged.

Directions: Take Beltway Exit 22 (the Baltimore-Washington Parkway) into Baltimore. Turn left on Lombard Street and continue west to Poppleton; go left to the museum.

143. Ellicott City B&O Railroad Station Museum

It was August 28, 1830 when the first cars were attached to the steam engine "Tom Thumb" for the run from Baltimore to Ellicott City,

13 miles away. On another later run of this little engine as the train passed the coach Relay House on the return trip, a race was on between the train and the coach. Guess who won? It looked as though "Tom Thumb" would be the victor, as he had already passed the horse, but mechanical difficulties changed the outcome of the race. The engine slowed and the horse surged ahead—and won!

A replica of the "Tom Thumb" is in the Baltimore & Ohio Transportation Museum in Baltimore but it's also worth a trip to visit the terminus at the other end of this historic line. At the Ellicott City B&O Railroad Station Museum a model of the 13-mile trip has been built, with an authentic scale gauge model layout. A "sight and sound" show also depicts the creation of the railroad and its first terminus, Ellicott Mills. Both are in the restored Freight Station (circa 1885) at the B&O complex in Ellicott City.

The old stone station, built in 1831, houses a Visitor Center, restored Station Master's quarters, Superintendent's Office, Ticket Office, Waiting Room and Engine House. A partially excavated turntable is located between the two buildings and a restored caboose is also open for inspection.

The museum hours are 11:00 to 4:00 Saturday and Sunday from January to the end of March. From April through the end of December the museum is open Wednesday through Saturday from 11:00 to 4:00 and Sunday from 12:00 to 5:00. Admission is charged.

Directions: From Beltway Exit 30 (Route 29), take Columbia Pike to Old Frederick Road. Follow that to Ellicott City and the Ellicott City B&O Railroad Station Railroad Museum

144. Strasburg Rail Road

Imaginative visitors to historic reconstructions often feel they've stepped onto a Hollywood set. Strasburg Rail Road, in addition to its authentic credentials, does in fact have steam trains that have been used in the movies.

The coach "Willow Brook" is nearly 70 years old and was featured in the movie *Raintree County*. Four other coaches and an observation car were used for *Hello Dolly*. But Hollywood came to Strasburg for the very reason that those interested in early transportation visit this turn-of-the-century railroad—it is the oldest short-line railroad in the United States. For 150 years these steam trains have been running. The line was originally chartered in 1832.

The coaches that make the nine-mile run have been restored to their appearance in the late 1800s. Inlaid wood paneling and plush seats evoke the early days when travel by rail really was something special. Potbelly coal stoves in each car keep the passengers warm for night travel.

Travelers on the Strasburg Rail Road today still have their tickets punched by the conductor, who gives a brief talk on the early days of railroad travel. Strasburg also has a special car once owned by a railroad president which reveals the luxury in which business tycoons traveled in the 19th century.

The state-owned Railroad Museum of Pennsylvania is located directly across from Strasburg Rail Road and will further expand an appreciation for the early days on the iron road.

During the summer months Strasburg runs daily; it runs weekends the rest of the year with the exception of mid-December to mid-January, when it is closed. There is a charge to ride the trains.

Directions: Take Beltway Exit 27 (I-95) to the Baltimore Beltway. Go northwest towards Towson. Take Exit 24 (I-83) north around York. From there take Route 30 east through Lancaster to Route 896, go right and follow this to Lancaster. At the town square in Strasburg turn left and follow Route 741 to the railroad.

The Cumberland Road

No discussion of transportation in the early days of the Republic would be complete that did not include the Cumberland Road, or National Pike. This American Appian Way linked Cumberland, Maryland with Wheeling, West Virginia. It eventually extended as far as Illinois and was the main land route connecting the eastern seaboard with the west.

The Cumberland Road was built by the federal government between 1808 and 1829. Like the Chesapeake & Ohio Canal, this was a project that George Washington, a former surveyor, first proposed. Jefferson also was interested in this effort to expand the country's boundaries and make the interior more accessible. Once built, it was heavily used with Conestoga wagons and stagecoaches traveling over it until 1850. After that the railroad, having made the canal route obsolete, also diverted much of the traffic from the Cumberland Road.

Built as it was through the Allegheny Mountains, there was no problem obtaining stone for its construction, and in places the road was as wide as 80 feet. Large boulders were covered by smaller stones, which much later were macadamized and still later re-done in concrete. A keen-eyed passenger traveling along the National Pike will see many old buildings constructed of stone that was quarried when the road was dug out of the mountain.

The Cumberland Road is now part of U.S. Route 40. One of the interesting features still remaining from the old road are the great stone bridges spanning the mountain streams. The largest one still standing, erected in 1813, crosses the Castleman River in western Maryland.

Just west of Washington, Pennsylvania there is another interesting bridge. This one was built in 1818 in the noteworthy "S" shape. Engineers found it more economical and easier to build their bridges at an angle to the flow of the stream, so they snaked across in an "S" pattern.

Bridges are not the only interesting reminders of the early days along the Cumberland Road. Even more closely associated with the first years of the National Pike are the toll houses. Only three remain, of which the most striking architecturally is the one just over the Maryland state line in Addison, Pennsylvania. Built of stone, this hexagonal building looks more like a tea house than a toll house.

Industries

Within a year of the settlement of Jamestown in 1607 two profitable enterprises had begun: tobacco was being planted and a small glass factory was in operation. These early beginnings of American business were only two of the endeavors attempted by the settlers.

The middle-Atlantic area later prospered both in peacetime and wartime because of the iron industry and the manufacturing of machinery. The factory system began slowly prior to the War of 1812 but that conflict accelerated the process. With the English blockade and the federal government restrictions on trade, domestic manufacturing was essential. The iron industry also was vital to the production of weapons to fight the war and later to capitalize on the new status of the United States.

Advances in transportation—roads, canals & railroads—provided new markets for goods. Concurrent advances in industrial productivity demanded even more expansion so that new materials and manufactured goods moved back and forth smoothly from the western markets to the eastern manufacturing regions.

Larger businesses brought another change. Formerly the master craftsman had worked beside his apprentices. Now, with industrialization, the owner no longer stood side by side with the factory worker. A great chasm developed between the life of one and the other.

In the south, industrialization locked the planters into the slave system. Eli Whitney's cotton gin made slavery profitable because it could clean 50 pounds if operated by hand or 1,000 pounds using water power, whereas before that a laborer could only clean about one pound a day. Thus cotton plantations expanded and the economy of the south rested on "King Cotton."

By 1820 it was clear that the three sections of the country were developing differently. Agriculture was big business in the south, the independent farmer had staked a claim in the northwest and manufacturing prospered in the north. The regional interests were so vastly different that by 1830 citizens were loyal to the section in which they had a vested economic interest. This division of interest, this sectionalism, would sorely test the new nation.

145. Colvin Run Mill

Down By The Old Mill Stream is more than a nice old song in this area; it's a great destination. Colvin Run Mill was once the commercial center for a variety of neighborhood services. These 19th-century activities are recreated at the mill today.

The mill itself was built between 1794 and 1810, following the designs of Oliver Evans, who substituted waterpower for manpower in all but the first step, that of weighing the grain. George Washington also used this system for the mill on his Mount Vernon estate (see Colonial Period: Colonial Business).

Each floor of the mill serves a function in the milling process. The grain moves by elevators, chutes and sifters through the various steps. This smooth-running operation was particularly important for the larger merchant mills like Colvin Run.

At the mill the local farm community was served with a weekly "milling day" and grain and flour was also bought and sold. Colvin Run Mill produced large amounts of flour for foreign markets such as Europe, Canada and the West Indies.

Colvin Run Mill operates as it did in the late 18th and 19th centuries, solely by waterpower. The water is diverted into a lagoon and millrace, then flows over the waterwheel to provide the power for the milling process.

The mill is only one of the restored buildings at Colvin Run. An old General Store that operated years ago near the mill has been restored and re-opened. Here visitors can buy flour and corn meal ground at the mill. The 19th-century ambience of the store is carefully maintained.

Also restored is the Miller's House built in 1820 on a shaded hill overlooking the mill. Today the house serves as a museum for local artists and craftsmen. During the weekends in the spring, summer and fall there are a variety of craft programs at the mill. Perennial favorites include the Sheep to Shawl Weekend, Flapjack Day, All Hallows Eve and woodcarving lessons.

Colvin Run Mill is open Wednesday through Sunday 11:00 to 4:00, from March 15 to December 31. Tours are offered every half hour. Group tours are available. Admission is charged to the mill only.

Directions: Take Beltway Exit 10 (Route 7) for five miles to Colvin Run Mill in Virginia on the right.

146. Hopewell Village

Though countless movies have brought to life the antebellum plantations of the south, the iron plantations in the mid-Atlantic states have been ignored. They, too, were a paternalistic society with the ironmaster living in the Big House directing furnace operations.

Just as cotton dominated most southern plantations, iron ruled those of the north. Night and day the fire burned, the waterwheel that provided air blasts to the furnace creaked and turned and the roar of the blast could be heard by all in the village.

Hopewell Furnace at Hopewell Village was built along the banks of French Creek in 1771 by Mark Bird and operated until 1883. Today visitors see the village as it was in the years 1820 and 1840. One of the 17 stops along the Walking Tour is the Big House.

Furnished in the style of the 19th century and once the home of resident ironmasters, the Big House provides a good picture of the upper strata of village life. The ironmasters who lived in the Big House were industrial leaders of the area. Two brothers-in-law of Hopewell's founder were fellow ironmasters and signers of the Declaration of Independence—James Wilson and George Ross.

One of the main areas of interest at Hopewell is the furnace's "cast house" where the molten iron was cast into stoves, sashweights and many other products. Here also is the waterwheel that operated the huge blast furnace, the bridgehouse that dumped the iron into the furnace and the tuyere arch through which visitors can observe how the air blast entered the furnace.

The Visitor Center provides a detailed, easy to understand explanation of how the iron furnace works so that the various phases of the operation are more comprehensible. Throughout the Walking Tour taped messages provide information on each step of the process.

In addition to the restoration of the old iron furnace, visitors can see what life was like for the ironworkers who once labored at this furnace. Several company-owned tenant houses still survive and two are furnished to show the living conditions of the average worker. Some black workers were employed at Hopewell and neither the living quarters nor the school was segregated. Evidence suggests that one of Hopewell's ironmasters was interested in the cause of abolition. Some of the blacks may have been runaways, but those who were stayed only briefly in this village so near the southern border.

The village store was a nerve center of the community. Owned by the company, it supplied most of the needs of the workers at reasonable prices. Furnace employees received credit for their work and could then charge supplies at the store. The men labored in 12-hour shifts with no holidays and were paid only when they worked. Only the ironmaster and his family were likely to travel to Philadelphia or New York.

During July and August costumed interpreters demonstrate and explain the life and work of the early 19th century. The village is open daily year round except December 23 and January 1.

Directions: Take Beltway Exit 27 (I-95) to the Wilmington exit on Route 202 north; bear left on Route 100 to Route 23. Turn right (west) on Route 23 for approximately six miles to Route 345. Then turn right (north) on Route 345 for four miles. Hopewell Village is on the left.

147. Waterloo Village

Some places offer more than just historical interest; they provide a retrospective of a long series of historical epochs. Waterloo Village is such a place.

In precolonial days, this area was the ancient meeting place of the Munsee Indians. The ground was sacred to the Indians as it was used for tribal burials. Once it had been surveyed in 1743, disregarding Indian sensitivies, homesteaders, miners and those interested in the abundant timber began moving into the region.

The next phase of development coincided with the discovery of iron. By 1763 there was a forge, a gristmill and a sawmill. Spacious homes for the ironmaster and forgeman were also built here. The Andover Forge, as it was called, supplied armaments to the Continental Army. This old site is carefully marked for visitors exploring Waterloo Village.

The excessive amounts of iron needed for the Revolutionary cause resulted in deforestation as the wood was needed to fuel the forge. Consequently, the forge was abandoned and the land farmed. In 1812 Brigadier General John Smith bought the 282-acre forge for $13.37 per acre. He revived the ironworks, naming it Waterloo Foundary. There are five houses in Waterloo Village built by the Smith family. Three are currently open to the public and provide a glimpse of changing financial status as well as architectural styles as the village prospered and grew.

The principal cause of prosperity in this region was the Morris Canal, built in 1831. Waterloo was a lock and plane stop on the canal, planes being the inclined segments between locks. By 1844 Waterloo Village had emerged as a bustling inland port with forge, gristmill, sawmill, tavern, general store and various residences.

The blacksmith shop run by General Smith in the 1790s, the broom and cabinet shop, the General Store built in 1831 and the gristmill have been restored.

A number of the restorations are associated with the Morris Canal, such as the Canal House used by the lock tender, the canal lock that lifted the boats over the mill tailrace and into the lock pond and the Canal Museum.

Additional orientation for a leisurely stroll through Waterloo Village can be obtained at the Visitor Center. A slide presentation and maps of the village are provided. On summer weekends special arts, craft and musical events take place at Waterloo Village.

Waterloo Village is open from mid-April to the beginning of January, Tuesday through Sunday. It's closed on major holidays. The village is open on holiday Mondays and closed the next day. Hour are 10:00 to 6:00, with no admission tickets being sold after 3:00.

Directions: Take Beltway Exit 27 (I-95) north past Philadelphia, then continue on U.S. 1 to Route 287. Follow Route 287 to Route 206. Continue north to Stanhope, New Jersey and Waterloo Road, which leads to this historic village.

148. Wheaton Village

Wheaton Village is a sparkling recreation of a Victorian American glassmaking town.

To gain an appreciation of the art involved, the visitor's first stop should be the Museum of American Glass which houses the world's largest collection of glass made in this country. Displayed in period rooms is a wide array of glass objects including everything from missile nose cones to mason jars. The display starts with the early utilitarian phase of glass blowing when bottles were needed for medicinal and culinary purpose. Most of these tended to be the aqua color produced naturally from the iron in the unprocessed sand.

By about the middle of the 19th century, ornamental glass was being produced and the decorative items turned out have rarely been equaled for beauty. One room of the museum is the country kitchen of 1888-1920. Here visitors see glass products in the context in which they were used. Another room specializes in paperweights; the beauty and variety is amazing.

After exploring the museum, one really appreciates the 1888 Glass Factory. Here artisans use the old techniques to produce paperweights, bottles, pitchers and vases sold at the Paperweight and West Jersey Craft Shop. There is an entire arcade of crafts that demonstrate the old-fashioned arts.

Two attractions guaranteed to interest younger visitors are the Village Railroad and the Pharmacy. A steam train modeled after the 1863 C. P. Huntington of the Southern Pacific Railroad provides a look at other areas such as the Agricultural Museum known as "Farming the Garden State" and the Village Green. For a pick-me-up try the fresh dipped ice cream in season at the Pharmacy.

Twice a day during the afternoon there's a "patent medicine" show on the Village Green. Typical of the shows popular in small town America in the late 1880s and early 1890s, it combines music, vaudeville and old-fashioned con artistry. It evokes the Victorian era from the high-wheeled bike to the corny performance.

Wheaton Village is open year round from 10:00 to 5:00 except on major holidays. During January, February and March hours are somewhat curtailed. Admission is charged.

Directions: Take Beltway Exit 27 (I-95) to the Delaware Memorial Bridge. From there take Route 40 to Route 47. Go south on Route 47, then take Route 55 to Millville, New Jersey. Wheaton Village is on Glasstown Street in Millville.

149. Hagley Museum & Eleutherian Mills

The French and Irish workers were nervous as they began employment in 1802 at the Du Pont company's black powderworks that made military, sporting and blasting powder. The explosive nature of the powder made many cautious and reluctant to live and work in what they considered a dangerous environment.

Following the French tradition of sharing the dangers with the workers—and also hoping to convince them that mishaps were unlikely—E.I. du Pont built his home overlooking the powderworks. His gracious, wisteria-covered Eleutherian Mills was built in Georgian style on a hill above the Brandywine River. Unfortunately his objectives were undermined when explosions severely damaged his home on several occasions. After a particularly bad blast in 1890 the house suffered too much damage to be rebuilt and the family moved. The house has been restored and is now part of the Hagley Museum. It reflects five generations of this industrial family. Adjoining the house is a 19th-century garden. The first Du Pont Company office, built in 1837, is also open.

There's a great deal more to see, and an open-air jitney takes visitors to various spots along a three-mile route in the 200-acre complex. The main exhibit building is a former cotton spinning mill built in 1814. It contains models and dioramas of flour, paper, iron and textile mills. One of the most exciting models is a cutaway of the Oliver Evans gristmill. (See Colonial Period: Colonial Business—George Washington's

Gristmill Historical State Park and Era Between the Wars: Industries—Colvin Run Mill.) A section from an 18th-century gristmill formerly located elsewhere in Delaware is part of the exhibit. A "talking map" tells the story of industrial growth of the Brandywine Valley.

Another industrial building from the 19th century is the machine shop. Working models demonstrate the making of black powder, the world's only known explosive when the Du Pont works opened in 1803.

Nearby is Birkenhead Mill, with a full-size reconstructed waterwheel built between 1822 and 1824. On Blacksmith Hill, close to the powder yards, a worker's home, carriage house and 1817 Sunday school are also open.

This park-like area is fun to explore on foot or by jitney. The Hagley Museum and Eleutherian Mills is open year round, Tuesday through Saturday from 9:30 to 4:30 and on Sunday from 1:00 to 5:00. It is closed Thanksgiving, Christmas and New Year's Day. Admission is charged.

Directions: Take Beltway Exit 27 (I-95) to Wilmington. Take Route 52N exit and go north to Route 100. Follow Route 100 to Route 141 and make a right. Stay in the left lane on Route 141 because the Hagley Museum is on the left after only a few hundred feet.

150. Mercer Museum

The personal history of the people of the United States is captured in this collection of 40,000 objects that were a part of the daily life of citizens from 1700 to 1860.

Henry Chapman Mercer began the collection in 1897. To house his painstakingly collected artifacts Mercer built a six-story castle-like structure of reinforced concrete. This was the first use of reinforced concrete in construction.

Mercer called his collection the "Tools of the Nation Maker." The assortment is somewhat of a jumble but is roughly divided into areas. "Home Sweet Home" lets us see the minutia of bygone eras containing things as mundane as salt boxes, kitchen tools and utensils for making butter or cheese as well as 20 different kinds of apple peelers. Old looms vie for room with their products—quilts and samplers. Even bathtubs are part of this exhibit.

In the "Tradesmen" gallery there is a well-stocked country store. This section also includes tools used by blacksmiths, cobblers and hatters as well as almost every craft of early America. There is an entire section reflecting early community involvement with exhibits of

18th-century fire fighting equipment, old medical tools, a print shop and even artifacts from the criminal justice system in the 1800s—a prisoner's dock, gallows and hearse.

A lighter note is evoked in "A Child's World," where both work and play are represented, from a school room to early toys. Candy making and music making apparently interested the young of earlier generations as much as modern youngsters, as several examples of these pastimes are represented.

Major emphasis is placed on "Transportation." One of the biggest items in the collection is an old Conestoga wagon. There are also stage coaches, whale boats, sleighs and the tools needed to make these early conveyances.

The building trade requires another section in itself. There is a sawmill and lumbering tools. The mining industry is represented, as is iron casting, cooping and carpentry. All the tools needed to tame the wilderness and to build the towns of our forefathers have been collected in the Mercer Museum.

Henry Ford once said, "This is the only museum I've been sufficiently interested in to visit." There is enough variety here to interest all.

Located near the Mercer Museum are two other Mercer buildings, again of concrete. The Moravian Pottery and Tile Works which Mercer started in 1910 still makes ceramic tile using the method he developed in 1898.

The other building on the grounds is Fonthill, the castle Mercer built as his home. He lived at Fonthill from 1910 until his death in 1930. It is a remarkable structure, well stocked with items he collected from around the world.

All the Mercer buildings are open March through December and closed January and February. Hours are Monday through Saturday from 10:00 to 4:30, Sundays from 1:00 to 4:30. Admission is charged for each.

Directions: Take Beltway Exit 27 (I-95) to the Wilmington, Delaware area, then take Route 202 to Doylestown, Pennsylvania. In Doylestown, turn right before the church at Pine Street and go 1½ blocks to the Mercer Museum on the right.

151. Duvall Tool Collection

Dr. Hugh Mercer of Pennsylvania was not the only one in this area to become fascinated with the tools of early America. When you talk about old "tools of the trade," you must also mention the Duvall Collection at Patuxent River Park near Upper Marlboro, Maryland. William H. Duvall, a local collector, amassed more than 1,200 antique tools and farm implements suggesting a variety of 19th-century trades.

Through the living history approach, visitors will learn how some of these early tools were used. For instance, they can watch timber being chopped by a broad ax and then smoothed with an adze. Though more primitive than modern tools, the work turned out by these antique implements has in many cases survived for more than 200 years. Here visitors can learn how old-fashioned barrel makers, or coopers, could make a watertight container without using a ruler or relying on nails.

Tools of a wide variety of trades are part of the Duvall Collection. One of particular interest is the complete dentistry outfit of the "horse and buggy" era.

This collection is only one aspect of the park's historical interpretive area. The role of the Patuxent River in the development of Prince George's County during the past 300 years is highlighted at Patuxent Village. A primitive log cabin provides a glimpse of life along the river. The tools used to build these structures are demonstrated by park personnel.

Also in the village is a smokehouse, hunting and trapping shed and the Jug Bay Packing House. At the packing house various aspects of the tobacco industry are explained and demonstrated. Visitors are shown how tobacco was stripped and "prized" for shipping. Ocean-going vessels once docked at Jug Bay to obtain tobacco for Europe.

There are many special nature programs sponsored by Patuxent River Park. Hikes, marsh ecology boat tours and canoe rentals are all part of the fun and enable visitors to enjoy the abundant wildlife in the park. Bird watchers may be especially interested since the Patuxent River Park offers some of the most outstanding birding in the entire Chesapeake Bay.

Visitors to the park need either a permit or advance reservations. Groups are welcome. Permits are available on a one day basis or annually. To obtain additional information call (301) 627-6074 or write Patuxent River Park, Rural Route Box 3380, Upper Marlboro, MD 20772.

Directions: Take Beltway Exit 11 (Route 4) to Route 301 south. At Croom Road, Route 382, turn left. Take Croom Road for 3.1 miles to Croom Airport Road and follow that to the Patuxent River Park sign. Turn left at the park entrance road and follow 1.8 miles.

Shot Tower was built in 1828 with 1,100,000 handmade bricks. It turned out 100,00 bags of shot each year until it closed in 1892.

152. Shot Tower

The interior of Shot Tower is unprepossessing, and no guides are on hand to orient interested visitors; but a button, rather like in Alice in Wonderland, invites the curious to "push me." The lights go out, a ghost speaks and hot lead seems to fall from the tower above. It's the three-screen audio-visual presentation describing Shot Tower and the early process of making musket balls.

Charles Carroll, whose house is only a block away, laid the cornerstone of Shot Tower in 1828. It was built with 1,100,000 handmade bricks, rising 246 feet with no exterior scaffolding. The foundations alone were 10 feet deep. At the bottom the tower walls are four feet six inches thick, tapering up to 20 inches at the top.

At that time there were two techniques used to make musket balls, either the buck or drop. Buck shots were made by molding, or compression. The drop method, which was used at Shot Tower, let the hot lead fall from dropping stations at various heights in the tower. The further the lead dropped the larger the ball. The lead formed

227

cylindrical shapes in its free fall and then passed through a perforated iron ladle. The balls were then placed in a cistern of water, next a dryer and finally a polishing cask.

At Shot Tower 100,000 bags of shot were turned out each year at $.06 a pound until 1892, when the tower was closed down.

Shot Tower is open daily, at no charge, from 10:00 to 4:00.

Directions: Take Beltway Exit 22 (The Baltimore-Washington Parkway) then take a right at Pratt Street. Just past the Inner Harbor go left on Gay Street to Fayette. Shot Tower will be on the right on the corner of Fallsway and Fayette Street.

153. Carroll County Farm Museum

Though not an industry, farming was an important business in the late 1800s. At Carroll County Farm, built in 1852, this life-style is recaptured.

The self-sustaining, independent farmer had been the country's bedrock since its earliest days. This Carroll County farm shows the improvements the farmers enjoyed in the 100 years since the days on The National Colonial Farm (see Colonial Period: Colonial Agriculture).

Equipment had improved both for the farmer and for his busy farm wife. Some of the improvements, like the availability of glass jars for preserving, helped provide greater variety on the table but also, unfortunately, meant more time in the kitchen.

Six rooms of the old farm house have been restored. Though life on the farm was simple, it was more comfortable than in the early days. Floors and windows kept the family better protected from the elements, thus increasing life expectancy.

There are 140 acres on this working farm. A nature trail winds through the farmland and by the lake. There is a springhouse, smokehouse, blacksmith shop, sheds and barns as well as the farm animals.

The Carroll County Farm Museum is open weekends and holidays 12:00 to 5:00 from late April to the end of October. During July and August the farm is also open Tuesday through Friday 10:00 to 4:00. A nominal admission is charged.

Directions: Take Beltway Exit 33 (Route 185) to Route 97 north. Continue to Westminster; the farm is off Route 140 to the left, on Center Street in Westminster.

Civil War Period

Homes

The houses of the Civil War period are important because of what happened either in the house or on the grounds. Houses of earlier eras gained prominence and were restored because of the famous personalities associated with them, so they served as the backdrop to personalities rather than events.

Homes which have been restored from the Civil War period are of historic interest because of the battles that occurred in their front yards, like Belle Grove or because they served as a field hospital, like Chatham. Others are noted as the backdrops of conspiracy, as is the case with the Mary Surratt House and the Petersen House.

These homes became part of the events that took place in and around them. For instance, the Clara Barton House served not only as a home but also as headquarters and office for the American Red Cross.

This utilitarian emphasis is reflected in the architecture and furnishings of the homes of the Civil War period.

154. Boyhood Home of Robert E. Lee

By paying close attention it is possible to sort out the details of the connection between the marriage of George Washington Parke Custis and Mary Fitzhugh with the marriage 27 years later of their daughter and Robert E. Lee, who also happened to spend his boyhood in this house.

In 1804, when Martha Washington's grandson married Mary Fitzhugh, the Fitzhughs owned the house. But shortly after that it was rented to "Lighthorse" Harry Lee, who moved to Alexandria before the War of 1812 with his wife and their five children. The upstairs bedroom, with its view of the Potomac River which their son Robert

229

enjoyed for more than 10 years, has been carefully restored to evoke his presence.

He would later complete the circle by marrying Mary Anna Randolph Custis, daughter of George Washington Parke Custis and Mary Fitzhugh, at the Custis' home, Arlington House.

A second room is associated with an earlier military hero—General Lafayette. In 1824, when he returned to America to celebrate his Revolutionary War triumphs, he visited with the widow of his old comrade, "Lighthorse" Harry Lee, who had died in 1818. The guest room is called the Lafayette Room in honor of the French General.

The house had actually been built in 1795 by yet another American Revolutionary War hero, John Potts, who sold it in 1797 to the Fitzhughs. This house has stood on this shady Alexandria street for more than two centuries and the charm of that by-gone period is evident in its design, furnishings and garden.

As in so many of these historic homes, it is the small items which strike visitors as unusual. Some different items to watch for here are the miniature doll bed with canopy once used by cabinetmakers as a sample of their work, the military chess set and the Beau Brummel gentlemen's traveling wash stand. Often these reminders of the everyday facets of earlier times bring them most strongly alive.

The Boyhood Home of Robert E. Lee is at 607 Oronoco Street, across from the Lee-Fendall House in Alexandria. It is open Monday through Saturday 10:00 to 4:00 and Sunday from 12:00 to 4:00 with the exception of mid-December to the end of January. Admission is charged.

Directions: Take Beltway Exit 1 north (U.S. 1) into Alexandria. Turn right on Oronoco Street.

155. Booker T. Washington National Monument

A home that strikes at the very root of the Civil War is the Burroughs Plantation on which Booker T. Washington spent the first nine years of his life—in slavery. The young boy, five years of age when the Civil War began, was born on April 5, 1856 to the Burrough's family cook, Jane Ferguson. Even at his young age he experienced the hard life of a slave. He chores included feeding the animals, toting water and sweeping the yard at the "Big House."

This certainly wasn't a lavish colonnaded manor house, but rather a five-room log house where 12 members of the Burroughs family lived.

Though the house no longer stands, its location is marked on the Plantation Trail at the Booker T. Washington National Monument. Taped messages provide some insights as to what it would have been like to live on a small 19th-century tobacco farm.

Further along the trail is the Kitchen Cabin, which has been reconstructed to evoke the actual cabin that was once situated on the Birthplace Site. Since Jane Ferguson was the cook, she and her three children lived in this cabin. At night they slept on the dirt floor covered by a few rags.

Life on a farm this size was hard. Even the Burroughs worked out in the tobacco fields beside the slaves. Although Lincoln issued the Emancipation Proclamation effective January 1, 1863, Booker and his family were not freed until April 1865 at the end of the Civil War. Having no last name, he picked "Washington."

His life was not substantially improved as a free black. He moved with his family to Malden, West Virginia and worked in a salt mine. The one overwhelming difference was that he could now learn to read and write, something that had been forbidden him as a slave.

Incredible determination enabled him to educate himself, then travel to the Hampton Institute in Virginia. Only 16 when he arrived, he graduated three years later. His efforts so impressed General Samuel Armstrong, founder and Principal of Hampton Institute, that he recommended Washington to head a new school for blacks in Tuskegee, Alabama.

Booker T. Washington's outstanding accomplishments as a black educator brought him national prominence. His advice was sought by Presidents—McKinley, Theodore Roosevelt and Taft all appreciated the accommodating stance Washington had adopted in his "Atlanta Compromise." This address stressed the need for interracial harmony at the expense of immediate social equality.

The first chapter of Washington's well known autobiography, *Up From Slavery*, returns in print to the same roots visitors can observe when they visit the Booker T. Washington National Monument. It is again a working farm as it was when he was born. The hogs and chickens and the tobacco in the fields all reflect the atmosphere of his early days as a slave.

Perhaps the story of the nine-year-old boy who traveled so far from his slave origin tells a lot about what some men died for in the Civil War. Visitors can judge for themselves as they walk this southern soil.

The Booker T. Washington National Monument Visitor Center is open daily at no charge from 8:30 to 5:00 except Thanksgiving, Christmas and New Year's Day. A film on the life of Booker T. Washington, exhibits and maps of the Plantation Trail around the historic area and the one-and-a-half mile Jack-O-Lantern Branch Nature Trail are available at the Visitor Center. Living History demonstrations with costumed personnel bring to life farm activities of the 19th century from mid-June to Labor Day.

Directions: From the Beltway take Exit 8 (Route 29) south to Lynchburg. From Lynchburg take Route 460 west to Bedford, then pick up Route 122 to the Booker T. Washington National Monument.

156. Barbara Fritchie House and Museum

Throughout all of our country's conflicts there have been individual moments of courage and valor, but they have often been relegated to footnotes or a fleeting reference amidst the telling of the larger battle or event. Fortunately one such moment was immortalized by John Greenleaf Whittier and the heroine has lived on, recognized for her patriotism and spirit. In this excerpt from Whittier's poem *Barbara Fritchie* the moment of confrontation between North and South is captured:

Up rose old Barbara Fritchie then,
Bowed with her fourscore years and ten,

Bravest of all in Frederick town,
She took up the flag the men hauled down;

In her attic-window the staff she set,
To show that one heart was loyal yet.

Up the street came the rebel tread,
Stonewall Jackson riding ahead.

Under his slouched hat left and right
He glanced; the old flag met his sight.

"Halt!" — the dust-brown ranks stood fast,
"Fire!" — out blazed the rifle-blast.

It shivered the window, pane and sash;
It rent the banner with seam and gash.

Quick, as it fell, from the broken staff
Dame Barbara snatched the silken scarf;

She leaned far out on the window-sill,
And shook it forth with a royal will.

"Shoot, if you must, this old gray head,
But spare your country's flag." she said.

A shade of sadness, a blush of shame
Over the face of the leader came;

The nobler nature within him stirred
To life at that woman's deed and word;

"Who touches a hair on yon gray head
Dies like a dog! March on!" he said.

Residents of Frederick still talk of the time Winston Churchill, cigar in hand, stood in the Barbara Fritchie House and recited with great animation the entire poem. Many others have come to pay tribute to this gallant, gray-haired legend. Barbara Fritchie was a genuine character. She married for the first time at 40. Her husband was 14 years her junior, a young 26-year-old glove maker named John Caspar Fritchie. Despite the disparity in ages she outlived him by 30 years.

Their home has been reconstructed and is furnished with period pieces from the Civil War era. Many of the items belonged to Barbara Fritchie, including the bed in which she died and one of her own quilts.

The Barbara Fritchie House is open weekdays, except Tuesday and Saturday from 9:00 to 5:00 and Sunday from 1:00 to 5:00. It is closed for the season from December through March. Admission is charged.

Directions: Take Beltway Exit 35 (I-270) to Frederick. The Barbara Fritchie House is at 154 West Patrick Street.

157. Belle Grove

At five o'clock in the morning on October 19, 1864, the Confederate General Jubal Early led a surprise attack on the Union soldiers sleeping on the grounds of Belle Grove Plantation. Belle Grove was General Philip Sheridan's Union headquarters, though at the time he was in Washington conferring with Secretary of War Stanton. Fighting had been going on in the Shenandoah Valley throughout the fall, but despite superior strength, the Union forces couldn't score a decisive victory.

General Early hoped to reverse the odds by tactical surprise. His plan almost worked. By mid-day the Confederate troops were celebrating the rout of the sleepy Union force. But their optimism was premature; Sheridan, hearing the distant firing as he returned via Winchester, galloped back to the front and led the regalvanized Union men to victory in what came to be known as the Battle of Cedar Creek. More than 6,000 men lost their lives in the see-saw battle fought that day.

Belle Grove was built in 1794 by Isaac Hite, who had married James Madison's sister, Nelly. Madison referred Hite to his good friend, Thomas Jefferson, for help in designing Hite's Shenandoah Valley estate. When James Madison married Dolly Payne, they honeymooned at Belle Grove.

This lovely Virginia home, more Federal than German though it was built by the grandson of the Valley's first German settler, has been completely restored and is a property of the National Trust for Historic Preservation. Belle Grove is a working farm, and a highlight of its year-round schedule is Farm Crafts Day celebrated the third weekend of July each year. The manor house is open April through October from 10:00 to 4:00 Monday through Saturday and Sunday from 1:00 to 5:00. Admission is charged.

Directions: Take Beltway Exit 9 (I-66) to I-81. Go north on I-81 two miles to the Middletown Exit. Belle Grove is one mile south of Winchester off U.S. 11, just past Middleton, Virginia.

158. Chatham

The advantageous location of this gracious Virginia mansion overlooking the Rappahannock River proved to be its downfall during the Civil War years. The river was the northern frontier of the Confederates during some phases of the war from 1862 to 1864, and Chatham's central position between Richmond and Washington made it ideal as Federal headquarters. In fact, during the two major battles in the Fredericksburg area the grounds served as an artillery position and the house as a field hospital. Both Clara Barton and Walt Whitman nursed the wounded in this hastily converted Southern home.

Chatham, which had been built by William Fitzhugh in 1771 and had been the focal spot for entertaining many of the leading figures in colonial Virginia, was restored after the Civil War. It is the only existing home where both Washington and Lincoln were entertained. Beautiful gardens were added to the estate early in the 20th century.

Today Chatham is part of the Fredericksburg Battlefield Tour (see Battlefield Sites). Five rooms of the mansion are open, and three have exhibits that enlarge on Chatham's colorful history. The grounds are also worth exploring; there is a Rappahannock overlook that shows where the Northern engineers built a pontoon bridge during the Battle of Fredericksburg.

Chatham is run by the National Park Service and is open 9:00 to 5:00 daily. There is no admission charged.

Directions: Take Beltway Exit 4 (I-95) south to Fredericksburg. Follow Visitor's signs to Battlefield Visitor Center. Chatham is two miles further on the tour route, off Route 218.

159. Clara Barton House

At age 40 Clara Barton, one of the very few women permitted behind the lines by the Union army, tended the wounded on the bloody battlefield of Antietam. She operated from the front lines and was often under fire. Once, while holding a wounded soldier in her arms, a bullet pierced her sleeve and killed the young boy. Clara Barton became known as the "Angel of the Battlefield" for her gallant determination to go where needed to relieve the suffering of the wounded.

She was also quick to spot necessary reforms. Observing that in army convoys the ambulance wagons with medical supplies were preceded by the ammunition and the food and clothing wagons, she made sure her wagons, filled with bandages, stimulants and food, arrived early. After only a short time at the front she realized that the shortage of lanterns prevented the surgeons from continuing to treat the critically wounded into the night. Her wagons were stocked with lanterns from that time on and lives were saved.

Clara Barton's reforms were not limited to the battlefield. Another cause she espoused was to locate the missing and identify the unmarked graves of the many fallen soldiers of the Civil War. The war dead totaled 359,528; of these only 172,400 were identified. Before Clara Barton received authorization from President Lincoln and began her work, there were 143,155 unmarked graves. She was able to locate and identify 22,000 in four years of grueling work. She also was instrumental in having the infamous Andersonville prison, where 14,000 Union soldiers were marked only by number, declared a National Cemetery. She helped identify the nine acres of numbered graves and was on hand to first raise the American flag over this former charnel house.

Shortly after publishing the list of Andersonville dead, Clara Barton suffered an emotional breakdown and went to Europe at age 48 to recover. It was in Europe that she discovered the great cause of her life. She became aware of Jean Henri Dunant and the International Red Cross. It was a matter of great concern to her that because of the U.S. fear of entangling alliances her country was not a signatory to the Geneva Convention supporting this relief organization.

During her European "convalescence" Clara Barton again became involved in front line duty, this time in the Franco-Prussian War of 1870. Afterwards she returned to America exhausted and depressed

235

The Clara Barton House in Maryland was home to a woman who devoted her entire life to public service.

but determined to establish an American Red Cross. It would take almost 10 years of frustration, rebuffs and heartbreaking setbacks before she first established the society from her own home at Dansville, New York, in August of 1881. Early relief work by the New York group aiding fire victims brought eventual success, and on March 1, 1882, President Chester Arthur signed the treaty allying the United States with the Geneva Convention.

When the Red Cross aided the victims of the Johnstown flood in 1889, they erected a hotel for the homeless. At the conclusion of the relief effort Clara Barton had the lumber shipped to Washington via railroad and then brought by wagon to Glen Echo, Maryland, where she erected a similar structure to serve as a warehouse for Red Cross supplies. The house had 72 concealed closets, some deep enough to store large wheelchairs.

In 1897 she moved into this Glen Echo house, making it her home. The house was expanded to 36 rooms, providing bedrooms on the third and fourth floor for her belongings and those of numerous visitors. The house has an intriguing architectural design. Looking up from the main hallway, two balconied floors rise above with a sitting room in the center at the top overlooking the floors below and "hung" from the sides with no visible means of support. It is an excellent example of Victorian eccentricity.

After the American Red Cross efforts in the Spanish-American War, it was felt Clara Barton was too old at 83 to manage such a large organization. She was forced to resign in 1904. There was even talk of a Congressional investigation of her financial records but the efforts to initiate it were dropped when she resigned. She was extremely bitter at this repudiation. But even this did not stop her. She went on to establish the National First Aid Society.

Clara Barton died at her home in Glen Echo on April 12, 1912. She was an incredible woman; her entire life, spanning some 90 years, was devoted to public service.

The Clara Barton National Historic Site is open at no charge daily from 10:00 to 5:00. There is a 20-minute movie that sheds further light on her many activities.

Directions: Take Beltway Exit 40 (the Cabin John Parkway) to Glen Echo. Exit at the MacArthur Avenue exit and turn left on MacArthur Avenue. Proceed to sign on right for the Clara Barton House.

160. Ford's Theatre National Historic Site

The light comedy *Our American Cousin* was playing to a full house on April 14, 1865. In the balcony was a young actor who knew every line of the play. He had planned his own scene well, waiting for a slow spot when only one actor was on the stage and the audience was laughing. At that moment, John Wilkes Booth entered the unguarded President's Box from the Dress Circle and shot Abraham Lincoln. He struggled with Major Henry Rathbone, who was also in the box, then leapt to the stage, injuring his leg, but making good his escape.

Shock and horror paralyzed the audience. Doctors in the theater rushed to the President's Box and carried Lincoln next door to Petersen House, where he died the next morning.

Public outrage forced Ford's Theatre to close and the Federal government acquired the building. For a time it housed the files of Union soldiers and the Army Medical Museum. On June 9, 1893, a second tragic incident occurred here—the third floor collapsed, killing or injuring a number of Federal workers.

In the 1930s the Oldroyd Collection of 3,000 items associated with

Lincoln was moved into this old theater. It wasn't until 1968, however, that Ford's Theatre was restored to its 1865 appearance and reopened. Visitors will see the presidential box as it was on that fateful night. The rocker used by Lincoln and his wife's straight back chair are reproductions of the originals. But the red sofa and framed engraving of George Washington that decorated the front of the box are original. This historic box is never occupied.

Downstairs in the theater basement is the Lincoln Museum, which uses the Oldroyd Collection as its basis. One area is devoted to Lincoln's early years. Farm tools from the period in which he worked the Illinois soil, his old surveying equipment and some of his books plus a long wooden bench on which he often rested are part of this section.

Next Lincoln's public career is spotlighted in an exhibit including the desk and chair from his Springfield home, as well as some of his law books. Early campaign literature from Lincoln's political contests is also included.

Items from the presidential years are the focus of the third area. Some White House furniture and china are on display, as are copies of letters Lincoln wrote and a shawl he draped over his shoulders on his frequent walks from the White House to the War Department.

Finally there are reminders of the assassination. Clothes worn that night by both Lincoln and Booth are on display. Flags and pictures from the funeral can be seen and, finally, the single-shot Deringer pistol used by Booth to kill Lincoln rests alone in a display case.

Ford's Theatre is open 9:00 to 5:00 daily, except Christmas Day. During the active theatrical season the theater is closed Thursday and Sunday afternoons for matinee performances, but the Lincoln Museum is still open. There are 15-minute talks on the history of Ford's Theatre and the Lincoln assassination once an hour on the half hour from 9:30 until 4:30, with a break for lunch.

Directions: Ford's Theater is at 511 10th Street, N.W., in Washington, D.C., and the Petersen House is directly across the street at number 516.

161. Petersen House

The commotion outside the Petersen House the night of April 14, 1865 caused Henry Safford, a roomer at the boarding house, to rush out on the porch to investigate. He saw soldiers carrying a bleeding President Lincoln out of Ford's Theatre. He yelled to the men, "Bring him in here! Bring him in here!"

Safford guided the men to the empty back bedroom, where Lincoln was placed on the small cottage bed, with his feet off the bed and his injured head protected by pillows.

Mrs. Lincoln, who had followed her husband across the street, moved from the bedroom to the parlor where she was joined by her eldest son, Robert. She kept a night-long vigil. Friends attempted to comfort her as they faced the fact that there was no way Lincoln could be saved.

A young physician who had been attending the performance at Ford's Theatre, Dr. Charles Leale, monitored Lincoln's pulse all night. Along with other doctors he attempted to relieve the President's suffering.

When news of the assassination spread, Secretary of War Edwin Stanton hurried to the Petersen House and established the bedroom adjoining the parlor as a command post to begin the investigation of the shooting. Other government officials streamed through the house paying their last respects to the unconscious and dying President.

It was at 7:22 the next morning that the vigilant Dr. Leale no longer felt Lincoln's pulse beat. The official party quickly left, taking Lincoln's body to the White House. One of the boarders took a photograph of the bed on which Lincoln had just died. The existence of this picture was not publicly known until almost 100 years later. It was useful in the restoration that has attempted to reproduce this "Death Room" as it was on April 15, 1865. Only two other rooms on the first floor are open to the public: the parlor and the room used by Secretary Stanton.

As is so often true, those touched by this tragedy were never the same. It marred many of their lives. The house owner, William Petersen, died from an overdose of drugs in 1871. His wife died four months after that of a heart attack. Because both William Petersen and his wife died without a will, their children were forced to auction off the original furnishings of the house. The house was the focal point of popular curiosity and was finally sold to the government in 1896.

It is open at no charge from 9:00 to 5:00 daily, except Christmas Day, on a self-guiding basis.

Directions: Petersen House is located at 516 10th Street, N.W., Washington, D.C., and Ford's Theatre is directly across the street at number 511.

162. The Mary Surratt House

The house and tavern John Surratt built in 1852 became a popular gathering place for the local community. It would have been better for his family if this had not been true, because as events in the country became more turbulent discussions at the tavern became more fiery. The tavern became a favorite meeting place for Confederates who strongly believed in the cause of states rights and supported slavery.

In 1860, when Abraham Lincoln became President, the Surratts' eldest son left to join the Confederate army. The tavern became a safe house for agents of the Confederate underground that operated in southern Maryland, in what was officially a Northern or Union state.

In 1862 John Surratt died, leaving his widow, Mary, to handle the growing complexities of the time, plus the responsibility for the family business. Her youngest son returned home from college to help her, but soon got involved in Confederate espionage activities. He met John Wilkes Booth and became part of a plot to kidnap President Lincoln. One ramification of this plan was that weapons were hidden at the Surratt's tavern, now rented to John Lloyd. The Surratts had moved to Washington, 541 H Street (now number 604), where Mary Surratt ran a boardinghouse.

After failing to kidnap Lincoln, the conspirators plotted assassination. This plan, of course, was carried out. After shooting Lincoln at Ford's Theatre, John Wilkes Booth and an accomplice, David Herold, stopped at the Surratt's tavern and picked up one of the guns hidden there, as well as some whiskey. According to the testimony of the tenant, John Lloyd, earlier that day Mary Surratt had left a package at the tavern. In contained Booth's fieldglasses. She also told Lloyd to have the "shooting irons" ready to be picked up later that night.

This testimony was significant enough to influence the military tribunal that heard the case against Mary Surratt. Along with three other conspirators, she was hanged on July 7, 1865. She was the first woman to be executed by the Federal government. There are still questions about the extent of her complicity in the assassination.

The costumed volunteers at the Mary Surratt House provide more information on this complicated and infamous page of American history. They also portray the way of life in 19th-century Maryland. The house and tavern are furnished with antiques from the early- to mid-Victorian era.

The Mary Surratt House is in Clinton, Maryland. It is open March through December on Thursday and Friday from 11:00 to 3:00 and weekends 12:00 to 4:00. There are candlelight tours in mid-December. Admission is charged.

Directions: From the Beltway take Exit 7 (Route 5, South Branch Avenue) to Woodyard (Route 223, Clinton). Take a right, then take a left at second traffic light. The Mary Surratt House is on the left at 9110 Brandywine Road.

John Wilkes Booth Escape Route

Benedict Arnold, Aaron Burr, Edward Teach, John Wilkes Booth—there is a continuing fascination with these historical villains and their treacherous activities. This accounts for the popularity of The Surratt Society's biannual John Wilkes Booth Escape Tours. Each spring and fall a bus full of history buffs are escorted on the route Booth took after he assassinated President Lincoln at Ford's Theatre.

While it is undoubtedly enjoyable to travel in a group, the tour also can be done on one's own, keeping in mind, of course, that many of these stops are private property. There is a sense of drama to be felt in literally tracing the footsteps of history. The day's adventure begins in downtown Washington at Ford's Theatre at 511 10th Street (see Ford's Theatre National Historic Site). Booth shot Lincoln at 10:15 p.m. on April 14, 1965. After grappling with Major Rathbone he leapt to the stage, tangling himself briefly in the "Treasury Guard" flag. This slight miscalculation resulted in a fracture of his left leg as he landed. The injury slowed his escape and provided clues that helped those tracking him.

Mounting a horse he had arranged to have standing at the back of the theatre, Booth galloped down "F" Street and crossed Judiciary Square to Pennsylvania Avenue. He was spotted as he rode just south of the Capitol. Following Booth on his ride from the now hostile city was another conspirator, David Edgar Herold, who had been involved in a plan to kill Secretary of State Seward while Booth shot Lincoln.

Both men crossed the Potomac at the Navy Yard Bridge at the bottom of 11th Street. The Federal guard, Sergeant Silas Cobb, stopped each of them but after asking their destination permitted them to cross. The purpose of the guard was to prevent unauthorized entry into the city, not out of it, so it wasn't surprising that they were permitted to leave.

They continued up what is now Good Hope Road through Anacostia (formerly Uniontown) and then between the Civil War fortifications Fort Baker and Fort Wagner near Branch Avenue. After riding eight miles outside Washington, Herold caught up with Booth at Soper's Hill, which according to historians' best guess is the high ground just outside the Beltway at Exit 7.

The two fugitives stopped two miles before Surratt's Tavern around midnight. A young boy, George Thompson, and Henry Butler, a black man who worked for Dr. Joseph Blanford, the brother-in-law of Dr. Samuel Mudd, were stuck in a broken wagon where Branch Avenue now intersects with "Jenkins Corner." Booth asked them if there was a doctor in the area as his leg was giving him trouble after riding almost two hours.

They next stopped at Surratt's Tavern (see Mary Surratt House). Booth did not dismount. He had dropped off a pair of field glasses earlier in the day at Mary Surratt's boarding house in Washington. She took them down to the tavern and left word that they were to be given to the travelers who would stop by that night along with the guns that had been hidden in the tavern. Only one of these guns was taken that night by Herold. Booth was having too difficult a time with his leg to carry a carbine. The remaining gun was hidden in the dining room ceiling at the tavern.

After just a few minutes at the Surratt Tavern they continued on to the town of T.B. Though their next stop is known, the route is uncertain. From T.B. they next showed up at the farm of Dr. Mudd, a southern sympathizer and local doctor. Their probable route leads past St. Peter's Church.

St. Peter's also played a role in the larger drama. At Sunday service on April 16, Dr. Mudd asked his cousin to inform the authorities that two strangers had been at his farm the preceding day. Dr. Mudd's use of the term strangers was significant, as he had met Booth in November of 1864 at St. Mary's Catholic Church just down the road off Route 231 outside Bryantown. (The route passes St. Mary's, the site where Dr. Mudd would much later be buried.) Booth and Mudd met again in December at the Bryantown Tavern on Routes 5 and 232 and later in the month in Washington on business relating to various Confederate agents. Though he may not have known that Booth assassinated Lincoln, it is highly probable Dr. Mudd was at least aware of the Lincoln kidnap plot.

While at St. Peter's Church it is worth noting that this is also the burial spot of Edman Spangler, another of the convicted conspirators in the Lincoln plot. Spangler served time but was pardoned by President Johnson in 1869. He moved into the Mudd household and lived there until his death in February 1875.

It was 4:00 a.m. when Herold and Booth arrived at the Mudd farm, located where Route 382 and 232 meet. Dr. Mudd set Booth's injured leg. They left the farm Saturday afternoon but Mudd didn't suggest the authorities be contacted until after service on Sunday morning.

Making their way through the Zekiah Swamp, now part of Cedarville State Park, the fugitives were seen in the vicinity of "Oak Hill," the home of Dr. Mudd's father, on Route 232. Actually only Herold was spotted when he asked directions from one of Mudd's employees.

Still needing directions, they stopped at the farm of Oswell Swann, which was at that time situated one mile south-southwest of what is now Hughesville. They hired this black tobacco farmer to lead them to "Rich Hill," the farm of Samuel Cox at Route 6 and Bel-Alton Newtown Road. There was conflicting testimony as to whether Cox let them come into the house. He denied it, but their guide said they were inside three or four hours.

The tired assassins did spend the night in the pine thicket several miles from "Rich Hill" off what is now Route 301. Booth and Herold stayed hidden in the woods for several days. Cox had his son contact Thomas A. Jones of "Huckleberry," a Confederate agent who was to get the two men across the Potomac River as soon as it was safe to do so.

It wasn't until Thursday, April 20, that they attempted to cross the Potomac into Virginia. Their first attempt failed. They tried again the next day and landed up Gambo Creek just south of the Route 301 toll bridge at a house along the water. They got food and were put in contact with a guide to take them to "Cleydael," the summer home of Dr. Richard Stuart. Word had been circulated of the assassination of the President and Dr. Stuart was wary of the two strangers. Though he gave them food, he would not let them come in nor would he treat Booth's leg. He sent them for refuge to a free black, William Lucas. The racially bigoted Booth was highly insulted. He sent a bitter note to Stuart with a meagre sum to pay for the food. His surly temper forced the Lucas family out of their own cabin for the night. Booth and Herold did hire Lucas' son to take them by wagon to the Port Conway ferry for $20.00.

While waiting on arrangements to get across the Rappahannock River, they met three Confederate soldiers. Herold's boasting talk soon revealed that they were the men who killed Lincoln. The three southerners agreed to help them make good their escape. The addition of three more members to the group, men who were known in the area, eventually made the capture of Booth and Herold easier.

The five of them crossed the river and found a hiding place for Booth at a local farm owned by the Garretts. Booth stayed there while the other four went on into Bowling Green. The next day they returned and left Herold at the farm with Booth. As the soldiers started north they saw the Federal cavalry heading in their direction. Federal agents had learned at Port Conway that the fugitives were in the area. The cavalry had crossed the Rappahannock and were on their way to the Garrett farm.

At 2:00 a.m. Colonel Baker posted his men around the barn while Booth and Herold slept inside. When they woke up they were trapped. Despite an hour of threats Booth refused to come out. When Baker threatened to burn the barn, Herold surrendered but not Booth. At 4:00 a.m. they set fire to the barn. Booth, limping and with a pistol in one hand and a carbine in the other, started for the door. Before he came out one shot was fired, hitting Booth in the neck.

The shot paralyzed Booth and Federal soldiers dragged him out of the burning building. He died before dawn. A soldier named Corbett admitted firing through the barn siding and evidence indicated this to be the shot that killed Booth. Rumors continued, however, that Booth shot himself or was shot to prevent him from revealing a government conspiracy to kill Lincoln.

Neither the Garrett house nor barn is standing today. A marker on the Fort A.P. Hill military base marks their former location.

With Booth dead the main villain could not be punished. But the lesser band stood trial. Herold, Mary Surratt and two other plotters were hung. Dr. Mudd was given a prison sentence for his role in the tragic events, as were three additional bit players. From Dr. Mudd's connection with this plot comes the expression, "Your name will be mud(d)."

For those interested in joining The Surratt Society tours, advance reservations are required. For additional information call (301) 372-6945 or write the Surratt Society at 9110 Brandywine Road, Clinton, MD 20735.

Civil War Forts

The Confederate firing on Fort Sumter in Charleston, South Carolina actually began the Civil War, but the stage had been set when Lincoln won the presidency in 1860.

Not even waiting to see what action Lincoln would take to heal the profound differences separating north and south, seven states seceded before his inauguration. They justified their decision by the fact that Lincoln's Republican party had not received a single popular vote in 10 of the southern states. South Carolina was first to leave in December 1860, followed by Mississippi, Florida, Alabama, Georgia, Louisiana and Texas in February.

Virginia, Arkansas, Tennessee and North Carolina held off. They awaited Lincoln's inauguration to see what action the government would take regarding the seceded southern states.

On March 4, 1861, Abraham Lincoln provided some answers. In his inaugural address he declared that there would be no invasion of the South, but also that the Federal union must be preserved. He told the South, "You have no conflict without being yourselves the aggressor."

Events would not wait long to test that judgment. The day after his inauguration Lincoln received an urgent communication from Major Robert Anderson telling him that Fort Sumter was woefully low on supplies and ammunition. Only Fort Sumter and Fort Pickens in Pensacola maintained a Federal presence in the South. All other Federal forts had been given into Confederate hands without resistance.

Lincoln faced a problem. If he sent supplies, Confederate President Jefferson Davis would undoubtedly take it as an invasion of Confederate sovereignty and attack the fort. But failing to provision the fort would be a sign of weakness and lead to its loss. Lincoln reluctantly decided to send supplies by naval expedition on unarmed ships. He then informed the Governor of South Carolina of his peaceful purpose; food and supplies would be sent without any additional men or munitions.

This attempt to smooth over a difficult impasse failed. When Major Anderson refused to surrender the fort a rocket was fired in the early morning hours of September 12, 1861. The Civil War had begun!

163. Fort Ward Park

It was May 23, 1861 when the state of Virginia seceded from the Union. Consternation reigned in the capital; Washington was on the front lines of a divided nation, completely unprotected. The realization of the city's peril brought quick action. On the very day that Virginia's secession became effective Union troops crossed the Potomac River and seized Alexandria and Arlington Heights to build defensive forts. Work was begun immediately on three sites south of the river.

When the South won the first major battle of the war on July 21, 1861, at Bull Run (Manassas), the work to defend Washington intensified. Forts were begun that would encircle Alexandria, Washington and Georgetown. These fortifications were modeled on 17th-century fieldworks designed by the French military genius Sebastien Le Prestre Vauban. By the end of 1861 more than 40 forts had been built.

With this degree of protection Federal confidence was restored until August 1862 when the South won the Second Battle of Bull Run. Some of the forts were enlarged, more guns were added and new forts built. By the end of 1862, Washington was the most heavily defended location in the Western Hemisphere. There were 68 forts and batteries bristling with over 900 guns. Over 30 miles of trenches and roads linked these fortifications.

Fort Ward was the fifth largest of the forts surrounding Washington. It was begun in September 1861 and named for Commander James Harmon Ward, the first Union naval officer killed in the Civil War. Today visitors can see much of Fort Ward as it was over 100 years ago during the Civil War. There is a replica of the 1865 Ceremonial Gate to the fort. Also the Northwest Bastion has been carefully restored, complete with exact duplicates of the Civil War cannons. Using old Mathew Brady photographs, an Officer's Hut and Civil War Headquarters building have also been reconstructed. Fort Ward Museum contains a large collection of Civil War items. The museum hosts frequent special exhibits relating to the Civil War period in addition to its permanent displays.

Fort Ward Park is open daily at no charge from 9:00 to sunset. The museum is open from 9:00 to 5:00 and on Sunday from noon to 5:00. It is closed on Mondays, Thanksgiving and Christmas.

Directions: Take Beltway Exit 1 (U.S. 1) north into Alexandria. Turn left on King Street and proceed west on King Street (State Route 7) for approximately three miles to T.C. Williams High School. Turn right onto Radford Street for one block, left at first traffic light onto West Braddock Road. Proceed for approximately one mile—park entrance will be on your right.

164. Fort Marcy

While Richmond was a psychological prize coveted by the North and defended by the South, the city of Washington was viewed even more covetously. If the South could capture the capital of the United States it would give their cause greater legitimacy, perhaps even persuade European countries, still anxious for Southern cotton, to support them in this internal struggle.

Recognizing the strategic importance of Washington, the Federal government made sure that it was heavily fortified. One of the 48 forts that protected the city was Fort Marcy on the old Leesburg Pike on the Virginia side of the Potomac River. Along with Fort Ethan Allen on the other side of Chain Bridge Fort Marcy secured the bridge. Confederate access across Chain Bridge would have also jeopardized the C&O Canal, the principal supply link for Washington.

Though Forts Marcy and Ethan Allen were on Confederate soil, the land was seized during the opening stages of the war. Federal troops under General W.F. Smith crossed the Potomac on September 24, 1861 and began construction of both earthwork forts.

Visitors today can still clearly see this ground defense. It is worth keeping in mind that this form of defense was considered in many ways stronger than bricks. Forts constructed of bricks were rigid and when struck by cannonballs collapsed, while earthworks would merely be loosened but would still provide protection.

General Smith's command was staffed by West Point graduates considered the best engineers in the world. They were well trained in the technique of defensive fort construction. A fellow graduate, Robert E. Lee, realized the efficacy of these fortifications and for the most part did not choose to risk his men against them.

Though the fort was first named in honor of the commanding officer as Fort Baldy Smith, in the late fall of 1861 the name was changed to Fort Marcy. General Randolph Barnes Marcy was not only a chief on General McClellan's staff, he was also McClellan's father-in-law. Marcy's daughter, Nellie, had been courted by West Point roommates, George McClellan and Ambrose Powell Hill. Her rejected suitor served the Confederate cause so well that one of McClellan's men is supposed to have remarked once in exasperation, "Nelly, why didn't you marry that man?"

Fort Marcy sits 275.4 feet above the Potomac at low tide. There were once 18 guns—a 10-inch mortar, two 24-pound mortars and 15 smaller cannons—in place during the Civil War. The perimeter of the fort was 338 feet. Though no structure exists, the remaining earthworks of this fort can be visited during daylight hours and make an interesting outing close to Washington.

Directions: Fort Marcy is located four miles north of Key Bridge. Access is from the northbound lane of the George Washington Memorial Parkway. The fort is situated on top of Prospect Hill just one mile west of Chain Bridge.

165. Fort Monroe

Fort Monroe stands on Point Comfort, so named by Captain Newport of the Virginia Company in 1607 because the peninsula afforded protection from the rough seas. It was comforting to the Jamestown settlers to know that the fort built there in 1609 would protect them.

A later fort built in 1819, Fort Monroe, would not prove as comforting to Jefferson Davis. Falsely implicated in the plot to assassinate Lincoln, he was captured on May 22, 1856 and imprisoned in a casemate cell at Fort Monroe.

Shackled in this dank, cool cell for almost five months, the ex-President of the Confederacy was humiliated by this abrupt end to all his grand plans. On October 2, 1865, he was moved to a more comfortable residency in Carroll Hall. The location of this house is marked on the walking tour of Fort Monroe. Jefferson Davis spent two years imprisoned at Fort Monroe before the charges against him were dropped.

This is not Fort Monroe's only association with the Civil War. It was the only Federal bastion in the upper South that was still in Union hands. As such it was used as the launching point for many of the amphibious operations planned by the North. In 1862 the *Monitor* and the *Merrimac* fought their famous four-hour battle of the iron-clads in Hampton Roads off Fort Monroe. As part of the fort's Casemate Museum there is a model and battle plan of this encounter.

It was at Fort Monroe that General McClellan landed the Army of the Potomac when he began the Peninsula Campaign with Richmond as the objective. Abraham Lincoln took part in the planning of the attack on Norfolk and stayed at Quarters Number One (Stop 9 on the walking tour) from May 6 to 11, 1862. The last offensive against Richmond planned by General Grant also began in April 1864 from Fort Monroe.

Another interesting stop along the fort's tour route is the quarters once occupied by Robert E. Lee. From 1831 to 1834 he served as an army engineer and assisted in the construction of Fort Monroe. Perhaps it was his knowledge of just how well what was often called the "Gibraltar of Chesapeake Bay" was built that discouraged the South from launching an attack during the Civil War.

The fort was designed by General Simon Bernard, former aide-de-camp to Napoleon. It was the largest stone fort ever built in North America as well as the largest enclosed fortification in the United States at the time it was completed. The seven-sided fort was surrounded by an eight-foot moat, making it practically invincible.

Before the Civil War, Fort Monroe had served as the home for the Army's first professional service school, the Artillery Corps for Instruction. In 1907 it again housed a school, the Coast Artillery School. The fort is still operational today. It serves as the U.S. Army Training and Doctrine Command Headquarters for all army service schools, ROTC programs and training centers. Because of this long association with the artillery, Fort Monroe has an impressive collection of artillery pieces. At the West Bastion there are two original 32-pound casemate cannons. Also interesting is the Lincoln Gun, cast in 1860 and used against the Confederate batteries on Sewell's Point. It was the first 15-inch Rodman gun and weighed more than 49,000 pounds. The cannonballs fired from this massive gun were 15 inches in diameter. The balls were of two sizes, 450 pounds and 330 pounds, and had a range of more than 5,700 yards. Fort Monroe had seven more Rodman guns in use in 1865 and 1866.

Fort Monroe and the Casemate Museum are open at no charge from 8:00 to 5:00 on weekdays and weekends and holidays from 10:30 to 5:00. They are closed on Thanksgiving, Christmas and New Year's.

Directions: Take Beltway Exit 4 (I-95) to Route 295, the Richmond By-pass, then Route 64 to Hampton.

166. Fort Delaware State Park

During the War of 1812 a primitive earthwork fortification designed to protect Philadelphia and its harbor was built on Pea Patch Island in what is now Fort Delaware State Park, just one mile from the present Delaware City. This fortification was dismantled and in 1819 a masonry fort was built, but it was destroyed by fire in 1832. In 1848 work began on a fort that surpassed even Fort Sumter in size. Fort Delaware was not completed until 1859, just two years before the Civil War.

The fort covers six acres and is surrounded by a 30-foot moat. Considered by knowledgeable architects as an example of the finest brick masonry work in the country, the fort has solid granite walls that are 30 feet thick and 32 feet high in certain spots. There are three tiers for guns and circular granite staircases. Entrance to the fort is by a drawbridge. It is an impressive structure.

Fort Delaware was first occupied in February 1861. After the battle of Kernstown in 1862, some 250 prisoners from General Stonewall Jackson's Virginia force became the first Civil War prisoners and were housed on Pea Patch Island. Space was limited so wooden barracks were built in 1862 for 2,000 men. The prisoners of war kept pouring in; by June 1863 there were 8,000 men imprisoned on Pea Patch Island, which was equipped for 10,000. This still proved insufficient. After the Battle of Gettysburg Confederate prisoners, from General James J. Archer to foot soldiers, brought the total population to 12,500. Of these, roughly 2,700 died at Fort Delaware. All were buried at Finn's Point National Cemetery in New Jersey.

Though the fort was modernized in 1896 in preparation for the Spanish-American War and garrisoned during World War I, it never fired a shot during it's entire military history. The fort was closed entirely in 1944 and later turned over to the state of Delaware.

Visiting Fort Delaware is fun as well as educational. Getting to Pea Patch Island is an experience in itself, as the only way is by boat. The *Miss Kathy* leaves Delaware City, Clinton Dock on Saturday, Sunday and holidays from 11:00 to 6:00 at frequent intervals for the 15-minute trip. There is a nominal round trip fare but the fort itself is open at no charge from the last weekend in April through the last weekend in September. Once on the island, a jitney transports visitors the short distance to the fort's entrance or "Sally Port" as it's called. A good way to get acquainted is to view the 30-minute film on *The Story of Pea Patch Island* before exploring the fort.

Various groups maintain museums within the Fort Delaware complex. Another point of interest is the difference in quarters for various soldiers. Those of high ranking Confederate officers were spacious; the more crowded area with its three-tiered bunks was for those over the rank of captain and the "dungeons" were used for solitary confinement of difficult prisoners. The rank and file were quartered in temporary barracks which no longer remain.

A walk along the ramparts provides an overview of the island as well as the emplacements for artillery. If time permits, visitors should also take the nature trail on the island. It leads to an observation platform overlooking one of the largest nesting areas for egrets, herons and ibis in this part of the country.

Directions: Take Beltway Exit 27 (I-95) north. Exit on Route 77 east to Route 13. Exit on Route 72 east to Route 9 into Delaware City.

Battlefield Sites

There are a great many similarities between the Confederacy during the Civil War and the self-proclaimed independent colonies during the American Revolution. Like the colonies, it seemed the South could win the conflict by holding out, by fighting defensively on their home ground. But no single battle could break the South as there was not a vital center that would paralyze the Confederate States of America. This had proved to be the case during the American Revolution also, to the frustration of the British.

French aid had helped make the difference during the Revolution, but during the Civil War the South ended up fighting alone. They had been confident that England, at least, would come to their aid. Seventy percent of the cotton used in British textile mills came from the South and there was every hope that "King Cotton" would save the South; but it did not.

The position of the North during the Civil War had many parallels with that of England in 1776. Both enjoyed superior resources—more men, money, transportation facilities, manufactured goods and food. Also, both had established systems of government and trade, while the Confederacy, like the colonies, was just in the process of organization. But if the war had been as short as most predicted these Northern advantages would not have proved significant. At the beginning of the war the armies were essentially equal in size. It would not be until after 1863 that Southern losses would deplete manpower and there would be no reinforcements.

The American colonies had more able military and civil leadership than the British sent to wage the war. The Southern military leadership—Lee, Jackson and Stuart—were the finest graduates of West Point. They provided inspired leadership in the field. The North had trouble finding generals to stand up to this triumvirate. On the other hand, the Northerners fared better on the political scene; Lincoln proved more effective than Jefferson Davis at running a country fighting for its life.

The Civil War was a transitional type of conflict, having elements of older styles of warfare as well as being in many respects a "modern" war. It was the last of the old wars in which chivalry played a role.

Officers of both armies had studied together at West Point; in some battles roommates who once worked on such projects together as homework assignments planned battle strategy for life and death struggles. These men treated each other with respect even though they showed no mercy. This attitude of respect extended to the men in the field. It was quite common for pickets to exchange tobacco and coffee with those they were supposed to be on guard against.

New inventions were changing the methods of warfare. Railroad lines were vital to both sides during the Civil War. It was the first time that armies arrived at the battlefield by train, and enormous field armies were supplied by rail. Telegraph lines, ironclad ships, observation balloons and long-ranged rifles with telescope sights all marked this as a new style of fighting. Trench warfare, which would later be so significant in World War I, was really inaugurated in the long sieges of the Civil War.

This was also the first instance in America of "total war." The civilian population of the South was not exempt from their own kind of combat. For 10 months the people of Petersburg fought their own battle against starvation. The women of the South took over the job of providing food and running the farms and businesses while almost all the able-bodied men from 17 to 50 served in the army. As the war dragged on the North adopted a scorched earth policy to compel the South to surrender. The extent of the losses both in terms of manpower and economics was overwhelming. Much of the war was fought in the South and the landscape was devastated by the conflict. Recovery would prove to be long and slow.

167. Harpers Ferry National Historical Park

Seventeen months before the Civil War began an event occurred that shattered all hopes of reconciliation between the abolitionists and slave-owners. John Brown, a former free-soiler in Kansas who had gained a reputation as a murderer of Southern sympathizers, led 18 men on a plan to invade the South to free the slaves.

To obtain arms for his crusade, John Brown and his small band raided the Federal arsenal at Harpers Ferry, Virginia, on October 16, 1859. Before the townspeople were aware of what was happening the raiders had seized several strategic points. When the alarm was given John Brown and his followers barricaded themselves in the armory fireengine house, called John Brown's Fort since that time. It is one of the many ironies of the Civil War, that the two men who came leading the U.S. Marines were Lieutenant Colonel Robert E. Lee and Lieutenant J.E.B. Stuart. Both officers would shortly resign their commissions and become effective leaders of the Confederate army. Brown lost 10 of his men when the Marines stormed the fort and no Virginia slaves rallied to his banner. Four raiders managed to escape but Brown and the remaining four were captured. Brown was tried, convicted and hanged two months after the raid, on December 2, 1859. John Brown's Fort still stands at Harpers Ferry where it commands greater interest than it did at the Chicago World's Fair. The fort had been shipped to the Fair brick by brick but only 11 people paid the $.50 admission to tour it. When it was sent back to Harpers Ferry it was not returned to the original site but to its present location.

At the Harpers Ferry Visitor Center there is an introductory movie about the town. Maps of the historic area, which is roughly three restored streets, are also available.

The Master Armorer's House serves as a museum that reveals the story of how guns were made. President George Washington had established a gun factory at Harpers Ferry in 1796. The Civil War totally disrupted this industry. When the Federal soldiers retreated from the town, unable to hold their position, they burned the arsenal and armory. The town seesawed between the two sides. In September of 1862 Harpers Ferry was in Federal hands when it was attacked by Stonewall Jackson who defeated the small Union garrison. Fighting here was over in two days, enabling Jackson to rejoin Lee just in time to adequately defend the Confederate position at Sharpsburg and salvage the Southern line at the Battle of Antietam.

Various historic homes in Harpers Ferry have been restored to their pre-Civil War appearance. The Marmion Row Houses are three buildings erected between 1832 and 1850 that evoke the years before the war.

During the summer months, living history programs populate the town with soldiers and shopkeepers who bring to life the year 1864. Escorted walking tours reveal the stories and legends that make events memorable.

The town is built in the Appalachian Mountains where the Shenandoah and Potomac Rivers meet. A walk up the stone steps leads behind St. Peter's Catholic Church to Jefferson Rock. In 1783, Thomas Jefferson said the view was "worth a voyage across the Atlantic." Also to be explored is Harper House, a short way up the stone steps. Built by town founder, though not original settler, Robert Harper between 1775 and 1782, Harper House is open during the summer.

There are several nature trails at Harpers Ferry and information about these trails is also available at the Visitor Center. The Loudoun Heights Trail connects with the Appalachian Trail for those interested in a longer hike. The park is open daily but special programs do occur in the summer months.

Directions: Take Beltway Exit 35 (I-270) to Frederick then Route 340 into Harpers Ferry.

168. Manassas National Battlefield Park

The story goes that on July 21, 1861, *the* thing to do was pack a picnic lunch and journey by carriage or horseback to rural Virginia to see the Union soldiers put an "end" to the rebellious Confederacy. Everybody wanted to see the fun. By four o'clock the outing was a rout with picnickers as well as soldiers in a panic. Warfare was not what anybody expected.

Neither side was ready to fight in July. Both were still training their recruits, but the Northern army under General Irvin McDowell was made up for the most part of three-month volunteers who had signed up in April after Fort Sumter. Their time was almost up and they were getting ready to head home. McDowell had to fight while he still had an army. There was also considerable pressure from Washington to get started—the battle cry "On to Richmond" echoed throughout the capital. So McDowell headed south with his 35,000 untrained men.

They encountered the Confederate force at Manassas, defending the vital railroad junction leading to the important regions of the South. The Southerners, numbering about 20,000, were led by General P.G.T. Beauregard. He was seeing action for the second time though the war had hardly begun. He had led the Southern troops which captured Fort Sumter in April. As would be the case in so many battles in the next four years, the men leading the opposing armies were friends and classmates. Both McDowell and Beauregard graduated from West Point in 1838.

Another Southern army of about 12,000 men under General Joseph E. Johnston, which was supposed to be pinned down in the Shenandoah Valley near Winchester, was moved to Manassas. When Johnston was informed of the Northern activity at Manassas, he transferred his brigades by train to this Virginia railroad center in order to bolster Beauregard's force. This was the first time an army was ever moved to battle by railroad—and the trains were on time. Some of the soldiers went directly from the train to the battlefield.

The opening shots of the first major battle of the Civil War were fired soon after dawn on July 21, 1861. The Union army, in a diversionary tactic, attacked the Confederates positioned at a stone bridge over Bull Run (this is Stop 1 at Manassas National Battlefield Park). There is a hiking trail from the bridge to Farm Ford where General William T. Sherman's troops crossed Bull Run during the morning's fighting.

Colonel Nathan Evans, who was guarding the stone bridge, saw the dust from the Union force as it tried to move around the Confederate position. Evans, leaving a small force at the bridge, rushed with the bulk of his troops to Matthews Hill (Stop 2) to halt the forward advance of McDowell's men. He was reinforced by two brigades under General Bernard Bee and Colonial Francis Bartow, but the Confederates were still pushed back and the men broke ranks. The retreat became a rout with soldiers turning and running from the fighting.

As the troops were pushed back to Henry Hill, General Bee spotted General Thomas J. Jackson's brigade drawn up in orderly ranks behind the crest of the hill. He shouted to his men, "There stands Jackson like a stone wall! Rally behind the Virginians!"

The brigade held firm against the Union onslaught and was afterward called the "Stonewall Brigade" while its general became known as "Stonewall" Jackson. They held the line for more than three hours until even the Stonewall Brigade began to weaken. But at that crucial junction the last train carrying Johnston's men arrived at Manassas. The addition of fresh troops was too much for the tired Union soldiers. They panicked and ran, the picnickers were in full retreat as well, and the army became a mob. Lincoln himself watched the wild flight into Washington from the White House windows.

One additional point of interest which figured not only in this battle but would also play a role in the Second Battle of Manassas was the Stone House (Stop 2) that served as a field hospital. Originally a turnpike inn for teamsters, it provided some protection for the wounded. Though the thick stone walls could protect the injured from the battle raging ouside, it couldn't protect them from the inadequacy of the surgeons responsible for helping them. Many regiments had only one surgeon and one assistant. This was not nearly enough to handle the volume of wounded. Seriously injured men were left to die, and those with arm or leg wounds had the limb removed in a five minute operation that lacked antiseptic or sterile refinements. Surviving this brutal surgery was difficult; death usually occurred within three days of "surgical fever." The casualties after Second Manassas were even greater. Nearly 20,000 men were wounded and many languished on the battlefield for days without attention. Today there are guided tours of the Stone House Field Hospital during the summer months.

One year later the Union and Confederate armies were back once more on the battlefield at Manassas, but this time they were no longer untrained recruits, they were battle-trained troops.

In the summer of 1862, Lee had driven McClellan's Army of the Potomac from the Richmond battle lines into a fortified camp on the James River. The Confederacy was at its zenith, both in terms of morale and military strength—all things still seemed possible. Though Lee had but half of McClellan's strength in numbers, he never hesitated to take a gamble, and he split his force in half, sending Jackson north to deal with the new Army of Virginia.

The War Department in Washington was not pleased with McClellan's showing and so created a new Army of Virginia under the command of Major General John Pope. This army would fight only one battle, that of Second Manassas. Their dismal showing caused them to be disbanded subsequent to that encounter. Pope, a collateral descendant of George Washington and a relative of Mary Todd Lincoln by marriage, was not a popular or effective leader. He was a self-proclaimed fighter who declared his headquarters would be his saddle. A military joke of the day had it that Pope didn't know his headquarters from his hindquarters. His stubborn refusal to accept military intelligence and his complete mishandling of Northern troops at Manassas caused him to be sent to Minnesota to fight the Indians.

But he was riding high before Manassas, determined to defeat Jackson and bring new laurels to the north. When McClellan was ordered to proceed north to join with Pope, Lee decided to attack before the two forces could be combined.

In order to achieve this objective, Lee ordered one of the boldest military movements in history. On August 24, he sent Jackson with 24,000 men on a 54-mile flanking march around Pope's right flank. Their two-day march took them between Blue Ridge and Bull Run Mountain and east through Thoroughfare Gap to seize Manassas Junction. Jackson and his men reached their objective by August 26 and destroyed Pope's supply base. Pope felt that Jackson, with only 20,000 men, could easily be taken with his own 55,000-man army. Jackson had meanwhile found a secure defensive position in the same area where the First Battle of Manassas had been fought. In an unfinished railroad bed, Jackson deployed his men to await the arrival of Lee and Longstreet.

To prevent Pope from moving east of Bull Run and merging with the rest of McClellan's troops, on August 28 Jackson revealed his position by firing on Pope's troops (Battery Heights, the scene of the opening attack of the Second Battle of Manassas, is Stop 1 on the 12-mile auto route that covers the three-day battle). It was 5:15 p.m. when Jackson ordered the three Confederate artillery batteries to open fire. With less than 100 yards between the two sides, casualties were heavy. When darkness fell the losses were tallied and it became apparent that the Stonewall Brigade had suffered heavily; they had started the battle with 635 men and had only 100 left standing. Of the 2,800 Federal soldiers who saw action that afternoon, over 1,100 were hit. Word was sent to Pope that Jackson and his 20,000 men had been pinned down. Pope assumed Jackson was trying to escape to the mountains and made plans to wipe out this Confederate nuisance once and for all.

The next morning Jackson strung out his three Confederate divisions for two-and-a-half miles along the unfinished railroad bed

(Stop 3). Here Jackson's men held the line against numerous Union assaults as they waited to be reinforced. All day the Confederates held their position, until darkness ended the Northern attacks.

On August 30, Pope still felt he had a weakening Confederate force trapped, despite various dispatches that told of large Confederate forces on the march toward Manassas. The orders Pope gave his generals on the 30th were to pursue the supposedly fleeing Jackson and "capture the whole lot of them." It was to be the shortest pursuit on record, as Pope would be heading into the cleverly planned trap that Lee had set (Stop 4, the Deep Cut Trail, is a one-mile hiking trail that covers much of the action on the afternoon of August 30). The Confederates were spread out like two huge jaws ready to swallow the unsuspecting Union line. The fighting was so intense that Jackson's beleaguered force ran out of ammunition and resorted to throwing rocks at the Yankees only 20 yards away. With Lee and Longstreet now on the field, the jaws closed and the Union lines crumbled. It was the second debacle at Bull Run, with Pope losing 14,462 men, plus his command. The Army of Virginia was disbanded.

The victory at Manassas, though it cost Lee 17 percent of his men (9,474 men had fallen), still provided the impetus for the South to carry the war into the North—the next battle would be on the banks of another creek, this time in Maryland at the village of Sharpsburg.

Tour Stops 4 and 5, the Sudley Church and the Stone House, both served as Union field hospitals. Other stops mark isolated incidents in the three-day fighting. At Stop 8, Henry Hill, there is a Visitor Center where two audio-visual programs provide orientation to the major battles that took place at Manassas. Living History programs are scheduled for the summer months. The Manassas National Battlefield Park is open daily in the summer from 9:00 to 6:00 and in the winter from 9:00 to 5:30, except Christmas Day. There is no charge to visit the park.

Directions: Take Beltway Exit 9 (I–66) west 17 miles to the intersection of Route 234 north, where the battlefield is located.

169. General Stonewall Jackson's Headquarters

General Thomas Jonathan Jackson's career as Lee's ablest general was short-lived. Jackson served only two years before being tragically shot by his own troops in a moment of triumphant victory at Chancellorsville.

Jackson's military strategy in the "Valley Campaign" that he planned from his Winchester Headquarters is regarded so highly that it is still studied in military academies both in America and in Europe. The able strategy, rapid movement and brilliant execution are high points of the Confederate army campaign.

As Commander of the Army of the Shenandoah in late May and early June, Jackson marched with his men nearly 400 miles in 32 days, fighting almost daily, including five major battles. They defeated three Union armies, capturing 20 much needed artillery pieces and taking 4,000 Federal prisoners. In this "Valley Campaign" fewer than 1,000 of Jackson's men were killed or wounded. His troops were 15,000 strong while more than 60,000 opposed him.

This highly effective tactical campaign can be traced by car along U.S. 11 and Route 340 between Lexington and Winchester. There are 11 road markers that provide information on Jackson's "Valley Campaign."

When Jackson came to the Shenandoah Valley one of his officers, Colonel Lewis T. Moore, offered the use of his home on Braddock Street. Jackson spent most of the winter and spring quartered here, with Mrs. Jackson joining him for three months, their longest time together since he had left his teaching duties at Virginia Military Institute.

The house is a brick Gothic Revival cottage that was built in 1854. The room used by General Jackson as an office has been restored. His desk, prayer table, field chest and camp chair are all in place. The wall paper and floor matting are copies of those in use in 1861.

The house also has a collection of Jackson memorabilia as well as items from other leading Confederate figures. Battle flags, Civil War muskets and swords, paintings and prints complete the restoration.

An interesting aside—Colonel Moore was the great-grandfather of popular actress Mary Tyler Moore.

General Stonewall Jackson's Headquarters is open daily from 10:00 to 4:00 from April to December. Admission is charged.

Directions: From the Beltway take Exit 10 (Route 7) to Winchester, Virginia. The Headquarters is located at 415 North Braddock Street in Winchester.

170. Richmond National Battlefield Park

From the first days of the Civil War in 1861 Richmond was a prize sought by the North and defended by the South. Seven major Federal drives were launched against this symbol of the Confederacy. Both sides considered the city a prime psychological objective. Losing Richmond, the capital of the Confederacy, would be a devastating blow to the spirit of the South, also a military disaster because Richmond was the principal supply depot for Southern troops.

The first of the two Federal drives that came close to success was McClellan's Peninsula Campaign of 1862. At Richmond National Park's Chimborazo Visitor Center there is an audio-visual presentation that covers this campaign plus the climactic 1864 drive of General Grant that helped bring the Civil War to an end. Displays, information on the Park's frequent Living History programs and maps of the 100-mile battlefield tour ride are all available.

There are two distinct battlefield areas. Red dot markers indicate McClellan's campaign while blue dots represent the 1864 Grant offensive. General George McClellan had taken the ragtag, defeated Union troops after the First Battle of Manassas and forged them into the 100,000-man Army of the Potomac. His goal was to mount a combined land and water attack on Richmond.

On May 15, 1862, the federal naval attack on Fort Darling (Battlefield Tour Stop at Drewry's Bluff) was repulsed. Union ships numbered four gunboats and included the famous ironclad, *Monitor*. By repulsing this early effort the Confederates saved Richmond from being shelled and also protected the city from forays up the James River. There is a self-guided trail with explanatory markers that outlines the Civil War action around this fortification.

It wasn't until May 24, 1862 that McClellan reached the outskirts of Richmond, deploying his men on both sides of the Chickahominy River six miles from the city. From this position he waited for additional troops. The Confederates, seeing the Union army divided with half their force on each side of the river, decided to seize the initiative. On May 31, General Joseph E. Johnson attacked the Federal force at Fair Oaks and at Seven Pines (battle site markers indicate these locations on the Richmond tour map). Though the fighting itself was inconclusive, there were strategic results from this first confrontation. The Confederate initiative and showing made an already cautious McClellan even more careful, a disposition that would impede the Federal battle plan and eventually cause him to forego the chance to take the city. Secondly, Johnson was wounded in this encounter and was replaced by General Lee, who gave the troops new leadership and a new name, the Army of Northern Virginia.

General Lee summoned his trusted general, "Stonewall" Jackson, who had just wrapped up the Valley Campaign. These additional troops brought Lee's strength to 90,000, very near that of the Union force.

From this position of strength Lee decided to attack on June 26 and began what is called the Seven Days' Battle for Richmond. Watching from earthworks on Chickahominy Bluff (now a Battlefield Tour Stop with an audio interpretative marker), Lee oversaw the opening attack at Mechanicsville, where the Confederates were successful. A simultaneous attack north of the Chickahominy River on Beaver Dam Creek did not succeed and the Confederates suffered heavy losses. (Beaver Dam Creek is also a Battlefield Tour Stop.) To reach the Union position it was necessary to cross a waist deep mill-race in the face of artillery fire. It was an impossible situation and the Confederate attack at Beaver Dam failed.

During the night of June 26 the Union troops moved back from Mechanicsville to Gaines Mill, the location of the next day's fighting. There is now a self-guided trail around the battlefield at Gaines Mill. The Watt Farm House that Union General Porter used as his headquarters for the June 27 battle has been partially restored, though it is not open to be toured. The self-guided trail leads to Breakthrough Point where Texas and Georgia troops penetrated the Union line. From the trail the shallow trenches used by Union troops are still discernible. Union reinforcements enabled Porter to hold the line but McClellan, reflecting the cautious streak that would undermine his men, decided the battle was lost and ordered a retreat. If McClellan's will had been stronger it is very likely he could indeed have captured Richmond, as the Confederate force standing between him and his goal was only a thin line. But though not beaten in battle he was beaten in spirit.

General Lee felt the Union movement was part of a tactical strategy. He couldn't believe it was a retreat. When he learned that the Army of the Potomac was indeed leaving the battle, he started in pursuit. Skirmishes were fought at Savage Station, White Oak Swamp and Glendale (all marked, though not part of the Battlefield Park). The Union army made a stand on July 1 at Malvern Hill. They were waiting for the supply train to reach Harrison's Landing at Berkeley Plantation on the James River. (See Declaration of Independence: Berkeley.) The Union position on Malvern Hill was almost impossible to attack; in fact, so impregnable was it, surrounded by swamp and water and protected by the Union navy, that they needed no trenches. The Federal troops stood in lines of battle with their massed artillery and mowed down the Confederates attempting to advance up the open slope. One Confederate officer said later, "It was not war—it was murder." Lee lost more than 5,000 men to no avail.

Though they could not defeat the Union army at Malvern Hill, the Confederates felt victorious. They had stopped McClellan's drive to capture Richmond. The campaign cost 35,000 men, North and South. It would be repeated again in 1864.

For the next two years of the Civil War, though there was activity in Virginia, Richmond's entrenched position was not seriously challenged. After the savage Battle of the Wilderness and Spotsylvania, Grant moved south to find a new battlefield. On May 30, 1864, he was stopped in the vicinity of Mechanicsville by Lee's troops.

Grant felt that the Southern line was weak in the center near Cold Harbor and attacked there on June 3. What he didn't know when he ordered the dawn attack was that Lee had been reinforced during the night and had positioned the new troops at this precise point, fearing it would be attacked. After only 30 minutes of fighting Grant had lost 7,000 men and gained no ground. For 10 days Lee's men held the line, sweltering in the over 100 degree temperatures. At the end of the Battle of Cold Harbor Grant had 13,000 casualties, while Lee sustained a loss of 3,000 men. Grant conceded the position as hopeless and withdrew his men, moving next to Petersburg, the railroad connection for the South. After Cold Harbor the war around Richmond shifted from active encounters to a state of siege.

At Cold Harbor there is a Visitor's Center to provide orientation for this stage of the conflict. The 1¼ mile battlefield tour road passes well preserved field fortifications. The restored Garthright House served as a field hospital for wounded Union soldiers and after the Union retreat, for Southern casualties. The house is not open; only the exterior has been restored.

While the major portion of Grant's Army of the Potomac was involved in the siege of Petersburg, sporadic raids on Richmond still occurred. On September 29, 1864, a surprise attack by Union soldiers succeeded in capturing Fort Harrison, part of the Southern fort defense of Richmond. Federal troops occupied and enlarged the fort. They then built a second fort opposite Fort Darling on Drewry's Bluff. A self-guiding trail covers the Fort Harrison Battlefield area and leads to the second Federal bastion, Fort Brady. There is a Visitor's Center with exhibits at Fort Harrison.

When Lee retreated from Petersburg on April 2, 1865, Richmond's mayor informed the Union army that the Confederate army had abandoned the city. They burned warehouses and supplies as they left. Before the ruined buildings cooled, Lee had surrendered to Grant at Appomattox Court House.

Directions: Take Beltway Exit 4 (I-95) to Richmond. Heading south, use Exit 10A and follow signs to Richmond National Battlefield Park Headquarters and Visitor Center, 3215 East Broad Street. From the south, use Exit 10 to Broad Street and follow signs.

171. Antietam National Battlefield Park

The Union army seemed fated time and time again to snatch defeat from the jaws of victory. History abounds with "what ifs" but one cannot help feeling that if Lee had served the North rather than the South the war would have been far shorter. The generals he faced were not his equals. McClellan failed at Antietam, though he had everything going for him—advance information which gave him a decided edge, more men, and fresh troops when Lee's army stood on the ragged edge of exhaustion. Yet McClellan let all these advantages slip through his fingers and the only Northern gain was in preventing Lee from successfully invading the North.

The South needed to capitalize on their victory at the Second Battle of Bull Run. Lee hoped that if he could carry the war to the North it would achieve two important objectives: first, it might convince the North to work towards a negotiated settlement with the Confederacy and, second, it might persuade England and France to recognize the Confederate States of America. The Union blockade of the South was causing economic hardship not only in the southern cotton area but also in the English textile mills.

It was September 1862 when Lee crossed the Potomac into Maryland. Lee, the master of the bold stroke, decided to risk dividing his army, sending half his force under Jackson to capture Harper's Ferry and the remaining 20,000 under General James Longstreet continuing north. Longstreet with Lee headed for the eventual goal of Harrisburg, the capital of Pennsylvania. This risk was compromised when McClellan fortuitously obtained a copy of Lee's orders to Jackson and Longstreet on September 13 and learned the details of the Southern battle plan. The North now knew how thinly the Confederate forces would be spread over the Maryland countryside.

Once again the North had a chance to make a quick end to the war. They knew Lee's game plan! But rather than acting quickly on this information McClellan moved slowly, overcoming the small Confederate outposts in the South Mountain passes on September 14. Interpretive markers now indicate the skirmishes at Turner's, Fox's and Crampton's Gap on South Mountain.

Then McClellan with 50,000 men moved on September 15 into the Sharpsburg area where he *knew* Lee waited with only half the Confederate force. Still McClellan waited, while victory faded with the passing time. By September 16 the Union army numbered 70,000 with the Confederates fielding only 20,000. The other part of Lee's plan progressed smoothly. Jackson captured Harper's Ferry on September 15 and quick-marched his men all night to rejoin Lee at Sharpsburg the next day.

As the much needed reinforcements arrived to bolster the Confederate position, McClellan decided the time was right—not realizing he was at least one if not two days late for his appointment with destiny. At dawn on September 17 the bloodiest day of the Civil War began.

The opening attack was particularly brutal. From the Joseph Poffenberger Farm (Site 2 at Antietam Park) General Hooker's artillery attacked Jackson's force positioned in the Miller cornfield (Site 4). The line of battle crossed this field 15 times. Hooker, commenting on the encounter, reported, "every stalk of corn ... was cut as closely as could have been done with a knife, and the slain lay in rows precisely as they had stood in their ranks a few moments before." Jackson's men were subjected to almost an hour of constant shelling, but yielded only about one half mile until bolstered by additional troops around 7:00 a.m.

At 9:00 a.m. the Union army under General Mansfield counterattacked. Mansfield was wounded at the East Woods as he led his men into battle (Site 3). His men were cut off around the Dunker Church (Site 1) and General John Sedgwick's division lost 2,200 men in less than 30 minutes as they charged into the West Woods (Site 5) to extricate Mansfield's men. The morning fighting had taken a terrible toll. Neither side had made a substantial gain and the day had just begun.

Fighting diminished until Union troops under Sumner attacked the Confederates along the Sunken Road, afterwards called the "Bloody Lane" (Site 6). Almost four hours of continuous fighting resulted in 4,000 casualties. Sheer exhaustion stopped the battle at this point around 1:00 p.m. Neither side had profited, but neither side could continue. The Southern troops simply held their ground.

At the other end of the battlefield area the Union left flank under General Burnside had been trying to cross a bridge over Antietam Creek since 9:30 a.m. Burnside had four divisions and they were held back by 400 Georgia riflemen. Having this large number of men tied up and unable to reinforce Hooker in the northern sector of the battlefield certainly contributed to McClellan's defeat at Antietam. It was not until 1:00 p.m. that the Federal troops crossed what is now called Burnside Bridge (Site 7). After taking two hours to reform their lines, the Union force drove the Georgia troops towards Sharpsburg. Again their two-hour delay proved costly. Just as the Confederate line was being turned back additional reinforcements arrived—General A. P. Hill's division from the Harper's Ferry area. The Federal army was driven back to the fateful bridge and did not attack again.

The Hawkins Zouave Monument marks the spot where the battle ended at 5:30 p.m. on September 17. A foot path leads to this hillside monument which provides a view over the entire battlefield. It's a good place to put the day's events into perspective. Directly in the line of vision is the Antietam National Cemetery where 4,776 of the 12,410 Federal soldiers killed at Antietam are buried. Southern dead, numbering 10,700, lie elsewhere.

By late afternoon the Battle of Antietam was over. Losses were overwhelming and Lee had no more men to send into battle. McClellan, on the other hand, had 20,000 fresh toops still in reserve. If the North had made a big push the Southerners quite likely would have been defeated. But McClellan held back and Lee withdrew his army, recrossing the Potomac into Virginia. The South would fight another day—and another.

Antietam National Battlefield Park covers 12 square miles. Park tours start at the Visitor Center. There is an 18-minute slide presentation on the Battle of Antietam and the Maryland Campaign. At Stops 4 through 7 there is also a taped message. During the summer months daily rifle firing demonstrations take place and there are guided walks. The park is open daily from 8:00 to 6:00, except Thanksgiving, Christmas and New Year's.

Directions: Take Beltway Exit 35 (I-270) to Frederick. Continue on Route 70 until it intersects with Route 34. Take Route 34 to Sharpsburg; the Visitor Center is north of Sharpsburg on Maryland Route 65.

172. Fredericksburg National Military Park

In the bitter and tragic story of America at war with herself, Fredericksburg was indeed inopportunely placed, being midway between the two capitals. On four occasions the two sides fought bitterly in and around Fredericksburg. Within a 17 mile radius of this small Virginia town was a theatre of war so intense and continuous that it is unequalled on the American continent.

After General McClellan's poor showing at Antietam, he was replaced by General Ambrose Burnside. It was the bushy cheek whiskers of this gentleman which prompted the term "side burns." Burnside, recognizing that McClellan had been relieved of his command because he did not pursue Lee into the south after Antietam, was determined that the army under his command would advance to Richmond. Crucial to this plan was Fredericksburg. Burnside decided to cross the Rappahannock River by using pontoon bridges. When he arrived, anxious to leave Fredericksburg before the Confederate Army could unite and move up into position, there were no boats.

Though the pontoon boats arrived on November 25, Burnside had grown cautious and waited still longer—too long, as it turned out. The Confederates under General Lee moved into the area and positioned themselves in the hills behind Fredericksburg. On the night of December 10, the Rebel sentries on the town side of the river heard a voice from the other side yelling, "Yankees cooking big rations! March tomorrow!"

Before attempting to fight their way through the Confederate lines the Union army turned their cannons on the town and inflicted a brutal bombardment. When they crossed into the city they rampaged through the town destroying the belongings in the empty Fredericksburg homes. The Confederates, lying in wait in a seven-mile line on the hills behind the city, did not leave their entrenched position.

The real battle began on December 13 when 110,000 Union soldiers attempted to storm the Confederate-held hills west of the city. The Union army could not have picked a worse place to engage the enemy than Marye's Heights. At the foot of the Heights was a sunken road with a stone wall in front of it. Behind this wall were Confederate soldiers, four deep.

Like soldiers in earlier European conflicts, the Yankees marched in neat rows beneath the cannons on Marye's Heights. It was a slaughter. They were mowed down as they came on throughout the long, bloody day. Line after line, column after column and still they were ordered to advance up the deadly slope. Not one Union soldier got within 30 yards of the fateful stone wall. Over 6,000 men were casualties in a matter of hours. After eight hours General Burnside had lost 13,000 men either wounded or dead and was still going to order another attack when his staff officers persuaded him not to demand the certain death of any more brave soldiers. Two nights later Burnside recrossed the river using the protection of a heavy storm. The Battle of Fredericksburg, one of the most one-sided defeats in American military history, was over.

To gain an overview of Fredericksburg National Military Park, begin at the Visitors Center where there are exhibits and a short slide show. Maps and brochures also help to orient visitors. Directly in front of the Center is the Sunken Road, along which there is a well-marked walking route.

Across the Sunken Road is the National Cemetery where 15,000 Union dead are buried. On a hill is a large painting of the Battle of Fredericksburg. A taped message will provide additional information. Continuing along the Sunken Road, which originally ran for 600 yards along the edge of the Heights, visitors pass an area where the stone wall of the Southern fortifications has been reconstructed. A short segment of the original wall behind which the Confederates made their successful stand has been preserved. On the right is the Ennis House, which stood directly on the Confederate front line. The house sustained damage from thousands of bullets during the fighting on December 13. The Confederates, positioned only inches from the house, fired through the building. It was repaired and today a taped message continues the story of the battle.

There was another house next door, the Stevens House, which has since been destroyed. Martha Stevens did not leave her home in fear of the approaching battle like most Fredericksburg residents. She stayed and nursed the wounded soldiers outside her door. The night after this fierce battle Federal wounded lay beneath the guns of both sides. A young Confederate sergeant from South Carolina, Richard Kirkland, moved by their helpless cries for water asked leave to bring the dying men water from the Stevens well. Warned that no flag of truce could be shown and that he probably would be shot when he climbed the protecting stone wall, he nevertheless filled as many canteens as he could carry and jumped the wall to help the wounded Federal soldiers. A cheer came from the Union lines instead of the bullets he expected. Kirkland was called the "Angel of Marye's Heights" and today the Kirkland Monument honors this brave, compassionate soldier.

One final spot to be noticed is the Marye House, built in 1830 and called Brompton. From the grounds around the house the Confederate cannons leveled the Union lines. The house itself is not open.

After completing the walking tour there is an additional self-guided battlefield auto route along Lee Drive. At Stop 2 there is a short trail to the top of Lee Hill. From this vantage point General Robert E. Lee directed the Confederate forces, consulting with his subordinate officers "Stonewall" Jackson and James Longstreet. The guns that stand on Lee Hill are similar to those that were in place in December 1862 and which helped repulse the Union force. While Lee watched the battle a shell fell at his feet but failed to explode, sparing at least one Confederate general to continue the fighting.

The last major stop along the route is at the point of a major Federal breakthrough. Under General George G. Meade one division managed to break the Confederate line at least temporarily. They were driven back when Confederate reinforcements were brought in to augment General Gregg's command. Just a bit further down Lee Drive is Prospect Hill, where a large battery of Confederate guns continually assaulted the Federal line. Along the hilltop the fortifications constructed to protect the 14 guns that once stood here can still be seen.

There are other sites of interest within Fredericksburg National Military Park. The stately home, Chatham, which was used as both headquarters and hospital can be visited. (See Civil War Period: Homes.) At Chatham there is an overlook of the Pontoon Crossing Site. Other markers, monuments and cannons can be viewed in the park, which is open daily at no charge.

Directions: Take Exit 4 from the Beltway (I-95) to Fredericksburg. Signs will direct visitors to the Fredericksburg National Military Park.

173. Chancellorsville Battlefield

Lee's greatest victory, the Battle of Chancellorsville, was sadly diminished by the irreparable loss of General "Stonewall" Jackson, who was inadvertently shot by his own men at a moment of Confederate celebration.

Lee's victory was a triumph of vision over sheer numbers, determination over vacillation; he had the ability not only to dream the impossible but also the courage to carry out the dream. Actually it wasn't that General Joseph Hooker didn't come up with a good plan. He did; he had to, as he was very much aware that he was replacing General Burnside, who made such a poor showing at Fredericksburg. So Hooker was determined to beat Lee. After reorganizing the 120,000 Union troops during the winter camp he was ready. "My plans are perfect," said Hooker. "May God have mercy on General Lee, for I will have none."

His plan was to hold Lee's force at Fredericksburg with one part of the army and also move around Lee's left side with a larger force, thus compelling Lee to withdraw or surrender. But Lee, recognizing Hooker's intention, adroitly side-stepped and then executed the same maneuver on an army twice his size.

As Hooker moved to attack Lee's left flank with 75,000 men. Lee left only 10,000 men under General Jubal Early holding Fredericksburg and moved the rest of the army, 45,000 strong, toward Chancellorsville.

When Hooker met the advance troops he halted and dug in rather than attacking the inferior force, thereby metaphorically digging his own grave and burying his hopes of victory over Lee.

When Lee arrived and discovered the Northerners dug in, he decided to attack. Planning with his trusted aide, General Jackson (Auto Tour Stop 6, the Lee-Jackson Bivouac), he determined upon a bold and daring maneuver. With less than half his already outnumbered force he would hold the line, while Jackson, with 30,000 men, would march around the Union force and envelop Hooker's right flank. This surprise move was enormously effective, caving in the Federal line for two-and-a-half miles. It was at this time that the fates ceased smiling on the Confederates. Jackson, who had ridden out in front of his own line to reconnoiter the Federal position in order to plan the next day's offensive, was badly wounded—fired on by his own men as he returned.

Devastated, the Southern troops could not even stop to mourn their commander. Word had come in that a Northern attack had forced General Early to abandon Fredericksburg. Drastic measures were again called for. Lee left J. E. B. Stuart in Jackson's place and took 20,000 men east to recapture Fredericksburg.

Though it was a Confederate victory, the cost was high. Lee lost 12,000 men, plus the military genius of Jackson. Union losses were even higher, totaling 17,000. At the Chancellorsville Visitor Center (Stop 4, numbers 1-3 are part of Fredericksburg National Military Park 10 miles west) exhibits and displays bring this stirring Confederate victory, at two to one odds, dramatically to life. There is also a 12 minute film covering the conflict of May 1-4, 1863. During the summer months the park hosts special Living History Progams. Maps available at the center direct visitors to all the stops.

Stop 5, Chancellorsville Inn, served as General Hooker's Headquarters. In fact as he leaned against one of the inn's porch pillars he was painfully wounded by a Confederate shell. It did not prove as damaging as the loss of his nerve, though, which prompted him to withdraw and dig in to a defensive position on May 1, abandoning the offensive to Lee.

When the Confederates took the area around Chancellorsville on May 3, they realized victory was in their grasp. At Stop 8 on the Battlefield Tour fierce fighting occurred on May 3. This was one of the few high, open areas, called Hazel Grove. It was the location of Confederate artillery and placed the Southerners in a location to inflict continual damage on the retreating Union force.

The last major point of interest at Chancellorsville Battlefield is the clearly marked Jackson Trail, tracing the route he took to encircle Hooker's flank. This trail can be picked up at Stop 7, Catherine Furnace. Specific details of the drive are given on the map available at the Visitor Center.

An important footnote to the Battle of Chancellorsville is the small frame office building at Guinea Station. After being shot by his own men, Jackson's arm was amputated at Wilderness Tavern. He was then moved to a position well outside the battle area, the Fairfield Plantation. There he contracted pneumonia and died on May 10, 1863 of complications from his wound. The area is now the Stonewall Jackson Memorial Park. Guinea Station is on Route 606 just 15 miles south of Fredericksburg.

Directions: To reach the Chancellorsville Battlefield take Beltway Exit 4 (I-95) south to Fredericksburg, then take Route 3 to Chancellorsville. Both Stops 4 and 5 are on Route 3.

174. Gettysburg National Military Park

The bloodiest battle in American History, the high water mark of the Confederacy, the turning point of the Civil War—all these are phrases which attempt to describe the indescribable: the Battle of Gettysburg in July 1863.

This was the second and last time Lee attempted to invade the North. His first effort failed in September of 1862 at Antietam, Maryland. After his victory at Chancellorsville, Lee was ready to try again. His goals remained the same he had attempted to achieve the year before—to gain either a negotiated settlement with the North or, failing that, to secure from European allies aid in the continuing struggle.

In June 1863, to the utter consternation of officials in Washington, Lee, with the 76,000 men of his Army of Northern Virginia, moved west from Fredericksburg into Pennsylvania. By late June the Confederates held Chambersburg, York and Carlisle. Advance Southern troops were moving in on Harrisburg, the Pennsylvania capital.

Washington ordered General Hooker's Army of the Potomac to pursue Lee, who continued north with no real idea of how close the Union line was to his troops. His normal reconnaissance unit, J. E. B. Stuart's cavalry, was not with the main force, but had moved north to the area around Baltimore.

It was thus purely accidental that the two armies ran into each other around Gettysburg on June 30, 1863. Hooker was no longer in command of the Northern forces. He, too, failed to measure up to Lee and had been replaced just three days before by General George Meade.

The Battle of Gettysburg began on the morning of July 1, just beyond McPherson's Barn (Stop 10 on the Gettysburg Battlefield Auto Route). General John Reynolds commanded the Union infantry that held this line. The Federal forces were out-numbered here and at Oak Ridge (Stop 12) but held out until the afternoon when Jubal Early's Confederates broke through the Federal line at Barlow Knoll (Stop 13). This collapsed the Federal line north of Gettysburg and the Union forces were driven back to Cemetery Hill (Stop 16) south of Gettysburg. This ended the first day's fighting.

Dawn on July 2 found the two armies positioned one mile apart on two parallel ridges—the North on Cemetery Ridge and the South on Seminary Ridge. Lee's plan of attack called for General Richard Ewell and General A. P. Hill to make secondary attacks on the Union position while General Longstreet enveloped the left flank.

The only problem with this battle plan was that Longstreet and his men were still en route to Gettysburg. They were not in position to attack until afternoon on July 2. This gave the North time to reinforce their line. Once Longstreet's men began the attack they cleared the Union troops from Devil's Den (Stop 4) to the peach orchard (Stop 6). Between these two points was a wheatfield (Stop 5) which was the scene of a great deal of the fighting that day. It was left strewn with dead and dying men.

By late afternoon Longstreet's right flank began to climb two hills, Round Top and Little Round Top (Stop 3). These hills would give the South a commanding position from which to encircle the entire Federal line. But heavy artillery fire halted Longstreet's men before they reached the crest. The presence of two Union brigades at the peak of Little Round Top was the result of quick action on the part of General Warren, chief engineer of the Union Army. He had watched the action in the peach orchard and realized the crucial need for an adequate defense of the hilltop position. If Warren had not commandeered two brigades the North could well have lost the Battle of Gettysburg on July 2.

Longstreet's drive on Little Round Top was halted at dusk. A. P. Hill had broken through General Sickles' line in the Petzer Woods (Stop 7) and Ewell's attack on Culp's Hill (Stop 14), though briefly successful, was pushed back. The Confederates did seize Spangler's Spring (Stop 15) but lost it on July 3.

July 3, 1863 was the last day of the Battle of Gettysburg. Lee had decided to attack the center of General Meade's line on Cemetery Ridge. In an effort to weaken the Federal position, 160 cannons bombarded the Union troops for two hours. As the smoke from this barrage settled, the Northerners saw facing them a long line of Confederate soldiers, battle flags flying. These were 12,000 of Lee's finest; only one out of every three would make it back. As the infantrymen under George E. Pickett began crossing the open field they were met by a salvo from more than 200 guns. Though some faltered and fell, they kept marching into this killing fire. Lee, who was watching (from Stop 8), realized he had made the worst mistake of his military career. In 50 minutes 10,000 men lay dead and Pickett's Charge entered the pages of history.

For one brief moment during the charge it seemed as if they might breech the Federal line. General Armistead, holding his black hat on his sword, urged the men on over the wall. When Pickett's Charge was turned back at the ridge, where the same Copse of Trees still stands, the tide turned irrevocably for the Southern cause. Never again would they come so close to victory. The war from then on would be a defensive attempt to hold out and wear the North down. There is a one-mile trail at the High Water Mark (Stop 1 on the Auto Route). It takes about an hour to walk the trail but it is worth the time. The chance to stand at the very spot where Pickett's Charge was repulsed, see the many poignant monuments to these courageous soldiers, as well as Leister House, which served as Meade's headquarters, should not be missed.

When Pickett's Charge failed the Battle of Gettysburg was over. Though Meade should have pursued the retreating Confederate force, he let them withdraw. Losses for both sides were heavy; each side lost more than 20,000 men. More Americans died than in any other single battle in American history.

The last stop on the auto tour, which takes two to three hours to cover adequately, is the National Cemetery (Stop 17). When the Army of the Potomac left Gettysburg many Union soldiers did not. Remaining were the 21,000 casualties and the 8,000 dead soldiers either lying unburied or covered over in shallow temporary graves. Pennsylvania Governor Curtin was appalled at this carnage. He appointed a local attorney, David Wells, to establish a national cemetery. Only the 3,512 Union soldiers were buried there. The 3,320 Confederate dead were buried where they fell. After the war the Southern dead were removed to cemeteries in Richmond and other Southern capitals.

Reburial of Union soldiers began on October 27 and was less than half finished by November 19, 1863 when the Soldier's National Cemetery was dedicated. Abraham Lincoln had accepted David Wells invitation to attend the ceremonies. The train on which Lincoln arrived can be seen on Carlisle Street just north of Gettysburg Square. Lincoln spoke after the main address, which lasted over two hours. His remarks took only two minutes but are remembered to this day as the Gettysburg Address. In 1869 the Soldiers' National Monument, the first of 1,000 monuments that would be built at Gettysburg, was erected on the site where Lincoln delivered his simple message. The original two page handwritten copy of the address is in the Library of Congress.

During the celebration of the 75th Anniversary of the Battle of Gettysburg soldiers who had fought here gathered for the last time. In their nineties, these 1,800 men listened while President Franklin Roosevelt dedicated the Eternal Light Peace Memorial (Stop 11).

There is so much to see at Gettysburg National Military Park that the best way to begin a visit is at the Visitor Center. Auto route maps, hiking trail maps and an Electric Map orientation program will help fill in the details of this three-day battle. There is a charge for the 30-minute topographic map program.

Adjacent to the Visitor Center is the Cyclorama Center. A free 10-minute film, "From These Honored Dead," is worth seeing before starting out. In the large circular auditorium built to house the 356-foot cyclorama, painted in 1881 by Paul Philoppoteaux, there is a sound and light program. A small admission is charged for this but it shouldn't be missed. The 26-foot high oil painting of Pickett's Charge is remarkably dramatic.

In the days before movies cycloramas were very popular. The Gettysburg Cyclorama is one of only three in North America. It was purchased by the United States Government in 1942.

Gettysburg National Military Park also operates the Granite Farm. Located near Big Round Top at the southern end of the park, this living history farm provides a glimpse of Pennsylvania farm life in the 1860s. The farm, which was used as a hospital during the Battle of Gettysburg, is still operated by costume-clad interpreters who describe their rural life to visitors. The farm is open daily during the summer from mid-June until Labor Day. It is open weekends during the spring and fall. Park roads open daily from 6:00 to 10:00, but the Visitor Center and Cyclorama doesn't open until 9:00 and closes at 5:00. It is also closed Christmas, New Year's and Thanksgiving.

Directions: Take Beltway Exit 35 (I-270) to Frederick, then follow Route 15 to Gettysburg. Or take Exit 31 (Route 97) to Westminister and on into Gettysburg.

175. Wilderness Battlefield

West of Fredericksburg was a dense tangle of forest and underbrush called the Wilderness. Here the opposing armies engaged in "bushwacking on a grand scale," to quote one old veteran.

In this overgrown terrain armies could not maintain regular lines and many soldiers were actually either shot by their own men or discovered, to their eternal regret, that they were completely surrounded by the enemy. A further problem produced by the heavy but dry vegetation was fire—muzzle flashes set the tinder ablaze and it raged out of control killing impartially Union and Confederates in a deadly inferno.

Losses in the two-day Wilderness fighting were 18,000 Union men shot or burned and an estimated 8,000 Confederate men lost. Lee could no longer accept that many casualties, as he had only half as many men as General Grant. So this marked the end of the reckless Confederate charges that had turned the tide of the Second Battle of Manassas and again at Chancellorsville. General Lee now had to husband his dwindling army.

The Battle of the Wilderness ended when General Grant began pulling out his men on May 7, 1864. The Army of the Potomac had withdrawn from every encounter with Lee. As the lead column reached the intersection which would indicate either retreat or a continued battle, the men raised a rousing cheer to Grant because they realized they were heading farther south to engage Lee's force once again.

In Wilderness Battlefield there are interpretive road signs and an Exhibit Shelter at Wilderness on Route 20, just 1.3 miles from the intersection with Route 3. The Exhibit Shelter will provide a picture of the position of the opposing armies. General Grant had attached himself to General Meade's Army of the Potomac to map an overall strategy to end the three-year conflict in Virginia. The Union army wanted to position their force between Lee and Richmond, cutting off supplies and gradually winnowing away his command. As the Union army moved from their Culpeper camp on May 4, 1864, they entered the Wilderness area and were in a vulnerable position, unable to master an organized defense. Lee moved in and engaged them. For two days the armies clashed.

Moving down Route 20 for .3 mile to Hill-Ewell Drive, one can turn left and find a drive with trenches along the road which were built by the Confederates during the Wilderness Battle on May 5. From the intersection of Hill-Ewell Drive and Route 621 turn right (west) for .2 mile to an interpretive stop at Tapp Farm where Lee had attempted to lead a counterattack after his men had suffered a heavy barrage. Seeing their revered leader in danger at the head of the column the soldiers set up a cry, "Lee to the rear!" Realizing his mortal danger he did relinquish the lead position.

Both sides indicated their loyalty to their commanding officer and neither side suffered a decisive loss or stunning victory at the Battle of Wilderness, but still the young men died and the woods burned and the fighting moved on to Spotsylvania.

Directions: Wilderness Battlefield is a self-guided auto route. From the Beltway take Exit 4 (I-95) south to Fredericksburg, then west on Route 3 to Wilderness where the battle trail begins.

176. Spotsylvania Battlefield

When Grant's soldiers cheered as they left the overgrown Wilderness Battlefield to engage Lee farther south, they did not envision the encounter at Spotsylvania Court House.

The Spotsylvania Exhibit Shelter will provide orientation for the brutal two-week stalemate that cost about 29,000 casualties—10,000 Confederates and 19,000 Union soldiers. Heaviest fighting took place at the center of Lee's line where it jutted into the Union position. At this point called the "Bloody Angle," assault after assault was launched to break through. Fighting was hand to hand, with soldiers firing at point blank range, clubbing and bayoneting each other in savage frenzy. Spotsylvania's unfortunate distinction is that the "Bloody Angle" climax was the single most terrible 24 hours of the war. It was an unequaled, close quarters death struggle.

To reach the Bloody Angle from the Exhibit Center continue on Grant Drive from the Center for .9 mile to a parking area. There is a 30-minute loop trail that covers the Bloody Angle Battlefield.

On the Spotsylvania Battlefield the sites of several houses used as headquarters are marked for visitors. The Landrum House Ruins, from which General Winfield S. Hancock directed the Union forces, is on the Bloody Angle trail. The McCoull House Site served as headquarters for Confederate General Edward "Allegheny" Johnson. On May 10 heavy fighting occurred around this house, and later Lee led a counterattack against Union forces at McCoull House.

Realizing finally that neither side could break the other, General Grant decided on May 21 to shift to a more southern position. He moved into the Richmond area and the confrontation at Cold Harbor which would cost him dearly. Grant lost 13,000 men in the Battle of Cold Harbor, while Confederate losses numbered only 3,000.

There are two additional points of interest at Spotsylvania. The present Court House stands on the location of the earlier structure which was badly damaged during the Civil War. Also the Spotsylvania Confederate Cemetery is here, where 570 soldiers who fell during this battle are buried.

Directions: Take Beltway Exit 4 (I-95) south to Fredericksburg, then continue for 12 miles on Route 208 to the Court House at the junction of Route 613 (Brock Road). Go right on Brock Road to the intersection with Grant Drive and the Exhibit Center.

177. New Market Battlefield Park

Some say that the older, battle-worn regulars of Breckinridge's command jeered as the young cadets joined the Confederate force at New Market in their newly issued uniforms. If they did, by the end of the battle they had changed their tune from "Rockabye Baby" to loud cheers for the 157 young V. M. I. soldiers.

By what set of circumstances did these 15- to 17-year-old boys get involved in actual combat? Lee and the Army of Virginia were bogged down at Spotsylvania Court House by Grant's Army of the Potomac. In an effort to gain control of the crucial Shenandoah Valley area, which not only provided wheat and livestock to provision the Confederate army but also gave the Southern forces a line of invasion into the north, Federal military plans called for Major General Sigel, former Minister of War for Germany, to take 7,000 men and capture Staunton, Virginia.

To thwart the Northern plans, the South called on a latecomer to the Confederate cause, General John Breckinridge. He was a Senator from Kentucky when that state seceded, and had made an unsuccessful bid for the presidency in 1860. He was also the youngest Vice-President, serving with James Buchanan when only 35. Breckinridge waited until October 1861 to join the Confederate army, but he quickly made up for lost time. By 1864 he had seen service in more states than any other Confederate officer.

When Breckinridge gathered his force at Staunton there were 4,500 Confederates, leaving them outnumbered by the Northern forces. To equalize the ranks Breckenridge ordered the cadets of the Virginia Military Institute from their classrooms. After marching for four days, through constant and sometimes torrential rain, the 157 students joined the seasoned ranks.

Early on May 15, 1864 the Battle of New Market commenced. The Confederate forces were on Shirley's Hill and the Federal line on Bushong's Hill. To attack the Federal position the long grey line, strung out so it would seem a more substantial force, had to advance up an open slope in the face of heavy artillery fire. Breckinridge himself led the assault. The Confederates won the first round with the courageous assistance of Woodson's Missouri Rangers, a crack 65-man company that, at the cost of 60 casualties, picked off the Federal gunners.

As the Confederate army prepared for the counterattack it was obvious that they were short of men. The center of the line was weak and there were no replacements, only the V.M.I. cadets. When one of Breckinridge's staff, Major Charles Semple, advised putting in the cadets, General Breckinridge responded, "No, Charley, this will not do, they are only children and I cannot expose them to such fire as our center will receive." But time ran out and it was the cadets or almost certain defeat, so asking God to forgive him, Breckinridge ordered the young boys into the center.

The cadets positioned themselves out in front of the line, along a fence by the Bushong farm house. Their actions along this line helped repulse Sigel's counterattack, meaning ultimate Confederate victory. A poignant footnote to this tale was added by the incessant rain. It created a virtual quagmire of the Bushong farm, which has come to be called "The Field of Lost Shoes;" the mud literally sucked off soldier's shoes as they tried to make their way through under lethal fire.

275

Though not a major battle in terms of the outcome of the Civil War, New Market is a battle that is not forgotten. It was the last Confederate victory in the Shenandoah Valley and it was the first and only time the entire student body of an American college not only marched into battle but helped win the day.

The events of the May 15 battle are brought vividly to life at the New Market Battlefield Park's Hall of Valor Museum. As visitors peruse the letters written by cadets both before and after the battle to their parents and see their young faces in the photographs, the cadets become individuals with whom we all can identify. The short film, "New Market—A Field of Honor," is particularly poignant as it follows the cadets from classroom to conflict. When the entire corps of V. M. I. call the roll of the 10 cadets killed at the Battle of New Market it is indeed moving.

But this is certainly not a southern museum. Both sides of the Civil War conflict are presented, as is the entire war from beginning to end, with photo murals and maps. The museum has a second film that focuses on "Stonewall" Jackson and the Valley Campaign so highly considered by military strategists. It gives the amateur historian an idea of what made this campaign noteworthy.

But this million dollar museum is just part of the 160-acre park. Also of interest is the Bushong Farm that has been restored to provide a complete picture of a typical farm of the Civil War period. Nine dependencies of ths 19th-century farm have also been reconstructed.

A park walking tour traces the path of the V. M. I. cadets. A battery of Civil War cannons still stands on top of Bushong's Hill. Each year on the Sunday prior to May 15 the Battle of New Market is reenacted.

New Market Battlefield Park is open daily 9:00 to 5:00, closed Christmas. Admission is charged. Bushong Farm House is open from mid-June to Labor Day from 10:00 to 4:30.

Directions: Take Beltway Exit 9 (I-66) to Route 81. New Market Battlefield Park is on Route 81 one mile from the New Market Exchange.

178. Sayler's Creek Battlefield Historical State Park

Seventy-two hours before General Lee surrendered at Appomattox he lost over half his army in the botched and bloody Battle of Sayler's Creek. Total Confederate losses were estimated at 8,000, with 6,000 taken prisoner—the largest number of men ever to surrender in a single action on this continent. Six general officers also were captured and almost all of Lee's dwindling supplies were lost.

What caused such a debacle? A combination of factors bedeviled Lee's ragged and starving army as they fled Petersburg and Richmond. Heavy spring rains caused frequent rerouting and mudsoaked roads were often impassable for the wagons, resulting in loss of communication. The army was heading for Amelia Court House where they hoped to be reprovisioned. When supplies did not arrive, a day was wasted on a fruitless search for food. This gave Union forces time to catch up and set the stage for the last major battle of the Civil War in Virginia.

On April 6, 1865, a third of Lee's army under General Anderson and General Ewell bogged down—literally—in the swampy bottom land of Sayler's Creek and were overtaken by Federal troops under General Wright. Though the Richmond clerks, sailors and artillerymen who made up the Confederate forces repulsed the first attack, they came under the Union artillery batteries and were stopped. The entire force surrendered.

The wagon column under General Gordon that the Confederates were trying desperately to salvage had already crossed the creek but here, too, they were stopped by superior Union forces commanded by General George Armstrong Custer. While General Gordon and a few men escaped, the wagons and three-fourths of the column were captured.

The defeat of the Confederate army at Sayler's Creek was the first step to Lee's surrender of the Army of Northern Virgina. Three days later Lee would admit defeat at Appomattox Court House. .

Today there is an Interpretive Auto Route at the Sayler's Creek Battlefield Historical State Park. Overlooking the site of the Battle of Sayler's Creek is the Hillsman House. This house was used as a field hospital by both North and South. The floors, marked even now by bloodstains from the operating tables, still bear silent testimony to the many wounded. Although the Hillsman House is not open to the public, interpretive signs and an audio program tell visitors the exciting story of this climactic encounter. Sayler's Creek Battlefield Historical State Park, open Memorial Day through Labor Day at no charge, is operated by Virginia's Division of State Parks.

Directions: From the Beltway take Exit 4 (I-95) south to Richmond. Continue west on Route 360. Then take Route 307. This will lead to Route 617. The Interpretive Auto Route at Sayler's Creek Battlefield Historical State Park is marked at intervals on Route 617.

179. Petersburg National Battlefield

Serving as the industrial and transportation hub of the Confederacy, Petersburg became a victim of its own success. Because of its commercial and strategic importance to the south Grant felt that "The key to taking Richmond is Petersburg." After failing with the direct assault approach at Cold Harbor in June of 1864, the Union army turned south to Petersburg.

Their confidence undermined by the series of confrontations with Southern troops at Wilderness, Spotsylvania and Cold Harbor, the Federal commanders did not press their assault. They also realized that a frontal assault on a well-constructed fortification was suicidal. This lapse gave Lee an opportunity to move his army to Petersburg from the Richmond area.

It also led to the longest siege in American history—no other American city has ever suffered through an ordeal of this length (see Civil War Museums; Siege Museum). Just maintaining the armies in the field was the largest military operation of the 19th century. At one point there were more than 100,000 men in the Army of the Potomac. At the Petersburg National Battlefield Visitor Center there is a 17-minute map presentation every hour that details events during the long siege, highlighting the battle in June of 1864 when Grant tried to break through the Confederate defense, and the climactic Confederate offensive in April 1865.

A short walk from the Visitor Center leads to a Confederate battery that fell into Union hands during the first day of the opening battle. It was here that a 17,000-pound Union mortar called the "Dictator" fired 200-pound shells into the city only two-and-a-half miles away.

Stops 1, 2, 3 and 8 are near Confederate forts built to protect Petersburg. They were areas of bitter fighting during the struggle to gain control of this Confederate stronghold. Stops 5, 6 and 7 were part of the Union siege line. In fact Stop 5, Fort Stedman, was the last objective Lee attempted to seize. Realizing that the Northern stranglehold was growing even tighter as the railroad links with Petersburg were broken, Lee decided to attack Grant at Fort Stedman hoping to force a Union shift to the eastern sector of the siege line. This would ease the pressure on the last Confederate railroad link into Petersburg. This railroad was also Lee's best escape route. For a brief time it looked at though Lee would succeed, but a strong Federal counterattack doomed the offensive.

Grant, seeing victory at last, ordered General Sheridan to attack five miles west of Petersburg at Five Forks on April 1. Union victory here cut the last supply line into the city and at last Lee had to withdraw.

Indeed he would not have had the chance to evacuate his army were it not for the gallant stand of the 450 men left to hold back the Federal advance at Fort Gregg. It was 450 against 5,000 but they bought enough time to prevent the war from ending on the streets of Petersburg. It would end for Lee seven days later at Appomattox. Fort Gregg is one of 11 forts on the 16-mile drive of the siege line that begins at the Crater.

The Crater is one of the most unusual strategic battle approaches employed during the Civil War and it almost worked. The Battle of the Crater came in the early days of the siege and the idea behind it was ingenious. Pennsylvania coal miners dug a tunnel under the Confederate line. Four tons of explosives were placed in the tunnel and literally exploded beneath the unsuspecting Southerners. When the explosion went off on July 30, 1864, it caused a crater 170 feet long, 60 feet wide and 30 feet deep. The idea was for an assault division to lead the charge penetrating the Confederate position through the gap left by the explosive, with the entire Ninth Army Corps to follow. However, Union concern that the black regiment trained to carry out the mission might all be lost and lead to accusations that the Federal command was trying deliberately to kill black soldiers, prompted them to substitute an unprepared division for this all important assault. Federal soldiers poured into the crater instead of going around the gap left by the explosion until they created a bottleneck and became perfect targets for the Southern troops to pick-off. The Union lost over 4,000 men to 1,500 for the South. They also lost the chance to end the siege.

One final point of interest at Petersburg National Battlefield is Stop 3, Meade Station, where a three-fourths mile loop trail leads to this important stop on the U.S. Military Railroad. During the siege 500,000 tons of supplies were shipped on this line, providing the Army of the Potomac with food and uniforms to endure the coldest weather this area had experienced in years. Southern troops were not so fortunate, as the Union cut the city's vital supply link, railroad line by railroad line. The Meade Station Trail has interpretive markers to explain the role of the railroad in the siege of Petersburg. Maps of this walking tour and of the extended battlefield siege line drive are available at the Visitor Center. During the summer months visitors can also find the times for various artillery firing demonstrations and other Living History programs at the Center.

Petersburg National Battlefield is open daily except major holidays at no charge.

Directions: Take Beltway Exit 4 (I-95) south to Petersburg. Proceed east on Route 36 towards Hopewell. Route 36 goes right by the entrance to Petersburg National Battlefield. The Visitor Center is on the left, the park drive is on the right.

180. Appomattox Court House National Historical Park

It was fitting, but still a magnanimous gesture, to end the fratricidal war that cost the lives of over a half million soldiers, more Americans than were lost in World Wars I and II combined, in a manner that allowed the defeated to return to their homes with their horses and personal possessions, and so begin the job of restoring their lives and their country.

The surrender of Lee's Army of Northern Virginia, the Confederacy's most successful field army, at Appomattox Court House was a surrender made with honor and dignity. Grant's terms left the men with not only the means of resuming their civilian life but also with the feeling that though they had lost the battle they were not disgraced. When the Confederates rode and marched between the Federal lines to lay down their arms, their former opponents presented arms. Responding to this unexpected tribute, the Confederates returned the salute in a moving moment on that day of formal surrender.

On a more practical level, when news of the Confederate surrender was passed among Federal camps, men emptied their haversacks to share their rations with the starving Confederate soldiers.

It had been a long road to Appomattox. Lee left the small Virginia town on the anniversary of the firing on Fort Sumter four years earlier. With his surrender the Civil War was all but over, the hopes of the Confederacy ended. The unity of the United States was secure.

The last encounter of Lee and Grant came after the bitter Virginia campaign of 1864 when Lee halted Grant's drive toward Richmond. Grant, realizing it was futile to persist in his objective, shifted to attack Petersburg and the long 10-month siege of that city began.

When the Petersburg defense finally cracked in April 1865, it was the beginning of the end for Lee and his men. There would be only seven days between their withdrawal from Petersburg and the surrender at Appomattox Court House. The savage fighting at Sayler's Creek on April 6 cost Lee nearly one-fourth of his army, and his oldest son was captured.

By the time Lee was camped outside the small village of Appomattox Court House on April 8, 1865, he was operating without supplies. The headquarters of this general of the Confederate Army had no tent, no chairs, no bed or table. It was here, at the site marked Lee's Headquarters (a 20-minute walk from the parking lot leads to the campsite), that the last council of war was held and Confederate options explored. Lee rejected the idea of continuing the conflict through guerrilla tactics. The officers decided to make one last attempt to break through the Union lines. General Gordon's veteran infantrymen were to try to crack the line early the next morning. After Gordon left he realized he didn't know how far he should lead his men if he broke through. Sending a message back to Lee he received this answer, "Tell him that I'd be glad for him to halt just beyond the Tennessee line."

But Lee realized that no hope really existed and when he appeared before his startled officers on the morning of April 9, he was in full dress uniform, embroidered belt and gold spurs. He believed that before the day was out he would be Grant's prisoner. When word came that Gordon had failed, Lee resigned himself to surrender, saying, "Then there is nothing left me to do but to go and see General Grant and I would rather die a thousand deaths."

Lee sent word to Grant and arrangements were made to meet at the McLean House. There is a certain irony to their choice as it had been the fighting at Manassas which prompted Wilmer McLean to move to this out-of-the-way Virginia town. He wanted a place where his family would be safe, and where the armies would be unlikely to appear. The first battle of the Civil War occurred right in his front yard, and when the Second Battle of Manassas returned the fighting to his neighborhood, he felt compelled to seek a haven at Appomattox Court House, little dreaming that the war would come to an end in his parlor. Grant and Lee met and, observed by Grant's staff officer, agreed to a cessation of hostilities. Lee was pleased with the terms of surrender and felt that it would do much toward conciliation of the defeated Southerners. When the Federal artillerymen began a 100 gun salute to victory, Grant had them stop. "The rebels are our countrymen again," said Grant, "and the best sign of rejoicing after the victory will be to abstain from all demonstrations in the field."

If the leaders in Washington had followed Grant's generous approach to victory the scars of this internecine war would have healed much more rapidly. But with Lincoln's assassination five days after the surrender at Appomattox, the hot-heads inflamed rather than soothed the wounds of the country. There was even an attempt by a small group to hang Lee for treason. This was rebuffed by Grant's soldierly intervention. Lee went on to assume the presidency of Washington College in Lexington, Virginia. It was renamed Washington and Lee University after his death in October 1870. Grant went on to assume the presidency of the United States from 1869 to 1877.

Today Appomattox Court House looks the same as it did in 1865, except for the absence of the people to fill the village streets, to tend the fields and enjoy a respite in the tavern. It is the quiet of Appomattox that induces a reflective mood and a sombre realization of how important this really was for our country's future. Thirteen of the original buildings in the town are still standing, and have been carefully restored. Nine other buildings, including the McLean House, have been reconstructed where they once stood.

Visits should start at the reconstructed courthouse which serves as the park's Visitor Center. It was once a Confederate recruiting station. During the climactic events in April 1865 the courthouse played no role in the drama. Two 15-minute slide shows give different perspectives on the surrender of Lee's army. One is a chronological account of the events from April 1 through 12. The second, called "Honor Answers Honor," uses first person accounts of the surrender to dramatize the action on April 12 at Surrender Triangle.

The village, with its twin major buildings and other sites, is easily covered on foot. Of paramount interest is the McLean House, where Lee surrendered to Grant. The furnishings are not original; actually, most of the pieces in the parlor where the famous meeting occurred were bought or stolen as souvenirs immediately after the papers were signed. General Ord purchased the table where General Lee sat. The small oval table used by General Grant was sold to General Sheridan for $20.00. McLean didn't want to part with the chairs but when he wouldn't sell them they were taken by two cavalry officers. The painting by Louis Guillaume of this historic meeting has enabled historians to reconstruct the room.

Outside the McLean House are a number of dependencies including the log kitchen and servants quarters, the gazebo well in front of the house and an icehouse on the side. Across the street are several commercial establishments such as Meek's Store, built in 1852 and one of the social centers of the community; the one-room frame law office of John Woodson; and the Clover Hill Tavern with guesthouse and tavern kitchen. It was here that many of the 28,231 individual Confederate paroles were printed. Also restored is the county jail with the sheriff's office and quarters on the first floor and the cells on the top two floors. There are four restored private residences that were part of the local scene in 1865. On the opposite side of the village from Lee's Headquarters is the site of General Grant's Headquarters.

Appomattox is symbolic of a new beginning for the United States. This obscure village marks the spot of one of the great watersheds in American history. It is open daily, except Thanksgiving, Christmas, New Year's Day and Washington's Birthday. There is a small per car charge. During the summer months interpretive programs are given.

Directions: Take Beltway Exit 9 (I-66) west then Route 29 to Amherst. At Amherst take Route 60 east to Route 26, then south to Appomattox. Appomattox Court House National Historical Park is three miles north of Appomattox on Route 24.

Civil War Museums

The repositories of the mosaic of American history are the museums throughout the United States. Testifying to the enduring interest and popularity of the historical museums, approximately one new history museum opens every week in the United States. There are over 2,500 history museums throughout the country. Those described in this section relate to the Civil War.

The first museum in the United States opened in 1784 when noted portrait artist Charles Wilson Peale opened his Philadelphia home so that the public could enjoy his work. This proved to be only the beginning. Undoubtedly the largest and most inclusive collection is housed in the 152-year-old Smithsonian Institution's 13 museums. They contain an estimated 78 million items, many of which languish in the vast storage space of never visited rooms. It is often called the nation's attic.

Just as America's first museum was in Philadelphia, so was the first historical museum. Again, it was in a private home, this time that of amateur historian Pierre du Simitiere. In the 1780s he opened his house so others could see his collection of historical artifacts, documents and portraits.

There has been a boom in history museum attendance as a result of the interest in finding one's roots. To experience a sense of the past, the feeling of being part of a continuing series of events is essential. Museums like the Siege Museum in Petersburg vividly bring to life the courageous actions of everyday people with whom visitors can identify.

The best way to approach any museum is to discover its purpose and how it is laid out. Many museums are organized chronologically and a visit that is begun haphazardly will not be as interesting or as informative. If the museum provides an orientation film, see it before touring. If not, try to obtain a brochure or at the very least question the museum attendant to obtain basic guidelines for getting the most out of the museum.

181. Museum of The Confederacy & The White House of The Confederacy

We might speculate on why, though there are any number of Confederate museums, there are no "Union Museums." Perhaps it is simply that the winners do not feel a compulsion to tell their side of the story. History may be written by the winners but museums are founded by the losers. Within a decade after the surrender at Appomattox numerous communities launched efforts to preserve a record of the Confederate cause.

Not until 1890 did a movement begin to salvage the White House of the Confederacy. It served as the official residence of the first and only President of the Confederate States of America, Jefferson Davis, who lived there from 1861 to 1865. The city of Richmond, capital of the Southern states, had rented for the Davis family a private residence built in 1818. After the war the house was used as a Union army headquarters and then for 20 years as a public school. By 1890 there was talk of razing the then dilapidated structure.

Concerted action saved this historic building and efforts were begun to rebuild the gutted interior. In 1896 it opened as the "Confederate Museum." The White House of the Confederacy is currently undergoing restoration to its wartime appearance. The Museum of the Confederacy is housed in an adjacent building added in 1976.

The museum contains the largest existing Confederate collection. Its poignant effects of prominent Confederates remind visitors of the gallant men who fought so hard and lost so much. Effects include the sword that General Robert E. Lee wore at Appomattox, the suit Jefferson Davis was wearing the morning he was captured by Union cavalry in May 1865 and tattered battleflags from Gettysburg and Missionary Ridge.

The original furnishings of the White House of the Confederacy are part of the collection as are numerous paintings of the Civil War. There is also an extensive library.

The Museum of the Confederacy is open Monday through Saturday from 10:00 to 5:00 and Sunday from 2:00 to 5:00. It is closed on major holidays. Admission is charged.

Directions: Take Beltway Exit 4 (I-95) to Richmond and then Exit 10. The museum is adjacent to the Medical College of Virginia, north of East Broad Street at the corner of 12th and Clay Street. The address is 1201 East Clay Street.

182. Warren Rifles Confederate Museum

Throughout the South there are many small museums commemorating the Confederate cause. For dedicated Civil War buffs these local efforts, with their mementos of local Confederate heroes, provide a sidebar to history. Warren Rifles Confederate Museum is an excellent example of this phenomenon.

The museum collection includes weapons, cavalry equipment, uniforms and battleflags. Both officers and soldiers are represented. Personal possessions from Mosby's Rangers, General Jackson and others are highlighted. Old pictures and maps help tell the story of the bloody conflict.

Warren Rifles Confederate Museum is open from April 15 to November 1 on weekdays from 9:00 to 5:00 and on Sundays 12:00 to 5:00. Admission is charged.

Directions: Take Beltway Exit 9 (Route 66) to Front Royal. The museum is at 95 Chester Street in Front Royal, Virginia.

183. The Valentine Museum

A treasure trove of unusual collections surprises first time visitors to the Valentine Museum in Richmond, Virginia. One room of the museum is devoted to Robert E. Lee and the Civil War Period. The plaster model for Edward V. Valentine's recumbent statue commemorating Lee is on display. Lee's trusted aide and co-strategist "Stonewall" Jackson is also remembered by the death mask made while Jackson lay in state at the Governor's mansion.

Dealing with an earlier chapter of American history there is an Indian collection that includes displays on all major Indian cultures found in North America, with particular reference to the East Coast tribes (see Indian Epoch). Artifacts go back to Prehistoric groups dating from 10,000 B.C.

A popular favorite at the museum is the costume collection, which provides a glimpse of changing fashion through the various eras. The earliest item is a 1668 linen Christening dress. Accessories supplement the outfits.

The history of Richmond is interpreted through a series of rotating exhibits, and the building that houses the museum is itself of historical interest. It was built in 1812 for John Wickham, the lawyer who represented Aaron Burr in his treason trial. The house is only a part of the museum but it is maintained as a typical 19th-century Richmond residence. The oval ladies' parlor is considered one of the most beautiful rooms in America. The gardens located outside the oval parlor are the oldest in continuous use in Richmond. They are still kept up according to the original landscape specifications.

The Valentine Museum was founded in 1892 and has been intriguing visitors since 1898, when it first opened. The museum hours are 10:00 to 5:00 Monday through Saturday and 2:30 to 5:00 on Sunday. Admission is charged.

Directions: Take Beltway Exit 4 (I-95) to Richmond. The Valentine Museum is at 1015 East Clay Street.

184. Siege Museum

For 10 long months from July 1864 to April 1865 the people of Petersburg withstood the Union siege. It was the longest ordeal any American city has ever undergone in any war. The unusual focus of the Siege Museum makes it unique among 19th-century museums. Here visitors see the human side of the Civil War.

General Grant decided that "the key to taking Richmond is Petersburg." Efforts were begun by the Union forces to sever the five railroad lines that served Petersburg. As each link was broken, the people of the city suffered further privations. The stories of the difficulties these shortages provoked is told in personal accounts. Their position as the front line of battle for the Union and Confederate armies is testified to by fragments of houses torn by shells. This, though, is not a military museum, but rather a collection that reflects the effect of a military campaign on the civilian population.

Petersburg at the start of the Civil War combined the best of the industrial North and the hospitable South. Unlike most Southern cities, thriving industries operated including iron foundries, cotton and flour mills and tobacco warehouses. There were more free blacks in Petersburg than in any other city in the South. Theaters, colleges and churches all flourished here. This antebellum period is represented at the Siege Museum in varied ways. There are examples of the cotton patterns and moulds from the ironworks that during the war converted its facilities to making the much needed munitions for the South. There is also a typical Victorian parlor and an office that might have existed in the Bank of the City of Petersburg in the 1860s. Early photos reveal examples of the Greek Revival style so popular during the antebellum period. In fact, the museum itself is designed in that style and once served as an Exchange Building. Farmers would bring in their tobacco, wheat and rye; buyers on the upper gallery would survey the available commodities and make their choices.

A 20-minute film that recaptures this time of courageous fortitude and, indeed, the undaunted spirit of the Confederacy throughout the war is narrated by actor Joseph Cotten, a native of Petersburg. It was from Cotten's grandfather's farm that General Lee viewed the final day of the Battle of Petersburg. The film contrasts Petersburg in its heyday before the war with its struggles during the siege.

The Siege Museum provides a feeling for the spirit of the city. It is open at no charge Monday through Saturday from 9:00 to 5:00 and Sunday 1:00 to 5:00. It is closed major holidays.

Directions: Take Beltway Exit 4 (I-95) past Richmond to Petersburg. The Siege Museum is at 15 West Bank Street.

185. Portsmouth Naval Shipyard Museum

In May 1862, after a year in which the number of Union ships blockading Southern ports had increased to 700 and reduced Southern trade to a mere trickle, a strange new vessel sailed out of Norfolk harbor. The South, with great ingenuity, had come up with a new weapon to fight the wooden ships of the North. Over the hulk of the federal steam frigate *Merrimac* they had built an iron superstructure with a large ram. This formidable sailing weapon, now called the *Virginia*, easily sank two Union ships. Tremors were felt in the North, but the North wasn't the industrial center for naught; the next time the ultimate Confederate iron-clad emerged she was met by a new federal iron-ship, the *Monitor*, that was technically easier to manipulate and had guns placed on a revolving turret. The classic fight between these two behemoths lasted four hours and, although neither scored a decisive victory, it resulted in ultimate triumph for the North. The *Virginia* never reappeared, while the North produced dozens of iron-clads.

The Portsmouth Naval Shipyard Museum is home of the C. S. S. *Virginia*, which was the original *Merrimac*. The details of its development, first forays and climactic battle with the *Monitor* are outlined in the museum.

The range of the exhibits extends far beyond the years of the Civil War. Ship models, uniforms, weapons and flags from the first naval ship through the Polaris missile are on display.

There is no charge to visit this museum which is open Tuesday through Saturday from 10:00 to 5:00 and Sunday from 2:00 to 5:00.

Directions: Take Beltway Exit 4 (I-95) to Richmond, then Route 64 to Hampton. Take Route 17/258 across the James River and follow Route 17 into Portsmouth. The museum is on the waterfront of the Elizabeth River at the foot of High Street.

186. Culpeper Cavalry Museum

On June 8, 1863, General Robert E. Lee reviewed Major General J. E. B. Stuart's Confederate Cavalry. He said it was, "the most brilliant cavalry display in history." This might have been an exaggeration, but the next day's battle, near Brandy Station in Culpeper County, Virginia, was certainly the largest cavalry engagement ever fought in the Western Hemisphere.

This battle, as well as the almost 40 other skirmishes that occurred in Culpeper County during the Civil War, is responsible for the formation of the Culpeper Cavalry Museum. It is located in what was once the boyhood home of A. P. Hill, the distinguished Confederate general.

Many of the items in this collection of weapons, relics and artifacts were found on local battlefields and camp grounds. They represent both Union and Confederate forces. Visitors interested in old weapons will be particularly intrigued because this collection includes a Colt revolving rifle and a Colt pistol, a 10 pound Confederate Parrott cannon, a Fayetteville and Mississippi Rifle, as well as the numerous side arms and hand weapons carried by the common soldier in the Civil War.

Other items in the collection include old maps, portraits, and flags, plus a complete 1825 Naval officer's uniform.

The Culpeper Cavalry Museum is in the Chamber of Commerce Headquarters in Culpeper, Virginia. It is open weekends June through September on Saturday from 11:00 to 4:00 and Sunday 1:00 to 4:00. It is open year-round on weekdays from 10:00 to 4:00. Although no admission is charged, donations are accepted.

Directions: Take Beltway Exit 8 (Route 50/29). Stay on route 29 to Warrenton, then Route 15/29 south to Culpeper. The museum is in Suite C of the A. P. Hill Building on Main and Davis Street.

Recent History

From 1607 to 1865 the Middle Atlantic region had, for better or worse, a front seat in American history. Wars were fought in front yards, illustrious figures lived, shopped in and frequented the growing towns. Those exploring our country's past will find spots here that highlight every aspect of these long ago years.

When the Civil War ended the stage shifted, and history happened someplace else. A new chapter opened. America spread beyond this section of the country. The United States developed and expanded westward, while in the east big business began to rival the government in power.

This chapter suggests these epochal developments in modern American history. One of the greatest of the industrialists was John D. Rockefeller who, after amassing his great wealth through shrewd business practices, went on to plow his money back into society. The Rockefeller Foundation was responsible for the restoration of Colonial Williamsburg and the Rockefellers' gracious home, Bassett Hall, evokes the era of great wealth. Economics also comes to mind at Camp Hoover where Hoover tried to escape from the growing economic problems of a country headed towards the Great Depression.

Concurrent with undisciplined economic growth was international expansion. The United States became involved in world politics. It is fortunate that the Civil War is the last conflict that permits us to walk the battlefields. The later conflagrations wrought far more havoc as war became more mechanized and death less personal. The role of the United States in the military struggles of the last 115 years is traced in various military museums. In no other part of the country is there the opportunity to explore such diverse aspects of the U.S. military machine. The military museums included here all shed light on the U.S. role in foreign affairs through the uniforms, equipment and reminders of the deadly conflicts in which American soldiers have fought.

Woodrow Wilson, who was President during World War I, is represented twice in this section. His two homes reflect the man who was such a pivotal figure not only in the United States but also in world history.

One of the most colorful periods from our past, the "Roaring Twenties," is represented by the Blue Blazes Whiskey Still. And to bring this exploration up-to-date there is Dwight Eisenhower's Gettysburg Farm.

187. The Woodrow Wilson Birthplace

Just as those born on a farm may remain to some extent "country folk" though they live their adult lives in the city, so Woodrow Wilson always reflected the influence of the moral values and intellectual life of the Presbyterian Manse in which he was born. He was a scholar and a humanitarian, and his great objective as President was to create the League of Nations, which he believed would insure world peace.

Thomas Woodrow Wilson was born on December 28, 1856. His mother was the daughter of a minister, his father the pastor of the Presbyterian Church in Staunton, Virginia. The Wilsons lived in this Manse from March 1855 until November 1857 when Mr. Wilson accepted a post in Augusta, Georgia.

The Staunton Manse now known as the Birthplace is a handsome Greek Revival mansion built in 1846. The three-story portico on the western facade overlooks the lovely garden, while the two-story front entrance is on Coalter Street.

The interior of the house has been recently restored on the basis of extensive research to suggest its appearance at the time the Wilson family lived there in the 1850s when Staunton was the commercial center of the Shenandoah Valley and the largest town in western Virginia. The rooms are furnished with Empire and early Victorian furniture, some of which belonged to the Wilsons, and some simply period pieces. Mid-19th century reproduction wallpapers, and both period and reproduction window treatments, carpetings and other floor coverings complete the decoration of this historic house.

On the ground level the Wilsons had their kitchen, workroom, servant's bedroom, and their family dining room. The main floor contained the parents' bedroom where the future president was born, the pastor's study, the parlor where the family gathered for musical evenings, and the formal dining room. The upstairs floor contained bedrooms for the older Wilson children and guests, and storage area.

Before the conducted tour of the Manse, visitors go to the Reception Center adjacent to the Manse, where they see exhibits relating to Wilson's life and political career, and where they view an 18-minute film, "Spokesman for Tomorrow," which was made from newsreels of Wilson's term as the 28th President. On the tour guides will point out the desk Wilson used while President of Princeton University (1902-

Built in 1846, this Presbyterian Manse was the birthplace of our 28th President, Woodrow Wilson.

1910), the Wilson family Bible where all the children's birth dates were recorded and mementos associated with Wilson's presidency.

Beneath the West Portico is the Victorian town garden. The century-old boxwoods form bow-knot flower beds. They are set among brick walkways on the terraced lawn to provide a charming vista year round.

In the Carriage House is the 1919 Pierce-Arrow limousine used by Wilson when he was President and which he purchased from the government when he left office in 1921. The Wilsons used the car until his death in 1924.

The Woodrow Wilson Birthplace is open daily from 9:00 to 5:00 except Sundays of December, January and February, and New Year's Day, Christmas and Thanksgiving. Admission is charged. There is a large area for free parking in the back.

Directions: Staunton can be reached by either Route 81 or Route 64. For either take Beltway Exit (Route 66). Then, for Route 81 go west on Route 66 to I-81 and down to Exit 57 for Staunton. For the alternative route, pick up Route 29 south to Charlottesville then go west on I-64 and backtrack briefly up I-81 to Exit 57, Richmond Road (Route 250). The Woodrow Wilson Birthplace is at 24 North Coalter Street.

188. Woodrow Wilson House

The high cost of living in Washington is nothing new. Those who would like to indulge their own knack for design should take heart—even ex-Presidents have found the rates prohibitive. When Woodrow Wilson left the White House in January 1921, one of his greatest hopes was to be able to build a home from his own plans. But even Wilson found he couldn't afford to realize his dream.

Though the Wilsons considered other cities for their retirement, they decided to remain in Washington as the former President required the accessibility of the Library of Congress for his scholarly writing.

As in so many families, it was Edith Bolling Galt Wilson who did the house hunting. After weeks of searching, she chose a Georgian revival townhouse on S Street. She described it as "an unpretentious, comfortable, dignified house, fitted to the needs of a gentleman." She was surprised on their fifth wedding anniversary when Wilson escorted her to the house and gave her the key to the front door and soil from the garden, an old Scottish custom. He had bought the house for her.

Like a time capsule, the house preserves upper middle-class life in the 1920s, with the very special addition of the mementos of Wilson's two terms as President. Wilson's favorite room and the one that reveals most about his personal tastes is the library. Here this learned, former President of Princeton University, was surrounded by his personal collection of 8,000 books, all familiar to him. He was the author of nine books and numerous articles and, until sickness precluded it, continued to write during his retirement.

The library contains two poignant reminders of World War I—the pen Wilson used to sign the proclamation of a state of war between the United States and Germany and a microphone marking Wilson's last public address, from this room, on Armistice Day, November 10, 1923. Within three months he would be dead.

But Wilson wasn't all work and some of his recreational interests are also represented. Until his health confined him to the S Street house, he enjoyed Saturday night movies at the RKO Keith's. Once it became difficult for him to get out, friends provided a graphoscope so that he could see movies at home. Also in the library is a Victrola Talking Machine which played records with a wooden needle.

Many of the decorative items in the house were given to the Wilsons by other countries, reflecting the enormous role foreign relations played in Wilson's career and his tireless crusade for the formation of the League of Nations. A Gobelin tapestry made for the Wilsons was a gift of the French government; the Belgian royal family gave them hand-painted plates and the Italian government, a painting and desk. Throughout the house Wilson's wife tried to recreate aspects of their White House life. Nowhere was this more evident than in Wilson's bedroom which was an exact replica of his White House room. The bed is a copy of the Lincoln Bed and over the mantel is an empty brass shell. It held the first shot fired by an American soldier in World War I.

Because of Wilson's semi-invalid state this was not only a residence but a refuge. It is clearly apparent as one tours the house that here is where the Wilsons spent their time. Mrs. Wilson lived on in the house for 30 years after Woodrow Wilson died. When she died in 1961 it became the property of the National Trust for Historic Preservation.

It truly has been preserved. Even the green plants Edith Wilson so loved still infuse the house with life. The Woodrow Wilson House is open Tuesday Through Friday from 10:00 to 2:00 and from 12:00 to 4:00 on weekends. Admission is charged.

Directions: The Woodrow Wilson House is at 2340 S Street, N.W., Washington, D.C.

189. Frederick Douglass Home

It was a long journey from fugitive slave to U. S. Marshall—but Frederick Douglass made the transition. He was born Frederick Augustus Washington Bailey near Easton on Maryland's Eastern Shore in 1817. Though he received little food and no education he grew, both physically and intellectually, teaching himself to read and write despite his owner's objection. At the age of 17 he was sent to a professional slave breaker by his nervous owner. The slave beat the professional, but the incident went unreported as it would have destroyed the reputation of the slave breaker.

When Douglass was sent to Baltimore in the 1830s to learn ship caulking, he escaped north. He was 21 and began a life long involvement with the abolitionist cause. Changing his name to Douglass to escape arrest under the fugitive slave law, he married Anne Murray, a freedwoman. They settled in New Bedford, Massachusetts. As a spokesmen for antislavery groups Douglass was so articulate that many doubted he was ever a slave. To set the record straight, he daringly published his life story in 1845, thus putting himself in jeopardy as a known fugitive slave. Forced to flee the country, he continued his abolitionist crusade in England.

When he returned to the U. S. in 1847, supporters from England helped finance his abolitionist paper *The North Star*. During the Civil War Douglass recruited black troops for the Union. His own sons served with the Federal army. He did not approve of the extreme approach of John Brown and had counselled him against the Harper's Ferry raid.

It was in 1877 that Frederick Douglass moved to Washington as U. S. Marshall in the District of Columbia. He purchased the John Van Hook house, built in 1855 and situated on a hill overlooking the Federal City. The two-story brick house known as Cedar Hill was spacious but not elegant. Douglass added a library and an extra bedroom and settled in. The furnishings and grounds reflect this period.

In 1881 Douglass became the District's Recorder of Deeds. His wife died the same year and 18 months later he married a secretary for the Office of the Recorder of Deeds. Though theirs was an interracial marriage, his second wife was a staunch supporter of his beliefs. After he died on February 20, 1895, she spent the rest of her life preserving their home as a memorial to her husband's work. In 1962 the National Park Service took over stewardship of the house.

Cedar Hill is open 9:00 to 4:00 September through March and 9:00 to 5:00 April through August.

Directions: The Frederick Douglass Home (Cedar Hill) is at 14th and W Streets, S.E., Washington, D.C.

190. Sewall-Belmont House

This is a house with a history as diverse as its architecture. The land on which this Capitol Hill residence stands was granted by King Charles to Cecilius Calvert, second Lord Baltimore, in 1632. While the land was owned by the Calverts, it was managed by Margaret Brent of the St. Mary's settlement (see Colonial Period: First Settlements). She was the executrix of the Calvert estate and also owned property. These joint concerns prompted her to ask for a voice in the General Assembly of the New Colony, but her request was refused. It is singularly appropriate that the land she once oversaw should become the headquarters of the National Woman's Party, which achieved the vote for women so many years after Margaret Brent failed.

Though there was a house built on the land in the late 1600s or early 1700s , it was not until Robert Sewall purchased the land in 1799 that an impressive home was erected. Since the 18th-century house incorporated the early structure it makes the Sewall-Belmont house one of the oldest in Washington.

During the Jefferson and Madison administrations, Albert Gallatin, the Secretary of the Treasury, rented the house. It is thought that he arranged the financial details of the Louisiana Purchase from here. A year after Gallatin moved out, men from Commodore Barney's flotilla stationed themselves in the Sewall house and fired on the British. This is believed to be the only armed resistence the British experienced as they took Washington during the War of 1812 (see War of 1812: 1814 British Invasion Route).

The Sewall family owned the house for 123 years, after which it changed hands several times before becoming the property of the National Woman's Party in 1929. The numerous owners, plus the fact that the house was partially burned by the British during the War of 1812, created a mixture of architectural styles. Some experts love it as an eclectic survey of architectural periods, encompassing as it does the early primitive colonial farm house, Georgian, Early American, Federal, Queen Anne, Classic Revival, Victorian and the French Mansard periods. Some view the house as devoid of architectural integrity for the same mingling of styles. None dispute its historical interest.

The Sewall-Belmont House's greatest historical significance is that it is a living monument to Alice Paul, who founded the National Woman's Party in 1913 and led women all across the country in support of the 19th Amendment, which gave women the vote. In 1923, Alice Paul wrote the Equal Rights Amendment that many women are still attempting to get ratified.

After the 1929 purchase of the Sewall-Belmont House by the National Woman's Party, Alice Paul directed the fight for ERA from this house. It was her battle for equal rights and suffrage that led to the house being designated a National Landmark. It is the only house in the U.S. from which the contemporary women's movement can trace its roots.

The Hall of Statues at the house recognizes women leaders from Jeanne d'Arc to American leaders like Lucretia Mott, Susan B. Anthony, Elizabeth Cady Stanton and Alice Paul. If these names don't strike a responsive chord, then exploring this collection associated with the women's rights movement will provide a great deal of background.

Originally the house was named for Alva Belmont, President of the National Woman's Party in 1929. When it was declared a National Landmark the name was changed to the Sewall-Belmont House. Mrs. Belmont provided funds for the organization's first headquarters. The dining room furniture is from the Belmont's Long Island home. The furniture has interesting associations as most of the pieces have been donated in memory of illustrious women activists.

The library collection was opened in 1943 and was the first feminist library in America. The library has been closed for several years, but is being reopened for serious research use. Included in its resources are microfilms of more than 450,000 pages of suffrage and equal rights history.

The Sewall-Belmont House is open Tuesday through Friday from 10:00 to 2:00 and weekends and holidays, with the exception of New Year's Day, Memorial Day, Fourth of July, Thanksgiving and Christmas, from 12:00 to 4:00. There is no charge.

Directions: The Sewall-Belmont House is located at 144 Constitution Avenue, N.E., Washington, D.C.

191. Frying Pan Farm

The farming way of life holds a mystical attraction for many urban residents. There is an abiding interest in what it was like to live on a farm. It is indeed fortunate that it is possible to follow the growth of agriculture in this area from its very beginning in the 1660s at the Godiah Spray Farm in St. Mary's City through the other four 18th-century colonial farms. There are also the battlefield farms of the 1860s—Bushong's Farm and Granite Farm. With Frying Pan Farm at Frying Pan Farm Park representing a working farm of the 1920s, the picture moves into modern times.

This small family farm could have been found in rural Virginia well into the 20th century. The fields of corn, oats and hay are worked with horse-drawn machinery. Draft horses pull the farm wagon. The cows are milked by hand once a day and the eggs collected and sold at the farm. Frying Pan's livestock includes sheep, pigs, ponies, goats, rabbits, geese and turkeys.

Repeat visits will enable interested observers to see the fields being prepared for planting, the crops harvested, wheat threshed and corn shucked. Also part of the 88-acre Frying Pan Farm Park is the Moffett Blacksmith Shop. This preserves one of the last blacksmith shops operating in northern Virginia. Many summer weekends visitors will be able to watch this old craft being demonstrated.

The park has an Equestrian Center, where horse shows and livestock judging are frequently held, and a large Indoor Activities Center for a variety of events from Bluegrass concerts to flea markets and antique auto shows. The park is open daily from 10:00 to 6:00 at no charge.

Directions: Take Beltway Exit 9 (Route 66) west to Chantilly. Then turn right on Centreville Road, then right on West Ox Road. Frying Pan Farm Park is at 2709 West Ox Road in Herndon, Virginia.

192. Blue Blazes Whiskey Still

As the story goes, it wasn't that Frederick County Sheriff Clyde Hauver didn't know about the whiskey still operating in the Catoctin Mountains, he just didn't know officially until an informer reported the Blue Blazes Whiskey Still in July 1929. Now it could not be ignored, and on a hot Saturday afternoon authorities of Frederick County raided the still. During the shoot-out Sheriff Hauver was killed by one of his own men. There is still a lot of talk among old-timers in this area about exactly what happened. Many feel the wrong man got shot and the wrong man went to jail. It's a story right out of the pages of America's past. The tale is told to this day at the old whiskey still the National Park Service runs at the site of the Blue Blazes Whiskey Still. The original distillery was destroyed two days after the 1929 raid.

In 1970 when the National Park Service decided to operate a whiskey still at Catoctin Mountain Park so that visitors could see what a real moonshiner's still looked like, there was a great deal of opposition. The Women's Christian Temperance Union, which played a large role in the passage of the 18th Amendment, establishing Prohibition in 1933, was outraged.

The acquisition of a still from the Smokey Mountains in Tennessee resembled one of the old moonshiner runs, except, of course, that it was completely legal, being run by the Federal government. Published reports indicate that the still was transported in an unmarked truck to avoid protesters or demonstrations. But though some objected, the Blue Blazes Whiskey Still fascinates visitors. It is one of the biggest attractions in the Catoctin Mountains.

Some question whether the still provides "how to" information for illegal entrepreneurs, as moonshining is still illegal though profitable. No alcoholic beverage may be made and sold without proper licensing and without paying alcohol taxes.

The Blue Blazes Whiskey Still is nestled in a grove of beeches. Stills were always positioned so as to be as inconspicuous as possible in hopes of evading federal officers. This still is made of hewn stones and copper, protected from the elements by a wooden lean-to. It is operated on weekends from 11:00 to 4:00, though a denaturing agent is added to the whiskey to make it undrinkable. Instead of a 'snootful,' visitors get an earful—the legends and lore of the Prohibition era.

Directions: To reach Catoctin Mountain Park take Beltway Exit 35 (Route I-270) to Frederick, then take Route 15 to Thurmont to Route 77 and follow the signs.

193. Camp Hoover

When a president visits a vacation spot away from Washington between April and October someone in the press is bound to call it the "summer White House." From George Washington forward, presidents have sought a refuge from the incessant demands of their office. It was Herbert Hoover who built the first get-away exclusively for the purpose of serving as a "summer White House," an escape from both Washington weather and worries.

Hoover, chafing at his fish-bowl existence in the White House, said that the American public allowed their presidents privacy only when fishing or praying. To capitalize on the former, he built a fishing camp on the Rapidan River in the Blue Ridge Mountains of Virginia. Purchasing the land and paying for the construction of 12 cabins out of his own pocket, he still ran into complaints from irate, economically depressed taxpayers because Camp Rapidan (later known as Camp Hoover) was built by Marine Corps labor and a Marine guard stationed at the camp was paid for by the taxpayers.

Hoover spent many weekends fishing for trout and walking the mountain trails. Some weekends were more relaxed than others. One October weekend before the stock market crash of 1929 he spent the entire weekend on the phone.

When Herbert Hoover left the White House he also left Camp Rapidan to the National Park Service to be used by his successors and their cabinets. But Franklin Roosevelt was an enthusiastic sailor and, until the German U-boats curtailed this pursuit, did not visit Camp Rapidan. When he did spend a weekend there he found that it was not convenient for his wheelchair, and the low elevation affected his summer asthma.

Roosevelt then had a weekend retreat built in the Catoctin Mountains for $15,000. Roosevelt's Shangri-La is now known as Camp David and is still frequently used. Hoover's camp is also a periodic weekend retreat for the White House extended family. Many of Nixon's aides escaped to Camp Hoover. Both the Mondales and the Carters vacationed there.

The austere lodge is only open to the curious two days a year, though the forested campsite can be seen from the hiking trail. Once a year, to celebrate Herbert Hoover's birthday on August 10, the National Park Service hosts a "Hoover Days" weekend. Visitors don't have to hike the five miles to Camp Hoover because throughout the two-day event buses run from Byrd Visitor Center to the campsite. Photographs show the camp as it was when Hoover stayed here. Building tours are enlivened by stories about the camp's illustrious visitors.

On those two days there are guided hikes for the more adventurous.

It's possible to walk to the camp and then ride back. As this is now part of Shenandoah National Park, there's always a chance of spotting a deer, fox, skunk or wild turkey.

Directions: Take Beltway Exit 9 (I-66) west to Gainesville. Follow Route 29 to Warrenton, and Route 211 to the Skyline Drive, at the Thornton Gap Entrance of Shenandoah National Park. Camp Hoover hikes and buses leave from Byrd Visitor Center 20 miles down Skyline Drive at Milepost 51.

194. Dumbarton Oaks

There are no battlefields, no Flander's Field, no war-scarred bombed cities—we are fortunate that the places associated with World War II in the United States are those sites where the peace talks were held. Wartime diplomacy brought an urgency to the goal of establishing a new international organization. On April 25, 1945, there was a meeting in San Francisco attended by representatives of 50 anti-Axis nations. They drafted the Charter of the United Nations.

The groundwork for that meeting took place at Dumbarton Oaks in Washington where diplomats from the United States, Great Britian, the U.S.S.R. and China met to make detailed plans concerning the establishment of an international organization. Their sessions continued from August to October 1944.

The idea of the San Francisco Conference was to avoid the difficulties the drafters of the League of Nations had encountered in 1918 and 1919 when they tried to arrange the peace treaty ending World War I and establish the League at the same time. The San Francisco Conference was held while the countries were still united in their wartime alliance; the peace treaties would come later.

The Dumbarton Oaks mansion where this historic meeting in preparation for the San Francisco Conference took place is today owned by Harvard University. The estate has changed hands frequently since the original land grant over 275 years ago. The first house was built on the grounds in 1801. Today's mansion and gardens were created by Ambassador and Mrs. Robert Woods Bliss. They acquired the estate in 1920 and donated it to Harvard in 1940.

Ambassador and Mrs. Bliss also donated their collection of Byzantine and Pre-Columbian art which still can be viewed while touring the house. The superbly maintained gardens are considered the finest open to the public in the Washington area.

Just the names of the various garden areas are evocative: Forsythia

Hill, Cherry Hill, Crabapple Hill, Lover's Lane Pool, Camellia Circle and the Pebble Garden. Probably the most popular, and the Bliss' personal favorite, is the Rose Garden.

The gardens are open daily from 2:00 to 5:00 except on national holidays. They are closed Mondays and all major holidays. There is an admission charge to visit the gardens between April and November. The museum observes the same hours but is closed on Mondays.

Directions: Dumbarton Oaks is located at 1703 32nd Street, N.W., Washington, D.C., in the heart of Georgetown.

195. Bassett Hall

Though Bassett Hall was built in the mid-1700s and as such is linked to the colonial chapter of American history, its real historical significance comes from its association with John D. Rockefeller, Jr. The Rockefellers acquired this estate in the mid-1930s and it is as their home that it is now available to be toured.

The family wealth originated with John D. Rockefeller, Sr., whose name is almost synonymous with the rise of big business in America. He literally rose from "rags to riches." Starting in Chicago as a bookkeeper in a grocery store, he earned $15 a week. In three years he had saved $800. He then went into business for himself, increasing his capital to $100,000 by 1865. Rockefeller invested all of that in a new field—oil. His Standard Oil Trust enabled him to amass one of the world's largest fortunes.

This enormous wealth engenders an active curiosity about the lifestyle of the Rockefeller family. The Bassett Hall estate is a 585-acre woodland tract in the heart of colonial Williamsburg. It was one of Rockefeller's abiding interests; in fact, the spot on the grounds where Reverend Godwin and John D. Rockefeller, Jr., first discussed restoring the old colonial town in 1926 is marked by an enormous oak tree.

John D. Rockefeller, Jr., and Abby Aldrich Rockefeller moved into Bassett Hall in 1936 and personally decorated this colonial treasure. The interior continues to reflect their taste. The house not only contains much of the folk art they collected, but there are also some pieces that Mrs. Rockefeller made, such as the three needlework rugs. Their porcelain collection is composed of many rare pieces and is also very striking.

Visitors will want to explore the grounds as well. The Bassett Hall "homestead" contains three original outbuildings: a smokehouse, kitchen and dairy, plus a guest house. The lawn is particularly enjoyable viewed from the Orangery which overlooks the oak allée.

Tickets to tour Bassett Hall are available at the Reception Building off Francis Street near the Capitol. Tours run from 10:00 to 6:00 daily.

Directions: Take Beltway Exit 4 (I-95) to Route 295, the Richmond By-pass, then follow Route 64 to historic Williamsburg.

196. Eisenhower National Historic Site

Dwight David Eisenhower owned only one home in his life, his Gettysburg Farm. His choice of the rolling Pennsylvania farmland reflected his ancestral ties to this area of the country. Jacob Eisenhower, his grandfather, had moved the family from this part of Pennsylvania back in 1879 in hopes of finding more fertile soil in the west. Coincidentally, when Ike was given his first command after West Point in 1918, it was to Camp Colt, just a few miles from Jacob's old farm.

While Eisenhower was serving as Supreme Commander of Allied Forces in Europe he thought longingly of retirement after the war. It would be a long while before he realized that objective. In 1950 the Eisenhowers did purchase the 189-acre farm on the edge of the Gettysburg Battlefield. Eisenhower, serving as President of Columbia University, still frequently talked of retirement.

But President Truman co-opted him from Columbia to serve two years in Paris as Supreme Commander of NATO. While he was acting in this capacity the Republicans urged him to become Truman's successor. The fact that a great many Americans did indeed 'like Ike' postponed still further a move to Gettysburg.

But Mamie Eisenhower moved ahead with the construction of a new house incorporating the south portion of the old house. When the modified Georgian farmhouse was complete in 1955, the Eisenhowers began spending every available weekend at their new retreat; it was indeed their "summer White House." After Eisenhower's first heart attack in late 1955 he recuperated at his new home.

On January 20, 1961, Ike left office. Retirement had finally arrived. He and Mamie drove to their Gettysburg home. He would remain active writing his memoirs, supervising the farm and receiving the many delegations and distinguished guests who came to Gettysburg. Among the notables to drop by were Sir Winston Churchill, Indian

301

Prime Minister Nehru, British Field Marshal Bernard Montgomery, German Chancellor Konrad Adenauer, Soviet Premier Nikita Krushchev and French President Charles de Gaulle.

The home they visited is very livable. Eisenhower would frequently host backyard barbecues or entertain on a glass-enclosed sun porch, where he also set up his easel and painted. The upstairs walls display seven of Ike's oil paintings.

The furnishings suggest that the Eisenhowers have just stepped out and may return at any time. The open closet doors of Mamie's pink, green and gold room display a huge collection of dresses. The General's robe lies at the foot of the bed on which he would often nap. The living room fireplace is also part of history. It stood in the White House until President Grant ordered it removed to storage. Later auctioned off, it was found and given to the Eisenhowers on their 38th anniversary.

Theirs is a warm and friendly house and hospitality is still offered to visitors who explore on a self-guided basis. Maps of the farm are available at the Gettysburg National Park Service Visitor Center. Buses run back and forth from the center to the farm.

Directions: Take Beltway Exit 35 (I-270) to Frederick, then follow Route 15 to Gettysburg. Or take Exit 31 (Route 97) to Westminister and on into Gettysburg.

197. George C. Marshall Library and Museum

Giving the Nobel Peace Prize to a professional soldier? Surely that's unusual. And it only happened once, in 1953 when George Catlett Marshall received it. But then he was more than a soldier; he was also a statesman and the author of the Marshall Plan to aid the economic recovery of war-torn Europe.

The George C. Marshall Library and Museum in Lexington, Virginia, provides visitors with a look at the many facets of his brilliant career. As one enters this imposing memorial to Marshall, the Nobel Prize, the speech outlining the Marshall Plan which was delivered at Harvard University in 1947, as well as some of the decorations he received from 16 foreign countries all attest to the magnitude of Marshall's achievements.

The rest of the rooms detail some of his many accomplishments, starting as a young VMI cadet and continuing through his early days as a soldier. In 1913 he distinguished himself in the Philippines. The chief of staff fell ill and Marshall stepped in, dictating an entire battle plan of attack without a single hesitation or error. Major General Bell, the army chief of staff, commented on Marshall's field orders by saying, "He is the greatest military genius since Stonewall Jackson."

The museum explores Marshall's service as chief of operation of the First American Army in France during World War I. He once transferred 500,000 men and 2,700 guns from St. Mihiel to the Argonne Front in a two-week period without the Germans discovering the shift.

Between the wars he spent four years as military aide to General Pershing and rose steadily in rank. In 1939 he was advanced over 34 higher officers to become the second non-West Pointer to be named Chief of Staff. He was sworn in on September 1, 1939, the same day Hitler invaded Poland.

Under Marshall the army grew from 200,000 men to eight million during World War II. The museum has a "talking map" of World War II, with moving lights and a recorded narrative that outlines the major action of the war. There is also a collection that includes General George Patton's helmet, Field Marshal Rommel's own map of El Alamein and General Gerow's operation map of Omaha Beach.

After relinquishing his post as Chief of Staff in 1945, Marshall's career as a diplomat began. He was sent by President Truman as a special emissary to try to arrange a truce between the Nationalist Chinese under Chiang Kai-shek and the Communist Chinese under Mao-Tse-tung. He was unable to reconcile the two factions but counseled against U.S. involvement in that civil war. He became Secretary of State in 1947 and, by a special act of Congress, at the age of 70 became Secretary of Defense in 1950, making him the only man in U.S. history to occupy three of America's highest nonelective offices. Marshall died on October 16, 1959, and was buried at Arlington National Cemetery.

The library connected with the museum has an extensive collection of research books and personal papers on Marshall's life and on the Marshall Plan. The lower floor of the museum is devoted exclusively to the Marshall Plan. Murals, maps and explanatory notes detail the concept and scope of this historic program.

The George C. Marshall Library and Museum is open Monday through Saturday from 9:00 to 5:00. From mid-October to mid-April it closes at 4:00, and on Sundays it is open from 2:00 to 5:00.

Directions: Take Beltway Exit 9 (Route 66) west to I-81. Go south to Lexington. The museum is across the parade ground from the Virginia Military Institute barracks.

198. General Douglas MacArthur Memorial

In January 1880 the Norfolk newspaper reported that, "Douglas MacArthur was born January 26, 1880, while his parents were away." Surely a medical first! Actually, what the article meant was that the MacArthurs were in Arkansas rather than in their family home in Norfolk. Though not a new record medically, Douglas MacArthur would go on to achieve many firsts. He graduated first in his West Point class of 1903 with the highest average of any student in the previous 25 years. He was the youngest general in the American Expeditionary Force in World War I, the youngest Superintendent of West Point and, at 50, the youngest to become Army Chief of Staff and a full general.

At the MacArthur Memorial in Norfolk, every phase of his brilliant military career is detailed. The museum is only one part of MacArthur Square. There is also a library, archives and a theatre. Before exploring the museum itself, see the 24-minute biography of MacArthur. The mementos and displays will then be appreciated in the context in which they were used during MacArthur's life.

In the museum the famous corncob pipe, cap and decorated tunic recall so many photographs of MacArthur. Also displayed are the numerous medals and awards given not only by the U.S. government but also by other nations. When he received the Congressional Medal of Honor, it marked another first. His father, Lieutenant General Arthur MacArthur, had also received it, making them the only father and son recipients.

Reminders of MacArthur's years in Japan, Korea and the Philippines can be found in the museum, which also has the original manuscript of his autobiography, *Reminiscences*. The museum's 11 galleries have a diverse collection of artifacts recapitulating MacArthur's career in World War I, World War II and the Korean War. Highlights include a model of the PT-41 that carried MacArthur out of Corregidor in 1941 when he made the famous promise, "I shall return." The General's own collection of canes, pipes and Japanese swords is on display. Murals of the great moments of MacArthur's life include the Japanese surrender on board the U.S.S. *Missouri* on September 2, 1945, as well as MacArthur's speech before the Joint Session of Congress in April 1951 after being relieved of his command by President Truman.

MacArthur is buried in the crypt in the Memorial's Rotunda and the walls are carved with quotations from his famous speeches. The memorial is open Monday through Saturday from 10:00 to 5:00 and on Sunday from 11:00 to 5:00. There is no charge for admission.

Directions: Take Beltway Exit 4 (I-95) to Route 295, the Richmond By-pass, then go east on Route 64 to Norfolk.

199. Paul E. Garber Facility

One of the most popular attractions in town is the National Air and Space Museum. But there is a companion museum, the Paul E. Garber Facility, which is less well known, considerably less crowded and well worth exploring. Air enthusiasts will enjoy this "no frills" display where the actual preservation and restoration takes place.

Of the 280 aircraft in the Smithsonian collection, 76 are exhibited at the Mall Museum and 92 at the Facility. Astronautical artifacts, kites, models and the restoration shop itself all make for a fascinating tour.

The Garber complex has been putting planes back together for the Smithsonian since the 1950s at this 24-building facility. In January 1977 it opened for the first time to the public. In the cavernous aluminum sheds a behind-the-scenes look at aviation restoration is possible.

The Garber collection includes a British Hawker Hurricane 11C of the type used in the Battle of Britian during World War II, a German Messerschmitt Me. 163 and a SPAD XIII flown by Eddie Rickenbacker that still bears the marks from German bullets.

Many of the foreign planes came to this country as war prizes. The U.S. Army Air Forces collected them from all over Europe and the Pacific Theater at the end of World War II with the idea of incorporating them in an aviation museum. The technicians at the Garber Facility have been restoring these antiquated planes.

There are also planes that mark advances in the aviation field, such as the Bel VTOL, a vertical takeoff and landing aircraft; the Bell Model 30, the first successful two-bladed helicopter; the Ryan X-13, the world's first vertical takeoff jet; and the Stinson Sr-10F, which made the first human pickup by aircraft.

In addition to planes, the Garber Facility has an extensive collection of artifacts from the astronautical field. The Able-Baker nose cone from the Jupiter launch vehicle that carried two monkeys into space on May 28, 1960 is here, as are a J-2 engine, one of the power plants for the Saturn launch vehicles and a number of early guided missiles. Rockets, satellites and even kites complete the collection.

Tours are given seven days a week, at 10:00 Monday through Friday and at 10:00 and 1:00 on Saturdays, Sundays and holidays. All tours require at least two weeks advance reservations. Call (202) 357-1400 or write to the National Air and Space Museum, Smithsonian Institution, Washington, D.C. 20560.

Directions: Take Maryland Beltway Exit 4 (St. Barnabas Road) towards Suitland, Maryland. Cross Silver Hill Road and take Old Silver Hill Road to the Paul E. Garber Facility adjacent to the Silver Hill Volunteer Fire Department.

200. Shannon Air Museum

Many older citizens can vividly recall their first sight of a plane flying over their farm or town. The thrill such new-fangled "flying machines" brought was experienced throughout the country. To recapture some of that early excitement visit the Shannon Air Museum in Fredericksburg, Virginia.

Many of the mementos from the first days of flying, as well as most of the aircraft, are from the collection of Sidney L. Shannon, who, with Eddie Rickenbacker, helped develop Eastern Airlines. Unlike the huge Smithsonian monument to the science of aviation on the Mall, this museum reflects the individuality of one of the adventurous young men who was part of those halcyon days.

One of the still air-worthy antiques that make up this exhibit is the 1914 Standard E-1. This is one of only two existing Standard E-1s left from the 150 that were built as World War I training planes. This plane's Le Rhone rotary engine turns the same number of revolutions as the propeller. It's hard to reconcile this simplicity of operation with planes as we know them today. Another World War I plane is the 1916 SPAD VII, a fighter built by the French. This is the only SPAD VII in the world that can still fly. A 1927 Pitcairn Mailwing Model PA-5 demonstrates the peace time uses of aviation. It was built to carry mail in a covered compartment forward of the cockpit. "Old Elephant Ears" was the nickname of the 1927 Travel Air 2000 because of the large balance horns on the ailerons. Other models represent planes from the 1930s and 1940s.

At the museum there is a replica of an early aeronautical machine shop. Aviation slides and movies show some of the planes in action. Displays, exhibits and aeronautical gear, including the only World War II Civil Air Patrol uniform on display in the U.S., makes this an interesting afternoon diversion. The Shannon Air Museum is open daily from 9:00 to 5:00.

Directions: Take Beltway Exit 4 (I-95) to Fredericksburg. The museum is just south of Fredericksburg on Route 2 and U.S. 17. It is adjacent to the Shannon Airport.

201. U.S. Marine Corps Aviation Museum

Marines may be tough, but at Quantico when winter winds start blowing through the metal hangars that were salvaged from the marine intervention in Nicaragua back in 1927, the U.S. Marine Corps Aviation Museum is shut down. Several times a day trains roar past these metal hangars, as the museum is situated on the main line of the RF&P Railroad. It sounds very much like an enemy attack, delighting the young and making their elders shudder.

Within these drafty reminders of the marine presence on other shores there are 11 planes, most in flying condition—but too valuable to risk in the air. Two Japanese planes of interest are the single surviving Zero fighter plane used in December 1941 in the attack on Pearl Harbor plus an "Ohka." This rare plane was the only flyable Japanese suicide bomb to survive intact. They were used in kamikazi missions from which, for obvious reasons, they could not be recovered.

The museum also has the last Grumman F4F-3 Wildcat fighter. In the World War I section visitors can see a reproduction of a 1911 Custiss pusher, a DeHavilland DH-4 bomber and a Boeing F8-5 fighter. This unique display offers planes not seen even in the National Air and Space Museum.

The U.S. Marine Corps Aviation Museum is located on the Quantico Marine Base and is open Tuesday through Friday from 10:00 to 4:00, Saturday from 10:00 to 9:00 and Sunday from 10:00 to 5:00. The museum closes on November 28 and opens April 1.

Directions: Take Beltway Exit 4 (I-95) to the Quantico exit for the U.S. Marine Corps Aviation Museum.

202. Marine Corps Museum and Historical Center

Visitors will indeed travel from the Halls of Montezuma to the shores of Tripoli at the Marine Corps Museum. It's part of the "Historic Precinct" at the Washington Navy Yard. With expected military efficiency the Marines have their museum well in hand. The main exhibit is the time tunnel that chronologically reviews the more than 200-year history of the United States Marines.

On the left are weapons, uniforms and equipment. On the right are personal reflections on the various conflicts in which Marines have fought. In the Civil War section there is a letter written by a young Marine officer who traveled with Lincoln to Gettysburg. There are other letters, photographs, paintings, war souvenirs, guns and mementos from Marine Corps actions throughout America's history.

The museum also has a continually rotating display of combat art. The work is either by or about Marines and evokes feelings of pride and loneliness and bravery and fear in those who view it. Far more than Hollywood heroics, this art comes to grips with men in combat.

The museum and historical center contains an extensive collection of military music as well. Musical scores, recorded music, band uniforms, instruments and related artifacts make this a unique repository of martial musical lore. The collection spotlights the U.S. Marine Band and the music of John Philip Sousa.

The Marine Corps Museum can be toured at no charge Monday through Saturday 10:00 to 4:00 and Sundays and holidays 12:00 to 5:00. There are some parking spaces in front of the museum and others in marked visitor parking areas. The Museum Shop stocks historical material and memorabilia of the Marine Corps.

Directions: The Marine Corps Museum and Historical Center is in Building #58 inside the gates of the Washington Navy Yard off M Street between 8th and 9th Streets in Washington, D.C.

203. U.S. Army Engineer Museum

Somebody has to build the bridges armies march across and clear the jungles for helicopter landing pads and the beaches for amphibious assaults. The job frequently goes to the U.S. Army Corps of Engineers whose motto, "Let Us Try" ("Essayons"), embodies the spirit with which they approach their tasks.

The U.S. Army Engineer Museum's varied collection includes the original maps prepared by French engineers at the siege of Yorktown in 1781, as well as items from all the subsequent conflicts in which the U.S. has been embroiled. From the Spanish-American War comes the original ship's wheel of the U.S.S. *Maine* sunk in Havana Harbor in 1898. "Remember the Maine" was the rallying cry that got us into that struggle, though arguments still continue as to whether the Spanish sunk her or she simply suffered an accident. The Army Engineers raised her from the harbor in 1912 and towed her to open water where she was again sunk, after a commemorative ceremony honoring the ship and its deceased crew members.

From a later war there is a German glass anti-personnel mine and photographs of various corps tasks in Vietnam. More than 600 Engineer insignias are part of the collection, as well as a number of rare small arms weapons.

Engineering equipment, uniforms, photographs, maps and flags complete the picture of the Army Corps of Engineers. Many of their civil works assignments, like the building of the Panama Canal, are also represented.

The U.S. Army Engineer Museum at Fort Belvoir, Virginia, is open during the week from 8:00 to 4:30, and Saturdays from 1:00 to 4:00. It is closed on Sunday. There is no admission charge.

Directions: Take Beltway Exit 1 (U.S. 1) south to Fort Belvoir. The museum is in Building 1000 at Sixteenth and Belvoir Roads.

Alternate Route: Take Beltway Exit 4 (I-95) south to the Belvoir-Newington exit at Backlick Road (Route 617); follow to Route 1, turn left (north) on Route 1 and follow to the main gate (Pence Gate). Enter at Pence Gate and follow Belvoir Road to the Engineer Museum.

204. U.S. Army Transportation Museum

"Moving out" takes on new meaning when visiting the U.S. Army Transportation Museum at Fort Eustis. The army moves by rail, air, ship, truck, wagon, helicopter, and, of course, by foot.

The motor convoy supplying the battlefields of World War I, World War II and Vietnam was the most vital link between the men in the field and headquarters. Food, medical supplies and military equipment were delivered. Though the army has tested "flying jeeps," it still uses the wheeled variety.

A number of the army's experimental vehicles are on display at the Transportation Museum. It has tried air-cushion vehicles, cybernetic walking machines and a one-man helicopter in addition to the flying jeep. Army aircraft are important tools of the trade. The museum collection includes the first helicopter to land at the South Pole, a vertical take-off-and-land vehicle and the "Flying Crane." The latter is the army's largest helicopter. The army uses aircraft for medical evacuations, aerial observation reconnaissance flights, heavy equipment lifts and to transport manpower when needed.

As early as the Civil War the railroad's role in warfare was exploited. Both men and supplies could be moved faster by rail. The U.S. Army has operated railroads not only at home but in Korea, Europe and

North Africa. The museum display park contains steam locomotives, troop cars, freight cars and a rolling hospital.

The last phase of the army's 200 years of transportation history deals with the sea-going soldier. There's even a ship that flies, the SK-5 Hovercraft, plus the World War II DUKW, an amphibious carrier.

A film gives a history of the Army's Transportation Corps. Models, displays, dioramas and many vehicles similar to those shown in the film are included in this museum. It is open at no charge from 8:00 to 5:00 on weekdays, Saturday and holidays from 10:00 to 5:00 and on Sunday from 12:00 to 5:00.

Directions: Take Beltway Exit 4 (I-95) to Route 295, the Richmond By-pass, then Route 64, 11 miles east of Williamsburg. Turn off Route 64 at the Fort Eustis Gate.

205. U.S. Army Quartermaster Museum

The movie *Close Encounters of the Third Kind* opens with a mystifying scene of a World War II plane being found in the desert. The military is keeping a low profile and the intriguing possibilities of this plane's fate are developed throughout the movie. A similar true-to-life experience was the discovery in 1960 of the *Lady-Be-Good* bomber 17 years after she disappeared over the Libyan Desert in 1943. At the U.S. Army Quartermaster Museum, or QM Museum as it's called, they have the uniforms, equipment and rations from that ill-fated craft. A poignant notation in a diary found on the plane laments, ". . . could make it if we had water, just enough to put our tongues to . . ." It certainly makes one stop and think about the fate of these brave men.

Over the years the army quartermaster has provided housing, clothing, food and transportation. These varied tasks are reflected at the museum. One part of the collection is made up of items connected with famous generals including the uniform General Eisenhower wore in World War II, General Pershing's office furniture, the modified jeep used by General Patton and some personal military mementos of General Maxwell Taylor.

The flag collection features the Presidential banners used by Taft, Wilson, Harding, Truman, Eisenhower and both Roosevelts. The Hall of Heraldry has an extensive array of patches, unit crests and military plaques. At the QM Museum there is one of the most complete displays of military uniforms to be found anywhere in the United States.

The Quartermaster Corps' role in the ceremonial handling of military funerals is represented by the drum used in John Kennedy's cortege and the architect's original model for the Tomb of the Unknown Soldier, which was built at Arlington Cemetery.

Another of their functions deals with the quartering and equipping of animals used by the military. Saddles, boots and bridles are represented in this exhibit. The era of the horse soldier is further explored in a saddler's workshop, a blacksmith's shop and even a horse stall. There is a camel bell from the California camel barns that were used when the army was experimenting with the use of camels in the southwest United States.

The U.S. Army Quartermaster Museum is open at no charge Monday through Friday from 8:00 to 5:00, weekends and holidays from 11:00 to 5:00. It is closed on Thanksgiving, Christmas and New Year's.

Directions: Take Beltway Exit 4 (I-95) to Petersburg. Shortly before reaching Petersburg there will be an exit for Fort Lee and the U.S. Army Quartermaster Museum. The museum is located on Route 36 one mile east of Petersburg just inside the main gate of Fort Lee. After the gate, go to the first stop light, turn left and the museum is the second building on the left.

206. Navy Memorial Museum

Up the periscope, man the guns, launch the bathyscaphe—it's definitely a "hand's on" approach at the Navy Memorial Museum. Enthusiasm runs high even before entering. It looks like a submarine is surfacing right in front of the museum, though all one can see is the conning tower. As with the other large outdoor exhibits in Willard Park, children are welcome to touch and climb on the intriguing assortment of munitions. The park has a collection of captured guns, Civil War cannons, shipboard missile launches, tanks and a huge propeller from the battleship *South Dakota*. It's hard to turn one's attention inside, but there the atmosphere is the same: touch, explore and get to know the exhibits.

The museum is situated in the longest hall in Washington. This 600-foot building is located at the Navy Yard, which began operation in 1799. It was the first shipbuilding facility of the young American navy. By 1879 the shipyard had turned out 22 naval vessels.

Naval history from the American Revolution through the later conflicts is presented here. Vital to the story of naval involvement in

The fighting top of the frigate U.S.S. *Constitution* is on display at the Navy Memorial Museum at the Navy Yard in Washington, D.C.

this country's conflicts is the history of fire power, so there is a collection which spans the growth of naval ordinance. From Revolutionary War muzzle loaders to the Poseidon missile, a wide variety of weapons are on display. Some guns are large enough to actually climb on; others, on a gundeck, swing around when cranked by the big brass wheel.

Smaller visitors can fit comfortably inside the pressure sphere of the 25-ton bathyscaphe, *Trieste*, which descended to a record ocean depth of 35,800 feet. Adventurous adults will marvel at those who went so deep in something so small.

The museum's ship models run the gamut from child-size to those almost as large as the craft itself. Perennial favorites at the museum include Admiral Byrd's Antarctic Hut, a fully rigged foremast fighting top from the frigate *Constitution* and the submarine room with working periscopes that permit visitors to monitor water traffic on the Anacostia River.

Paintings of great naval figures and battles together with battle flags add color to the museum's collection of over 5,000 naval artifacts. Often referred to as the 'Navy's attic,' there is an informal atmosphere perfectly appropriate for this easygoing museum. It certainly dispels the myth that all museums have to be dusty and static.

The Navy Memorial Museum is open at no charge weekdays 9:00 to 4:00 and weekends and holidays 10:00 to 5:00. It is closed Thanksgiving, Christmas Eve, Christmas Day and New Year's Day.

Directions: From inside the Beltway the Navy Memorial Museum is located in Building #76 at the Washington Navy Yard at 9th and M Streets, S.E., Washington, D.C.

207. U.S.S. *Torsk*

The "Japanese Fish Fry" may sound like one of the many ethnic restaurants in Baltimore, but it actually refers to another attraction at the Inner Harbor. It is what someone jokingly called one of the navy actions of the U.S.S. *Torsk*.

It happened on August 13, 1945. After sinking a Japanese freighter in the morning, the submarine's crew found a large freighter on the periscope. To come within firing range the submarine had to surface. When the *Torsk* came up she was surrounded by a fishing fleet of 75 Japanese boats. Moving through this floating obstacle course in a zigzag pattern, the *Torsk* wreaked havoc among the small boats and fishing nets, thus earning the dubious title the "Japanese Fish Fry." The end of the story is also interesting. The target which had prompted action of the *Torsk* had moved close to shore; in fact, the freighter was only two miles from the beach. The *Torsk* fired a spread of torpedoes, or "fish" as they were called, and turned out to sea. One of the torpedoes hit the beach while another continued on and hit a railroad bridge. It just so happened that an ammunition train was crossing the bridge when it hit and the explosion was enormous. Two Japanese warships took off after the *Torsk* but, though the anxious crew could hear the exploding depth charges, they escaped unscathed.

The next day, August 14, was the *Torsk's* most successful day of battle. Within 10 minutes she sunk two Japanese men-of-war. On August 15 the *Torsk* was again ready to attack. She had the torpedoes ready to fire at a carrier when word came that the war was over. The "fish" were pulled out of the tubes and the *Torsk* ended her combative career. This submarine has an all-time world record for submersions, with 11,884 dives to her credit.

It is amazing to experience first hand the claustrophobic atmosphere of a submarine. Neither war movies nor books can really provide the sensation of the enclosed space. It gives one a new appreciation for the valor of those who sailed these submarines. It is hard to believe that a 36-man crew slept in a room 14' × 30'. The bunks are only 18 inches apart and hardly wide enough for a young boy. To think about spending months in such space is overwhelming.

The young volunteers of the Del Marva Chapter of Submarine War Veterans and the city of Baltimore Department of Recreation & Parks act as guides and explain the torpedo room and sonor system. The U.S.S. *Torsk* is available to be toured Memorial Day to September 30 on Monday through Thursday from 12:00 to 8:00 and October 1 to Memorial Day from 10:30 to 4:30. Admission is charged.

Directions: Take Beltway Exit 22 (the Baltimore-Washington Parkway) to Baltimore and follow the signs to the Inner Harbor where the *Torsk* is anchored.

208. Arlington National Cemetery

Linked to George Washington through his foster son, George Washington Parke Custis, Arlington National Cemetery stands on part of the 1,100-acre Arlington estate (see Colonial Period: George Washington and the Washington Family Homes). The land was purchased by the U.S. government in 1883 for $150,000 and is now administered by the U.S. Army Military District of Washington.

Actually, the use of the Arlington land to bury slain soldiers was initiated by happenstance. In May of 1864 President Lincoln and General Meigs were visiting the wounded in the tent hospital on the Arlington grounds. They realized that with the number of Civil War fatalities mounting daily a new burial site would be needed, so they decided to bury the dead at Arlington. Thousands would rest there before the end of the Civil War.

Buried at Arlington are the known and the unknown, the famous and the ordinary citizen soldier. All our country's wars are represented, including the American Revolution, the War of 1812 and the Mexican War, though Arlington officially began during the Civil War. Subsequent military deaths in the Indian campaigns, Spanish-American War, the Philippine Insurrection, World Wars I and II, the Korean War and Vietnam all are represented by soldiers who lie at Arlington National Cemetery.

There are many special memorials to soldiers who died in battle and could never be identified, but the most famous is the Tomb of the Unknown Soldier. On October 22 in 1921 four unknown American where slain soldiers from World War I were buried. A highly soldiers were exhumed from separate military cemeteries in France decorated soldier, Army Sergeant Edward F. Younger, placed a spray of white roses on one casket on October 24, 1921 and this became the unknown soldier of World War I. The following month on Armistice Day, November 11, President Warren G. Harding headed the dignitaries on hand to officially inter the soldier at the plaza of the Arlington National Cemetery amphitheater.

During the Eisenhower administration unknown soldiers from World War II and Korea were interred at Arlington on Memorial Day, 1958. Americans from all across the country come to pay tribute to these valorous soldiers guarded around the clock by the Tomb Guards from the 3d U.S. Infantry (The Old Guard). The impressive changing of the guard ceremony takes place every 30 minutes during summer hours, every hour during the winter and every two hours at night.

This was not the earliest monument honoring unknown soldiers. The first unidentified battle dead came from the fields at Bull Run. There are 2,111 Unknown of the Civil War in a vault beneath a massive sarcophagus south of Arlington House. From the Spanish-American War, the mast of the battleship *Maine* is adjacent to the burial spot of 167 unknown soldiers who went down with the ship in Havana Harbor.

Names enshrined in American military history are found throughout Arlington National Cemetery—Philip H. Sheridan, William Jennings Bryan, Robert Todd Lincoln, John J. Pershing, George C. Marshall, Walter Reed, Robert E. Peary, Richard E. Byrd, James V. Forrestal, John Foster Dulles, Virgil Grisson, Roger B. Chaffee and two presidents of the United States.

William Howard Taft, who was not only Chief Justice of the U.S. but also the 27th President, is buried at Arlington. There is also a special memorial with the eternal flame marking the spot where John Fitzgerald Kennedy, the 35th President, is buried. Two children who pre-deceased their father are also buried at the Kennedy gravesite. Robert Kennedy is buried nearby.

North of the cemetery, a long hike away, is the often photographed Iwo Jima Memorial. Carved to duplicate the photo of the Marines raising the U.S. flag during World War II, the 78-foot sculpture is imposing. On Tuesday evenings during the summer months the Marines have a dress parade and color ceremony at this memorial.

Arlington National Cemetery is open October through March from 8:00 to 5:00 and April through September from 8:00 to 7:00. Maps at the Visitor Center indicate specific burial sites and orient visitors. The cemetery is not open to general traffic. Cars must be parked at the Visitor Center but tour buses are available for those who do not want to walk. There is a Metro stop about 100 yards from the main entrance.

Directions: Arlington House is directly across the Potomac from Washington via the Arlington Memorial Bridge.

Suggested Readings

Prehistoric Man

The First Americans, A Story of North American Archeology, C.W. Aram, Harcourt, Brace Jovanovich, Inc., N.Y., 1971.
The Prehistoric People of Accokeek Creek, Robert L. Stevenson, Alice Ferguson Foundation, Accokeek, Md., 1959.
Ancient Washington, American Indian Cultures of the Potomac Valley, Robert L. Humphrey and Mary Elizabeth Chambers, George Washington University, Washington, D.C., No. 6, 1977.

Fictional Reading:

The Clan of the Cave Bear, Jean M. Auel, Crown Publishers, Inc., N.Y., 1980.
Centennial, James Michener, Random House, N.Y., 1974.

Indians

The Indian Heritage of America, Alvin M. Josephy Jr., Alfred A. Knopf, New York, 1968.
The Piscataway Indians of Southern Maryland, Alice and Henry Ferguson, Alice Ferguson Foundation, Accokeek, Md., 1960.
A Short History of the Indians of the U.S., Edward H. Spicer, D. Van Nostrand Comp., N.Y., 1969.
The Eyes of Discovery, John Bakeless, Lippincott, Philadelphia, 1950.
Old Virginia and Her Neighbors, John Fiske, Houghton Mifflin & Co., Boston, 1949.
The Potomac, Frederick Gutheim, Rinehart Press, N.Y., 1949.
Colonial Piscataway in Maryland, Katherine A. Kellock, Alice Ferguson Foundation, Accokeek, Md., 1962.

Fictional Reading:

Chesapeake, James Michener, Random House, N.Y., 1978.

For literature by and about Indians, their legends, poetry and autobiographies:

The Portable North American Indian Reader, Frederick W. Turner, ed., The Viking Press, N.Y., 1974.

Colonial Period

Jamestown 1544—1699, Carl Bridenbaugh, Oxford University Press, New York, 1980.

Everyday Life in Colonial Maryland, George and Virginia Schaun, Greenberg Publications, Annapolis, Maryland, 1972.

Mount Vernon Family, Elswyth Thane, Cromwell-Collier Press, New York, 1968.

Affectionately Yours, George Washington, ed. Thomas J. Fleming, W.W. Norton & Comp., Inc., New York, 1967.

Mount Vernon is Ours, Elswyth Thane, Duell, Sloan and Pearces, New York, 1966.

Planters and Pioneers, Life in Colonial Virginia, Parke Rouse, Jr., Hastings House, New York, 1968.

Homes and Gardens of Old Virginia, ed. Frances Archer Christian & Susanne Williams Massie, Garrett and Massie, Inc., Richmond, 1960.

Tidewater Maryland, Paul Wilstach, Tidewater Publishers, Cambridge, Md., 1969.

Four Seasons on a Colonial Potomac Plantation, The Accokeek Foundation, Accokeek, Maryland, 1979.

American Colonial Mansions, Everett B. Wilson, A.S. Brown and Co., Inc., New York, 1965.

Historic Houses of America, ed. Beverly Da Costa, American Heritage Co., Inc., New York, 1971.

More Great American Mansions, Merrill Folson, Hastings House, New York, 1967.

Great Historic Houses of America, Phyllis Lee, Levin, Coward-McCann, New York, 1970.

Great Historic Places, ed. American Heritage, American Heritage Publishing Comp., Inc., New York, 1973.

Historic Churches of the South, ed. Mary Lorraine Smith, Tupper & Love, Inc., Atlanta, 1952.

Old Alexandria, Nettie Allen Voges, EPM Publications, Inc., McLean, Va., 1975.

Annapolis Houses, Deering Davis, Bonanza Books, New York, MCMXLVII.

Early America at Work, Everett B. Wilson, A.S. Barnes and Comp., New York, 1963.

Colonial Living, Edwin Tunis, The World Publishing Comp., New York, 1967.

America's Historic Inns & Taverns, Irvin Haas, Arco Publishing Comp., New York, 1972.

Stage Coach and Tavern Days, Alice Morse Earle, The Macmillan Comp., Detroit, 1968.

July 4, 1776, Donald Barr, Chidsey, Crown Publishers, Inc., New York, 1958.

Four Days in July: The Story Behind the Declaration of Independence, Cornel Adam Lengyel, Grosset & Dunlap, New York, 1958.

Monticello, Gene and Clare Gurney, Franklin Watts, Inc., New York, 1966.

Revolutionary War Years

1776 National Park Service Guide to the Historic Places of the American Revolution, James V. Murfin, National Park Service, Washington, D.C., 1975.

Landmarks of the American Revolution, Mark M. Boatner III, Stackpole Books, Harrisburg, Pa., 1973.

The Bicentennial Guide to the American Revolution, Vol. I–III, Sol Stember, Saturday Review Press, New York, 1974.

Decisive Battles of the American Revolution, Lt. Col. Joseph B. Mitchell, Fawcett Publication, Inc., Greenwich, Conn., 1962.

The American Heritage Book of Great Historic Places, ed. American Heritage, American Heritage Publishing Company, Inc., New York, 1973.

Bicentennial Philadelphia, Ruth L. Gales and Diane F. Loewenson, S.B. Lippincott Comp., Philadelphia, 1974.

America's Historyland, Landmarks of Liberty, National Geographic Book Service, National Geographic Society, Washington, D.C., 1967.

Philadelphia: The Unexpected City, Lawrence Lafore and Sara Lee Lippincott, Doubleday and Comp., Inc., New York, 1965.

War of 1812

The War of 1812, Reginald Horseman, Alfred A. Knopf, New York, 1972.

The War Nobody Won: 1812, Robert Leckie, G.P. Putnam's Sons, New York, 1974.

The Age of Fighting Sail—The Story of the Naval War of 1812, C.S. Forester, Doubleday & Company, Inc., New York, 1956.

The War of 1812—America's Second War for Independence, Don Lawson, Abelard-Schuman, Ltd., New York, 1966.

The Story of the War of 1812, Colonel Red Reeder, Meredith Press, New York, 1960.

1812 The War and the World, Walter Buehr, Rand McNally & Comp., New York, 1967.

Era Between the Wars—Presidential Homes

Historic Homes of the American Presidents, Irwin Haas, David McKay Company Inc., New York, 1976.
The White House, White House Historical Association, National Geographic Society, Washington, D.C., 1975.
A Tour of the White House with Mrs. John F. Kennedy, Perry Wolff, Doubleday & Company, Inc., New York, 1962.

Era Between the Wars—Homes

Great Houses of American History, Andrew H. Hepburn, Clarkson N. Potter, Inc., New York, 1972.
Great Houses, ed. Constance M. Greiff, The Pyne Press, Princeton, 1973.
America's Historic Houses, The Living Past, ed. of Country Beautiful, Country Beautiful Corporation, Waukesha, Wisconsin, MCMLXVII.
The City of Washington, The Junior League of Washington, Alfred A. Knopf, New York, 1977.

Era Between the Wars—Transportation

The Face of Maryland, A. Aubrey Bodine, Bodine and Associates, Inc., Baltimore, 1961.

Era Between the Wars—Industries

Mini-Vacations, Karen Cure, Follett Publishing Company, Chicago, 1976.
History: USA, Jack Allen and John L. Betts, American Book Company, New York, 1967.

Civil War Period—Homes

A Tour Guide to the Civil War, Alice Hamilton Cromie, Quadrangle Books, Chicago, 1965.
Discover Historic America, Robert B. Knokow, Rand McNally & Comp., New York, MCMLXXIII

Civil War Period—Civil War Forts

The United States in the Civil War, Don Lawson, Abelard-Schuman, New York, 1977.

Civil War Period—Battlefield Sites

The Military History of Civil War Land Battles, Trevor Nevitt Dupuy, Franklin Watts, Inc., New York, 1960.

First Bull Run, Peter Davis and H. John Cooper, Hippocrene Books, Inc., New York, 1973.

The Battle of New Market, William C. Davis, Doubleday & Comp., Inc., New York, 1975.

Chancellorsville Disaster in Victory, Bruce Palmer, The MacMillan Comp., New York, 1967.

The Battle of Gettysburg, Bruce Catton, American Heritage Publishing Comp., Inc., New York, 1963.

Appomattox Closing Struggle of the Civil War, Burke Davis, Harper & Row Publishers, New York, 1963.

Civil War Period—Civil War Museums

A Civil War Treasury of Tales, Legends and Folklore, B.A. Bolin, Random House, New York, 1960.

The Eyes and Ears of the Civil War, G. Allen Foster, Criterion Books, New York, 1963.

Recent History

Historic America Guide, Rand McNally and Company, New York, 1978.

The Best Free Attractions in the Eastern States, John Whitman, Meadowbrook Press, Deephaven, MN, 1981.

The One-Day Trip Book, Jane Ockershausen Smith, EPM Publications, Inc., McLean, Virginia, 1978.

Free Stuff for Travelers, ed. Tom Grady, Meadowbrook Press, Deephaven, Mn., 1981.

Weekender's Guide, Robert Shosteck, Potomac Books, Inc., Washington, D.C., 1979.

Annual Calendar of Events

January

Lee Birthday Celebration—Candlelight Tours of the Boyhood Home of Robert E. Lee—(703) 549-0205 LATE

February

George Washington Birthday Parade—Alexandria, Virginia— 549-0205 MID

George Washington Musicale—Montpelier Mansion—490-2596 MID

Revolutionary War Encampment, First Virginia Regiment of the Continental Line—Fort Ward Park, Alexandria, Virginia— 549-0205 MID

Antique Valentine Display—Mary Surratt House—868-1121 MID

Washington Birthplace Celebration—Pope's Creek Plantation—(804) 224-0196 MID

March

Tea, Tour and Lute Concert—Sully Plantation—941-5008— MID

Living History Weekend at Lee Corner—Alexandria, Virginia— (703) 549-0205 MID

Gunston Hall Kite Festival—(703) 550-9220 MID

Flapjack Day at Colvin Run Mill—941-5008 MID

Maryland Day Celebration—St. Mary's City—(301) 994-0779 LATE

April

Kite Day—Ash Lawn Plantation—(703) 293-9539 EARLY

Blacksmithing Day—Colvin Run Mill—941-5008 MID

Historic Garden Week in Maryland and Virginia—293-5350 (Virginia); (301) 269-3517 (Maryland)

John Wilkes Booth Escape Route Tour (advance reservations necessary)—Mary Surratt Society—868-1121 MID
Maryland Kite Festival—Fort McHenry—(301) 483-4776 LATE

May

Montpelier Spring Festival—Laurel, Maryland—(301) 779-2011 EARLY
Mother's Day at Mary Washington House—Fredericksburg—(703) 373-1776 EARLY
Spring Open House Tours—Philadelphia—(215) 864-1976
Flower and Plant Market at Shriver Homestead—Union Mills, Maryland—(301) 848-2288 EARLY
Market Square Fair—Fredericksburg—(703) 373-1776 MID
Re-enactment of the Battle of New Market—New Market Battlefield Park—(703) 740-3101 MID
Belle Grove Annual Needlework Show—(703) 869-2028 MID
"Plantation Daily Life"—Sully Plantation—941-5008 MID
Cavalier Days in Calvert County—Prince Frederick, Maryland—(301) 535-0144 MID
Chesterton Tea Party Festival—Chesterton, Maryland—(301) 778-1776 LATE
Annual Fort Frederick Rendezvous—Fort Frederick, Maryland State Park—(301) 842-2504 LATE
Horticulture Day at the London Town Publik House and Garden—Edgewater, Maryland—(301) 956-4900 LATE
Sheep to Shawl Festival—Colvin Run Mill—941-5008 LATE
Steam-Up Days, Carroll County Farm Museum—Westminster, Maryland—(301) 848-7775 LATE.

June

Alexandria Candlelight Heritage Tour—(703) 549-0205 EARLY
Summer Sunday Afternoon Historic Programs—Clara Barton House—492-6245
Gunston Hall Arts and Crafts Fair—(703) 550-9220 MID
Flag Day Ceremony—Fort McHenry, Baltimore—(301) 962-4290 MID
Antique Car Show—Sully Plantation—941-5008 MID
Victorian Wedding Reception—Mary Surratt House—868-1121 LATE
Maryland Forces in Garrison—Fort Frederick State Park—(301) 842-2504 LATE

July

Heritage Festival—Fredericksburg—(703) 373-1776   EARLY
Civil War Encampment—Antietam—(301) 788-7264   EARLY
Old Fashioned 4th of July Celebration—Colvin Run Mill—941-5008 EARLY
Summer Festival—Ash Lawn—(703) 293-9539   EARLY
Battle of Gettysburg Re-enactment—Gettysburg, Pennsylvania—(717) 334-6274   EARLY
Custis-Fitzhugh Marriage—The Boyhood Home of Robert E. Lee, Alexandria, Virginia—(703) 548-8454   MID
Woodlawn Candlelight Tour—(703) 557-7880   MID
Civil War Encampment—Mary Suratt House—868-1121   MID
Shenandoah Valley Farm Craft Days—Belle Grove—(703) 869-2028   MID
Children's Festival—St. Mary's City, Maryland—(301) 994-0779 MID
Militia Days—St. Mary's City—(301) 994-0779   MID
Military Field Days—Fort Frederick State Park—(301) 842-2504 LATE
Oatlands Plantation Children's Day—(703) 777-3174   LATE
Old Fashioned Quilting Bee—Colvin Run Mill—941-5008   LATE
Historic Philip Calvert Crab Feast—St. Mary's City—(301) 994-0779 LATE

August

Old Quilt Show—Rising Sun Tavern, Fredericksburg, Virginia—(703) 373-1776   EARLY
Old Fashioned Corn Roast Feast—Union Mill Homestead, Maryland—(301) 848-2288   EARLY
Re-enactment of Civil War Battle of Fort Stevens—Fort Ward, Alexandria, Virginia—(703) 549-0205   EARLY
Brunswick-Potomac River Festival Days—Brunswick, Maryland—(301) 663-8686   EARLY
Hoover Days—Shenandoah National Park, Luray, Virginia   EARLY
Loudoun August Court Days—Leesburg, Virginia—(703) 777-0519 MID
Jonathan Hager (House) Frontier Days—Hagerstown, Maryland—(301) 739-8393   MID
First Settlement Celebration—Kent Island—(301) 643-2617   MID
Corn Feast—The National Colonial Farm—(301) 283-2113   LATE
Maryland Forces in Garrison—Fort Frederick State Park—(301) 842-2504   LATE
Quilt Show—Sully Plantation—941-5008   LATE

September

Draft Horse Day—Belle Grove—(703) 869-2028   EARLY
Harvest Festival—The National Colonial Farm—(301) 283-2113 MID
Potomac Heritage Days—Riverbend Park, Great Falls, Virginia—941-5008   MID
John Wilkes Booth Escape Route Tour (advance reservations necessary)—Mary Surratt House—(301) 868-1121   MID
Defenders' Day Celebration of Battle of Baltimore—Fort McHenry, Baltimore (301) 962-4290   MID
Blessing of the Fleet—St. Clement's Island, Bushwood, Maryland—(301) 645-2693   LATE
Historic Tours of Fairmount Park—Philadelphia—(215) 686-1776 LATE

October

Waterford House Tours—Waterford, Virginia—(703) 882-3018 EARLY
Carriage Drive and Competition—Morven Park—(703) 777-2414 MID
Victorian Craft Fair—Mary Surratt House—868-1121   MID
Revolutionary Encampment—Gunston Hall—(704) 550-9220   MID
Battle of Cedar Creek Day—Belle Grove Plantation—(703) 869-2028 MID
Celebration of Lafayette's Visit to Alexandria—The Boyhood Home of Robert E. Lee., Alexandria, Virginia—(703) 548-8454   MID
Halloween Mardi Gras—Fredericksburg—(703) 373-1776   LATE

November

1880s Christmas at Oatlands—Leesburg, Virginia—(703) 777-3174 EARLY
Washington's Review of the Troops—Gadsby's Tavern, Alexandria, Virginia (703) 549-0205   EARLY

December

Scottish Christmas Walk—Alexandria, Virginia—549-SCOT EARLY
Candlelight Walking Tour—Historic Fredericksburg—(703) 373-1776   EARLY

Christmas Madrigals at Old St. Mary's—(301) 994-0779   EARLY
Christmas at Morven Park—Leesburg, Virginia—(703) 777-2414 EARLY
Carols by Candlelight—Woodlawn Plantation—(703) 557-7880 EARLY
Candlelight Tour—Montpelier Mansion, Laurel, Maryland—(301) 779-2011   EARLY
Decatur House Open House—387-4062   MID
Christmas Candlelight Tour—Mary Surratt House—868-1121   MID
Victorian Christmas at Frederick Douglass House—Washington— 889-1736   MID
Holiday House Tours—Beall-Dawson House, Rockville, Maryland— 762-1492   MID
Bringing in Christmas—Arlington House—557-0613   MID
Grand Illumination—Colonial Williamsburg—(703) 229-1000   MID
Victorian Christmas at Clara Barton House—Glen Echo, Maryland— 492-6245   MID
Octagon House—Washington—638-3105   MID
A Colonial Christmas at the Hammond-Harwood House—Annapolis, Maryland-(301) 267-8149
Victorian Celebration at the Woodrow Wilson House—Washington— 387-4062   MID
Carols by Candlelight—Gunston Hall—(703) 550-9220   MID
Christmas at the Miller House—Hagerstown, Maryland—(301) 797-8782   MID
Christmas at Belle Grove—(703) 869-2028   MID
Cut Your Own Christmas Tree—Ash Lawn—(703) 293-9539   MID
Old Fashioned Christmas at Colvin Run Mill—(703) 941-5008   MID
Christmas at the William Paca House—Annapolis, Maryland—(301) 267-8149   MID
Candlelight Tours—Sully Plantation—940-5008   MID
Christmas Evening at Hampton Mansion—Baltimore—(301) 823-7054   MID
Christmas Open House—Rising Sun Tavern, Fredericksburg, Virginia—(703) 373-1176   LATE
White House Candlelight Tours—Washington—456-2323   LATE

Geographical Cross Reference

St. Mary's

Washington

Williamsburg: Colonial Triangle

Index

Acknowledgments

With appreciation to:

Michael Humphries, St. Mary's Archeologist and Curator for the St. Clement's Island Interpretive Center—Potomac Museum, for his help with the Prehistoric Period.

Robert K. Evans for his extensive information on the Thunderbird Museum and Archeological Park.

John Rhodehamel and Ellen McAllister, Mount Vernon Librarians, for their help with the Washington family, with special thanks to the latter for her help in preparing the Washington family tree.

Karin Stanford, St. Mary's Public Education Officer, for her help in acquainting me with their "living history."

Helen Magargle and Carol Hurtig for introducing me to the world of colonial farms.

Joan Chaconas for her help throughout the book and especially on the Civil War Period.

Conny Clough and Jean Van Devanter for their willingness to keep me up-to-date on the many historic happenings in Fairfax County.

Marian Bellama and Pat Richards for their enthusiastic readiness to accompany me on so many of these excursions.

John August Smith for his unflagging willingness to encourage my efforts and edit my copy.

The many people whose names I have not mentioned but who shared with me their expertise and their interest in America's past.